T0228221

"How unions approach working-class politics has always been contentious, and CAW/Unifor is no exception. *Shifting Gears* explores the union's changing strategy from its inception. It should be read by all looking to advance the interests of workers through the political process."
  – **Wayne Lewchuk,** *School of Labour Studies, McMaster University*

"Succinctly written and deeply researched, *Shifting Gears* offers an important, lively, and timely re-examination of the Canadian autoworkers from the UAW to Unifor – Canada's largest and most influential private sector union – and how the labour landscape's dramatically shifting dynamics have had a tremendous impact upon politics, the economy, and ordinary working Canadians' lives."
  – **Dimitry Anastakis,** *Rotman School of Management and the Department of History, University of Toronto*

"*Shifting Gears* is an excellent read and rich in detail. It does a superb job of providing a historical background and setting the stage for the reader to understand the CAW's political strategy over the last forty years."
  – **Victor G. Devinatz,** *Department of Management and Quantitative Methods, Illinois State University*

SHIFTING GEARS

SHIFTING GEARS

*Canadian Autoworkers and the Changing
Landscape of Labour Politics*

STEPHANIE ROSS AND
LARRY SAVAGE

UBCPress · Vancouver · Toronto

Printed in Canada on FSC-certified ancient-forest-free paper (100% post-consumer recycled) that is processed chlorine- and acid-free.

UBC Press is a Benetech Global Certified AccessibleTM publisher. The epub version of this book meets stringent accessibility standards, ensuring it is available to people with diverse needs.

Library and Archives Canada Cataloguing in Publication

Title: Shifting gears : Canadian Autoworkers and the changing landscape of labour politics / Stephanie Ross and Larry Savage.
Names: Ross, Stephanie, author. | Savage, Larry, author.
Description: Includes bibliographical references and index.
Identifiers: Canadiana (print) 20240361547 | Canadiana (ebook) 20240361563 | ISBN 9780774870856 (hardcover) | ISBN 9780774870887 (EPUB) | ISBN 9780774870870 (PDF)
Subjects: LCSH: CAW-Canada – History. | LCSH: Unifor (Labor union) – History. | LCSH: Labor unions – Political activity – Canada – History.
Classification: LCC HD6528.A8 R67 2024 | DDC 331.88/12920971 – dc23

Canada Council   Conseil des arts
for the Arts   du Canada

Canadä

BRITISH COLUMBIA
ARTS COUNCIL

BRITISH
COLUMBIA

UBC Press gratefully acknowledges the financial support for our publishing program of the Government of Canada, the Canada Council for the Arts, and the British Columbia Arts Council.

This book has been published with the help of a grant from the Canadian Federation for the Humanities and Social Sciences, through the Scholarly Book Awards, using funds provided by the Social Sciences and Humanities Research Council of Canada.

UBC Press is situated on the traditional, ancestral, and unceded territory of the xʷməθkʷəy̓əm (Musqueam) people. This land has always been a place of learning for the xʷməθkʷəy̓əm, who have passed on their culture, history, and traditions for millennia, from one generation to the next.

UBC Press
The University of British Columbia
www.ubcpress.ca

CONTENTS

CONTENTS

ACKNOWLEDGMENTS

We have many people to thank for helping us to bring this book to fruition.

First and foremost, thank you to our editors, Randy Schmidt and Megan Brand, and to the anonymous reviewers at UBC Press, whose helpful insights and suggestions made for an improved manuscript.

The book draws on a larger program of research focused on union politics in the twenty-first century that is supported by the Social Sciences and Humanities Research Council. This support, along with a grant from Brock University's Council for Research in the Social Sciences, proved key to seeing the book through to completion.

Our research assistants, Chris Fairweather and Curtis Fric, proved incredibly helpful and dependable. Edie Williams, the Archives and Special Collections assistant at Brock University, and Lisa Jobling, of Library and Information Services at Unifor, were very accommodating and helped us to secure key primary documents during our research visits. Tim Fowler generously shared with us some of his own research notes on the CAW. Thomas Collombat kindly provided translation services. Wayne Lewchuk, Carmela Patrias, and Tom Dunk offered encouragement and very useful feedback on the first draft of the manuscript.

We are also incredibly thankful to those who participated in this research as interviewees, sometimes on more than one occasion. We conducted interviews with over two dozen key informants, including Jenny Ahn, Malcolm Allen, the late Ed Broadbent, Dave Cassidy, Brent Farrington,

Wayne Gates, Sam Gindin, Joel Harden, Buzz Hargrove, Pat Kerwin, Willie Lambert, Ken Lewenza, Michael MacIsaac, Danny Mallett, Sylvain Martin, Earle McCurdy, Gil McGowan, Hemi Mitic, Thomas Mulcair, Peggy Nash, Lana Payne, Carol Phillips, James Pratt, Herman Rosenfeld, Jim Stanford, Fred Wilson, Ritch Whyman, and Hassan Yussuff. Conversations with interviewees offered us rich insights, strong opinions, and revealing details about unions and politics.

Finally, thank you to our respective spouses, Derek and David, for their patience and good humour.

ABBREVIATIONS

ABC	"Anybody but Conservative"
AIF	annual improvement factor
ATU	Amalgamated Transit Union
BQ	Bloc Québécois
CAW	Canadian Auto Workers
CCF	Co-operative Commonwealth Federation
CEP	Communications, Energy and Paperworkers Union
CIO	Congress of Industrial Organizations
CLC	Canadian Labour Congress
COLA	cost-of-living allowance
CUPE	Canadian Union of Public Employees
GM	General Motors
MAPA	Movement Against Political Affiliation
MP	member of Parliament
MPP	member of provincial Parliament
NDP	New Democratic Party
NEB	National Executive Board
NPI	New Politics Initiative
OECD	Organisation for Economic Co-operation and Development
OEN	Ontario Election Network
OFL	Ontario Federation of Labour
OPSEU	Ontario Public Service Employees Union
OSSTF	Ontario Secondary School Teachers' Federation

PC	Progressive Conservative
PEL	Paid Education Leave
PQ	Parti Québécois
SEIU	Service Employees International Union
TCA	Travailleurs canadiens de l'automobile
TLC	Trades and Labour Congress
UAW	United Auto Workers
UFCW	United Food and Commercial Workers

SHIFTING GEARS

SHIFTING GEARS

An Introduction

On November 2, 2021, union members from across the province gathered virtually for the Ontario Federation of Labour (OFL) convention to pledge support for the New Democratic Party (NDP) in the upcoming provincial election.[1] Meanwhile, in Milton, Progressive Conservative (PC) premier Doug Ford, flanked by Unifor president Jerry Dias and Ontario Public Service Employees Union (OPSEU) president Smokey Thomas, was holding a press conference with members of Unifor Local 414 to announce a surprise boost to the minimum wage.[2] The pre-election announcement, which came three years after Ford scrapped the previous government's scheduled minimum-wage increase, immediately shifted the media spotlight away from the OFL convention. The fact that Ford was standing alongside two of the province's most well-known labour leaders made for headline news and left many labour activists scratching their heads. "Some people were raising eyebrows, and some people were raising bricks," according to Unifor retiree Tony Leah.[3] After all, both Unifor and OPSEU had campaigned hard against Ford in the 2018 provincial election and were historically harsh critics of the PCs. The idea that the leader of either union would stand alongside a PC premier at a press conference seemed anathema to the political aims and objectives of the labour movement. Dias, however, brushed off criticism from union activists. "I don't give a rat's a–," he told the *Toronto Star*.[4]

Dias's decision to stand alongside a Conservative premier as part of a pre-election news announcement demonstrated just how dramatically the landscape of labour and working-class politics in Canada had shifted. Since its founding in 2013, Unifor had been closely associated with anti-Conservative strategic voting, a tactic inherited from its primary predecessor union, the Canadian Auto Workers (CAW). A decade earlier, the CAW had shifted gears in terms of political strategy, leaving behind a partisan alliance with the NDP in favour of political independence that routinely manifested itself in strategic-voting campaigns, primarily to the benefit of Liberals both in Ontario and in federal politics.

This move away from the party-union alliance was a significant departure for the CAW. Not only had its predecessor union, the Canadian section of the United Auto Workers (UAW), helped to officially launch the social democratic NDP in 1961, but both the UAW and the CAW had also sustained the party through campaign donations and volunteer resources for nearly four decades. The partisan alliance was a key feature of the CAW's identity, as evidenced by the attention that it received at the union's founding convention in 1985. Initially named the UAW Canada, the new union declared that it had "long recognized that gains made at the bargaining table need to be backed up with laws to protect workers. For this reason, the UAW Canada is a strong supporter of the New Democratic Party at the municipal, provincial and federal levels."[5] NDP leader Ed Broadbent was the only political dignitary invited to address the September 1985 convention. Flanked by CAW founding president Bob White, Broadbent used the opportunity to attack the record of Brian Mulroney's PC government and trumpeted the union's record of achievement at the bargaining table. The NDP leader also praised the union for advancing the cause of working-class people generally and for its leadership in the fight against apartheid in South Africa.[6] Broadbent's comments underscored the fact that the union's politics had always been broader than the party-union relationship, a dynamic that remains true today.

What has changed is the union's political strategy. From the 1960s into the 1990s, the union saw politics as class-based, which led it to forge a partisan relationship with the NDP and to actively participate in broader social justice struggles. Although the union's philosophical commitment to social unionism remains intact, its political strategies have shifted significantly. In the face of a crisis in social democratic electoralism in the 1990s and amid the rise of neoliberal politics, the union pivoted to place a heavier emphasis on syndicalist-inspired direct action as an alternative to the traditional NDP-union relationship. This strategic repositioning, however, soon gave way to the pursuit of anti-Conservative strategic voting and tactical alliances with Liberal politicians as the political-economic context shifted around the turn of the twenty-first century. In the face of an unprecedented attack on union rights and freedoms and significant industrial job loss and de-unionization, a defensive and transactional labour politics rooted in sectionalism became more prominent in the politics of the union.

Sectionalism refers to the tendency of unions to limit their aims and objectives for the benefit of their dues-paying members, often to the exclusion of other groups of workers or the public more broadly.[7] Although all unions experience sectionalist pressures, how these pressures manifest themselves in the frames, repertoires, and internal organizational practices of labour organizations is dependent on both the choices of union leaders and the political-economic context in which they find themselves.[8] This book explains the *how* and *why* behind CAW/Unifor's political shifts and explores the implications for the labour movement and for Canadian politics more generally.

For much of the postwar period, the United Auto Workers' Canadian section found itself at the forefront of labour movement struggles in the workplace, on the streets, and at the ballot box. At the level of the workplace, the autoworkers struck to establish key labour rights like mandatory union recognition and union security (such as the Rand Formula, which settled the famous 1945 Windsor Ford strike), and they moved the yard stick for unions and the broader working class on a host of issues, including shift premiums, cost-of-living allowances, and better vacation entitlements. The union engaged politically by mobilizing its members to vote for social democratic political parties and to rally in the streets in response to policy changes. In this way, autoworkers played a key role in the fight for the welfare state, labour protections, the social wage, and redistributive public policies for all working-class people. In short, the union not only enjoyed a reputation for bargaining strong collective agreements for workers but also had political clout that extended beyond its own membership.

The union was catapulted into the media spotlight when the Canadian section broke away from the UAW to form the CAW in 1985. Building on the legacy of Canadian pulp and paper workers who broke away from their respective US-based international unions to form the Pulp, Paper and Woodworkers of Canada in 1963 and the Canadian Paperworkers Union in 1974, the CAW's dramatic breakaway from a powerful international union reinforced a growing trend toward Canadianization of the movement.[9] The timing and context of the break, and the sheer size of the CAW, inspired many union activists beyond its ranks to embrace militancy, a class-based discourse, and an explicitly political approach to labour relations.

In the years following its formation, the CAW absorbed dozens of independent unions that shared this vision of a militant and independent Canadian unionism and impressively grew the union through a combination of new organizing drives and raiding – that is, the attempt by one union to induce members of another to defect and become members of the raiding union. The CAW steadily diversified its membership beyond the automotive sector, a process that was further accelerated with the merger of the CAW and the Communications, Energy and Paperworkers Union (CEP) to create Unifor in August 2013.

The creation of Unifor rendered the union less Ontario-centric and less male-dominated than it had been when the CAW was founded. In 1987, 80 percent of the CAW's 143,000 members were based in Ontario, and the union's ten largest locals were all located in Ontario. By 2005, 64 percent of its 265,000 members were Ontario-based, and Local 114 in British Columbia was the only CAW local to break into the top ten.[10] Unifor is now the largest private-sector union in Canada and represents workers in over two dozen sectors of the Canadian economy. However, a majority of Unifor's members still live and work in Ontario. As of 2022, 58 percent of the union's 315,000 members were based in Ontario, and 72 percent were men.[11] Thus the history of the union is very much focused on Ontario, particularly southern Ontario. Manufacturing and the automotive and auto parts sectors, although no longer numerically dominant, continue to have outsized influence on the union as a whole.[12]

Although the CAW ceased to exist formally when it merged with the CEP, only its name has disappeared. Key CAW personalities, structures, practices, and cultures persist at Unifor, thus contributing to the sense, albeit contested, that the CEP was more or less absorbed into the CAW's basic structure and culture with the creation of Unifor. This absorption was perhaps most evident in the realm of political action, where Unifor more or less adopted the CAW's anti-Conservative strategic-voting tactic as a key pillar of its electoral strategy – one that has since evolved into a more sectionalist transactional approach to party-union relationships.

Unifor has unquestionably worked to establish itself as a political power-house. Given its size, reach, and institutional focus on political action, the union's approach to politics matters for Canadian politics as a whole. Unifor's politics also matter for the rest of the labour movement. Although it ceased to be affiliated with the Canadian Labour Congress (CLC) in 2018, Unifor's influence in central labour organizations has been significant, with numerous leaders elected to the presidencies of the CLC, provincial federa-tions of labour, and local labour councils. This outsized influence, combined with competition for members and political differences, has produced enduring rivalries with other unions like the United Steelworkers, the United Food and Commercial Workers (UFCW), and the Service Employ-ees International Union (SEIU). Unifor's unique status in the Canadian labour movement and its shifting political strategies are changing the landscape of labour politics.

STRUCTURE AND AGENCY IN LABOUR POLITICS

Why do unions pursue certain political strategies over others? What accounts for changes in union political strategy? The answers lie at the intersection of structure and agency. Structural frameworks for understand-ing labour politics focus on broad political and economic factors to explain how political choices and opportunities are shaped.[13] In contrast, for those who focus on agency, the strategic preferences and choices of individual leaders are the key explanatory variable. This approach is premised on the belief that union leaders and members are rational, pragmatic, and self-interested.[14] In the context of labour politics, union leaders are regarded as rational utility maximizers seeking to benefit their members through whichever political strategies might yield the most desirable outcomes. The same logic applies to the union-leader-as-sellout critique, which assumes that a union's choices and strategic direction can be radically altered through a simple change in leadership.

Structuralist approaches vary, but they do not altogether discount the importance of individual or collective self-interest. Rather, structuralists understand self-interest to be "embedded in an institutional structure of rules, norms, expectations, and traditions that severely limited the free play of individual will and calculation."[15] In short, union leaders become organizationally socialized into pursuing particular political strategies and alliances based on historical links, ideological alignments, and a general unity of purpose.[16]

Labour politics does not exist in a vacuum, and labour unions are not static entities. Although unions and their members have agency and real capacity to change the political and economic context, they are simultaneously constrained by it. The relationship is a dialectical one. As a result, unions' strategies and tactics must constantly be reformulated and reassessed in relation to what is politically possible. However, we also cannot understand political shifts as separate from what is happening in the workplace. Labour market restructuring and broader economic factors like deindustrialization and economic crises have an impact on what unions think is possible and achievable not just in the realm of collective bargaining but also in the political sphere.

The labour studies and industrial relations literature generally frames crises in union density and labour's declining political power in structural terms, but as social scientists Scott Aquanno and Toba Bryant correctly note, these explanations "are not so much wrong as they are overly simplistic and politically restraining: by ignoring the important role of union strategies and fixating on the laws of motion of capitalism or abstract economic shifts, they discern few of the organized forms of power impacting historical eventuation."[17] In the words of sociologist Pamela Sugiman, "Structure moulds and constrains, but it does not prohibit agency, in either thought or action."[18] In short, political-economic structure is a necessary but insufficient explanation for the choices that unions make about economic and political strategy.

LABOUR POLITICS IN CANADA

To contextualize the growth and development of the union's politics, it is necessary to consider this evolution in relation to the political history of the broader labour movement. Political action has always been part of unions' arsenal in Canada, and debates concerning unions' approach to politics date back to at least the 1870s. Since that time, union leaders have advanced a wide variety of political strategies, including partyism, labourism, syndicalism, socialism, communism, and social democracy.[19] Political scientist Martin Robin's historical analysis of competing forms of labour politics in Canada has revealed a pattern that shows that Canada's union movement alternated between conventional electoral strategies and syndicalist direct action between 1880 and 1930.[20] Although there was a strong tradition of independent labour political action in Canada, Gomperism steered craft unions' approaches to electoral politics for much of the early twentieth century.[21] Named after founding American Federation of Labor president Samuel Gompers and often referred to as business unionism, this approach is more narrowly concerned with securing the best possible economic deal for union members. Even if Gompers conceded that capitalists and workers did have some conflicting interests, he was well known for his political pragmatism, rejecting outright any suggestion that the capitalist system needed to be replaced or that workers needed a socialist party to promote their political and economic interests.[22] In the realm of electoral politics, Gompers argued that labour could strengthen its economic clout in the workplace by employing a strategy of rewarding friends and punishing enemies.[23] Generally, a business-unionist (or Gomperist) political strategy is geared toward protecting the interests of a specific group of union members rather than toward issues of wealth redistribution or justice with broader implications for the working class as a whole.[24]

The most widely embraced alternative to Gomperist labour politics in the early to mid-twentieth century was social democracy. Although social democratic thought and action took various competing and complementary forms, its most prominent electoral expression in Canada was undoubtedly the Co-operative Commonwealth Federation (CCF). Created in the midst of the Great Depression by socialists, farmers, labour organizations, and social reformers to challenge the capitalist economic orthodoxy of the Liberals and Conservatives, the CCF competed with the Communist Party to carry the mantle of working-class politics and managed to secure significant support from industrial unions, including the United Auto Workers.[25] In its first decade, the CCF managed to make inroads in British Columbia, Saskatchewan, and Manitoba, both federally and provincially, and would eventually emerge as the dominant electoral force on the left.

Union affiliation to the CCF peaked in 1944, with roughly 100 unions and 50,000 union members formally linked to the party.[26] However, these numbers were disappointing given the explosive growth in union membership and the effort put into recruitment strategies during the war. Decades of debate and division between unions about labour's political strategy impeded the CCF's ability to win over the broader labour movement as a formal partner. The labour movement was torn apart by internal political divisions, with communist, socialist, and Gomperist elements pulling unions in different directions and making a cohesive approach to politics impossible. In the case of the UAW in Canada, both CCFers and Communists had significant influence and bitterly battled for control of locals and elected offices.[27] Both of these parties were largely shunned by the much larger Trades and Labour Congress (TLC), which preferred a nonpartisan Gomperist approach to electoral politics in line with that of the American Federation of Labor. By 1952, union affiliation to the CCF had shrunk to just 15,000 union members, and labour movement efforts to build the CCF lost steam amid internal divisions and external threats.[28] Industrial relations scholar Richard Ulric Miller argues that "whether because of American influence and control, communist opposition, and alleged predilection of TLC leadership for the Liberals or further disillusionment with political action engendered by consistent electoral failures, the CCF did not become labour's parliamentary arm."[29]

The debate over whether labour needed its *own* party would not be resolved until the TLC merged with the Canadian Congress of Labour to form the Canadian Labour Congress in 1956. One of the CLC's first priorities was to throw a lifeline to the faltering CCF. After decades of disappointing results in federal elections, the party had been handed a near death blow in the 1958 federal election, capturing just 9.5 percent of the popular vote and holding onto just eight seats in the House of Commons.[30] Changes in the ideological composition of the labour leadership, strained relations between the Liberals and key labour leaders, and the ascendency of social democratic union leadership more broadly helped to create the conditions that allowed most unions to overcome their aversion to partisan politics and to support the establishment of a "New Party" out of the ashes of the CCF.[31] The CLC's successful resolution called for the establishment of "a broadly based people's political movement, which embraces the CCF, the

Labour movement, farm organizations, professional people, and other liberally minded persons interested in basic social reform."[32]

The most significant formal partisan attachment between organized labour and a political party in Canada was thus achieved in 1961 with the creation of the New Democratic Party. Canada's NDP was launched much later than similar parties in the United Kingdom, Australia, and across Europe. However, unlike the creation of these socialist-inspired labour parties, the emergence of the NDP did not fundamentally realign Canada's federal party system. In fact, the NDP has never formed a federal government and only briefly rose to the status of Official Opposition in 2011 before reverting to its traditional position as third or·fourth party in 2015. The party has proven more successful at the provincial level, having formed governments in six provinces. This provincial success is relevant insofar as most labour and employment law in Canada falls under provincial jurisdiction.

The initial response from affiliates to the CLC's call for the creation of a New Party was promising. In the late 1950s and early 1960s, a labour movement consensus emerged around the need to create a social democratic party that could act as a vehicle to advance unions' political interests. Every provincial Federation of Labour, except for that of Prince Edward Island, was officially on board. Nearly every industrial union, including the UAW, signalled support.[33]

Much has been written about the labour movement's relationship with the NDP in both federal and provincial politics. Contemporary academic debates have largely centred on the extent to which NDP provincial governments actually represent workers' interests.[34] Union experiments with strategic voting and the tactic's perceived negative impact on the NDP have also attracted scholarly attention.[35] Similarly, party and union activists, as well as researchers, have long debated whether the union link helps or hinders the NDP's electoral fortunes.[36] Some of these debates have been framed in normative terms. However, the ideological implications of strengthening or loosening labour ties to the NDP are complicated and uneven, in part because labour has had both left-wing and right-wing influences on the party, depending on the era, the issue, and the individual unions involved.[37]

Political scientists Matthew Polacko, Simon Kiss, and Peter Graefe contend that although union and working-class voters are historically more

likely to support the NDP than their nonunion or managerial-class counterparts, "the fact that the NDP has rarely won more than one in four working-
class votes speaks to its limited ability to carve out a distinct class electorate
in a country dominated by linguistic and regional divisions."[38] Whether
responsibility for the federal NDP's less-than-stellar electoral record rests
primarily with organized labour, party strategists, or the relative weakness
of class voting in Canada has been hotly contested.[39]

Union member affiliation to the NDP reached its peak of just 14.6 percent
in 1963, only two years after the party's launch.[40] Outside of major industrial
unions like those in the auto and steel sectors, affiliation rates remained
weak, and the individual locals of affiliated unions often resisted calls from
leaders to line up behind the party in any official capacity. The party's initial
lack of electoral success contributed to the idea that there was not much
to be achieved through partisan affiliation, but leaders of industrial unions
remained quite committed to the NDP. Although the NDP failed to achieve
much traction at the federal level, its leverage in minority parliaments
between 1962 and 1968 amplified its importance, and its relative success in
provincial politics in the late 1960s and early 1970s gave the union movement a reason to preserve its stake in the party.[41]

The federal Liberal government's imposition of wage and price controls
in 1975, after having campaigned against them in 1974, colossally damaged
any goodwill that remained between the Liberals and the labour movement.[42] This policy reversal drew unions closer to the federal NDP – a
staunch opponent of wage controls – and helped to increase the NDP's
seat count and share of the vote in the 1979 and 1980 elections. Although
the NDP remained a minor party, the labour movement could justify its
continued support by pointing to its positive electoral trajectory, its important role as a successful broker in minority parliaments, and its reliability
as an ally on the public-policy front.

Despite the central role played by the UAW in launching the NDP and
despite the CAW's strong support of the party for much of its history, the
politics of the union cannot be reduced to that of a partisan relationship
with the NDP. For the union, the party-union relationship was just one
expression of its politics, and the union never completely surrendered its
own political perspectives or priorities to the party. Writing in 1998, sociologist James Rinehart argued,

The social unionism of the CAW is manifested through building women's shelters, health clinics, child care facilities, and co-op housing; spearheading anti-FTA and anti-NAFTA coalitions; organizing a series of citywide work stoppages and mass demonstrations to protest the policies of the current Progressive Conservative government in Ontario; forging ties with South African, Mexican, and South and Central American labor movements; establishing a social justice fund to support progressive international projects; and broadening the scope of collective bargaining to incorporate demands that benefit the community (e.g., demands for reduced work time to create job openings).[43]

It is also important to note that, despite a sordid legacy of racism and sexism within its ranks, the leaders and activists of the UAW and the CAW also organized and took part in demonstrations, lobbying, boycotts, and community-union alliances in support of a range of progressive social and economic issues.[44] Coalition work in support of migrant farm workers, gender equity, anti-racism, and queer and reproductive rights all provide rich examples of how the union's notion of politics extended far beyond the confines of parties and elections.[45] Indeed, coalition building became more prominent in the CAW as relations between the union and the party became increasingly strained. The above highlights a central problem in categorizing union approaches to political action.

Debates about the labour movement's proper political direction often cast business unionism and social unionism as mutually exclusive union strategies, with social unionism – understood as engagement with social justice struggles beyond the workplace – generally considered the route most closely associated with social democratic electoralism. However, the counterposition of business unionism and social unionism is often based on simplistic understandings of these ideal types. In particular, strategies and tactics are often mistaken for a philosophical approach to unionism.[46] The reality is more complex. Because labour politics and strategic action are worked out in the course of contingent historical struggles both within unions and in relation to employers, governments, and political parties, the concrete patterns of unions' political claims and practices mix these two modes of action. Thus understanding the implications of union practices requires some careful and nuanced analysis. Unions are, in fact, complicated hybrids, often advancing collective action frames, repertoires, and internal organizational practices that do not conform to ideal types.[47] CAW/Unifor is no exception.

The union's shift in terms of partisan alliances is often misunderstood as a break with social unionism. Its enduring commitment to social justice projects in Canada and abroad, its public pronouncements on issues of human rights and income inequality, and its regular calls to protect and expand universal social programs that benefit all working-class people suggest a more complicated reality. A partisan alliance with the NDP is not a precondition for social unionism, nor is independent political action is not synonymous with Gomperism. However, there is still evidence that CAW/Unifor's politics have shifted over time in ways that have brought the union closer to the frames and repertoires traditionally associated with business unionism. Strategic political alliances with employers and with non-social-democratic parties are but two expressions of this shift. Meanwhile, repertoires traditionally associated with social unionism have gradually faded into the background, even though the union continues to frame and understand its own politics in social unionist terms. In short, CAW/Unifor represents a complex synthesis of business unionism and social unionism in the Canadian labour movement.

SHIFTING ELECTORAL STRATEGIES

A range of theoretical approaches has been applied to the study of relationships between organized labour and social democratic parties. The scholarly literature yields four theoretical strands. The first focuses on how macro-economic shifts influence and alter union-party relations. Political scientist James Piazza, for example, argues that social democratic parties have jettisoned their ties to organized labour because increased global capital mobility has hollowed out the membership of industrial unions and severely diluted the importance of organized labour as an electoral base.[48] Piazza's argument, however, is overly deterministic because it treats globalization as an exogenous threat that directs the actions of parties and governments rather than as a political project and terrain of struggle where parties and governments play active roles in both authoring and responding to

globalizing pressures.[49] Moreover, a considerable body of research empiric-
ally demonstrates that the impact of globalization is not uniform and that
the responses of social democratic parties have varied.[50]

The second strand of the literature is rooted in transactional politics,
where unions and social democratic parties operate with a view to maxi-
mizing utility.[51] This rational-choice approach treats unions and social
democratic parties as rational actors engaged in a mutually beneficial
exchange. Unions are expected to use their resources and to mobilize their
members to elect social democratic politicians, and in exchange, social
democratic governments are expected to deliver on labour's public-policy
priorities. Although there is no question that all labour politics is transactional to some extent, a utility-maximization framework wrongly down-
plays and even ignores ideology and personal ties as important motivating
factors in relationships between labour leaders and social democratic
politicians. Given that the relationship between organized labour and the
NDP in Canada endured even when the party seemed far from the halls
of power, the explanatory value of the rational-choice approach has rightly
been questioned.

A third strand of the scholarly literature offers "ideological affinity" as
the glue that holds together union-party relationships.[52] In their study of
NDP-union relations, political scientists Harold Jansen and Lisa Young
argue that, despite the adoption of campaign finance reforms banning
union donations to federal political parties in the mid-2000s, the party
and the labour movement maintained their links based on a joint ideological commitment to social democracy. In the words of Jansen and Young,
"Labour unions support social democratic political parties not in the hope
of improving the fate of unions or their workers but rather as a way of
furthering the objectives of social democracy – objectives to which trade
unionist leaders are generally personally committed."[53]

Jansen and Young's framework has not gone uncontested. In collaboration with political scientist Dennis Pilon, we have challenged many of the
assumptions associated with the ideological-affinity approach, including
the idea that unions and social democratic parties lack any sort of material
basis for their links. Instead, we offer up a critical political economy lens
to better understand both stability and change in union-party relationships.
Focused on the dialectical interplay between institutional structures and

social dynamics over time, we and Pilon argue that a critical political economy approach that is "non-determinist and historicized" is best equipped to reveal "the complexities, variations and evolving tensions" in the party-union relationship.[54]

It is important to note that the theoretical frameworks for understanding party-union relationships are not watertight compartments. For example, political scientist Katrina Burgess has combined insights from various theories of union-party relations to explain why unions in different national contexts confront "loyalty dilemmas" differently in their dealings with social democratic governing parties.[55] Specifically, although Burgess recognizes the importance of utility maximization as the central goal of party-union relationships, she relies on structural factors to contextualize her case studies and draws on ideological affinities to demonstrate how party-union relationships are heavily mediated and coloured by a range of factors, including historical legacies. Larry Savage and labour scholar and union activist Chantal Mancini rely on a similar integrated theoretical framework to explain both convergence and divergence in Ontario teacher union electoral strategy between 1999 and 2018.[56]

In the Canadian context, similar integrated insights reveal that labour's enduring ties to the NDP eventually weakened amid a crisis in social democratic electoralism. Strategic disagreements over how the party handled the free trade issue in the 1988 federal election exposed fissures in the union-NDP partnership, which was further strained by the Ontario NDP government's policy reversals in the early 1990s. Specifically, the Ontario NDP's anti-union Social Contract Act in 1993 precipitated a rupture that disoriented the labour movement and opened possibilities for alternative political outlets.

Owing to the twin external pressures of neoliberal globalization and the need to preserve jobs and investments in an increasingly anti-labour climate, the CAW's relationship with the NDP was further marginalized. Given the party's lack of influence at Queen's Park and in Ottawa, it could do little in practice to help the union weather the storm. And given the party's moderating tendencies, left-wing elements inside the union saw an opportunity to move beyond the party by embracing a more radical and independent political approach. On the one hand, the union found itself at the forefront of radical protest movements, as evidenced by its strong support for the Days of Action demonstrations in Ontario and for anti-globalization mobilizations in cities like Windsor and Quebec City. Counterintuitively, the union's electoral interventions during this period were leading to stronger links with Liberal politicians, largely at the expense of the NDP. Vacillation between competing and arguably contradictory political strategies in the late 1990s and early 2000s gave the impression that the union lacked a coherent approach to political action. Moreover, the NDP's natural tendency to put its own electoral ambitions ahead of the labour movement's public-policy agenda in minority-government situations beginning in 2004 further strained the party-union relationship.

The union's eventual turn away from the NDP as its primary political vehicle can be understood only within the broader political-economic context, where neoliberal policies threatened the union's organizational stability and its capacity to defend its interests. Having been shut out as a stakeholder by anti-labour governments, the union felt forced into a defensive position that required it to make some difficult decisions about how to weather the neoliberal storm. Although there were internal struggles over the union's political direction, these dynamics eventually resulted in a shift toward a more independent and transactional brand of political engagement that has now come to define Unifor's approach to parties and elections.

Thus the reorientation of party-union relations has shifted the landscape of labour politics in Canada but not in the direction of a more socialist or left-wing brand of working-class politics, contrary to what many in the union had intended. Rather, there has been a clear emergence of Gomperist strategies as the main alternative to traditional partisan links to the NDP in the realm of electoral politics.

These shifts in CAW/Unifor labour politics can be explained only by integrating insights from the various theoretical strands outlined above. Although ideology figures prominently, the parties in office, public opinion, and unions' own capacity to secure wins or to fend off losses all play a role in shaping political strategy. When the political-economic environment became more restrictive after 9/11, leaders used the union's centralized structure to manage expectations rather than to whip up discontent. External economic pressures were increasingly internalized by the union's leadership to justify shifting gears politically.

INTERNAL UNION DYNAMICS

Although the aforementioned political dynamics are strongly influenced by external pressures like deindustrialization, globalization, and financial crises, they are also internally driven by actors who see ad hoc alliances with employers and governments as key to weathering the negative effects of these external pressures. Internal dynamics unquestionably play a significant role in the formulation of unions' political strategies. As labour studies scholar Charlotte Yates reminds us, "collective identities and internal organizational structures shape how unions intervene in political debates and conflicts and are therefore critical in fully understanding the strategic choices made by unions."[57] Internal union dynamics – including the organization and distribution of power between leaders, staff, and members; political culture and collective identities; and the mechanisms of discussion, decision making, and political education and socialization – are central to understanding how political orientations are both reproduced and transformed.

In the case of the CAW, the union actively reproduced a culture of struggle that was rooted in its syndicalist politics and tactics, its toleration of dissent from the left, particularly at the Canadian Council, its internal educational program, and its recruitment of left activists to staff roles. Since the early 2000s, this culture has given way to defensiveness, as the union has pursued controversial cross-class alliances with both employers and non-social-democratic political parties.

A long-standing and underappreciated characteristic of the CAW's internal political structure was in fact its centralization. Although the CAW had a National Executive Board (NEB) made up of elected rank-and-file leaders, these leaders were mostly hand-picked by the president's office, and their elections were secured through a very disciplined caucus system, namely the Administration caucus descended from the days of UAW president Walter Reuther. Of note, UAW and CAW national leadership elections were formally conducted at delegated conventions rather than by a one-member–one-vote system. In the words of labour studies scholar David Camfield, "the Administration Caucus functions somewhat like a political party in a one-party system. Delegates and staff who attend one of its meetings are expected to support its decisions during debates on the convention floor."[58]

However, the union's position as a Canadian section in a US-based union created an incentive to allow for political ferment that denoted the Canadians' political independence and provided the leadership with a counterweight to pressures from the UAW's international headquarters in Detroit. The formation of the CAW in 1985 shifted the centralized power of the Canadian director into the office of the national president, and the left-nationalist dynamic that fuelled dissent at the Canadian Council was removed. As a result, decisions about political direction became increasingly top-down, as there were fewer counterweights from the membership. This concentration of power also meant that interpersonal relationships between leaders and key political figures took on greater importance. The CAW's culture and structure have largely persisted at Unifor. When the CAW merged with the CEP, the union retained the centralization of power in the president's office and in the Administration caucus (reformed as the Unity caucus after 2013), along with the command-and-control culture that flows from this centralization of power.

The president's assistants play a central role both in the day-to-day affairs of the union and in its broader strategic direction. Not only do staff carry the political message and authority of the leadership, but they also actively participate in the caucus system that reproduces this leadership. Although staff do not have the right to vote at Unifor councils or conventions, they do have the right to speak, often doing so in support of the leadership's priorities. The president's material ability to distribute rewards also helps to consolidate power. Staff positions at Unifor are highly coveted, and many of those recruited onto staff come directly from the ranks of the NEB. This situation creates a dynamic where members of the NEB risk losing out on staff positions if they find themselves offside with the national president, who has the exclusive authority to appoint staff. Thus, with the leadership having decided that a shift in political strategy was needed, there was little to prevent its implementation, despite the formal role played by the Canadian Council – often referred to as the union's parliament – in rubber-stamping the decision. In short, the centralization of power in the president's office and the increasingly marginal role played by the Canadian Council allowed the union to shift gears with little internal dissent.

It is worth noting that even if progressive reformers within the union have criticized the caucus system and the level of centralization in the president's office as undemocratic, the relationship between centralization, the caucus system, progressive political change, and union democracy is complicated. Although the command-and-control culture of the union stifles effective challenges to the union leadership's positions or priorities, a centralized structure has also allowed the leadership to push through progressive priorities, like support for gun control or same-sex benefits, that were initially met with resistance by some elements of the rank and file.[59] In other words, sometimes progressive change comes from the top down rather than the bottom up. Historically, the caucus system was also defended as the best mechanism to ensure that women and members of other equity-deserving groups, as well as smaller sectors and various regions, were represented in a union structure numerically dominated by men working in the automotive sector.[60] In short, the internal dynamics are complicated, and much hinges on the personal views and priorities of the union's president.

Given that the union has been dominated by a white, male membership, questions of gender and race have gained attention in academic treatments of autoworkers in Canada.[61] Labour scholars Carmela Patrias and Larry Savage have highlighted that the union was firmly committed historically to fighting racial discrimination in housing and other facets of society, despite its tolerance of sex-based discrimination in the workplace and in the union.[62] Similarly, in her study of the gender politics of the UAW in Canada, Pamela Sugiman has brought attention to the paradox of the union's outward focus on human rights and social justice in contrast to its internal ambivalence about sex-based discrimination in auto plants and collective agreements, like separate seniority lists and job designations.[63] Given its sectoral breadth, Unifor is much more demographically diverse than the CAW or the UAW, but as of 2022, women still made up only 28 percent of its membership.[64] Although women and members of equity-deserving groups have made great strides within the union through equity committees and by securing designated positions on the NEB as part of Unifor's founding constitution, there is little evidence that demographic shifts in the union's composition provide any clear explanations for the union's political transformations.

A final internal dynamic that is key to our analysis is the continued centrality of the automotive sector inside the union. The automotive sector was the bread and butter of the UAW and the CAW, and the continued significance of the sector to Unifor is impossible to deny. Although the automotive sector no longer composes a majority of the union's membership, it remains Unifor's largest subsector and still funds much of the union's education and job-transition programs.[65] Moreover, a higher share of dues is derived from members working at the (Ford, GM, and Chrysler) given the higher-than-average wages in this sector. Thus the automotive sector's continued centrality in the union's profile and priorities endures and still appears to drive much of the union's politics.[66]

METHODOLOGY AND ORGANIZATION OF THE BOOK

Our analysis relies on primary archival sources and on in-depth interviews with key informants to examine the evolution of the politics of the CAW and Unifor while situating the union in historical context and seeking to understand the organization in terms of its concrete practices rather than its stated objectives or values. This approach is key to revealing the dynamics that have driven change within the union over time. In this opening chapter, we have outlined the arguments and main themes of the book while situating CAW/Unifor within the broader labour movement and Canadian economy.

We chart these themes chronologically through an examination of key moments in the union's history. We begin in Chapter 2 by exploring the union's political history, starting with the founding and development of the Canadian section of the UAW. The chapter focuses on the interplay between political-economic conditions and internal union dynamics in shaping the union's political outlook. This outlook, we argue, also helps to explain how and why leaders of the UAW in Canada were able to pull off a successful breakaway that led to the creation of the CAW in 1985. This chapter also highlights the historical links between the UAW/CAW and the NDP, emphasizing the strong educational, organizational, and financial ties to the party while acknowledging the union's consistent desire to preserve its own political capacities and perspectives.

Chapter 3 explores the tensions that emerged between the CAW and the NDP in the late 1980s and early 1990s amid a crisis in social democratic electoralism and the rise of neoliberalism. Specifically, the chapter describes how the 1988 "Free Trade" election and the passage of the Social Contract

Act by Bob Rae's government in Ontario in 1993 exposed major schisms in the party-union relationship, leading to public denunciations and the CAW's significant withdrawal of funding and support for the NDP. The chapter also reveals how constitutional turmoil in the early 1990s led the union's Quebec section to forge a closer relationship to the sovereignist Bloc Québécois at the expense of the NDP. This period is critical for understanding the role that the union came to play as the NDP's most significant left critic and explores how the party-union dynamic was altered as a result.

Chapter 4 explores the CAW's role in fostering a syndicalist politics rooted in street protest and in global justice activism as an alternative to social democratic electoralism in the wake of the Ontario NDP government's defeat at the hands of Mike Harris's Conservatives in 1995. The chapter examines the contradictions, internal debates, and struggles that characterized this period of the union's history, focusing on the Days of Action demonstrations in Ontario and concluding with the defeat of the CAW-backed New Politics Initiative, which proposed the launch of a new left party at the 2001 federal NDP convention. The chapter reveals a union that was struggling with its own political identity and unsure of what strategies and tactics to adopt in the face of an unprecedented assault on workers' rights and a state-led crackdown on extra-parliamentary politics in the wake of 9/11.

The union's retreat from syndicalism did not drive it back into the arms of the NDP but rather fostered a defensive brand of politics heavily reliant on anti-Conservative strategic voting and closer relations with Liberals in Ontario and at the federal level. This strategy, explored in Chapter 5, was initially justified as a form of electoral harm reduction. However, strategic voting was gradually expanded to justify pragmatic and transactional relationships with key Liberal politicians and was bolstered on the economic front by unprecedented cross-class alliances with employers to protect jobs and investments in the face of economic crises, accelerated job loss, and devastating plant closures.

Chapter 6 highlights how these external economic pressures helped to precipitate the CAW's merger with the CEP in 2013. Although the question of political strategy was initially sidestepped in the merger process, it would not take long for the new union to resolve this question in favour of anti-Conservative strategic voting. The 2014 Ontario provincial election proved key in consolidating Unifor's political approach and validated strategic voting on a go-forward basis. We demonstrate, however, that the basis for strategic voting has continued to evolve along with the union, highlighting the transactional dimensions of Unifor's politics that are reminiscent of Gomperism but are pursued under the guise of anti-Conservative strategic voting.

Chapter 7 is focused on Unifor's founding president, Jerry Dias, and on the political stamp that he left on the union. A controversial figure, Dias cozied up to Premier Doug Ford and forged close ties to Liberal prime minister Justin Trudeau in an effort to boost Unifor's political clout. Dias's access and influence evaporated overnight in the wake of a kickback scandal that prompted his early retirement and a police investigation. The unprecedented campaign for the presidency of the union that followed Dias's fall from grace exposed deep political divisions within Unifor and opened the door to challenging the union's direction on a range of fronts, thus introducing a new chapter in the union's history.

Although the book's focus is on the CAW and Unifor, its themes have implications for all unions and movements seeking to build workers' capacities and to leverage workers' collective power both in the workplace and at the ballot box. Thus the book concludes by summarizing Unifor's political transformation and by considering how it affects the broader labour movement.

CHAPTER 2

IN THE DRIVER'S SEAT
The Birth of the CAW and the
Promise of Social Unionism

To understand how the politics of the Canadian Auto Workers (CAW) evolved over the course of its twenty-eight-year history, it is necessary to go back to the founding and development of its predecessor, the Canadian section of the United Auto Workers (UAW). This chapter briefly charts the political history of the UAW's Canadian section, emphasizing how internal union dynamics and external political-economic conditions shaped the union's approach to politics. We then turn to the breakaway of the CAW from the UAW in 1985, with a specific focus on the role that politics and the former's commitment to social unionism played in differentiating the goals and priorities of the two organizations. The chapter paints a picture of the strong party-union relationship that accompanied the development and founding of the New Democratic Party (NDP) in 1961. However, a closer look at the union's educational, organizational, and financial ties to the party into the 1980s reveals that the UAW/ CAW never uncritically farmed out its politics to the NDP and always understood politics to be broader than electoral activity.

THE UAW IN CANADA

Any analysis of the politics of the CAW requires us to take stock of the trajectory of the union, dating back to the establishment of the first locals in Windsor and Oshawa in the mid-1930s. Both locals were forged through workers' militancy, the first at Kelsey Wheel in the form of a two-week sit-down strike in 1936 and the second at General Motors (GM) via a strike in 1937. Both strikes were part of a wave of militancy that included the Flint sit-down strike, and they faced dogged opposition from employers. By 1939, with Local 199 representing the workers at McKinnon Industries (later to become GM) in St. Catharines, Canadian autoworkers had formed District Council 26 of the UAW.[1]

Canadian autoworkers' political orientations were strongly coloured by the ideas of UAW president Walter Reuther and what came to be known as "Reutherism." Reuther's philosophy about the proper role of unions in capitalist societies is best contrasted with that of Samuel Gompers, the long-serving president of the American Federation of Labor. Gompers eschewed partisan political engagement, emphasizing instead unions' primary role in delivering ever-increasing material benefits to their members through collective bargaining. Although he, too, believed in the power of collective bargaining to deliver the goods, Reuther argued that this "nickel-in-the-pay-envelope kind of philosophy" was too limited. The labour movement's purpose was "not to patch up the old world so you can starve less often and less severely; we are building the kind of labor movement that will remake the world so that the working people will get the benefits of their labor."[2] Reuther's vision of a modern and dynamic labour movement meant support for social democratic redistributive politics, civil rights, and anti-poverty movements.[3]

Reuther's ideas about the appropriate role of unions in politics thus created one of the foundations of the UAW Canada's social unionism. Many Canadians were inspired by and explicitly identified with Reuther's brand of politics. For example, in the late 1940s and early 1950s, a young Dennis McDermott (who would later go on to be elected UAW Canadian director) played an active role alongside Bromley Armstrong and Kalman Kaplansky on the Joint Labour Committee to Combat Racial Intolerance.[4] The committee developed anti-racism materials for the labour movement and carried out a series of test cases to challenge racist and discriminatory practices at restaurants and clubs in Ontario. The committee's work helped to secure the province's Fair Employment Practices Act in 1951 – one of the earliest pieces of human rights legislation in North America. Similarly, in 1959, Local 199 president John Ideson led a deputation to St. Catharines city hall demanding a housing bylaw that would make it illegal for landlords to refuse tenants on the basis of race, colour, religion, or national origin. The campaign helped to bring about a 1961 amendment to the provincial Fair Accommodation Practices Act that secured the coverage of apartment rentals.[5] In Atlantic City in 1957, while attending the UAW International's convention for the first time, future UAW Canadian director and CAW national president Bob White heard Reuther speak and "soaked it up like a sponge." He recalls, "Reuther's vision included the whole world. The sense I had of the UAW from Reuther was that the union was at the heart of everything that mattered, that it was enormous, that it was involved in every issue that touched on people's lives."[6] Buzz Hargrove, White's successor as the CAW's national president, was a member of the Reuther caucus in Windsor and also a great admirer of the Reuther brothers.[7]

However, the impact of Reutherism in Canada was complicated given the specific combination of internal union dynamics and external political-economic conditions. As Charlotte Yates recounts, Canadian autoworkers applied for a charter for a district council precisely to consolidate local control over union affairs in the context of an international union led from Detroit.[8] This structure interacted with the distinct political culture of the left among Canadian autoworkers. On the one hand, the interplay of social democrats, communists, and syndicalists influenced the character of the union's politics. On the other hand, the distinct role that the Canadian economy played with respect to the United States, the effects of international trade and the Auto Pact, and the dynamics of international unionism and the growing support for an independent Canadian labour movement all created space in Canada for greater ideological diversity and support for a different political orientation in opposition to US domination.

One expression of the UAW's social unionism in Canada was its important historical ties to the Co-operative Commonwealth Federation (CCF) and to social democratic electoralism. In the late 1930s and early 1940s, the UAW was part of a "new, young, aggressive industrial union movement in which enthusiastic CCFers held important leadership positions."[9] The first Canadian director of the UAW was Charles Millard, well known for his strong CCF allegiances and antipathy to communist influence in the labour movement.[10] Political scientist Gad Horowitz has argued that the UAW in

Canada was slower than others to fully embrace the CCF, but in June 1951 "the UAW District Council endorsed the CCF as the union's political arm and pledged full and active support to CCF candidates in future elections." This relationship was continually consolidated through appointments of staff to lead political action and through financial and volunteer support for CCF candidates, and it was evident in the 1951 Ontario provincial election, when seven UAW members ran under the CCF banner.[11]

However, these partisan ties were never completely dominant, as they became in other unions of the Congress of Industrial Organizations (CIO), like the United Steelworkers, nor did they represent the universe of political opinion within the UAW in Canada. From its inception, the UAW was the site of a protracted struggle between social democrats and communists, and it was not clear until the 1950s which faction would dominate the union's politics.[12] As Horowitz puts it, although "CCFers were an important faction" in the 1940s, "in the UAW the Communists had the upper hand."[13] In Windsor, communists controlled the executives of UAW Locals 195 and 200 and had been central to the efforts to organize Ford since the 1920s.[14] Local 199 at McKinnon Industries in St. Catharines was also deeply divided between communists and social democrats.[15] George Burt had been treasurer of Local 222 at General Motors in Oshawa during the 1937 strike and had ousted Charles Millard as UAW director in 1939. Although never a Communist himself, Burt was dependent on their support, and his positions on political activity reflected this reality. The UAW rejected affiliation to the CCF in September 1943, reflecting internal divisions between communists and CCFers.[16] In the 1940s, the UAW contained "very influential Communist factions," and the leadership was "dependent on Communist support."[17] Although support for the CCF and later for the NDP became embedded in the expectations of elected leaders and staff, communists were never entirely expunged from the union's political culture and continued to play a significant role in the union's life.

The UAW's institutional links with left parties did not completely eclipse relations with other political parties either. According to Yates, Liberal Party supporters "flourished within the Canadian UAW as this party seemingly offered greater access and influence to government than the social democrats did."[18] The openness of the Liberals to more progressive social policy and the relatively improved postwar environment for collective bargaining made "the need for a third party ... less urgent" for some in the union's orbit.[19] There was also a regional character to Liberal support, with a notable base in Windsor, Ontario, which in part reflected the more general religious and ethnic patterns in voting that one might expect in a French-Catholic working-class community.[20] It is worth recalling that leading Liberal Paul Martin Sr. was the member of Parliament for Essex East in the 1950s and would have been buoyed by many Windsor-area autoworker votes.

However, Liberal support was also politically complicated. In part, it reflected the enduring impact of the wartime alliance between the Liberals and the Communists, whose willingness to support a no-strike pledge after 1941 to support the war effort was opposed by the CCF, which made attempts to extract legal and economic gains for workers in this context.[21] In the realm of partisan politics, this dynamic was evident in the 1945 Ontario provincial election. The UAW endorsed three Windsor candidates – UAW Canadian director George Burt, Local 195 president Alex Parent, and former Windsor mayor Art Reaume – who were, in turn, endorsed by the communist Labour Progressive Party and ran as Liberals.[22] Support for the Liberals was also rooted in the enduring mistrust that some UAW members had for the CCF given the latter's attempts to meddle in internal UAW affairs and to encourage the purging of Communists, which fostered an "enemy of my enemy is my friend" political calculus. Finally, attachment to the Liberal Party was also pragmatic, as the Liberals were perhaps in a better position to form government and to deliver on the union's demands for improved labour legislation and social programs. Indeed, this was the premise on which the UAW accepted the overtures of Ontario Liberal leader Mitch Hepburn in the lead-up to the 1945 provincial election, despite the fact that, when premier in the 1930s, Hepburn had been an arch-enemy of the CIO and its organizing drive in Oshawa.[23] In exchange for an electoral alliance where the Liberal Party would support labour candidates and vice versa, supportive unions would be able to "appoint the minister for the Department of Labour" if the Liberals won. "In spite of their long history of animosity and conflict with Hepburn, the UAW saw this proposed alliance as a means to defeat the provincial Conservatives and achieve UAW goals of improved legislation and a greater role for labour in provincial government affairs."[24]

Also present in the Canadian UAW's political culture was a syndicalist orientation that often seemed to unite people of different partisan persuasions in the view that "social and political change emerg[ed] from union, rather than party, activism."[25] Economist and former CAW research director Sam Gindin characterizes the syndicalist orientation as one where "the union comes first always."[26] This perspective did not reject a role for party politics. Rather, there was a confidence in the union's ability to act politically and to represent workers' interests in a way that did not foster dependence on a particular party. This independence could manifest in a variety of tactics, ranging from workplace militancy and wildcat strikes to extra-parliamentary mobilization and lobbying members of Parliament (MPs). Even with its eventual strong relationship with the NDP, "the union never limited its definition of politics to electoral activity. The UAW developed and maintained an emphasis on independent lobbying in a number of ways. It sent cavalcades to Queen's Park and Ottawa, organized the unemployed, and buttonholed MPs."[27]

THE ORIGINS OF THE ADMINISTRATION CAUCUS

From its beginnings, the UAW featured competing factions vying for influence and control of the union. These factions would sometimes operate as formal caucuses, typically organized along ideological lines. Historian John Barnard describes these caucuses as "a coalition of diverse elements," noting that "shifts and realignments, with old alliances dissolving as new ones formed, sometimes occurred."[28] According to labour historian Nelson Lichtenstein, the caucuses' ideological bases were fragile, complicated by personal ambition, and vulnerable to internal factionalism and dissolution.[29] Among the most high-profile and enduring caucuses were the socialist- and communist-supported Unity caucus on the left and the liberal or social democratic Progressive caucus on the right, which was understood as representing its own faction within the ideological spectrum of a broadly left-wing labour movement.[30]

After narrowly winning the UAW presidency in a close race in 1946 against the backdrop of prolonged infighting between ideological factions, Reuther made no secret of the fact that he would accept "nothing less than the elimination of his rivals from all posts in the UAW hierarchy."[31] He accomplished this objective through the Reuther Administration caucus, which propelled him to victory by uniting disparate groups of workers within the UAW. Once Reuther took over as UAW president, the Administration caucus operated like a clientelist one-party state built on a combination of patronage and coercion. Its effectiveness at consolidating power cannot be understated. By 1947, all of Reuther's adversaries had been voted off the International Executive Board.[32] Some adversaries, like UAW Canadian director George Burt, allowed themselves to be absorbed into the caucus as an act of self-preservation. According to Horowitz, "Confronted with rising CCF strength in the Windsor locals and the Reuther victory in the international, Burt 'swung over' under pressure from Detroit: 'Reuther ... read the riot act to him [and told] him to stop playing footsie with the Reds or he'd be fired.'"[33]

The Administration caucus, however, was not merely an electoral machine. Loyal "Reutherites" were appointed to key staff positions, presumably to reinforce Reuther's grip on power.[34] There was also an element of coercion insofar as identification with and loyalty to the caucus became a prerequisite for both union staff and rank-and-file members seeking election to local leadership positions. As labour historian Roger Keeran explains, "Immediately after his sweep of the 1947 convention, Reuther purged all Communists, Communist sympathizers, and other leftists from the International staff." Keeran goes on to document how the new UAW president deployed his "subservient" Executive Board and union staff to move "quickly and ruthlessly against left-wing leaders of local unions."[35] The caucus did not take long to deliver the results that Reuther was seeking.

Although Keeran is critical of how Reuther used the caucus system to squash internal dissent, its efficacy in the realm of collective bargaining was also evident. The Administration caucus provided a unified agenda at the top of the union that seemingly paid dividends at the bargaining table, as evidenced by significant improvements to the terms and conditions of work for autoworkers. Signed in 1950, the Treaty of Detroit between the UAW and General Motors established the basis not only for large-scale pattern bargaining in the auto industry but also for the Fordist principle that, through ever-increasing wages and benefits, workers could expect a share of the productivity gains to which they contributed. This collective agreement established a 2 percent annual improvement factor, quarterly cost-of-living adjustments, pensions, and employer-paid health insurance for 50 percent of the cost of premiums.[36] Measured in constant dollars, autoworkers' average weekly wage of $56.51 in 1947 had more than doubled to $115.21 by 1960 and had tripled to $170.07 by 1970.[37] A union divided against itself was unlikely to deliver similar results, and the consolidation of power in the office of the president did not appear to elicit much rank-and-file opposition.[38] The caucus even outlived its charismatic founder. After Reuther's untimely death in 1970, a carefully managed transition orchestrated by the International Executive Board ensured that the Administration caucus persisted.[39] It became a fixture in the life and culture of the union. Indeed, "a wave of relief went through the locals when workers saw that the top was holding, that nothing had changed in any important way with Reuther's death," remarked Bob White decades later.[40]

The UAW's Canadian section featured an Administration caucus of its own. It, too, was dominant, but it existed alongside a Left caucus. Although some radicals were purged from Canadian locals, the Canadian District Council acted as a refuge for leftists within the union and provided a countervailing left-wing force that helped to preserve a wider ideological range within the Canadian section of the UAW.[41]

Because the left was not entirely marginalized in the Canadian section of the union, as it was in the United States, the UAW evolved differently north of the border. However, the Canadian director still wielded significant power and always managed to have his preferred successor approved. As an extension of the union leadership, staff also played an important role in advancing the leadership's agenda, and prospective candidates for leadership positions (often staff members themselves) recognized the importance of securing staff support if they were to be considered legitimate contenders. The director's role in hiring and firing staff complicated this dynamic. Bob White, for example, recounted how retiring director George Burt used intimidation tactics to suggest that White would lose his staff job if he did not fall in line and back Dennis McDermott, the union's Toronto-area subregional director, as Burt's successor.[42] Formally, elections were open, but in practice only candidates backed by the Administration caucus secured wins, usually through acclamation. On rare occasions, candidates would emerge to oppose the candidate who was backed by the Administration caucus, but the outcome of elections was never in doubt.[43] Although the Left caucus did not have the capacity to run a slate to challenge the electoral dominance of the Administration caucus, its activists did have influence as a voice of dissent at the Canadian Council, where its leaders would express alternative views and stir up collective anger in debates. Some articulate and dedicated Left caucus members were even pulled into staff positions, partly in recognition of their talent but also to blunt their opposition to the union leadership.[44]

Electorally, left caucuses proved more successful at the local level. There were competitive caucuses or slates in most local unions. Local 199 in St. Catharines, for example, featured an enduring social democratic Blue slate (formerly the Reuther Administration caucus) and a more radical Unity slate.[45] Over time, however, these local caucuses declined in importance.[46]

UAW POLITICS IN THE 1960S

Despite the enduring ideological influences, the union and its leaders appeared to settle on the NDP as its official electoral vehicle in the 1960s, even if this alignment was not the whole of the union's politics. Anti-communist sentiment associated with the Cold War, the Liberal Party's declining influence in Ontario politics, and key personnel changes within the UAW all contributed to the union's focus on building the NDP. The UAW played a key role in creating the party in 1961. George Burt served on the New Party's founding committee, and the UAW sent sixty delegates to the founding convention, surpassed only in size by the delegations of the United Packinghouse Workers of America and the United Steelworkers.[47]

The UAW and its successor union subsequently remained firmly committed to the party for the next forty years, at least monetarily. At the party's inception in 1961, 26 percent of the total donations to the New Party Fund used to transform the CCF into the NDP came from the UAW.[48] By 1962, 70 percent of UAW members were paying dues to the party through their local unions, and a report by the Political Action Committee of the Ontario Federation of Labour (OFL) noted that they led all other unions in Ontario in terms of their rate of affiliation to the NDP.[49] By 1966, thirty-three of the UAW's sixty-nine locals were affiliated to the NDP, but this figure represented 89 percent of the union's membership.[50] The union struggled with party affiliation the most in Quebec. By 1969, only one of its Quebec locals, representing just 534 workers, was affiliated to the NDP.[51] Nevertheless, the

UAW enjoyed significant weight among the NDP's union-affiliated members, accounting for 28.6 percent of the union caucus, their numbers exceeded only by the United Steelworkers, which represented 30.3 percent of the party's union-affiliated membership in 1966.[52] The relationship between the Canadian UAW and the NDP was solidified through the expectation that all elected leaders and staff would be NDP members, would make regular financial contributions to the party, and would actively participate in elections in support of the party's candidates.[53]

The creation of the NDP gave new life to those in the UAW who wanted to represent their fellow workers in Parliament, an effort fuelled in part by the union's support for their candidacies through financial backing and dedicated staff time. For example, the UAW contributed $36,000 to the NDP's 1965 federal campaign and assigned eight staff to work full-time.[54] Throughout the 1960s, a significant number of UAW members who ran for elected office did so under the NDP banner. For example, Cliff Pilkey, former president of both Local 222 in Oshawa and the Canadian Council, was elected to Queen's Park as the NDP member for Oshawa in 1967.[55]

Leadership changes in part explain the Canadian UAW's firmer embrace of the NDP in this period. After serving nearly thirty years as Canadian director of the UAW, George Burt retired in 1968 and tapped Dennis McDermott, his preferred successor, to replace him. McDermott came out of Local 439 in Toronto, having worked as an assembler and welder at Massey Ferguson, a manufacturer of farm implements. A fierce civil and human rights activist, McDermott served his local in several elected roles before joining the international union staff in 1954 as an organizer.[56] McDermott was a "lifetime NDP stalwart" and had close personal ties to federal NDP leader David Lewis and his family.[57]

According to Yates, "immediately upon taking office as the Canadian UAW regional director in 1968, McDermott made clear his intention to translate his personal commitment to social democracy into a renewed relationship between the NDP and organized labour."[58] McDermott served on the executive committee of both the federal and Ontario NDP and used his clout to demand "better communication between trade unions and the party and increased labour representation in party policy and decision-making structures."[59] The party responded positively, and at its 1969 convention, delegates voted to expand the size of the party's federal council to include one representative from each of the twelve largest affiliated unions. In short, McDermott was a going concern in NDP circles and worked diligently to bring the party and union closer together. Many observers and union activists themselves have characterized the typical union-party relationship as one premised on a division of labour with distinct roles and spheres of action. According to academic and political activist Robert Laxer, "The NDP model has tended to emphasize a distinction between the unions, which are supposed to act on economic issues, and the party, which is supposed to deal with political questions. The unions themselves, in this model, are not seen as potential centres for rallying workers to action on specific legislative or political issues."[60] However, given the multiplicity of political orientations inside the union, the UAW in Canada never strictly adhered to this formula and always retained some independent political capacity. In fact, there was always some discontent with the close relationship to the NDP that McDermott fostered in this period. According to Buzz Hargrove, McDermott

> believed there was a natural alliance between trade unionism and democratic socialism. But by insisting that the UAW draw closer to the NDP, he touched a nerve. Not all union members are comfortable voting for the NDP or being involved in politics. Some thought Dennis was trying to tell them how to vote. Others felt the NDP was too far to the left for their thinking; still others thought the NDP was not far enough left.[61]

This multiplicity meant that some independence from the party was always politically necessary, but how much independence and through what means varied over time.

THE POLITICAL ECONOMY OF THE NORTH AMERICAN AUTO INDUSTRY IN THE 1960S AND 1970S

External political economic and policy conditions also shaped the union's politics in important ways. The union had to face two key facts about the auto industry in Canada: first, its domination by US-based capital, namely the Detroit-based Big Three auto manufacturers Ford, GM, and Chrysler;

and second, its dependence on the US market for stable auto-sector employment. This dependence was also a problem for politicians and policy makers, whose ability to deliver on full employment and stable economic growth in the postwar era was constrained by the reality of Canadian economic dependence. Historically, Canadian governments had used tariff walls to incentivize US manufacturers to locate production in Canada. First established in 1879 by John A. MacDonald's government, the tariff wall of 35 percent on imported finished goods encouraged the development of a branch-plant economy where smaller manufacturing units of US-based parent companies were located in Canada in order to sell to Canadian consumers. Thus the Canadian auto sector was "a creature of the tariff."[62] By the early 1960s, the tariff rates had been reduced. However, the structural problems in the sector persisted. Canadian consumer demand for the full range of model choices made Canadian production increasingly inefficient, as it was not possible for Canadian plants to produce the same range of models as were available in the United States in a cost-effective way. Competition from cheaper European and Japanese imports was also undermining the viability of Canadian production and having a negative impact on jobs. Canada had developed a persistent trade deficit with the United States in auto sales, with little prospect of new investments in increasingly inefficient Canadian plants. Most importantly, Detroit automakers began to pressure the US government to negotiate with Canada for continental free trade in the sector. These converging issues led Lester B. Pearson's Liberal government to reconsider the tariff regime in the auto sector and to enter negotiations with the Americans in 1964.[63]

The resulting 1965 Auto Pact provided a new political-economic framework that would mitigate these inefficiencies and structural weaknesses in the Canadian auto sector. The Auto Pact replaced the tariff with a Canadian-content requirement as the basis for selling duty-free automobiles to the Canadian market. As business historian Dimitry Anastakis explains, "Imports to the United States could only come from Canada and had to have 50 per cent North American content to be duty-free." Furthermore, "specified manufacturers who maintained regulated Canadian content levels and continued to produce as many vehicles in Canada as they sold in Canada could import duty-free from any country, although the United States was the most likely source." Finally, "to be considered a Canadian manufacturer" and therefore to be able to import duty-free, "a company had to have been producing passenger vehicles in Canada in the 1963–64 base year" of the agreement.[64]

On the one hand, the Auto Pact was a form of managed trade that required US-based automakers to commit to Canadian production and hence to Canadian auto jobs in order to gain access to the Canadian consumer market. It certainly had this effect: by 1970, Canada's trade deficit with the United States in the auto sector had been replaced by a modest surplus. Furthermore, investments in the industry began to grow, as did Canada's share of North American auto production, rising from 7.2 percent in 1965 to 11.4 percent in 1971.[65] This increase also allowed for the rationalization of auto production on a North American scale, as it was no longer necessary to produce all of the models in Canada in order to sell them to Canadians.[66] On the other hand, this arrangement solidified the Big Three's role as employers of Canadians and strengthened the union's commitment to a continentally integrated economy. As political scientist Miriam Smith has put it in her analysis of the CLC more generally, "the Congress was skeptical of radical measures to heighten Canadian control of the economy which it feared might come at the expense of jobs."[67] Although this perspective was by no means universal in the labour movement, the new framework for trade shaped the economic militancy and political strategy of the UAW in Canada in the decades to come.

UAW POLITICS IN THE 1970S

The 1970s were a time of economic and political upheaval that tested the UAW's approach to both policy and politics. According to Gindin, by this point, "it was evident that this was a movement in decline" in the United States. "In Canada what was happening is we stopped looking to the US. We had caught up to the US through the Auto Pact, and we stopped looking to the US for our goals. We'd matched them. Now we were looking at other sectors and in particular ... the public sector, which was just emerging at the time."[68] In Gindin's view, although the UAW in Canada "had a lot of confidence going into the '70s," the union also struggled with the question of an independent economic path for Canada.[69] There was a growing desire for an independent Canadian unionism in the context of the continuing dominance of international private-sector unions, whose approach to collective bargaining was largely designed in the United States and placed primary emphasis on the interests of American union members. In response to this dynamic, McDermott moved the Canadian headquarters of the UAW from Windsor to Toronto in 1970, partly to create distance between the Canadian section and the international union leadership in Detroit.[70] That same year, McDermott also succeeded in convincing Walter Reuther to support a constitutional change that would automatically recognize the Canadian regional director as a vice-president of the international union.[71] However, this nascent politics of nationalism was complicated, and these struggles spilled over into the political arena in unexpected ways.

By the late 1960s, the Movement for an Independent Socialist Canada had emerged from within the ranks of the NDP to challenge continental integration and American control of the Canadian economy. Dubbed the Waffle, the movement included prominent left-wing academics Mel Watkins and James Laxer, socialist and union activists, and even members of the NDP caucus. The Waffle's manifesto, *For an Independent Socialist Canada* (1969), identified two problems facing Canadian workers: the American domination of the economy and its capitalist form. Canadian economic independence could therefore be won only through socialist politics, not merely by replacing Canadian capital with American capital.[72] Politically, then, the NDP's platform needed to prioritize the fight for "extensive public control over investment and nationalization of the commanding heights of the economy, such as the essential resources industries, finance and credit, and industries strategic to planning our economy."[73]

The UAW's leadership played a key role in helping the party establishment to quash the Waffle.[74] However, given the tension in the union over the economic policies needed to protect the auto industry, the UAW's relationship to rising left nationalism within the NDP was contradictory. On the one hand, some within the union viewed support of the Auto Pact as consistent with a left-nationalist politics and the desire to subject US investment to certain forms of public regulation. On the other hand, the union's dependence on US-based employers for jobs still provided some sectionalist economic basis for supporting continentally integrated production. Indeed, as Anastakis points out, the Auto Pact was seen by some – even within the union's membership – as reinforcing rather than lessening

Canadian dependence on American capital and as preventing the development of a truly made-in-Canada auto industry.[75]

Yates argues that "the struggle between international unions and the Waffle over party strategy and direction" was "the catalyst for the strengthening of ties between the UAW and the NDP."[76] The UAW supported Stephen Lewis for Ontario leader in October 1970, and McDermott "employed union resources to ensure a united UAW voice at the Ontario convention, a strategy which departed radically from earlier traditions of leaving union locals to make their own decisions independent of influence from the central union office." The UAW sponsored 265 of the 830 union delegates present at this convention, with unions in general representing 45 percent of all voting delegates, up from 20 percent in 1968.[77] This investment, as well as the close personal relationship between McDermott and the Lewis family,[78] helped David Lewis win the contest to replace Tommy Douglas as federal leader at the 1971 NDP leadership convention. After Lewis defeated Waffle-backed candidate James Laxer, McDermott also organized support for a motion by Stephen Lewis at the June 1972 Ontario Provincial Council ordering the Waffle to disband or leave the party.

Gindin argues that McDermott's opposition to the Waffle was aimed more at the challenge that its members posed to the party's organization and leadership than at the substance of its ideas.[79] McDermott's antipathy to the Waffle further intensified when, through its ties with the UAW's Left caucus, the group organized a conference on the Auto Pact in Windsor in January 1972. McDermott saw this as "attempted interference in internal union affairs," and it led him to work with Lewis to rid the NDP of the Waffle at the Ontario Provincial Council.[80] The left-nationalist threat seemed as much about who would control the UAW in Canada as about what its policy orientation would be, a dynamic that went back to the 1960s.[81] McDermott was known as a "right winger" organizationally, but in terms of substance, this label is less clearly appropriate. As Gindin elaborates,

> McDermott, in spite of him being seen as coming from the right, actually had nationalist sentiments and even had social justice sentiments because he was Irish Catholic and always felt stepped upon ... McDermott always had the sense of justice. He was actually a human

rights advocate. When he was in the Navy and they went to South
Africa, he consciously went on shore with Blacks and went into bars
with them to break ... the apartheid barriers and would get arrested.
And when he came back [to Canada], he was a major player with
Bromley Armstrong in creating the [Ontario] Human Rights Act.[82]

Indeed, McDermott adopted many of the Waffle's left-nationalist policy
priorities after the group was expelled from the party, including support
for the establishment of broader regulation of direct foreign investment
and the establishment of publicly owned Crown corporations in key strategic industries. Left nationalism generally became more prominent even
in the international industrial unions from the 1970s on as the growing
crises of Keynesianism and global economic restructuring led to industrial
job loss. As Miriam Smith puts it, "in the sixties, protecting union members
from job loss ... meant defending continentalism; in the eighties, job
protection meant economic nationalism."[83]

The UAW's enduring support for the NDP in this period was also rooted
in the ability of the party to deliver policy to the unions. NDP provincial
governments in British Columbia, Saskatchewan, and Manitoba in the
1970s, for the most part, delivered on a working-class agenda.[84] As Gindin
points out, "in office, or where it was influential, the NDP led in the introduction of health and safety legislation and progressive labour reform" in
the 1970s.[85] According to Robert Laxer, "In June 1974 McDermott told the
UAW that Canadians had never done so well as under the 1972–74 Liberal
minority government, pressured by the NDP, even though this contradicted
those labour leaders who claimed Canadian workers had suffered their
first major loss in purchasing power since the Second World War."[86] The
policy achievements that the NDP helped to usher in through its condi-
tional support of the minority governments of Pierre Trudeau in the early
1970s included the establishment of the Crown corporation Petro-Canada
and the Foreign Investment Review Agency, both of which spoke to the
UAW's growing support for left-nationalist economic policies.[87]

In this period, then, the loyalty of the Canadian UAW leadership and many
rank-and-file members to the NDP was unambiguous. "Nine times out of
ten Dennis would side with the NDP," explains Buzz Hargrove.[88] This loyalty
was reflected in affiliations and financial contributions. According to Robert

Laxer, "In 1975 ... the largest union affiliation [to the NDP] came from the USWA [United Steelworkers of America] and the UAW. These two unions contributed about half of the total monthly payments made by Canadian unionists to the NDP."[89]

As previously noted, NDP membership for elected leaders and staff was an expectation, if not a formal rule. As Hargrove puts it, "We didn't have a mandate, but it was understood, politically, that if you want to be on the staff of the union, then you have to join the NDP, and we had a certain amount of money we donated per year, as staff members and officers of the Union."[90] This expectation did not mean that all political debate was foreclosed. Gindin describes a national office where vigorous internal debate was normal, even if staff were expected to unify around the outcomes. However, as he explains, the question of the union's support for the NDP in the mid-1970s was seemingly settled, even if some felt that the party was not really advancing electorally:

> I wrote a memo saying the NDP ran, you know, a decent campaign [in the 1974 federal election]. But we were going nowhere with the NDP, and our members weren't being educated on left politics. And I thought that we should have a discussion about the NDP, a serious discussion, and since the election was over, we weren't harming them. This was the right time to have that kind of serious discussion about what kind of politics we want, and I'm thinking about at some point to raise the question of a socialist party, which wasn't going to happen. I got the memo back from McDermott, not a long memo, but the first page has two letters on it, written in dark, in a dark black pen, "NO," with an exclamation mark. No other comment. He never mentioned it to me. That was the end of it.[91]

Despite the shared political commitments and policy successes of the NDP and the UAW, tensions remained in the union-party relationship over the relative power and influence of the two groups. Rank-and-file union partisans often wondered whether the party valued union members beyond their money and volunteer labour at election time. Sam Gindin illustrates this tension as he recounts an early conversation that he had with rank-and-file members soon after joining the union's staff in 1974:

My first discussion with autoworkers on the NDP was in a hotel room in Port Elgin [in the mid-1970s] … and I think this is indicative of something. They were all from Windsor. And I was asking them about the NDP and running somebody from the union. And they said, "Well, nobody from the union can run for the NDP. The party wouldn't allow it. They think that workers can't win." And they said [that] openly. Like, all of them supported the NDP, all of them contributed money, all of them knocked on doors, all of them went into the plant to talk about it, [and] all of them felt that they were instrumental tools for the NDP. [But they said,] "The NDP didn't want to hear our ideas. They want our money, and they want us to knock on doors. They want us to organize."[92]

As Gindin argues, "even as ties with the CCF/NDP grew, a healthy level of skepticism prevented the relationship from being reduced to one of unconditional loyalty. The union would, when necessary, challenge the party's direction."[93] In Gindin's observation, although there was "an official hegemony of the NDP … [and] every staff member had to contribute dues to the party," this characteristic coexisted with a "syndicalist strain … which meant that, yes, you supported the NDP, but the union came first."[94] In this way, the UAW departed somewhat from how other unions with strong partisan ties to the NDP thought about union political action. In general, unions with partisan allegiances to the NDP contracted out their politics to the party.[95] However, this division of labour was not as clear-cut in the UAW insofar as the union always maintained its own political capacity to influence policy directly.[96]

This perspective was clearly in evidence during the strike wave of the early to mid-70s, which demonstrated that syndicalist politics were still alive and well in the UAW and that members had confidence in the ability of the union – or even themselves – to win things directly. The strike rate in Canada soared to levels not seen since 1946, fuelled by record numbers of tentative agreement rejections and wildcat strikes.[97] The UAW was in the thick of the unrest. In 1969, workers at the Oakville Ford plant wild-catted over the establishment of mandatory overtime that resulted in a fifty-six-hour work week.[98] Workers at GM in both the United States and Canada went on strike for two months in 1970, and in the decade that followed, GM saw 59 wildcats in its Canadian plants.[99] Budd's stamping plant in Kitchener, Ontario, had 150 wildcats between 1976 and 1979.[100] Bitter and lengthy strikes took place at Dominion Forge in Windsor, at De Havilland and McDonnell Douglas Aircraft in Toronto, and at United Aircraft in Montreal, the latter of which Yates characterizes as "one of the longest and most violent strikes in Canadian autoworkers' history."[101] Such militancy in the face of demands for concessions, speed-up, and threats of plant closure indicated that significant stock was put in the value of direct action. The attitude of the UAW leadership in Canada to such efforts was also interesting. According to Gindin, "Wildcats were led at the local level and, while McDermott did not sanction them, he made no concerted attempt to discredit the frustrations these protests reflected."[102] This response is contrary to what was seemingly the case in many other unions, where wildcats were as much an indictment of quiescent and "responsible" union leaders as they were of management and where leaders took steps to repress the actions of young workers who were no longer willing to "take it."[103]

The Trudeau government's wage and price controls, established by Bill C-73, the Anti-Inflation Act, which was in effect from 1975 to 1978, also had an impact on the Canadian UAW's political alignments and strategic repertoire. The legislation, which McDermott described as "the worst act of political immorality in Canadian history," disillusioned many of the partisan Liberals in the union's ranks and helped to consolidate UAW support for the NDP both federally and provincially.[104] In the 1975 Ontario provincial election, the UAW helped to propel the NDP to the status of Official Opposition by contributing more money to the party coffers than any other union.[105] The UAW even made financial contributions to NDP election campaigns in provinces like British Columbia, Nova Scotia, and Saskatchewan, where the union had very little presence but where the party was strategically well placed to make inroads or to win.[106] This financial link, however, belied tensions over how NDP governments in Manitoba and Saskatchewan approached the issue of wage and price controls. NDP premiers Edward Schreyer and Allan Blakeney tepidly supported Trudeau's Anti-Inflation Act over strong opposition from both organized labour and the federal NDP.[107]

Wage and price controls proved a lightning rod for labour. Some unions gravitated toward extra-parliamentary politics for a time, and the labour movement organized the National Day of Protest against wage controls in 1976. According to Robert Laxer,

> There was some evidence in the mid-seventies that unionists in English Canada were beginning to recognize the limitations of confining their political action to formal support for the NDP. The UAW, in its mass lobby in Ottawa in February 1975, and its promise of stepped-up actions in the future, was seeking some new form of political expression. Following the 1974 election, Morden Lazarus, former director of political education for the OFL, suggested that labour leaders should "perhaps ... consider a five-year moratorium on resolutions in support of the New Democratic Party and spend more time in active endeavours.[108]

The Canadian UAW's independent political actions here were in part an expression of the union's syndicalist political dimension, where workers take direct action to make political change, which was also reflected in the mood of the broader labour movement at the time.

Although the federal NDP was very strongly opposed to wage and price controls, the party was at best ambivalent about the Day of Protest, in line with its general reluctance to encourage extra-parliamentary activism.[109] However, debates over the utility of parliamentary versus extra-parliamentary politics did not shake the enduring alliance between the NDP and the UAW. The party and the union butted heads from time to time, but in this period most conflicts played out within the context of a solid relationship, with the union feeling a significant amount of responsibility toward the party. In April 1977, CLC vice-president Julien Major told members of the CLC's National Political Education Committee that, politically, the NDP premiers "could not be seen as giving up immediately to 'big labour'" on the issue of wage controls. McDermott agreed, adding that "labour wanted out of the controls but was not insisting the political party commit suicide."[110] Thus, despite occasional public criticisms of the party, the strategy that McDermott pursued was to increase labour's presence within the NDP so that union leaders could exert more influence. As Yates notes, "the conflicts between the party and organized labour in the 1970s ultimately drew the UAW closer to the NDP. The union saw itself as able to influence policies and direct the party."[111]

By the late 1970s, the UAW's political education programs were geared toward building rank-and-file support for the NDP. The union's Paid Education Leave (PEL) program was first negotiated in 1977 at the auto parts company Rockwell International and was later expanded to include cents-per-hours-worked contributions from collective agreements throughout the union, especially the Big Three auto manufacturers after 1979.[112] With four-week and one-week residential programs held at the union's Family Education Centre on the shores of Lake Huron in Port Elgin, Ontario, PEL rapidly became a space for reproducing and spreading an oppositional consciousness among union members. Officially, the program had a political orientation aimed at "understanding the economy and addressing broad social change," but it was also designed to provide "working people with an understanding of capitalism, their place in the system, the role of unions as independent working class organizations, the history of workers and their organizations, and the principles and philosophy of the Canadian UAW."[113] In other words, the goal of PEL was to develop a militant form of class consciousness among the union membership that would build the base for opposing capital's prerogatives.[114] In contrast to the UAW's version of PEL in the United States, where employers shared in the shaping of the curriculum, the Canadian region insisted on and fiercely guarded its right to shape the pedagogy independent of employer prerogatives.[115] In practice, in this period, PEL was oriented toward building NDP activists insofar as one was expected to sign a party card at the completion of the course. PEL's class-oriented education presented the NDP as the primary vehicle for class politics, even if there was more political diversity in the union than this emphasis implied.[116] Nonetheless, PEL's counterhegemonic curriculum was personally and politically transformative for participants, whatever the direction their politics took. As Bob White and CAW staffer Jane Armstrong put it in their review of PEL in 2006, "The saying exists that the 'head of our union is in Toronto; the heart is in Port Elgin.'"[117]

In 1978, McDermott was elected to the presidency of the CLC and continued to consolidate support for the party in his new role.[118] McDermott was succeeded as UAW Canadian director by Bob White, who had served as McDermott's assistant since 1972. White had a long history in the union, having joined the UAW in the 1950s as a teenager. Within a couple of years, White was elected a union steward at the UAW-organized Hay and

Company and led his first strike in 1957 at the age of twenty-two.[119] He was elected president of Local 636 two years later in 1959 before being recruited onto the international union's staff in 1960.[120] White maintained the UAW-NDP alliance that was so dear to McDermott, although he recognized, like his predecessor, that unique circumstances in Quebec required the union to adjust its political approach there.

QUEBEC NATIONALISM AND UAW POLITICS

The rising tide of Quebec nationalism also shaped the UAW's politics, both outside and inside the union. First, partisan alignments played out differently in Quebec, where the NDP never really caught on in its early years. The rise of Quebec nationalism in the late 1960s, fuelled by class conflicts and social inequalities related to language and culture, drew many union activists to support the upstart Parti Québécois (PQ), a sovereignist political party with an initially social democratic orientation. Among the PQ's early union supporters was Robert Dean, a UAW member and vice-president of the Quebec Federation of Labour. A year after the PQ's majority government win in 1976, the UAW Canadian Council passed a resolution "recognizing Quebec's historic claim as one of the founding nations of Canada."[121] Dean eventually ran successfully for the PQ in the 1981 provincial election and was appointed to Cabinet by Premier René Lévesque.[122]

Second, discontent among the UAW's Quebec membership shaped the Canadian region's relationship with both Quebec nationalism and the UAW International's office and was another source of pressure in favour of greater independence from Detroit. This dynamic often played out on the terrain of collective bargaining and in the UAW International's treatment of locals on strike. UAW activists in Quebec complained that the Canadian section of the union focused on Ontario at the expense of Quebec and that the US head office had even less knowledge or concern. Members of the GM local in Sainte-Thérèse, Quebec, were excluded from the GM master contract, were subjected to unilingual anglophone management, and suffered from poorer wages and working conditions compared to their Ontario counterparts.[123] But the most dramatic case of internal union conflict that pushed the Canadians to a more independent posture vis-à-vis the Americans was the previously mentioned strike at United Aircraft in Montreal in 1974–75. A subsidiary of a US-based company (later to become Pratt and Whitney), the local had long tried and failed to negotiate a union security clause on the model of the Rand Formula and made this achievement a priority in the 1974 round of negotiations. A lockout and long strike ensued that rallied Quebec society around the strikers. The UAW's International office intervened in an incendiary way: in August 1974, UAW secretary-treasurer Emil Mazey sent a letter to all UAW local and regional leaders in Canada accusing the strikers of fraud and threatening to cut off strike pay.[124] In McDermott's absence, White had to travel to Detroit to confront UAW International president Leonard Woodcock with the message that the strike would be destroyed unless he committed to continuing strike pay and dealing with any problems around alleged misappropriation of funds internally. The "sensitivities in Quebec," which the Americans did not appreciate, meant that McDermott publicly condemned Mazey for his intervention at the next Canadian Council.[125] In this way, Quebec nationalism and Canadian nationalism reinforced each other.[126] This incident was, in Gindin's words, the "first real crisis between the two sections of the union."[127]

The adoption of a modified union structure that recognized the specificity of Quebec's unique history and political orientation would address the Quebec membership's alienation from the union and would eventually facilitate UAW support for the PQ. As Canadian directors, both McDermott and White pressed the UAW's International office to allow the formation of a Quebec Council for years but to no avail.[128] In September 1981, Bob White, in his director's address to the union's Canadian Council, conveyed the frustration of Quebec UAW members:

Currently the facts are that very few of our Quebec locals participate in this Council. The distance for travel is great, the debate is conducted in English, and a majority of the issues discussed relate mainly to our activities in Ontario. I don't want to totally lose the impact that we have at this Council from Quebec – but I also want them to have a properly structured vehicle where they elect an executive and resolutions committee, discuss issues and make recommendations to my office in a more formalized way. They also need an avenue where they can take positions on important legislative matters in Quebec.[129]

46

The Quebec Council held its founding meeting in March 1983.[130] The modified union structures in the UAW and other unions, like the United Steelworkers and the Canadian Union of Public Employees (CUPE), were all
established for the same reason: to provide a forum where union members
from Quebec could meet and debate political, social, and economic questions specific to Quebec. The Canadian section of the UAW recognized
that the aspirations of its Quebec members could not be achieved within
the larger framework of a highly centralized international union or even
of a pan-Canadian national union. Given this important realization, which
manifested itself in a principled stand on self-determination, and given
the more practical fear of losing Quebec members to rival trade-union
centrals, the union was convinced to adopt a modified structure.[131]

LABOUR CALLING: THE 1979 AND 1980 FEDERAL ELECTIONS

Although the labour movement showed openness to doing politics differently in Quebec, its electoral alliance with the NDP continued to gain steam
in the rest of Canada as the political impact of wage and price controls
convinced unions to get involved in the 1979 and 1980 federal election
campaigns in an unprecedented way. Labour movement political strategy
was also shaped by the ascendancy of NDP partisan Dennis McDermott
to the presidency of the CLC in 1978. According to retired CLC staffer Pat
Kerwin, although previous CLC presidents were supportive of the NDP,
McDermott was "the strongest supporter" and "came in quite determined
to put political action at the top of his [priority] list."[132] Yates concurs: "With
McDermott at the helm of the CLC and union relations with the Liberal
party at an all-time low due to the 1975 wage controls, the stage was set for
a massive union mobilization behind the NDP."[133]

This mobilization took the form of a "parallel campaign" of on-the-job
canvassing that sought to have union activists do the work of mobilizing
the working-class vote in a more comprehensive way than they had done
in previous elections. As historian and NDP insider Desmond Morton
explains, ahead of the 1979 federal election,

the CLC's Dennis McDermott summoned a hundred union leaders
to Toronto to make sure that no one would ignore labour's political

47

intentions. Instead of its usual discreet role in staffing committee rooms and contributing to local candidates, unions would mobilize a "parallel campaign" to the NDP door-knocking; each union member and family would be canvassed.[134]

For long-time UAW/CAW staffer Hemi Mitic, supporting the NDP in this way was "part of the DNA" of the union.[135] However, the CLC's parallel campaign also converged with the lingering legacies of distrust toward the party in some quarters of the membership. According to Yates, the CLC's parallel campaign meant that the UAW could avoid "relying upon the NDP to activate workers, a strategy that had backfired many times due to workers' suspicions about the party."[136] For its part, the NDP was ambivalent about the prominent role that the labour movement was taking in the 1979 electoral mobilization, fearing that "residual Canadian hostility to unions was all the more easily deflected to the NDP."[137]

The 1979 campaign bore contradictory results. The Trudeau Liberals were defeated, and a Conservative minority government led by Joe Clark was elected. The NDP's seat count increased from seventeen to twenty-six, and its share of the popular vote was bumped up by 2.45 percentage points. From a partisan perspective, the CLC's campaign was a success both in punishing the Liberal Party and in strengthening the NDP caucus, even if it saw a Conservative government elected. Internally, however, the CLC's National Political Education Committee bemoaned the fact that labour's parallel campaign "was not able to produce even 50% coverage of the membership."[138]

It was not long before the country was back at the polls, and in 1980 the CLC adopted another parallel campaign, Labour Calling. However, some tactical tweaks were made: "Perhaps the key difference in the UAW's campaign was its use of 'job canvassing' – talking to workers about the NDP at their workplace."[139] The UAW set up eighteen phone banks, reached 45,000 members, and identified 20,000 NDP supporters. The party's share of the vote increased by almost 2 percentage points on election night, and it netted an additional five seats, but it was the Liberals who carried the day, recapturing a majority government with Pierre Trudeau once more at the helm.

The UAW continued to pump money into the NDP after 1980, but according to Yates, a more visible gap between the union and the party began to open in this period: "The NDP and UAW were seemingly moving in opposite directions. The party moved away from its social democratic principles towards a more conservative political image at the same time that the UAW was becoming more politically militant in its own action and more radical in its demands for government action."[140] For instance, when NDP leader Ed Broadbent delivered a speech in Hamilton in 1982 with distinctly neoliberal themes, arguing for "a reduction in the deficit and for encouragement of investment through such measures as corporate tax breaks ... The labour movement responded quickly and harshly to this reorientation, effectively putting a lid on it for the near future."[141] Gindin, for example, complained that the party's policy direction "conjured images of 'workers having to accept wage concessions, decreases in social services, a shift in the tax structure to help certain companies – and who's paying? Workers. It's a dead-end street.'"[142]

THE MACDONALD COMMISSION AND
THE COMING OF FREE TRADE

Canada's economic future was an especially pressing issue in the early 1980s given high levels of unemployment, rising inflation, and a recessionary slump. Within this context, the Liberal government launched the Royal Commission on the Economic Union and Development Prospects for Canada (the MacDonald Commission) in November 1982. Headed by former Liberal finance minister Donald S. MacDonald, the commission was tasked with developing a new social consensus on Canadian economic policy. Drawn heavily from the business sector and right-wing academics, commission members included just one representative from labour: Gérard Docquier, Canadian director of the United Steelworkers.[143]

The commission was presented with very different visions of Canada's economic future. The corporate sector encouraged the commission to embrace international competitiveness and advocated for the removal of trade barriers with the United States. Organizations like the Canadian Manufacturers' Association and the Canadian Federation of Independent Business called for a reduced role for government in economic affairs and for a smaller public sector. This dominant corporate perspective did not go uncontested. Unions and social movement organizations presented the commission with views from "the factory, office and farm; as seen from the unemployment line and the welfare office."[144] Progressive organizations argued that Canada needed to foster job creation through the development of an interventionist industrial policy.[145] They argued that the corporate sector's emphasis on free trade was misguided given its potential negative impact on Canadian jobs and autonomy. For example, in the UAW's submission to the commission, the union argued,

> Playing this game of "international competitiveness" therefore undermines Canada's autonomy to carry out a national program to improve our society ... Even well-meaning governments find that the real decision makers are the amorphous market and the multinational corporations who control production. At issue is a meaningful democracy and the collective ability to really – rather than just formally – shape our lives.[146]

The UAW stated that it opposed any economic strategy that would increase Canada's trade dependence. "Rather than hoping to get more jobs by increasing our exports of manufactured goods (an illusion), we focus more seriously on import replacement: producing more of the goods and machinery we ourselves use," the union argued in its brief.[147] The UAW further argued that the path of international competitiveness was a "dead-end street. We suffer through 'short-term pain' only to learn it will be long-term pain ... We must stop limiting our questions to 'How can we become more competitive?' and begin asking whether this is in fact the game we want to play."[148]

Commission chair MacDonald did not share the UAW's concerns. Even before the commission issued its final report, he indicated support for free trade with the United States on the basis that Canada needed to take a "leap of faith" in order to ensure that the country remained competitive internationally.[149]

While the commission continued its work, Trudeau took his famous walk in the snow on February 28, 1984, and announced the next day that he was retiring from politics amid sagging public support for his government. The Liberal Party hastily organized a leadership contest, and on June 16, John Turner, a corporate lawyer and former finance minister, won on the second ballot over future prime minister Jean Chrétien. Turner's tenure as prime minister was short-lived. On July 9, he triggered a snap election for September 4, 1984.

The labour movement leadership lined up squarely behind the NDP but shifted tactics in an effort to better leverage union support. Yates argues that the CLC, underwhelmed by the results of previous parallel campaigns, "replaced the full-scale mobilization attempted under the original parallel campaign with the strategic targeting of resources and constituencies where organized labour might have an effect on the outcome of the election."[150] This decision was made, in part, because the party's internal polling indicated that the "upsurge in PC strength and the national decline in NDP strength seem to dictate an almost exclusively defensive NDP electoral strategy for the next Federal election."[151] In the case of the UAW, this strategy meant focusing efforts in places like Oshawa, Windsor, and St. Catharines, where the union had a large number of members.[152] At the outset of the campaign, Turner's Liberals led the polls with 49 percent support, followed by the PCs at 39 percent and the NDP at 11 percent. Internal party fighting over constitutional issues and policy direction had taken its toll on the NDP. By election day, however, based primarily on the strength of party leader Ed Broadbent, the NDP had substantially recovered, salvaging 30 seats and 18.8 percent of the vote. After Turner faltered badly in response to Brian Mulroney's jabs in the leaders' debate, the PCs easily cruised to victory, winning 50 percent of the popular vote and 211 seats. The Liberals held onto just 40 seats and 28 percent of the popular vote.

Trade policy did not emerge as a significant campaign issue even though Mulroney had campaigned against free trade in his 1983 PC leadership bid.[153] Nevertheless, once he took over as prime minister, he signalled to Ronald Reagan's administration his government's support for a free trade agreement. Mulroney's policy shift was legitimized by the 1985 findings of the MacDonald Commission, which recommended a free trade agreement as part of a broader package of neoliberal policy reforms. While the UAW's Canadian section geared up for a fight with Mulroney's government on the economic and social policy front, an internal battle with the international union would consume much of the union's attention in the coming year.

THE BIRTH OF THE CAW

The breakaway of the UAW's Canadian section from the international union in 1985 was the product of two long-standing influences: differences in external political economic conditions and differences in the internal union politics that shaped how sections of the union dealt with these conditions. These influences had begun to culminate in the late 1970s in the form of divergent union responses to the crisis in the postwar Keynesian order.[154] The UAW and its Canadian region differed over how to respond to capital's attempts to radically restructure labour and industrial relations that, in the North American auto sector, had been "settled" by the Treaty of Detroit in 1950. These divergences over how unions should respond to concessions in the face of recession, plant closures, global restructuring, and the rise of neoliberalism accelerated the existing impetus for an independent Canadian union that had developed throughout the 1970s. As Gindin puts it, the breakaway "cannot be understood apart from the dynamics of struggle: that is, from the interaction between a favourable environment in Canada and ideology, leadership, structures for participation, and the specifics of recent struggles."[155]

By the late 1970s, the global economy was again in recession. The North American manufacturing sector began a wave of layoffs and plant closures that undermined the strength of the industrial unions to resist employer demands for concessions to save jobs.[156] The crisis was especially acute in the US auto industry. As Gindin points out, the much greater volume of layoffs in US auto plants – with one-third of the auto workforce laid off by the early 1980s – had a demoralizing effect on the union there.[157] The UAW's growing acceptance of concessions was most evident at Chrysler. In 1979, Chrysler filed for bankruptcy protection, making it infinitely more difficult for autoworkers to resist the siren song of concessions to save their employer. After the members initially rejected a two-year wage freeze to bail out the company in August 1979, UAW leaders convinced them that there was no other way to help the company to secure the required loan guarantees. The wage freeze was agreed to in November 1979, followed by a wage cut of $1.15 per hour a year later, and set off demands from both GM and Ford for similar concessions.[158] In 1980, the UAW joined the company in lobbying Jimmy Carter's administration for loan guarantees, for which members – including those in Canada – had to submit to more concessions. In 1981, the UAW agreed to more concessions at Chrysler, without government intervention, and because this was an international agreement where American and Canadian members voted together, the dissenting votes of the Canadians were swamped by the assenting votes of their US counterparts.[159]

In contrast, and despite the general political economic turmoil of the period, Canadian autoworkers were in some ways more confident than ever, transitioning away from being a union that, from its foundation until the 1960s, had looked to the United States for leadership and toward being one that had now "matched" the Americans and was beginning to look to other sectors in Canada for political and economic referents.[160] In short, Canadian autoworkers had increasingly stopped idealizing the UAW as that union opened itself up to concessions.

In Canada, the Auto Pact created a particular set of conditions that advantaged the Canadian section of the UAW in the early 1980s. The requirement that automakers make at least as many vehicles in Canada as they sold in Canada gave Canadian autoworkers the structural power to "say no" when employer concessions, free trade, and work reorganization arrived because they were less afraid of job loss. A certain floor sat under Canadian auto jobs if automakers wanted to sell cars in Canada. Added to this situation was the effect of rationalization and specialization at the North American scale, which meant that Canada was producing more popular models and which also made "the corporations more vulnerable, in the short-term, to work interruptions."[161] Since the Auto Pact had encouraged investment in new plants, they were much less vulnerable to closure than the older US facilities.[162] Furthermore, there were cost advantages to producing in Canada, linked both to the exchange rate and to Canada's public health care system, which meant that US capital would not have to provide a costly private welfare state for its employees.[163] According to Gindin, "Canadian Big Three wages were about twenty-five per cent above the national average, half the gap between American autoworkers and the rest of their community. The Canadian movement was more highly unionized and aggressive."[164]

Where autoworkers were suffering from plant closures – mostly in auto parts production – the Canadian director's response was to encourage resistance rather than concessions. Gindin describes the events at the summer 1980 Canadian Council: "Delegate after delegate stood up to recount cases of individual and community tragedy. The collective frustration called out for some kind of union response."[165] White's view was that the union needed a tactic that could make a difference since "there was no point putting pickets in front of a deserted plant." Recalling the Reuther brothers' use of plant occupations to stop scab labour, White concluded that "the only weapon we had against plant closures was to occupy the plants so the company couldn't get its equipment out." He told the delegates, "If it takes an occupation of plants to stop this ... then we'll occupy them."[166] A wave of occupations ensued, the most famous being at Houdaille in Oshawa and Bendix in Windsor.[167] Even where such direct actions did not keep plants open, the experience of fighting back built workers' confidence in themselves and the union leadership. Furthermore, the fight against concessions was not the resistance of a small labour aristocracy preserving its privileges relative to most other workers but something that many other Canadian unions were both doing and inspired by. Autoworkers in Canada thus had more access to associational power and were more connected with other working-class people and social movements than was the case in the United States. These elements gave Canadian autoworkers more structural power and willingness to resist concessions.

The distinct political environments, political parties, and partisan alignments of the two countries also gave the UAW in Canada a bulwark against concessions at the bargaining table and against neoliberalism in social policy. Gindin argues that "the NDP provided a countervoice that the Americans didn't have. And Canadian nationalism allowed for much more skepticism over the claims and demands of American-based multinationals."[168] US corporations could not appeal to Canadians to make concessions based on a shared patriotism. If anything, concessions were *less* legitimate and contrary to the national interest because they were being demanded by foreign capital.

As a result, Bob White's leadership of the Canadian region from 1978 onward was economically and socially progressive, militant, and radical, but in another strategically important way, it was also a kind of "stubborn conservatism." As Gindin puts it,

> White's period was very much dominated by saying no ... In other words, what was happening is that workers had expectations in the postwar period. And what was changing was that we were being told you had to make concessions, you had to lower your expectations. We said no to that, we said no to social service cutbacks, we said no to free trade. White actually could live and lead by saying no. You

know, in an articulate way. But through to 1992, that was basically our position, No, we weren't going to change, in a stubborn way. It was stubbornness. And we could sustain it.[169]

The concessions made in 1979 at Chrysler were soon shown to represent a new normal sought by the Big Three rather than an exception to stave off a temporary crisis. The Canadians sought to carve out a different approach, which brought them increasingly into open conflict with the UAW leadership in Detroit. Signs of divergence and defiance began to accumulate. In 1981, the Canadian leadership refused to weigh in with a recommendation on the concessionary tentative agreement at Chrysler, which Local 444 narrowly rejected but whose vote was swamped by the US membership voting in favour. Canadian Chrysler workers left the international agreement soon thereafter. Whereas the other automakers secured concessions from American workers on annual wage increases, a cost-of-living allowance (COLA), and paid personal holidays in 1982, the Canadians won "extra money over and above that awarded in the US to compensate for higher inflation," rejected profit sharing, and switched to a separate Canadian COLA.[170] In their solo 1982 negotiations at Chrysler, Canadians went on strike for six weeks and won COLA increases and an additional $1.15 an hour and brought US negotiations to a standstill. Although Chrysler workers in the United States also wanted to refuse concessions, their fear of a strike's impact on their employer's viability held them back rather than emboldening them. It was the Canadians' strike that opened the door to a (more modest) wage increase in the United States.[171] These successes were a double-edged sword: although the Canadians' efforts increasingly inspired US members to build opposition caucuses in order to fight concessions, they also threatened the US leadership, who increasingly needed to save face. As Yates puts it, "Rather than seeing a no-concessions strategy as viable, the International saw the solution to its problems as forcing the Canadian Region into line with International UAW policy."[172]

The 1984 round of Big Three bargaining brought these tensions to a head, particularly in GM negotiations. Whereas the Americans traded "built-in wage increases for lump-sum payments and profit-sharing," even after a nine-day strike at some GM plants in September, the Canadians prepared for a fight, building a no-concessions fund and coordinating local-agreement bargaining.[173] With negotiations being filmed by a crew from the National Film Board, the mounting pressure on Canadians to accept the US deal came from both GM and the UAW in Detroit. White made it clear that there was no way "lump-sum payments [were] going to fly in Canada" and that GM "better be ready for a helluva confrontation."[174] GM continued to table the US agreement with lump-sum payments instead of the annual improvement factor (AIF) in Canada in the face of a strike vote of 95 percent in favour and a looming October strike deadline. Local leaders refused to recommend the agreement to their members. UAW president Owen Bieber also threatened to call the International Executive Board together to withdraw the strike's authorization if White stood firm on getting the AIF in Canada. He insisted, "You can't be on strike for AIFs in Canada when we didn't get them in the United States."[175] Making matters more heated, Oshawa GM workers began a wildcat sixteen hours before the authorized strike deadline, soon to be joined by members in Sainte-Thérèse.[176] The strike was settled thirteen days later only after the AIF was relabelled as a "Special Canadian Adjustment" to allow the US leadership to save face.[177] Interestingly, Canadian autoworkers emerged more united from the 1984 GM negotiations than their US counterparts: "87 percent of production workers and 83 percent of skilled workers" ratified the Canadian agreement, whereas "only 58 percent of the GM workers" in the US ratified theirs.[178]

Although the 1984 bargaining round resulted in the Canadians winning their argument and their agreements, the damage to their relationship with the UAW was deep. Earlier calls from locals in St. Catharines, Sainte-Thérèse, and Oshawa to separate or to form "at least a committee to study the international tie" returned with greater vigour.[179] Support for a split was widespread within the Canadian section. In December 1984, on the heels of the GM conflict, White sought and was given a mandate by the Canadian Council to seek a restructured and more autonomous relationship with the UAW, premised on "Canadian control over collective bargaining and strike authorization and complete control over staff appointments in Canada."[180] White brought these proposals to a meeting of the International Executive Board later that month but was thoroughly rebuffed.[181]

Instead, the UAW put the Canadians on the path to independence. Preparations were made for local unions to vote on the proposal to form the UAW Canada, with educational materials anticipating their questions and concerns.[182] As Hargrove later recounted, "his role in the debate was 'firefighter.' He'd travel to locals that weren't onside with the leadership's position and convince them to join the movement."[183] These and other efforts were clearly successful, with all but one local opting to break away from the UAW and form an independent Canadian union. Other elements of the labour movement were also inspired by the actions of this large and strategically important private-sector union. The breakaway and the circumstances that produced it showed that it was possible to build an independent Canadian unionism and to fight against concessions through class-conscious and militant action.[184]

With no small amount of drama, then, an independent Canadian union was founded on September 4, 1985, in Toronto with the name the UAW Canada. The founding convention was replete with excitement and enthusiasm. As "president-designate," Bob White was met with a lengthy standing ovation – "a hell of a reception from the delegates" that made "shivers go up [his] spine" as he took the podium to deliver the opening speech.[185] The union's founding was also legitimized by none other than Walter Reuther's younger brother Victor Reuther, who in his closing convention speech called the initiative "a laudable objective, a long time in the making."[186] The union's formal name was subsequently changed to the National Automotive, Aerospace and Agricultural Implement Workers Union of Canada – more popularly known as the Canadian Auto Workers, or CAW – at a special convention in June 1986. At the time of the CAW's founding, it had about 120,000 members, mostly in Ontario, and collective agreements with about 300 corporations.[187]

THE IMPACT OF INDEPENDENCE ON
CAW STRUCTURE AND POLITICS

Independence from the United States meant a rethinking of the Canadian region's structure. The new union had to create not only a new constitution but also a new set of decision-making bodies, relations of accountability, and forms of representation. And, as in all unions, these decisions reflected ideas – whether explicit or implicit – about the union's purpose, its unifying identity, its understanding of democracy and power, and the kinds of structures and practices that would best enact these ideas.[188] These decisions were also to have powerful shaping effects on the union's internal power relations and strategic capacities. So what were the major differences between the structures of the Canadian region of the UAW and those of the CAW? And what impact did these changes have on the union's internal political life?

The first major change involved the transformation of the Canadian regional director into the national president and the creation of a National Executive Board (NEB), which did not exist prior to 1985. In an interview in 2010, where he reflected on the union's history, Bob White was asked how the CAW worked to "allay fears" that "the union would be ruled by a few at the top" and to ensure that it was a "democratic union." White recounted,

> Within the UAW, we had a Canadian Council, but we never had an executive board. Local unions had an executive board but we never had one, so we sat down as a small group. "Look," I said, "we're going to have an executive board which will include the Canadian council executive, the president, the secretary-treasurer, as two key positions, their closest assistants would be there with voice but no vote. We were going to have that board and the majority of that board are going to be rank and file local union leaders, who are elected and become council leadership." From the board what we got was great input, people felt they could participate and reach a collective decision.[189]

The advent of the NEB changed the relationship of the Canadian Council to the union's executive leadership. In the UAW, the Canadian Council was a source of national autonomy, which allowed Canadians to meet and develop a distinct perspective that was often in opposition to Detroit. The Canadian director could sometimes benefit from and had some vested interests in that oppositional dynamic given that the director could use membership dissent to leverage more autonomy or resources from the US leadership. The Canadian leadership could use internal opposition as a resource rather than seeing it as a threat.

In the CAW, this dynamic began to change as the executive leadership became Canadian, with the Canadian Council's president becoming a part of the NEB. Dissent in the Canadian Council was now directed at Canadian leadership, who could no longer point to Detroit as responsible. Over the nearly thirty years of the CAW's existence, the pressures at the Canadian Council to conform with the direction of the NEB and president intensified in the absence of the impetus to chart a separate course from the United States and in response to the need to "unify" around a now domestic leadership. Yates highlights the Canadian Council's repositioning in the union's decision-making structure in this way:

> Although the CAW president continues to be responsible for reporting to Council and the scope of the Council's duties remains the same, the six Canadian Council executive board members as well as the president of the Quebec Council now sit on the National Executive Board (NEB). This change facilitated coordination of activities and the flow of information between the NEB and the Councils. Nonetheless, it has transformed the Council from a separate parallel power structure to one interwoven with the union executive.[190]

The CAW maintained the UAW's dual structure of Canadian Council and Quebec Council. The union's Canadianization also meant a centralization that gradually lessened the counterweight provided by the Canadian Council. The extent to which dissent was encouraged was also somewhat dependent on who was the president, but there is no mistaking the CAW leadership's greater control over key strategic decisions related to collective bargaining, strike authorization, and political action.

A transition in the way that staff appointments were used in the union also took place, further shaping how dissent was organized and sustained. In the pre-CAW period, staff appointments were often used to placate or neutralize opposition, particularly from the Left caucus, which could still mount electoral challenges to the Administration caucus in some locals.[191] When dissent could meaningfully destabilize leadership goals, staff appointments brought such dissenters onto the staff both to channel their dissent and to contain the forms of power available to them. For instance, staff had voice but no vote in the union's various decision-making bodies. However, such staff played a role in sustaining internal debate about politics, policy, and strategy, both in their own proposals and in their relations with the rank and file. As Sam Gindin explains, Bob White "actually liked people who were in opposition and would hire them, partly because you took them away from their base. They were talented, the union did this consciously. Some of the best lefties became staffers."[192] As dissent in the Canadian Council became a less potent threat, staff appointments were increasingly used to reward "good soldiers" rather than to contain dissenters. Such staff did not always enjoy an independent base in the membership they could refer to, draw power from, or potentially mobilize around key ideas. They depended more wholly on the executive that appointed them.

On paper, the union featured a number of democratic checks and balances, including the rank-and-file National Executive Board, but in practice the president wielded incredible authority. Increasingly, a command-and-control culture was accepted as the norm. "We were very much a male hierarchical structure in the sense that we did revere our leaders," argues Carol Phillips, who served as an assistant to both Bob White and Buzz Hargrove.[193] In the early days of the CAW, Phillips says, there was space for debate and dissent, particularly at CAW Council, but "the National Executive Board itself eventually became a body that rarely debated the direction of the president."[194] Phillips recalls that "the leadership came with decisions they had made, put them on the table and asked the NEB to endorse them with some discussion … I can't really think of a major example of anything being brought to the National Executive Board clean, as in 'here are the pros and here are the cons.'"[195] One long-time staff member who did not want their views attributed explained that "the battle cry was democracy, but it was veiled because everyone wanted to be a staff member." Phillips agrees, although she believes that the architects of the CAW who came up with the NEB structure did not realize that this dynamic would emerge. "But once they realized how effective it was … they didn't want to change it," she adds.[196]

The formation of the CAW also led to a spate of expansion as other groups of workers who had been seeking independence from their US-based unions saw a new Canadian home. As Yates documents, the CAW's first ten years saw the union add "more than 100,000 new members to its ranks, almost doubling its membership within a decade."[197] These new membership groups included various unions of airline workers, the Fishermen, Food and Allied Workers Union, the United Electrical, Radio and Machine Workers, the Canadian Union of Mine, Mill and Smelter Workers, and the

Canadian Brotherhood of Railway, Transport and General Workers.[198] Although many new members came to the CAW through new organizing initiatives in airlines, casinos, and other auto parts manufacturers, the vast majority, at 75 percent, came from existing unions that merged with the CAW.[199] The CAW's politics and strong reputation in collective bargaining appealed to smaller unions that lacked the resources to defend against concessions or to make gains in bargaining. Nonetheless, these unions had to be integrated into the union in ways that allowed them to feel that they had a voice and some control over their economic destiny. Yates discusses the tensions inherent in expanding the union's membership to include occupational groups beyond those that formed the core of the UAW's historic identity and the risks in not taking seriously the need to integrate these groups into the union's decision-making structures, strategies, and identities in meaningful ways.[200]

THE CAW'S APPROACH TO POLITICS, 1985–88

Politically, the CAW doubled down on the social unionist orientation of the UAW and articulated it in more overt class terms than had perhaps been the case in the United States for some time. The union gave its social unionist commitment expression and pride of place in the Statement of Principles at the beginning of its new constitution, contextualized by the union's understanding of its role in a democratic – and capitalist – society. Given the centrality and uniqueness of this statement, it is worth quoting at length:

Unions and a Democratic Society

In our society, private corporations control the workplace and set the framework for all employees. By way of this economic power, they influence the laws, policies, and ideas of society. Unions are central to our society being democratic because:

Unions bring a measure of democracy to the place of work, which is so central to peoples' lives.

Unions act as partial counterweight to corporate power and the corporate agenda in society more generally.

Social Unionism

Our collective bargaining strength is based on our internal organization and mobilization, but it is also influenced by the more general climate around us: laws, policies, the economy, and social attitudes. Furthermore, our lives extend beyond collective bargaining and the workplace and we must concern ourselves with issues like housing, taxation, education, medical services, the environment, the international economy.

Social unionism means unionism which is rooted in the workplace but understands the importance of participating in, and influencing, the general direction of society.[201]

Social unionism thus meant political unionism. As articulated in the report to the new union's first National Collective Bargaining and Legislative Convention in 1987, "politics is fundamental to union activity because it shapes the environment in which we live. It influences our relative ability to make progress by setting laws and standards and influencing the economic environment in which we act. And it is an instrument through which we can achieve goals not achievable at the bargaining table."[202] This social unionism had important expressions in the union's support for pressure campaigns and other social movements, international solidarity work, internal political education, collective bargaining, and of course, electoral politics.

The CAW also continued the UAW's involvement in social democratic politics via the NDP. As evidence of the strength of this relationship, federal NDP leader Ed Broadbent addressed the union's founding convention in September 1985 and was the only federal leader in attendance.[203] For many within the CAW, the NDP was an extension of the union's commitment to "social unionism."[204] Bob White expressed the classic case for why the union's social unionism required not only electoral political action but also alignment with the NDP as workers' party of choice: "The NDP's issues are a natural extension of our concerns. You can't separate the bread box and the ballot box. We can solve a good many things around a collective bargaining table, but we can't do anything there about a rise in price of prescription drugs, or the lack of support for day care, or the damage that free trade will bring."[205] Former CAW staffer Peggy Nash echoes this sentiment, recalling the saying of an older labour movement operative: "To be part of the labour movement, you've got to be part of the party. Collective bargaining, collective balloting!"[206] These sentiments were also realized through the personal political commitments of the union's key leaders in the form of party memberships, campaign contributions, and elected positions in the party structure. White, for example, was a vice-president of the federal NDP throughout the 1980s.[207]

"The CAW was genuinely born recognizing the historic partnership with the New Democratic Party ... The connection was evident ... All of our eggs were in the basket of the New Democratic Party," explains former CAW president Ken Lewenza.[208] Long-time staffer Hemi Mitic agrees, explaining that part of his job as a rep was to promote affiliation to the NDP among local unions.[209] And, as previously noted, the union's PEL program at its education centre in Port Elgin continued to orient CAW members to the NDP despite the curriculum's more radical undertones. "Prior to the '90s, the four-week PEL program ... was driving you towards being a member of the New Democratic Party," argues long-time CAW activist and former NDP member of Parliament Malcolm Allen. "At the graduation ceremony in the four-week program, you signed a [membership] card for the New Democrats," he explains.[210] Former Local 199 president and NDP member of the provincial Parliament in Ontario Wayne Gates concurs: "Our education at Port Elgin was always about supporting the NDP, about what's important to our communities, what's important to our families, publicly funded health care – all those things we talked about. It kind of drove me right to the NDP. It was an easy match."[211]

CONCLUSION

The UAW's Canadian section had a complicated political history owing to a combination of internal machinations and external pressures, but a consensus of sorts appeared to emerge among the union's leadership in support of the New Party project that led to the birth of the NDP in 1961. Relations with the NDP were gradually strengthened under Dennis McDermott, and the union poured significant resources and effort into the party. However, as Gindin reminds us, even as ties with the NDP grew, "a healthy level of scepticism prevented the relationship from being reduced to one of unconditional loyalty."[212] In short, the union's commitment to social unionism was not entirely tethered to the party-union relationship. The CAW's politics were multifaceted, as evidenced by its decisions to spearhead campaigns against continental free trade, establish a social justice fund in the name of labour internationalism, and pursue campaigns to fight racism in the workplace and in society more generally.[213] "We are the lead social union in the country, and I believe the lead social union around the world, which means we draw our strength from our members and our families ... Our people support the social work of the union because we bring everyone along," asserted Buzz Hargrove in 2010.[214] This kind of bold pronouncement reinforced the CAW's rivalry with other private-sector unions, which reflected not only competition over members but also "different philosophies about collective bargaining and political action."[215] The CAW's bargaining breakthroughs, no-concessions policy, and rejection of worker-ownership schemes set it apart from other industrial unions and gave the CAW a reputation for being more militant and combative.

This reputation was clearly revealed in the fight against wage and price controls in the mid-1970s but would become more pronounced in later years when the durability of the party-union relationship would be put to the test in the face of tensions over free trade in the late 1980s and over the Ontario NDP government's Social Contract Act in 1993.

CHAPTER 3

BACK-SEAT DRIVER?
The CAW as Left Critic, 1988–95

" The difference between our party and the others has been measured by the courage and confidence with which we pursue the dreams and hopes of ordinary people. We have never held back from the challenges of a new era in social and economic justice – we never have – and we never will."[1] Ontario New Democratic Party (NDP) leader Bob Rae's speech to the party's 1986 convention opened with this bold claim – a claim that was representative of the high hopes that the NDP and union activists had for the party. The Ontario NDP held the balance of power at Queen's Park after the 1985 election, and the federal party was steadily climbing in public opinion polls before topping them for the first time in Canadian history in May 1987.[2] Many labour activists believed that their aspirations for progressive government and for the policies expected of the NDP were about to be fulfilled.

However, over the course of the next eight years, party and union activists experienced a roller coaster ride of jubilation and despair characterized by dashed hopes, triumphant and unexpected victories, and ultimately a deep sense of disappointment and betrayal. Between 1988 and 1993, tensions emerged between the Canadian Auto Workers (CAW) and the NDP that pushed the union into becoming an important left critic inside the party. Both the party's strategy in the 1988 "Free Trade" federal election and the passage of the Rae government's Social Contract Act in Ontario caused severe tension in the party-union relationship, leading to public denunciations and ultimately, in the case of the latter, to a significant withdrawal of funding for the NDP. Constitutional turmoil in the early 1990s also led the union's Quebec section to forge a closer relationship with the sovereignist Bloc Québécois (BQ) at the expense of the NDP.

Throughout this period, the union struggled with how to pursue its own political agenda while maintaining its partisan electoral alliance with the NDP and its larger presence within the broader social democratic movement. The CAW's experience illustrates the dilemmas facing unions when social democratic parties form government. This period is thus critical for understanding the role that the union came to play as the NDP's most significant left critic and how the party-union dynamic was altered as a result.

THE 1988 "FREE TRADE" ELECTION AND ITS AFTERMATH

Answering the MacDonald Commission report's call for a free trade agreement with the United States, the government of Brian Mulroney kicked off negotiations with Ronald Reagan's administration in May 1986. On October 4, 1987, the Governments of Canada and the United States reached agreement on the terms of a new trade deal, the Canada–United States Free Trade Agreement. The deal included provisions for the phased elimination of tariffs and for the reduction of other nontariff trade barriers, along with a mechanism for the settlement of trade disputes.

Unions and other progressive forces in Canada had been raising alarm bells about the potential impact of free trade on Canadian sovereignty, jobs, and social programs for years, but the announcement of the new trade deal gave the movement a renewed sense of urgency. CAW president Bob White and Council of Canadians leader Maude Barlow co-led a cross-country community mobilization against the free trade agreement and in April 1987 helped to establish the Pro-Canada Network, a coalition of thirty organizations opposed to the trade deal.[3]

Bob White's position at the head of the anti-free-trade coalition signalled an important change in direction. As discussed in Chapter 2, for many decades, industrial unions had been strong proponents of continental integration, to the extent that many opposed left nationalism when it arose within the ranks of the NDP. By the mid-1980s, however, the labour movement had made a significant move to the left-nationalist camp. Job loss as a result of global restructuring, capital flight, and deindustrialization provided a material basis for organized labour's gradual embrace of economic nationalism. In the words of Miriam Smith, the labour movement now "viewed continental integration and US multinational presence in Canada not as the indispensable conditions for Canadian economic development and employment for organized workers, but as obstacles to these goals."[4]

In late October 1987, the Canadian Broadcasting Corporation hosted a two-part debate on the trade deal, pitting Bob White and Maude Barlow against Business Council on National Issues president Tom d'Aquino and former Alberta Progressive Conservative (PC) premier Peter Lougheed. White and Barlow exceeded expectations. According to Barlow, whereas d'Aquino and Lougheed "wrapped themselves in the flag and spoke in generalities about how they loved Canada," she and White focused on "the technicalities of the agreement, arguing about secure market access, American omnibus legislation, proportional energy sharing, national treatment (which requires that a country not discriminate between foreign and domestic investors and companies), and the threat to jobs, social programs, and the environment."[5]

Most of corporate Canada strongly supported the deal, whereas organized labour and progressive social movements were staunchly opposed. The country was also regionally divided, with support for the trade deal higher in western Canada and Quebec than in the rest of the country.[6] Both the Liberals and New Democrats opposed the Canada–United States Free Trade Agreement. The Liberal majority in the Senate actively delayed the legislation needed to implement the deal, thus prompting Mulroney to call an election for November 21, 1988.

Conflicts soon emerged between the CAW and the NDP over how vocally to oppose the trade deal in the 1988 campaign. By 1987, three-quarters of the NDP's union affiliate members were from Ontario, and more than half came from either the steel or auto industries.[7] This demographic reality created a very strong anti-free-trade constituency within the party. However, although the NDP was opposed to the policy of comprehensive free trade, the ensuing campaign dynamics made strategists reluctant to place the free trade issue at the centre of the party's platform and messaging. NDP strategists reasoned that playing up opposition to the trade deal would benefit the Liberals, who were better positioned to capitalize on the issue.

NDP members of Parliament (MPs) also worried that free trade was not a winning issue in western Canada, where most NDP MPs held seats, and that prioritizing opposition to the deal would pose a threat to their re-election. White's key advisor, Sam Gindin, recounts that in the run-up to the 1988 campaign, he and White met with the NDP caucus to emphasize the importance of opposing free trade as the central election issue. According to Gindin, "Everybody in the NDP caucus, except [Toronto NDP MP] Dan Heap, said, 'That's impossible. The West will kill us, and that's where all our seats are. We can't take on free trade as the main issue.'" In response, White and Gindin argued, "'Yeah, that may be true right now, but we can turn that around.' And then White went on a tour of the West, and every word that he spoke, he was met as a hero. He was on talk shows. He spoke to big rallies. And this was a reflection of our politics being ahead of the party."[8] White's leadership during the breakaway from the UAW and in the fight against free trade made him a household name. Beyond the ranks of the CAW, workers would routinely send messages to White seeking his support for unionization efforts or advice on how to resolve workplace issues.[9] In short, the CAW president enjoyed the status of a working-class hero during this period.

White's credibility and sway certainly extended to NDP circles. Not only did he serve as a vice-president of the federal party, but he also chaired the Political Action Committee of the Canadian Labour Congress (CLC).[10] Despite White's personal standing and the seeming popularity of the anti-free-trade message, the NDP ultimately decided against highlighting the free trade issue. According to former CLC chief economist Andrew Jackson, Broadbent's decision to kick off the campaign with a speech that did not even mention the trade deal was met with "palpable shock" in labour movement circles.[11] In retrospect, Ed Broadbent rationalizes downplaying free trade on the basis that "if the election became an up or down vote on the trade deal, that would really favour the Liberals."[12] In Broadbent's estimation, because both Liberal leader John Turner and Ontario's Liberal premier David Peterson were opposed to the trade deal, they were much clearer conduits for opposition to free trade. After all, Peterson's Liberals won an overwhelming majority in the 1987 provincial election fuelled, in part, by opposition to the deal, and it was the Liberal majority in the Senate that delayed the deal's implementation. Given this dynamic, Broadbent argues that the NDP "had to offer a broader range of social democratic options, and not just opt for opposition to the trade deal."[13] This approach, according to Broadbent, also recognized that different regions of the country had different views of free trade. Although these strategic considerations may have appeared sound to those running the NDP campaign, former CAW chief economist Jim Stanford argues that "the NDP was seen as opportunistically downplaying the fight against free trade."[14] The party's decision alienated important segments of the Canadian labour movement that had spent the better part of a year organizing against the trade deal.

It did not take long for NDP strategists to realize that the party had miscalculated, as John Turner's Liberals succeeded in making the election all about free trade and became the party most clearly associated with opposition to the deal. According to James Laxer, the NDP altered its strategy midway through the campaign, and Broadbent "joined the Liberal assault on free trade."[15] In Laxer's estimation,

> This combined Liberal-NDP attack on the Tory position turned public opinion polls around and Turner's Liberals gained the lead over the Tories. This was the pivotal moment of the election campaign and Broadbent had a crucial choice to make. Should he keep attacking Mulroney or should he also mount an attack on Turner and the Liberals? Broadbent and his advisers made a strategic decision that was to infuriate key labour leaders like Bob White, president of the Canadian Auto Workers Union.[16]

By turning his guns on Turner, Broadbent took the heat off Mulroney and arguably served to divide the anti-free-trade vote in a way that helped to re-elect the PC government. In the end, the NDP captured a record high 20.4 percent of the vote and forty-three seats. This achievement, however, was overshadowed by the re-election of the Mulroney government and the NDP's failure to win a single seat east of Ontario. Expectations were high, and the party was unable to deliver the win that so many union activists had hoped for. Quebec was a particular sore spot. According to author Lynn Gidluck, "Many party members were upset that Broadbent seemed to be spending a lot of time and money catering to Quebec. Since many people in Quebec were in favour of free trade, NDP opposition to that had been toned down, even though trade unionists and NDP rank and file were bitterly opposed to a free trade deal."[17] But no one was more disappointed by the Quebec result than Broadbent. He had expected the party to win a half-dozen seats in the province. As measured against expectations, the party's failure to break through in Quebec was a "colossal disappointment." He decided that night to resign as leader but held off on making an official announcement.[18]

Others, however, were keen to see changes sooner rather than later. Shortly after the campaign, both Bob White and Ontario United Steelworkers head Leo Gerard openly criticized the party's top strategists for their handling of the free trade issue. The latter described the campaign as a "betrayal of everything a social democratic party is supposed to stand for,"[19] and the former declared that "the results of the most recent federal election, and the strategies used in that election are so disastrous that they warrant a full debate within the party."[20] White went on to highlight the unprecedented "level of disappointment and anger" from labour movement activists and leaders, pointing out that the union's "financial and people support is accepted gratefully, but its ideas and leadership are completely ignored."[21] According to White, there was a common thread in the frustration felt by activists, "and that is the NDP, our party, never really came to grips with the importance of free trade, were scared of it as an election platform, and while it was mentioned in the campaign, it certainty did not get the priority or attention, or emotion it deserved."[22]

Broadbent recalls that within forty-eight hours of speaking out, Gerard called him to offer a "heartfelt personal apology for making an open criticism."[23] No such apology ever came from White. Broadbent suspected that "some leadership politics were underway," with White testing the waters for a run at his job. Many interviewees confirm that White was interested in becoming NDP leader, but his lack of bilingualism[24] and opposition from other union leaders aligned with the NDP[25] made it clear that his aspirations could not be fulfilled. "Had White been younger, he might have contemplated it," argues Gindin, adding that "he wanted to hear from somebody like Stephen Lewis ... and he wanted to hear from somebody like the Steelworkers, who said, 'Yes, it's time to have a labour party.' And he didn't hear from any of those people."[26] The ordeal "got messy, and I found the whole thing unpleasant to live through," recounts Broadbent.

White's letter was "a very sad development because, up until the '88 election, Bob White and I had been very collaborative ... We had been friends, not just collaborators."[27]

Thinking back to the fight against free trade and the fallout from the 1988 federal election, Gindin argues that "the labour movement seemed to be rebelling against past notions that the NDP had all the political savvy and labour's role was to provide the bodies and money."[28] For Herman Rosenfeld, the free trade election cemented his long-held perspective as a CAW staffer that "when the union supports the NDP, it's because the party aligns with the union and not the other way around."[29] These realizations, however, did not lead to a total breakdown of the party-union relationship. Rather, as Ken Lewenza explains, the union always had debates and discussions and differences of opinion with the NDP, "but our position was we were genuinely partners with the New Democratic Party in our approach to political action."[30]

Even though White ultimately decided against running for the leadership of the federal NDP, the CAW was engaged in the process to select a new leader to replace Broadbent. Initially, White tried to persuade Ontario NDP leader Bob Rae to run, but once this overture was rejected, he gradually decided to back the eventual winner, Yukon MP Audrey McLaughlin, who also enjoyed the support of Leo Gerard, Canadian Union of Public Employees (CUPE) national president Jeff Rose, and Ontario Federation of Labour (OFL) president Gord Wilson.[31]

THE ONTARIO NDP COMES TO POWER

When Ontario Liberal premier David Peterson called an early election in the summer of 1990, no one expected that it would result in an NDP majority government. Peterson's decision to trigger the election was panned as opportunistic and fed into a growing perception that he led a government that was arrogant and out of touch. These allegations dogged him for the entire campaign, along with hard-hitting negative attack ads and gaggles of protestors from the labour and environmental movements.[32] Given the unpopularity of the Conservatives in Ottawa, Bob Rae's New Democrats managed to capitalize on Ontario voters' pent-up anger and secured a majority government with just 37.6 percent of the vote.

"Maybe a summer election wasn't such a bad idea after all," declared Rae on election night.[33] Long-time party activists and labour movement leaders were euphoric. The party's hastily cobbled together platform, *Agenda for People*, read like a laundry list of NDP opposition demands, including public auto insurance, increased corporate taxes and minimum-wage rates, pay and employment equity, rent control, the adoption of an Environmental Bill of Rights, and investments in nonprofit housing, social assistance, and education.[34] The platform also contained commitments long championed by the CAW, including the establishment of a fund for wage and benefit protection and the introduction of plant-closure legislation mandating a jobs-protection board that would be responsible for determining whether a plant closure was justified.[35]

The NDP's election brought many union leaders and staffers into government, promising a close relationship with the labour movement. White's long-time assistant, Carol Phillips, for example, joined the Premier's Office. Of the seventy-four NDP members elected to the provincial Parliament as part of the Rae government, one-third came from the labour movement.[36] Among them were five current or former CAW members and staffers: Pat Hayes, George Dadamo, Randy Hope, Larry O'Connor, and David Christopherson.[37] Union movement figures were also prominent in Rae's Cabinet, including Frances Lankin of the Ontario Public Service Employees Union and Bob Mackenzie of the United Steelworkers.

Although unions had more influence around the Cabinet table than ever before, this did not translate into labour dominance of the government's agenda. Their high expectations were tempered by Rae, who sent a clear message about his changed responsibilities. In March 1991, while the government was still riding high in the polls, Premier Rae reminded union supporters and NDP activists that his government did not feel obliged to carry out all party policies as dictated by NDP conventions. "When a government is formed, the premier is no longer simply the leader of the party," Rae told convention delegates. "I have now a wider responsibility, to all the people of the province, many of whom – indeed, I think it's fair to say, most of whom – are not necessarily members or supporters of the NDP."[38] This dynamic of moving from the representation of a labour constituency when in opposition to prioritizing the "national interest" when in government was repeatedly observed in social democratic parties the world over and was the source of serious tensions with such parties' labour movement base.[39] Nevertheless, the Rae government did move forward on a number of files important to the labour movement, including investments in public works, reforms to the Labour Relations Act, pay equity, and anti-poverty measures.[40]

However, very early in the government's mandate, Buzz Hargrove, then assistant to Bob White, claimed that the CAW felt "frozen out of serious deliberation on government policy."[41] He offered the example of the government's first budget in 1991, which introduced a gas-guzzler tax. According to Hargrove, "Our members were furious. 'Here's our government,' they said, 'and it's imposing a tax that might cost us our jobs. Not even the Tories would have threatened our jobs!'"[42] The union brokered a deal with the government to back off from some components of the tax, but according to Hargrove, "the political damage was done. There would be no erasing the bitterness."[43]

Despite these tensions, NDP fortunes were on the rise across the country. In October 1991, NDP majority governments were elected in Saskatchewan and British Columbia. For the first time in history, a majority of Canadians were governed by New Democrats at the provincial level, and the federal NDP surged to first place in public opinion polls.[44] The party's popularity, however, would not last long. The Ontario NDP had come to power just as the province's economic fortunes were turning.

The effects of the free trade agreement hit working-class communities particularly hard, leading to plant closures, layoffs, and a deep economic recession. The *Windsor Star* described Labour Day 1990 as a "solemn celebration," pointing to the fact that "plant closures have doubled in the past year, putting 14,009 people out of work in Ontario."[45] In June 1992, the union claimed that a hundred CAW plant closures had occurred since the trade deal was enacted in 1989.[46] The CAW had built up its reputation in bargaining by saying no to concessions and by securing meaningful contract improvements, but the new economic landscape made this reputation more difficult to sustain amid accelerated job losses and plant relocations.[47] Even in this increasingly hostile context, some local unions put up militant resistance against such closures, the most notable of which took place in April 1991 at Caterpillar's tractor plant in Brampton, Ontario. Two hundred members of CAW Local 252 occupied the plant for six days after the company refused to negotiate a closure agreement. The Ontario NDP labour minister's intervention resulted in Caterpillar making modest improvements to the severance package but did not stop the work from being moved to Raleigh, North Carolina.[48]

In response to the economic slowdown, the NDP government boldly announced that it would use its first budget to fight the recession through deficit spending. Finance Minister Floyd Laughren forecast a then record-setting budget deficit of $9.7 billion – triple the amount of the previous year's deficit. The party's decision to challenge the prevailing economic orthodoxy generated a strong backlash as bond-rating services openly mused about the possibility of downgrading Ontario's AAA credit rating.[49] Media pundits and the corporate sector howled their disapproval of the NDP budget, and public confidence in the government began to wane.[50]

Amid these growing economic and political challenges, the CAW underwent a major internal transition. In June 1992, Hargrove took over the leadership of the CAW, and White made his way to Ottawa to take over the presidency of the CLC. In many ways, Hargrove, who came out of Local 444 in Windsor, was the logical successor. He was very experienced, having been appointed to staff in 1975 and promoted to become White's assistant in 1978.[51] "He was a very working-class guy who read a lot, worked hard, and I think people really appreciated his toughness in bargaining," explains Peggy Nash, who served for some time as Hargrove's assistant.[52] In his first address as president, Hargrove assured members that his election would constitute "a continuum of our history and policies."[53] Hargrove, like White, was a long-time card-carrying New Democrat.[54] However, Hargrove was different from White in important ways that began to reshape the union's approach to politics.

If White's relationship with Rae was tense, Hargrove's was best described as openly antagonistic. Hargrove's speech to delegates at the December 1992 CAW Council meeting exemplified the latter dynamic. The focus of the speech was worker frustration with the Rae government. As a courtesy, Hargrove sent the premier an advance copy so that Rae would not be blindsided. The speech criticized the Rae government's record of broken promises, highlighting the party's U-turn on public auto insurance in the face of opposition from the insurance industry. "They were getting all this pressure from the Right and nobody from the Left was raising issues at all,"

Hargrove later explained.[55] What was needed, he concluded "was a little push" from the Left for balance.[56] However, as legal scholar Patrick Monahan points out, "if Buzz Hargrove thought he was doing Rae a favour with his 'little push from the Left,' the Premier didn't see it that way."[57]

In his 1996 autobiography, Rae recounted receiving the advance copy of Hargrove's "gratuitous" speech. "I couldn't believe Hargrove's attitude, and called him … I blew my stack, and let fly a string of four-letter words," wrote Rae. "Something snapped in me that day," he added. "My resentment at the lack of perspective, the lack of solidarity, the absence of any sense of responsibility for the financial (and political) health of the government, the sense of a never-ending series of demands that would always be disappointed welled over."[58] Rae felt betrayed by Hargrove, especially because his government had played an instrumental role in saving the CAW-represented de Havilland plant earlier that fall.[59] Hargrove, however, was unrepentant. "Because of our union's traditional ties to the New Democratic Party, the CAW was slow to react. We kept hoping the government would recognize the dead-end street it was taking us down. The government, in turn, kept thinking we would fall in line," he recounted in his own autobiography.[60]

With the CAW-NDP relationship on the ropes and several other unions expressing disappointment with NDP governments' perceived abandonment of social democratic policy commitments, Bob White invited the three NDP premiers and federal leader Audrey McLaughlin to meet with the CLC executive in January 1993 in order to clear the air and figure out a way to mend fences. The meeting, however, ground to a halt when White went toe to toe with the premiers over how best to tackle growing provincial deficits. According to Rae, White did not hold back. "Why the hell should working people see all their benefits and everything we've been fighting for all these years go down the drain because you guys have bought into all this neo-conservative economics. You're elected to fight for our people, not to stick your nose up Mulroney's ass," he said. According to Rae, "After that exchange there was nothing more to be said. The gulf was wider than when we went in."[61]

Although White and Hargrove had established themselves as prominent left critics of the Rae government, some powerful segments of their union were challenging the government and the union-party relationship using right-wing talking points. In 1993, an organized group within Local 222 in Oshawa calling itself the Movement Against Political Affiliation (MAPA) emerged to push for the local to disaffiliate from the NDP. Although the local had a history of strong ties to the NDP – with its former president Cliff Pilkey elected as an NDP member of the provincial Parliament (MPP) in the late 1960s and with Ed Broadbent having served as an NDP MP for the Oshawa riding from 1968 to 1990 – it had also been internally divided over politics for much of its history. Able to galvanize right-wing sentiment in the local, MAPA won the motion to disaffiliate.

According to journalist Thomas Walkom, "many reasons were given, including dissatisfaction with government economic policy. But fear of employment equity played a major role."[62] In a piece for *Canadian Dimension*, autoworker activist Jay Casey described MAPA as a right-wing group led by skilled trades workers with contradictory class positions. "In MAPA's view our natural allies are our employers (in this case, GM), landlords and those investors who might put their capital into job-creating investments if the political climate were congenial."[63] The perception that the NDP government was hostile to employers, particularly in the context of a major recession when manufacturing jobs were disappearing daily, helped to drive support for disaffiliation from the party. But it was not the only driver. According to Casey, MAPA's disaffiliation campaign combined "three elements: an attack on the NDP and its policies, advocacy of traditional 'business unionism,' and the libertarian rhetoric of individual rights and freedom of choice."[64] In his estimation, the three pillars of MAPA's campaign were a potent mix that "simply hijacked the anger of the rank and file and directed it against both the NDP and the CAW leadership."[65] For his part, citing the example of employment equity, Gindin acknowledges that "some workers rejected the NDP for the 'wrong' reasons." For Gindin, the "backlash was rooted in the fact that these issues were not placed in the broader context of working-class struggles. The party's overall language and direction did not clearly identify it as fighting on behalf of working people."[66]

Arguably, the NDP's reaction to the disaffiliation only made matters worse. Hargrove says that he was attending a conference on jobs and the environment with Frances Lankin, Rae's minister of economic development and trade, when he got the call that Local 222 had voted to disaffiliate from the party. He whispered the news to Lankin because he wanted her to know before media started asking questions. According to Hargrove, Lankin was "disgusted" and told him, "We'll see how they feel when I turn down the request sitting on my desk from General Motors for financial support for the new product." Hargrove was furious with Lankin's response, which he perceived as a threat. He recalls that another Cabinet minister had to intervene to quell an open argument between the two at the conference.[67] Tensions aside, the national union moved quickly to counter Local 222's message, with the union's Skilled Trades Council, Locals 444 and 1973 in Windsor, and Local 1520 in St. Thomas all passing resolutions reaffirming support for affiliation to the party.[68] Their attempt at reconciliation would not last long, as the government soon put forward an approach to managing ballooning government debt and deficits that would widen divisions between the union and the party.

THE SOCIAL CONTRACT ACT

As the provincial debt and deficit continued to mount, the business community applied intense public pressure on the government to cut public services and rein in spending. The corporate sector effectively used the growing debt and deficit as a cudgel against the NDP to reinforce the stereotype that the party could not be trusted to manage the public purse. Pressure from the business community succeeded. As Thomas Walkom argues, "other NDP governments had tried to make peace with business. But none had done so with such a combination of enthusiasm and naïveté as Rae's."[69] Even after the Rae government backed off and began to bend over backward to reassure business through cuts to social spending, the corporate lobby did not let up.[70] The prolonged recession meant that deficits continued to mount. The government felt under siege not only by business leaders but also by media outlets, which began to report on economic doomsday scenarios, like the possibility that the province would hit the debt wall. These predictions were alarmist but succeeded in convincing the public that the debt and deficit were out of control.[71] A poll by Environics in April 1993 revealed that 84.3 percent of Ontario voters disapproved of the way that the provincial government was handling the deficit.[72]

The Rae government eventually succumbed to this growing pressure and announced the introduction of its now infamous Social Contract

Act, a fiscal austerity program that rolled back public sector workers' wages through unpaid days off (dubbed Rae Days by critics) and suspended collective bargaining rights in the broader public sector. The Social Contract Act was designed to rein in spending while preserving jobs, but it was met with fierce opposition by public-sector unions, whose members saw the legislation as a violation of their collective bargaining rights.[73] Private-sector unions were more divided. Although none were particularly supportive of the Social Contract Act, many expressed mixed feelings about the decision to attack the NDP government over the legislation since it had delivered on other key labour priorities, such as a reformed Labour Relations Act.[74]

Hargrove harboured no such mixed feelings. "If we take the idea of social democracy seriously, then we have a *responsibility* to criticize this government, challenge it, make demands on it, and yes, mobilize against its direction," he argued.[75] Hargrove further pledged to "stand side by side with the Public Sector Unions against any attacks on their rights by the Government of Ontario."[76] Delegates to the CAW's May 1993 National Collective Bargaining and Political Action Convention in Toronto endorsed this general direction in a report titled "Hard Times, New Times: Fighting for Our Future." "There is one very important lesson that many of us have learned lately: changing governments, in itself, does not transform power in our society," read the report.[77] It went on to assert that "maintaining and developing our own independent ideology is today as important – or more so – than it ever was. Without it, we have no compass, no sense of direction, no protection from getting absorbed into the agendas of others."[78]

Behind the scenes, public-sector labour leaders worked furiously to avoid a legislated wage rollback. They proposed raising corporate taxes as a solution to the government's revenue problem and pressed the government to grant a minimal wage increase along with job guarantees as something that they could sell to their memberships.[79] Gindin, who was at one of these high-level meetings between Rae and labour leaders, claims that Rae would simply not budge, even though the cost difference between the unions' plan and the government's plan was "peanuts in the scheme of things." In Gindin's view, Rae was "sending a message to the business community that I can control you guys [i.e., the unions]. And that's what's important to me. I can take your votes for granted."[80]

In an effort to convince the roughly two dozen NDP MPPs with labour movement connections to oppose Rae's bill, Hargrove joined Bob White and Leo Gerard at a press conference in late June 1993 "to warn that there would be trouble if the NDP overrode existing collective agreements with a legislated settlement."[81] The "trouble" promised was not specified but implied that the unions would pull their material support for these MPPs' re-election bids. However, this strategy yielded little success. In the end, only four NDP MPPs voted against the legislation, and the other sixty-six voted in favour.[82] All five CAW-affiliated MPPs in the NDP caucus voted in favour of the Social Contract Act, which passed on July 7, 1993.

In response to the bill's passage, the CAW announced in August 1993 that it was withdrawing its support for the government and would reduce its contributions to the provincial party to the bare minimum required to maintain affiliate status.[83] From the union's perspective, Rae's bill was a monumental betrayal. "It's one thing for a corporation or right-wing government to try to take away workers' hard-won rights to bargain their contracts. It's quite another when a supposedly 'labour-friendly' government tries the same thing," argued Hargrove.[84] Political scientists Leo Panitch and Donald Swartz agree, arguing that "what distinguished the NDP's attack on trade union rights in the form of its Social Contract Act ... was the particularly perverse and dangerous fashion in which it attempted to conceal coercion as consent."[85] As a result, the legislation had significant implications for social democratic politics and for party-union relations across the country. As political scientist Stephen McBride points out,

First, the exercise was coercive and involved setting aside the provisions of negotiated collective agreements in the public sector. Secondly, the Rae social contract represented a qualitatively different approach to social contracts. Its goal – deficit cutting through contraction of the public sector – was identical to that of the neoconservatives. Focusing on the deficit and targeting the public sector as the party primarily responsible for it are two of the hallmarks of neoconservatism. All that remained of a distinctively social democratic approach to managing Ontario's political economy was the effort, unaccompanied by real dialogue, to enlist public sector union support for the notion that cuts were necessary.[86]

Many in the labour movement shared this assessment that the NDP government was not much different from Liberal or Conservative governments. At the OFL's November 1993 convention, a majority of delegates voted in favour of a resolution stipulating that no money or volunteers would be made available to the party in the next provincial election unless the Social Contract Act was repealed. The resolution further called upon affiliates to "increase the involvement of labour activists in the nomination process and ensure that the 66 members of the NDP Caucus that supported Bill 48 are challenged at nominations meetings."[87]

However, the resolution was hotly contested. Twelve private-sector unions opposed to the resolution and loyal to the NDP circulated their position, titled "Political Action and Ontario Labour," to delegates on a pink piece of paper.[88] The "Pink Paper" unions, as they would become known, argued that the Social Contract Act was only one (albeit significant) blight on an otherwise pro-union legislative record and that public-sector unions would have faced a much worse situation under a Liberal or PC government. In the words of industrial relations scholars Yonatan Reshef and Sandra Rastin, "even if it had erred, the NDP was still their best emissary in provincial politics ... These unions were unwilling to tear down the government in the process of fighting it."[89] However, when it became obvious that the resolution would pass, Pink Paper union delegates left the convention hall in protest. The resolution then passed overwhelmingly.

Looking back on the debacle of the Social Contract Act, Hargrove maintains, "Our biggest mistake was that we waited too long before we started pushing from the left."[90] Rae drew a completely different set of lessons: "I learned that the leadership of the public-sector unions were more interested in the 'sacredness' of contracts than they were in the importance of jobs, more concerned with protecting the full benefits of the survivors than the fate of the people tossed overboard. They, as does Buzz Hargrove, think this makes them better socialists. I disagree."[91] But for Hargrove, Rae was simply a victim of his own naïveté:

> These people actually believed you could sit down and bargain $2 billion of takeaways from the public-sector unions. I don't know how or where you could ever, ever get that idea. I mean, there is no corporation that can get [wage rollbacks] without the threat of a plant closure

or a threat of a lockout. There's no way they can get anything out of a union with just saying let's sit down and talk.[92]

For McBride, the Rae government's lack of a social democratic alternative to the Social Contract Act rendered it a prisoner to right-wing hegemonic ideas. Citing Margaret Thatcher's famous line "There is no alternative," McBride argues that the NDP "claimed a new reality had imposed its inexorable logic on governments of all political persuasions. To this it added the calculation that the electorate would reward only those parties in tune with the new reality."[93] However, the government had clearly mis-calculated. As argued by Peter Kormos, one of the NDP MPPs who opposed the bill, "it was Tory types who agreed with the social contract. That doesn't mean they were going to vote for New Democrats."[94] Kormos had a point. In the wake of the Social Contract Act, an Environics poll found that support for the NDP remained stagnant.[95] Hargrove puts his criticism of the party leadership's attempt to please others outside the social democratic camp this way: "The power brokers in the NDP do not seem capable of understanding the simplest rule of politics: you protect and please and listen to your friends, even though this will antagonize your adversaries."[96]

For Hargrove, the Social Contract Act marked a clear break with the CAW's partisan approach to the NDP-union relationship that was consolidated in the 1960s. Although the union had always maintained its tendency to critically engage with the party when interests diverged, the legislation was a game changer. According to Hargrove,

> We learned a valuable lesson. From here on, the CAW will not support NDP candidates unless they declare their personal commitment to protect the rights of unions and workers, preserve social programs, and support programs such as public housing, child care, public education, and care for the less fortunate. Henceforth, the CAW will check the philosophical teeth of every NDP candidate.[97]

Interestingly, despite the strong sense of betrayal, the CAW did maintain its affiliation to the NDP throughout, albeit at the lowest level possible. The union was clearly walking a tightrope between complete abandonment of the party, which risked extinguishing its influence over the NDP's direction, and loyalty despite everything, which would have left the party off the hook for abandoning core labour principles. It was not clear, however, that this strategy was tenable over the longer term.

RECONSIDERING THE NDP-UNION RELATIONSHIP: THE 1993 FEDERAL ELECTION

In the wake of the Social Contract Act, the federal NDP's electoral prospects went from bad to worse. The CLC's decision to join forces with the NDP in 1992 and to campaign in favour of the Mulroney government's ultimately failed Charlottetown Accord led to the dramatic rise of the Reform Party and Bloc Québécois and further disorganized an already tenuous class politics.[98] Regional and linguistic cleavages and anger at provincial New Democrat governments ravaged federal NDP candidates across the country. When Essex–Windsor NDP MP Steven Langdon released an open letter criticizing the Rae government's then-proposed Social Contract Act in April 1993, Audrey McLaughlin stripped him of his critic portfolio, further complicating the federal NDP's already tense relationship with the labour movement.[99] The CAW strongly backed Langdon's position, and the national office withheld campaign contributions from candidates who did not adopt a similar view. The union even donated $500 to Dennis Drainville, the former Ontario NDP MPP who voted against the Social Contract Act and resigned his seat to run as an independent in Victoria-Haliburton in the October 1993 federal election.[100]

In the end, the federal NDP lost official party status, holding onto just 9 seats and 6.9 percent of the vote – an all-time low. The NDP did not win a single seat east of Manitoba and secured just 6 percent of the vote in Ontario. Only the governing PCs fared worse, capturing 16 percent of the vote but only 2 seats. The Liberals vaulted from Official Opposition to government, winning 41.2 percent of the vote and 177 seats. The right-wing populist Reform Party captured 18.7 percent of the vote and 52 seats, and the BQ took over as Official Opposition, securing 54 seats. In Quebec, where the NDP won a paltry 1.5 percent of the vote, the Bloc emerged as the clear electoral vehicle for left-wing forces and labour movement activists in that province. The expanded BQ caucus included several high-profile unionists: Gilles Duceppe, Osvaldo Núñez, Francine Lalonde, and Suzanne Tremblay. Buoyed by the defeat of the Charlottetown Accord in the 1992 referendum, by the BQ's success in the 1993 federal election, and by the Parti Québécois's majority government win in the 1994 provincial election, Quebec's labour movement began mobilizing like never before in support of independence.[101] The CAW's Claude Ducharme, who served as the union's Quebec director and as vice-president of the Quebec Federation of Labour from 1981 to 1995, was a leading sovereignist voice.[102] His successor as CAW Quebec director, Luc Desnoyers, was equally committed to the sovereignist cause.[103] The dramatic rise of the BQ not only complicated the union's relationship with the New Democrats but also reinforced the NDP's growing irrelevancy as a political force in Quebec.

With the federal NDP in tatters and provincial NDP governments on the ropes, the CAW's August 1994 Constitutional Convention walked a tightrope between being critical of the party and remaining affiliated – a balancing act that *Toronto Star* reporter Tony Van Alphen described as "confusing."[104] In short, although the NDP had recently proven an ineffective vehicle for promoting working-class interests, the union was signalling that it was not ready to entirely sever its relationship with the party given its historical attachments and achievements.[105] Instead, the union resolved that it would focus greater effort on workplace-based political action and alliances with social movements.[106] The CAW was not the only labour organization re-examining its relationship with the NDP in the early 1990s. With the federal NDP having lost official party status and the Ontario NDP languishing badly in public opinion polls, many union activists were increasingly angry and demoralized at the state of labour politics. However, to avoid a bitter fight at the CLC convention in May 1994, labour leaders shepherded through a compromise resolution directing the CLC to set up a working group to investigate the party-union relationship.[107]

THE 1995 ONTARIO ELECTION: MIKE HARRIS COMES TO POWER

As the 1995 Ontario election campaign approached, Hargrove appeared content to have the CAW sit on the sidelines. Citing the union movement's track record of having secured the Rand Formula, pensions, and severance pay legislation from previous Liberal and Conservative governments, Hargrove reasoned, "We can't be worse off with them than we are today. We've had less input with the NDP than with the Tories and Liberals."[108]

The CAW was not altogether absent from the campaign. The union officially backed a handful of NDP incumbent MPPs, most notably those who had opposed the Social Contract Act. However, of those endorsed, only Welland–Thorold MPP Peter Kormos managed to retain his seat. The union also supported a number of new NDP candidates on record as opposed to the Social Contract Act, like CAW Local 1256 member Willie Lambert in Oakville, Arlene Rousseau in Windsor West, and Dave Maris in Essex South.[109] Lambert claims that he ran "more of a socialist campaign" that consciously disassociated itself from Rae.[110] He won just 8.7 percent of the vote, and Rousseau captured 25 percent in a Windsor riding that had elected a New Democrat with over 54 percent of the votes in 1990. Maris took 16.3 percent of the vote in Essex South, and CAW left activist Joe Flexer, who ran as independent against NDP MPP Tony Rizzo in Toronto, won just 1.7 percent of the vote. Left electoral challenges, whether internal or external to the party, clearly did not pay dividends in the 1995 election.

It did not help that the NDP campaign was built almost entirely around Rae. The NDP made no bold commitments to recapture working-class support during the election. Indeed, the party's most significant commitment was that it would not make any promises.[111] In contrast, the Conservatives campaigned on a set of very audacious ideas outlined in its Common Sense Revolution platform. The Mike Harris Conservatives unapologetically called for big tax cuts, the repeal of the NDP's labour law reforms, the reversal of employment equity legislation, cuts to social assistance, deficit reduction, and the establishment of a system of work for welfare.[112] The Liberals, who entered the campaign as the odds-on favourite to win, began to falter badly after the leaders' debate, with their supporters moving to the PCs, not the NDP.[113] As the campaign wore on, it became increasingly clear that the Conservatives were gaining popularity – even among working-class and union voters – and had a real chance of winning.[114] This possibility began to raise the stakes for those unionists who were withholding support from the NDP on the basis that the other parties were essentially no different.

Labour leaders scrambled as the likelihood of a Conservative victory grew. OFL president and former CAW staffer Gord Wilson ignited a firestorm when he announced that he was personally supporting the Rae government despite the OFL's policy of nonsupport.[115] Several CAW locals followed suit once the Harris Conservatives started gaining in the polls mid-campaign. In Windsor, the local CAW leadership remained aligned with the NDP, with Local 444 president Ken Lewenza telling the *Windsor Star* that Education Minister Dave Cooke "deserves re-election because of all the good he has done for Windsor."[116] Gabe MacNally, vice-president of CAW Local 199 in St. Catharines, called on Hargrove to endorse the NDP. "As a responsible leader, I think there's no option but for him to come out and support the NDP in this campaign," McNally told the media.[117] Hargrove was not swayed, even though it was becoming increasingly clear that Harris was no Bill Davis Conservative. However, Bob White, in his capacity as CLC president, did offer what Bob Rae calls "a half-baked endorsement of the NDP ... which blew in and out of the air in thirty seconds."[118]

Any change of heart in the labour movement was too little, too late. On June 8, 1995, the Mike Harris Conservatives swept to power, winning eighty-two seats with 44.8 percent of the vote. The Liberals finished second with thirty seats and 31.1 percent of the vote. Rae's New Democrats fell to third place, capturing just seventeen seats and 20.6 percent of the vote. The Common Sense Revolution was about to begin.

According to Gindin, as individuals, many CAW activists "decided they had no choice but to cast their ballots for the NDP." But Gindin also maintains that "the union as an institution could not endorse the party's role in government by endorsing them in the election."[119] A few years after the election, Hargrove offered a stinging indictment of the Rae government:

[It] not only reneged on many of its election promises but did everything it could to keep the province's corporate sector satisfied. It refused to honour major pledges, such as public auto insurance. It chose to fight the deficit by slashing social programs rather than engaging seriously in job creation. It made deals with doctors, and cut nurses' wages. It made concessions to multinational drug manufacturing firms, raising the cost of drugs and medicine for the elderly, the poor, and the infirm. It slapped heavy taxes on the few perks a working person has – cigarettes, beer, wine, and gasoline – and let corporations and the wealthy off light. It legislated out of existence legal collective agreements covering almost one million public service employees. It violated provincial employees' basic right to bargain collectively and offered their unions the worst choice possible: accept wage rollbacks or expect compulsory wage cuts.[120]

The NDP's "no promises" approach also backfired. In Hargrove's words, Rae's campaign "reconfirmed for many voters that the NDP had nothing more to offer."[121] Hargrove went so far as to argue that "the controversy, bitterness, and soiled policies left behind by the Rae government opened the gates and made it easy for the Harris-led Tories to implement one of the cruelest right-wing legislative agendas this nation has ever seen."[122]

THE 1995 QUEBEC REFERENDUM

While union leaders in Ontario were bracing for a fight with the Harris Conservatives, union leaders in Quebec were building support for sovereignty in the referendum to be held on October 30, 1995. Back in February 1995, delegates at a special convention of the Quebec Federation of Labour had voted overwhelmingly to endorse a yes vote in the referendum, placing the organization squarely in the sovereignist camp along with the rest of the province's labour movement. The special convention was the first of many events launched by the federation and its affiliates, including the CAW, as part of an elaborate campaign to deliver the votes of union members to the yes side.[123] In the words of former CAW Quebec director Sylvain Martin, the province's autoworkers were "all in" for the yes side.[124] Bob White addressed delegates at the Quebec Federation of Labour convention with several strong statements in favour of the principle of self-determination and even suggested that, in the event of a yes victory, the Government of Canada should respect the democratic will of Quebecers and calmly negotiate the terms of separation with a sovereign Quebec. According to White, "A decision for sovereignty has certain economic implications but economic blackmail and doomsday scenarios must be seen for what they are – blatant attempts to interfere with and influence the course of democratic decision-making."[125] White continued, "If the referendum results in a Yes vote ... it would mean serious, undoubtedly tough negotiations on a multiplicity of issues. But those negotiations would have to proceed on the basis of mutual respect and recognition of the new reality."[126]

Union activists and officials in Quebec were ecstatic with White's bold statements, which stood in stark contrast to the meandering of the federal NDP on the question of Quebec sovereignty.[127] The party's position – that it would respect Quebec's right to self-determination but would prefer that Quebeckers not exercise this right – went over like a lead balloon in a province where the party had no seats and little credibility. A few years earlier, the small provincial wing of the NDP in Quebec had voted to disaffiliate from the federal party over policy differences largely related to constitutional issues.[128] When the leadership of the Quebec NDP endorsed sovereignist Gilles Duceppe's candidacy in a 1990 by-election in the downtown Montreal riding of Laurier–Sainte-Marie, the federal NDP voted to sever all ties to the Quebec NDP, which eventually changed its name.[129] The subsequent rise of the BQ virtually wiped the federal NDP off the map in Quebec as trade union activists rallied around the new sovereignist party.[130]

In mid-October 1995, New Democrats gathered in Ottawa to choose a new federal leader to replace Audrey McLaughlin. Hargrove endorsed BC MP Svend Robinson, a self-described socialist running to bring the NDP back to its left-wing and social movement roots.[131] Robinson led after the first ballot at the delegated leadership convention but withdrew when it became clear to his campaign that he did not have a path to victory on subsequent ballots. Former Nova Scotia NDP leader Alexa McDonough emerged the winner. However, her victory barely registered in the public mind, as the country was fixated on the impending Quebec referendum.

When it became clear in the final week of the referendum campaign that the yes forces might be headed toward victory, Liberal prime minister Jean Chrétien, under enormous pressure from federalist forces, promised that after a no vote his government would restore Quebec's constitutional veto power, recognize Quebec as a distinct society, and transfer responsibility for labour market training to the province. Chrétien's desperate televised plea to "preserve the economic and political union we already enjoy" helped to deliver the narrowest of victories to the no forces.[132] When all the ballots were counted, 49.4 percent voted yes; 50.6 percent voted no. Quebec premier Jacques Parizeau resigned soon afterward, and the province's labour movement expressed bitter disappointment at the result.

CONCLUSION

The battle over free trade and the election of Ontario's first NDP govern-ment revealed and, in turn, cemented tensions in the relationship between the party and the CAW. In the wake of the 1988 federal election, the CAW publicly berated the NDP for turning its back on the labour movement and for allowing the Liberal Party to own the anti-free-trade position.[133] More significantly, after Bob Rae's surprise victory in the 1990 Ontario provincial election, the CAW emerged as one of the government's most vocal critics on the left, pushing the party to follow through on the implementation of its ambitious social democratic platform amid widespread opposition from the business community. The Rae government's policy reversals in the context of a global economic recession drew intense criticisms from the CAW. In particular, the union spoke out against the NDP's decision to tackle the province's growing debt and deficit through the imposition of the Social Contract Act. The party-union relationship seemed irreparably harmed by the legislation. As Gindin laments, "The tragic impact of the Ontario NDP government's reign was, unfortunately, to further destroy hope and to demoralize, divide, and ultimately demobilize rather than activate working people."[134] The Ontario NDP government's defeat at the hands of the Mike Harris Conservatives in the ensuing 1995 provincial election was decisive. In Quebec, the union movement also gravitated away from the federal NDP and toward the Bloc as constitutional tensions mounted in the run-up to the 1995 Quebec referendum. The left was demoralized, and the future of working-class politics was uncertain. But just when labour activists thought that things could not get any worse, Ontario premier Mike Harris declared war on the labour movement as part of his so-called Common Sense Revolution.

CHAPTER 4

WINDING ROAD
Rebuilding the Left, 1995–2003

In the wake of the Ontario New Democratic Party (NDP) government's defeat at the hands of Mike Harris's Conservatives in 1995, the Canadian Auto Workers (CAW) focused on building extra-parliamentary opposition to the government and its aggressive right-wing agenda. This period featured several strategic political shifts as the union struggled to forge a coherent path to rebuilding the left and reasserting working-class power. The union's syndicalist approach to political action – highlighted through its leadership in the Days of Action protests and global justice activism – emerged as an alternative to social democratic electoralism. Although this dynamic further marginalized the union's relationship with the NDP, it did not result in the union's retreat from the electoral arena. Rather than focusing on electing New Democrats, the CAW concentrated on blocking Conservatives as part of a strategic-voting effort. This new strategy – which involved supporting Liberal candidates where electorally viable – proved controversial both within the union and among union activists more broadly. When the Harris Conservatives were re-elected in 1999 with an even larger share of the popular vote, the union did not make amends with the NDP. Instead, at the 2001 federal NDP convention, it supported the New Politics Initiative's proposal to replace the party with a new electoral formation on the left, to be backed by labour and social movements.

THE ECONOMIC LANDSCAPE

The performance of Ontario's automotive industry in the 1990s was highly paradoxical. On the one hand, as discussed in the previous chapter, the recession of the early 1990s, combined with the effects of free trade, contributed to a shrinking market share for the Big Three and to initial job losses.[1] On the other hand, the sector as a whole was growing, as evidenced by the fact that vehicle production was up by 27.6 percent between 1991 and 1995.[2] This growth was driven by a lower Canadian dollar, popular product lines, strong manufacturing capacity in recently updated plants, and relative labour peace.[3] Industrial relations scholars Pradeep Kumar and John Holmes have detected the same trend in auto parts production, noting that 18,000 jobs were lost in the sector between 1989 and 1991, before seeing record high production and investments between 1991 and 1995.[4] Whereas automotive manufacturers and parts suppliers saw increased productivity and profit margins, workers struggled to secure a fair share of the profits that they helped to generate, not least because the union footprint in the auto sector was beginning to shrink.[5]

This dynamic unfolded against the backdrop of a sharp turn to the right by Ontario's provincial government. The Harris Progressive Conservatives (PCs) moved immediately to gut the province's Labour Relations Act, repealing the previous government's anti-scab law and replacing the system of card-based union certification, first introduced by Bill Davis's PC government, with a system of mandatory votes. These anti-union legislative reforms made it much more difficult for workers to exercise their rights to unionize and bargain collectively.[6] The labour movement was under siege.

THE ONTARIO DAYS OF ACTION AND EXTRA-PARLIAMENTARY POLITICS

With the Harris government moving quickly on its destructive legislative agenda, Ontario's labour movement confronted the urgent problem of how to stop a majority government from tearing apart the province's social fabric when the next election was years away. With little capacity to slow the Common Sense Revolution at Queen's Park, significant sections of Ontario labour turned to mass mobilization. The CAW emerged as a leading proponent of this approach, pursuing a fightback strategy based on coalition building, street protest, and economic disruption. Although it did not abandon electoral politics for good, the CAW would never again rely exclusively or even primarily on the NDP to represent its political interests.

For the CAW, the years between 1995 and 2001 saw a resurgence of the union's tradition of syndicalist direct action and reinforced the sense that the CAW played a key leadership role among progressive forces. According to former CAW staffer Herman Rosenfeld, Hargrove "saw the union as the left," particularly during the years of Bob Rae and Mike Harris.[7] The union's former chief economist, Jim Stanford, elaborates on this point, arguing that the CAW saw "itself as a political vehicle," not just a collective bargaining agent. The dominant view was that "the union shouldn't outsource its politics to a party" and should "act as an important independent force in political debates, beyond what particular parties do."[8] The politics of the moment reinforced this perspective: if ever there was a time when unions had to produce their own political strategies, this was it.

According to political economist James Laxer, the CAW acted as a countervailing force in this period by combining "effective unionism, in an extremely difficult economic environment, with a new brand of social and political unionism. As a result, the public sector unions and the CAW have been involved in an expanding network of social movements."[9] Sam Gindin, who served as an assistant to both Bob White and Buzz Hargrove, described this new brand of movement-based unionism as including "the shape of bargaining demands, the scope of union activities, the approach to issues of change, and above all, that sense of commitment to a larger movement that might suffer defeats, but can't be destroyed."[10] These unions were bolstered by the coalition-building experience gained during the mobilization against free trade in 1988 and during the formation of the Public Services Coalition to challenge Rae's Social Contract Act.

The new emphasis on movement and coalition building at the CAW and at the Canadian Labour Congress (CLC), now under White's leadership, made the NDP nervous. "[White] wanted to build coalitions; we were finding women's groups, youth groups, all kinds of groups across the country, much to the chagrin of the NDP, who said, 'Hey, you're not paying any attention to us,'" says Danny Mallett, who worked under White at the

CLC.[11] Long-time NDP backroom strategist Michael Balagus argued in 1994 that labour's shift to coalition politics threatened the effectiveness of both labour and the NDP. "Bob White was fundamentally wrong," he said. "The NDP exists today because labour as a social movement recognized that it needed a parliamentary voice ... This is a real serious problem for the NDP. How do you address the fact that hard-core New Democrats are putting their time, energy, creativity and money into coalitions?"[12]

Deep divisions over political strategy remained among Ontario's unions themselves in the wake of the 1995 election. As Yonatan Reshef and Sandra Rastin put it, "The ill feelings between the pink unions, on the one side, and the public-sector unions and the CAW, on the other, smouldered."[13] NDP stalwarts were furious that some unions, like the CAW, had basically sat out the election, thus leaving the door open for Harris's election. For their part, the public-sector unions and the CAW blamed Rae and the NDP for the outcome. If the government had not betrayed its social democratic principles and union base with the Social Contract Act, they argued, the result may have been different. As it stood, the experience of a social democratic government attacking public-sector wages and free collective bargaining fostered a disillusionment with electoral politics among many labour movement activists, who were actively seeking a new approach. Regardless of who was responsible, the labour movement urgently needed a common political strategy for countering the legislative onslaught that began with the anti-union rewrite of the Labour Relations Act.

The November 1995 convention of the Ontario Federation of Labour (OFL) was the site of a contentious debate over how to respond. The factions lined up in much the same way that they had over the Social Contract Act. The Pink Paper unions argued for a parliamentary strategy and "opposed mass mobilizations and collective protests, which they argued were illegal and could turn public opinion against the unions and the NDP."[14] Their main concern was how mass mobilization, especially if it was disruptive, would shape the NDP's prospects in the next election. In contrast, the public-sector unions and the CAW were convinced that some urgent intervention was necessary to counter the Harris government and make the implementation of its neoliberal policies more difficult. One unnamed CAW executive member directly criticized the passivity of the electoral approach: "The vast majority wanted to do nothing except just to educate our members to vote NDP the next election. That was, more or less, the consensus. But we had a strong sense that that wasn't going to work."[15] Many began calling for province-wide mobilizations. For Sam Gindin and Jim Stanford, this debate over union political strategy reflected larger and "profound differences within the labour movement over how to respond to neoliberalism."[16]

To craft a compromise that would satisfy both NDP partisans and those desiring immediate interventions in the streets, the OFL convention approved a resolution titled "Fight Back," which committed the OFL to organizing demonstrations against the government. As these mobilizations were to be explicitly nonpartisan, the resolution did not mention the NDP, nor did the actual events necessarily feature NDP leaders as speakers – a standard part of most previous labour movement protests. However, to get the support of delegates from the Pink Paper unions, the OFL publicly reversed its 1993 decision to cut ties with the NDP. In a separate resolution, the OFL recommitted to supporting the NDP in future elections.[17] In backroom discussions about these resolutions, the Pink Paper unions made it clear that they would "only clear the way for the OFL's financial support of Days of Action strategy in exchange for revisiting disaffiliation from the NDP and on the condition that they themselves would not be expected to support the mobilizations financially or organizationally."[18] According to union organizer Marsha Niemeijer, the unions insisted that "this lack of commitment" was not to be "politicized in any way."[19] Unanimous approval did not mean unanimous participation. From a CAW executive member's perspective, "the labour movement was dragged into this protest kicking and screaming."[20]

The first Day of Action protest in London, Ontario, on December 11, 1995, drew between 12,000 and 20,000 people, and a subsequent protest in Hamilton in February 1996 saw this number balloon to 120,000.[21] The movement had momentum. The list of communities targeted for Days of Action protests grew quickly, with actions planned in Kitchener–Waterloo and Peterborough. The CAW played a leading role in organizing the Days of Action centrally, and CAW activists also played important roles at the local level, serving as co-chairs for the one-day community-wide strikes in London (Rick Witherspoon of Local 200), St. Catharines (Ed Gould of Local 199), Kitchener–Waterloo (Bob Cruikshank of Local 1451), Peterborough

(Thomas Veitch of Local 1987), Kingston (Charlie Stock of Local 1837), and Windsor (Gary Parent of Local 444).[22]

The Days of Action created a climate of mobilization that worked to politicize collective bargaining in ways that had rarely been seen in Ontario, and these labour relations conflicts also fuelled the protests. Over the course of 1996, several major strikes took on a more political and militant character. Participation in the Days of Action was further galvanized by the harsh approach that the Harris government took to the five-week strike of provincial civil servants represented by the Ontario Public Service Employees Union (OPSEU), which began in February 1996.[23] Months later, on October 4, 1996, the CAW began a strike of its own at General Motors (GM) in Oshawa and occupied the fabrication plant to prevent the company from relocating dies and moulds to another plant in order to keep production going. GM capitulated, and the strike was settled.[24] The use of scab labour during a 1997 strike by CAW members at PC World in Scarborough prompted an occupation backed by the national union and 1,000 workers in nearby workplaces. The action helped to secure a negotiated settlement and inspired more workplace occupations by CAW members at Molson's in Barrie and at Johnson Controls in Stratford in 1999. In the case of the latter, the occupation resulted in fifty-seven layoff notices being rescinded.[25]

The CAW's embrace of street politics was reflected in a theme paper tabled at its June 1996 National Collective Bargaining and Political Action Convention in Toronto. Titled "False Solutions, Growing Protests: Recapturing the Agenda," the paper offered a stinging critique of the limits of social democratic electoralism, arguing that "social democracy assumed that *capitalism would continue to provide steady growth*. The role of the NDP was, therefore, no longer to challenge the system but to moderate it."[26] The paper went on to argue that "social democrats didn't challenge the basic agenda of competitiveness but argued for a naïve 'progressive competitiveness.' When social democrats dealt with the deficit, they questioned neither the basic inequality in society nor the undemocratic power of the banks, but argued for 'humane cuts.'"[27] Finally, the paper asserted that "developing alternative policies is critical to any social movement. But the more fundamental issue is developing an alternative politics – the power to implement our alternatives. At this point in time, when we are very much on the defensive, the essence of an alternative politics is build-ing an effective opposition."[28]

THE 1996 ONTARIO NDP LEADERSHIP RACE AND THE POLITICS OF SOCIAL DEMOCRATIC ELECTORALISM

While elements of the labour movement were increasingly embracing syndicalist-inspired strategies, the Ontario NDP was searching for a new leader. The leadership convention took place in June 1996 against the backdrop of growing Days of Action protests. Four former Cabinet ministers – Howard Hampton, Peter Kormos, Frances Lankin, and Tony Silipo – vied to replace Bob Rae as leader. The CAW backed Welland–Thorold MPP Peter Kormos, the only one of the candidates who had opposed the Social Contract Act.[29] His populist campaign revolved around three key themes: restoring the party's relationship with the labour movement, respecting party policy, and reconnecting with the NDP's democratic-socialist roots. Although Kormos enjoyed the support of Hargrove, Sid Ryan at the Canadian Union of Public Employees (CUPE), and former Ontario Secondary School Teachers' Federa-tion (OSSTF) president Liz Barkley, the influence of the latter two leaders on the leadership contest was marginal because their unions had low or nonexistent affiliations to the party. Many CAW locals, in contrast, sent full delegations to the convention. Pink Paper unions, for their part, were well represented at the convention, splitting their support between Hampton and Lankin, the perceived frontrunners. When Kormos finished a better-than-expected third on the first ballot, Hargrove attempted to move the CAW contingent to Lankin in a bid to block Hampton from consolidating his first-ballot lead. However, CAW delegates rebelled, insisting that as long as Kormos was on the ballot, he had earned the union's support. A shouting match ensued as part of a hastily organized hallway caucus, and Hargrove and some of the CAW delegates eventually agreed to disagree.[30] Hargrove went to Lankin, but most CAW delegates stuck with Kormos, thus consoli-dating Hampton's lead after the second ballot. A significant portion of Kor-mos's delegates declared that they would spoil their ballots in the third and final round, guaranteeing Hampton's victory.[31]

Hargrove was unimpressed by the result. And the Ontario NDP's new leader appeared to do little to mend fences with the CAW in the wake of his third-ballot victory. In fact, after the Toronto Days of Action protest in October 1996, Hampton quickly allied himself with the United Steelworkers' leadership in opposition to continued CAW-backed street protests and demonstrations, arguing instead for the left to rally around the NDP.[32]

According to journalist John Ibbitson, the Toronto demonstration, which reportedly involved at least 250,000 participants, "represented the zenith of the labour movement's campaign against the Harris government."[33] With a new provincial NDP leader now in place, the Pink Paper unions wanted to wind down the Days of Action and to reorient labour movement efforts toward rebuilding support for the party in anticipation of a provincial election in 1999. Among other things, Pink Paper union leaders were furious that local demonstration organizers would not readily provide a platform for NDP leaders to address crowds.[34] In the eyes of these union leaders, if the Days of Action could not effectively build support for the NDP, they no longer served a useful purpose. As United Steelworkers District 6 director Harry Hynd wrote,

> Giving up on electoral politics won't get rid of Mike Harris, Ralph Klein or the more apologetic versions represented by the Liberals. Neither will street protests and demonstrations. They may anger the government. They may embarrass them and may make all of us who take part feel better. But there is only one way to get rid of right-wing governments: Defeat them at the polls.[35]

Debates over the wisdom of continuing with the Days of Action set the stage for the race to replace Gord Wilson as OFL president in 1997. The CAW and most of the public-sector unions who had fought the Social Contract Act pinned their hopes on Paul Forder. A former co-vice-chair of the Workplace Health and Safety Agency, Forder came out of the CAW and played a prominent role in coordinating the Days of Action protests as an OFL staffer. His candidacy was immediately backed by the CAW, CUPE, the OSSTF, and the Ontario English Catholic Teachers' Association.[36] Sid Ryan argues that Wilson and the Pink Paper unions "scoured the entire labour movement looking for a candidate to run against Forder. Many names were floated, including Dave Christopherson (CAW), a decent guy who had been a member of Bob Rae's cabinet." The choice of a CAW-affiliated candidate may have seemed odd, but Ryan argues that the Pink Paper unions were being "Machiavellian" because Christopherson was viewed as being more loyal to the party than to his union. Although Christopherson had come out of the CAW, he had also sided with Rae on the Social Contract Act. In Ryan's words, the Pink Paper unions "figured Christopherson would split the CAW vote," thus leading to Forder's defeat.[37] Hargrove confirms that Christopherson, then a sitting NDP MPP from Hamilton, was indeed interested in the job of OFL president and sought his union's support. Hargrove turned down Christopherson and threatened to come out against him if he put his name forward. "He was really pissed," recalls Hargrove.[38]

With Christopherson out of the running, the Pink Paper unions decided to put forward United Steelworker and NDP stalwart Wayne Samuelson, who also enjoyed the support of OPSEU president Leah Casselman.[39] In the end, delegates to the November 1997 OFL convention elected Samuelson over Forder by a vote of 1,251 to 1,046.[40] The result signalled the beginning of the end for the Days of Action, which were losing momentum after Toronto and were slowly wound down.

Hargrove looks back on the Days of Action as an important bulwark against Harris's Common Sense Revolution, arguing that the protests slowed down the government's agenda.[41] He points specifically to the government's 1997 decision to back off from proposed changes in Bill 136, the Public Sector Transition Stability Act, that would have allowed the provincial government to suspend municipal, health care, and school board workers' right to strike. "The polls made the government pause, but there's no doubt the key element in slowing the Harris juggernaut was the willingness of members in the labour movement, along with coalition partners, to fight back with the Days of Action," Hargrove argues.[42]

However, this reprieve from the government's assault on organized labour proved the exception rather than the rule. Harris charged ahead with restructuring the highly unionized education sector through Bill 160, the Education Quality Improvement Act. Among other things, Bill 160 removed the taxing powers of school boards, increased the number of instructional days, placed teacher union bargaining under the Labour Relations Act, and removed principals and vice-principals from teacher union bargaining units.[43] Because the law represented a significant threat to working conditions, it set off a firestorm of protest, ultimately culminating in a two-week province-wide walkout of teachers in October 1997 described as a political protest by teachers' unions. However, despite public support for the walkout, the action ended due to internal tensions among teachers' unions. The government made only small amendments to the legislation, which ultimately passed.[44]

In June 1998, the Harris government pushed through Bill 31, the Economic Development and Workplace Democracy Act, which removed the ability of the Ontario Labour Relations Board to grant automatic union certification as a remedy for unfair labour practices and made it easier for employers to be released from their existing obligations to construction trade unions.[45] These continued legislative assaults cast doubt on the effectiveness of direct action as a strategy to combat the government. Days of Action protests in St. Catharines and Kingston in 1998 drew relatively few participants, and eventually the Days of Action were shelved completely.[46] The movement had not rendered the province ungovernable, nor had it forced the Conservatives to back down.

However, for Hargrove, the Days of Action were never about making the province ungovernable; he just wanted the government to sit down with labour and listen to union concerns. "Open the door and talk to us. Let's see the problem you've identified. Let's work together to fix it," Hargrove says.[47] But even based on this measure, the unions were seemingly unsuccessful. Gindin's assessment is that "the union came up against its political limits." Hargrove, in Gindin's estimation, dwelled on the limitations of the Days of Action rather than focusing on the capacities that the union had managed to build through the city-by-city strike actions. "At the end of the day, Buzz took a look at it and said, 'Well, we just did the ultimate, general strikes across communities. This is our union leading this. And nothing changed.' And that was part of his conservative turn to a kind of corporatism within bargaining, a corporatism politically," argues Gindin.[48]

Corporatism emphasizes the essential common, rather than conflicting, interests between workers and employers while promoting cooperation with employers and the state as opposed to adversarial relationships. Proponents of corporatism believe that unions are able to exercise greater influence when their role is structurally legitimated.[49] Although a form of corporatism or tripartism has been institutionalized in labour relations frameworks in some European countries, this has not been the case in Canada. Nevertheless, some unions have sought greater legitimacy and influence by acting as junior partners to capital, effectively conceding that this is as good as it will ever get.

Gindin argues that the CAW's turn away from syndicalist strategies during this period "reflected the broader weakness of the left." He adds, "I think options got polarized. You either had to become very radical or you're going to be in real danger and Buzz wasn't going to become really radical without a base pushing him."[50] Others associated with the CAW have offered a range of views. Rosenfeld argues that the Days of Action "faded out because it didn't have a strong enough base in the union movement."[51] Peggy Nash, a former assistant to the CAW president, agrees: "We had a lot of people out, a lot of local people came, but remember we also bussed people in from all over … If the strategy was to somehow make the province ungovernable with a series of rolling days of action, there needed to be much more broad-based support and participation."[52] This is not to suggest that the CAW did not benefit in any way from the Days of Action. The protests, for example, helped to build activist capacity and to revive a syndicalist streak in the union, as evidenced by the consolidation and expansion of cross-union and cross-constituency solidarity.[53]

However, as the provincial election approached, unions turned their attention to defeating the Conservatives at the ballot box. This focus did not necessarily translate into support for the NDP. Pink Paper unions certainly backed the party, but other unions went in different directions. In the case of teachers, as Larry Savage and Chantal Mancini explain, the unprecedented political protest staged in opposition to Bill 160 had "politicized thousands of education workers across all teachers' unions and convinced the unions to step outside their comfort zones and embrace anti-Conservative strategic voting in order to defeat Harris in the 1999 provincial election."[54] Given that these unions had never shared close ties to the NDP, this strategy was unsurprising. However, the CAW's decision to join teachers' unions and building and construction trades unions as part of a union-backed strategic-voting campaign did send shockwaves throughout the labour movement.

THE CAW ADOPTS STRATEGIC VOTING

With the promise of the Days of Action in the rear-view mirror and the 1999 Ontario provincial election approaching, Hargrove turned his attention back to electoral politics. With the NDP languishing a distant third in public opinion polls, some CAW members were unenthused at the prospect of working for the NDP. Others argued for neutrality vis-à-vis parties. Hargrove, however, writes in his autobiography that "personally, leaving the party is not an alternative."[55] Hargrove explains that, despite his antipathy to the Ontario NDP, any decision to break ties would have been complicated because of the NDP's federated structure and because of the impact that it would have on other sections where the union, in his estimation, still enjoyed strong influence and good relations.[56] At a February 1998 meeting of the union's National Executive Board, members decided by a slim margin to continue the union's affiliation to the party. According to Hargrove, "The decision took into account that, notwithstanding current difficulties, our union had enjoyed a long relationship with the NDP." Hargrove also argues that "the CAW had to remain in the party to make sure there was a strong, progressive voice representing working Canadians. But the decision to stick with the NDP was very close, and many of our leaders are still wary."[57]

Over the course of that year, however, the Ontario NDP's standing in public opinion polls did not improve.[58] The real prospect of Harris's re-election prompted Hargrove to embrace anti-Conservative strategic voting as an electoral tactic for the first time in the national union's history. In a highly polarized debate at the December 1998 CAW Council meeting in Toronto, delegates officially adopted a strategic-voting plan that would see the CAW endorse and support NDP incumbents and NDP candidates in winnable ridings while extending support to the candidates best able to defeat Tory candidates in other ridings. Although there was virtual unanimity among CAW activists on the need to defeat the Tories, activists were sharply divided over strategy. Both Local 1837 president Charlie Stock and Marine Workers Federation/CAW financial secretary Les Holloway were vocal opponents of strategic voting, fearing the negative impact on the NDP.[59] Others, like Local 1990 president Anne Davidson, were more worried that the NDP might split the anti-Conservative vote and allow the Harris Tories to be re-elected.[60] Hargrove unquestionably drove the debate, arguing forcefully in favour of strategic voting. He warned that winning re-election would embolden the Harris government in its anti-union agenda and that labour could not survive another four years of Tory rule.[61] However, he was careful not to frame the decision as support for the Liberals, even if that was the logical conclusion. The *CAW Contact* newsletter described his position on the strategic-voting paper as follows: "CAW president Buzz Hargrove said the paper is first and foremost about defeating Harris. But it's also about the CAW supporting the NDP and is about supporting NDP incumbents and other NDP candidates where they have a real chance of winning."[62] Hargrove was more direct years later in justifying the union's approach: "There was no way, given the fresh memories in the electorate's minds, that Harris and the Conservatives would be booted out in favour of a refreshed NDP party ... Since an NDP victory was clearly out of the question, our main goal became limiting the Conservatives."[63]

The union's official plan called for:

1) Defeating as many Harris Tories as possible with the objective of defeating the government. This will mean tough anti-Harris canvasses and messaging with the knowledge that this may bolster the Liberal campaign in that riding.
2) Identifying winnable ridings and electing as many NDP candidates as possible. This means concentrating our resources in those ridings only and not resourcing NDP campaigns without a chance.[64]

Ken Lewenza describes the debate at the December 1998 CAW Council meeting as "very painful ... It was not an easy meeting for Buzz Hargrove, I can tell you that." Retirees in particular were angry with Hargrove's recommendation on strategic voting. "You've got to understand, all of our training programs, all of our educationals, all of our conferences ... all of our building of local unions and community activism was tied to the NDP. We had people that literally thought as highly about the New Democratic Party as they did about their union," explains Lewenza. "The retirees were born with the partnership with the New Democratic Party," he adds.[65]

Peggy Nash also attended the meeting in her capacity as Hargrove's assistant. "The preference of our political activists, the people who had really been organizing to defeat Harris, was the NDP, but I don't think people had a lot of confidence that the party could do it," she explains. "The right was so much more confident and revolutionary than the left. The left was very weak and meek, and people didn't seem to have confidence. I think it made sense, initially, for people to say, 'Listen, we've got to get these guys out of here. They're doing a lot of damage to the province,'" she says. However, strategic voting was a risky strategy. "When you have a government like the Harris government, people will do whatever they can to defeat that government. That was the logic behind strategic voting, but it confused people," explains Nash. "In essence, strategic voting to me was code for telling people how to vote, but not vote for the NDP."[66] Lewenza disagrees, asserting that the tactic was "in the best interest of our members ... In retrospect, I support the decision today as much as I did back then."[67]

Looking back, Jim Stanford acknowledges that the union's endorsement of strategic voting was a "controversial moment" but rejects the idea that it was a defining moment for the union. "The union had been moving away from the NDP for the better part of a decade, so it's not like it happened overnight. The key goal there was to get Mike Harris out, and it seems to me that's a no brainer for 99 percent of progressives," he argues. Stanford further defends the decision on the basis that "the credibility of the NDP as being the voice of workers or the political expression of the union movement was in tatters because of what the [Rae] government had done. And then the relationship with the NDP had not gotten any better in the years the NDP was in opposition."[68]

Sam Gindin was more ambivalent about the union's decision to embrace strategic voting in the 1999 Ontario provincial election. "My position on the NDP was because the NDP wasn't building an alternative, it was only an instrumental vote. And I think generally it's the right instrumental vote, but it was an instrumental vote. So when there was a danger of something really significant, whether it was free trade or something else, you should vote strategically," he argues.[69] At the time, Gindin did not think the tactical endorsement of strategic voting would morph into a more enduring electoral alliance with the Liberals. Similarly, Herman Rosenfeld did not think of the union's embrace of strategic voting in 1998 as an ideological shift but as a "tactical move to survive" a particular moment in time. It wasn't presented as a new direction but as "the best of a buffet of bad decisions." In retrospect, however, Rosenfeld considers the decision to pursue strategic voting to have been a "rabbit hole" for the CAW. Once the union committed to this strategic approach, it needed to "justify being on this path."[70]

Gindin credits the centralized power of the president's office with carrying the day on strategic voting:

> Buzz had the resources and the power and the ammunition and talking points ... about the limits of the NDP. He could present this,

because he was smart enough to do it, as a modest temporary thing ... The opposition wasn't strong enough to challenge him because they couldn't defend the NDP ... and the other thing is, a big part of the membership was itself already agnostic ... They had to be convinced to vote for the NDP, and that was probably the majority.[71]

CAW activist Willie Lambert looks back on the decision as a turning point for the union. For him, strategic voting "hurt our capacity to build the NDP ... I always believed the NDP could be a vehicle ... I still believe that."[72] Although Gindin acknowledges that there were many NDP partisans like Lambert in the union, "they weren't strong enough. And I think the reason they weren't strong enough is that there were enough people who didn't care."[73]

As for Hargrove, he was unrepentant, arguing in his 2009 autobiography, "The attitudes and actions of Mike Harris and his Tories justified, in my mind, a new approach to politics by the CAW, and that's what I recommended to the union leadership."[74] Although divided, CAW Council delegates agreed. According to Reshef and Rastin, 60 percent of the 750 delegates present supported the strategic-voting proposal.[75] Hargrove estimates that roughly 80 percent of delegates voted in favour. "I knew there'd be no backlash from the rank and file. The backlash we had was from the NDP and the labour movement," he says.[76] Indeed, the CAW's decision to pursue strategic voting triggered opposition from both the party and the Ontario Federation of Labour. The OFL's director of legislation and political action, Ross McClellan, wrote to Hargrove to challenge the union's new direction. In his letter, McClellan, a former NDP member of provincial Parliament (MPP), castigated Liberal leader Dalton McGuinty as anti-union, noting that prior to taking over the party leadership, he had voted against the NDP's anti-scab law and had proposed a private member's bill to curtail teachers' right to strike.[77] Hargrove, however, was unmoved.

THE 1999 ONTARIO ELECTION: HARRIS RE-ELECTED

The CAW was certainly not alone in pursuing strategic voting in 1999. Under the umbrella of the Ontario Election Network (OEN), the CAW worked together with the Toronto-based Citizens 4 Local Democracy, the teachers' unions, OPSEU, the Ontario Nurses' Association, and building trades unions to target two dozen key ridings, endorsing a roughly equal number of Liberal and NDP candidates.[78] By defeating the Tories in ridings targeted for strategic voting, the unions reasoned that they could deny Harris a majority in a reconfigured 103-seat legislature.

Harris, however, proved a formidable foe. The Tories significantly out-fundraised and outspent the other parties, thanks to the government's rewriting of campaign finance laws to increase donation limits.[79] They used their massive war chest to launch a pre-election negative ad campaign designed to paint McGuinty as woefully unprepared for the job of premier.[80] In contrast, the Tories largely ignored the NDP, no doubt hoping that the party would rise in the polls at the expense of the Liberals and thus help to split the anti-Conservative vote.

The NDP had been trailing badly in third place in public opinion polls under Howard Hampton's leadership, and pundits had basically written off the party in advance of the campaign.[81] Part of the problem for Hampton was that he was working hard to turn the page on the Rae years despite leading a caucus made up mostly of former Rae government Cabinet ministers. Given the legacy of the Social Contract Act and the NDP gov-ernment's decision to jettison key progressive policy initiatives like public auto insurance, Hampton's attempt to rebrand the party arguably came off as lacking in credibility.

Whereas unions that were committed to strategic voting had engaged in high-level cooperation in an effort to defeat Conservatives, Hampton had been uninterested in playing along. Throughout the campaign and in the leaders' debate, he went after the Liberals just as much as, if not more than, he went after Harris and the Tories. McGuinty complained that Hampton and Harris were teaming up against him as part of a "conspiracy" to siphon Liberal votes to the NDP and keep the Tories in power.[82] NDP campaign director Rob Milling addressed this very dynamic in an internal party post-election analysis: "Those who may argue that we made a strategic error in attacking McGuinty and targeting Liberals overlook the fact that our only chance of growth, and of winning any seats, was to win and keep votes that would otherwise go Liberal."[83] However, the NDP campaign's decision to target the Liberals did not go over well with the unions associ-ated with the OEN.

The OEN's strategic voting effort was ultimately unsuccessful insofar as the Harris government was re-elected with an even greater share of the popular vote.[84] The Tories won fifty-nine seats and 45.1 percent of the vote. The Liberals increased their vote share by 8.8 points to 39.9 percent and captured thirty-five seats, and the NDP secured just 12.6 percent (a drop of 8 points from 1995) and managed to win just nine seats. Admittedly, the OEN's strategic-voting campaign was considered a qualified success by some. Political scientist Brian Tanguay argues that the OEN campaign had a modest effect compared to strategic-voting efforts in past electoral contests in Canada and helped to defeat key Cabinet ministers in the process.[85] Both Patrick Monahan and journalist John Barber argue that the OEN's success was limited to the City of Toronto.[86] However, Reshef and Rastin summarize the factors that hurt the OEN's strategic-voting effort as follows:

> The unions did not communicate their strategy and their choices well enough; they often did not endorse the same candidate in a given riding; they only targeted their members and did not inform the general public of the strategy; they waited to release their official list of endorsed candidates until only days before the election; NDP supporters were "touchy" about backing Liberals and could not detach themselves from their long-established partisan allegiance; the non-endorsed candidates refused to give up without a fight, causing the Liberal and NDP candidates to battle each other directly; and finally, many voters (and media reporters) interpreted "strategic voting" to mean "vote Liberal."[87]

Overall, Reshef and Rastin conclude that strategic voting "likely damaged the NDP's capacity to represent labour adequately and voice its concerns in parliament. Clearly, it did not prevent the Conservatives from attaining a second majority government."[88]

This last point was used by NDP activists to argue that strategic-voting efforts had not only re-elected the Tories but also worked to drive down NDP support, costing the party official status at Queen's Park in the process. Hampton openly accused the CAW of having handed Harris a second term through its ill-conceived efforts at strategic voting.[89] Hargrove rejected Hampton's assertion, noting that a riding-by-riding analysis demonstrated that in every riding where the party lost, it was by at least 10 percent.[90] In actual fact, the party had come a very close second in several ridings, but in general, Hargrove had a point: the Ontario NDP would almost certainly have lost seats in the 1999 election with or without the full backing of the CAW. Take, for example, the riding of Windsor–St. Clair, where the CAW backed NDP MPP Wayne Lessard.[91] Lessard had lost his seat to Liberal Dwight Duncan in 1995 by just 380 votes but was returned to the legislature two years later after winning a by-election in Windsor–Riverside, called after the resignation of NDP MPP Dave Cooke. Changes to riding boundaries, brought about by a significant cut in the number of MPPs, meant that Duncan and Lessard squared off once again in the 1999 provincial election in the new riding of Windsor–St. Clair. Lessard lost by more than 4,200 votes and blamed strategic voting for the outcome, even though he had the CAW's endorsement.[92]

Overall, it's not clear that any union endorsements actually helped individual candidates. In the twelve ridings where the OEN endorsed NDP candidates, the party finished third and lost vote share in eight of them, including Oshawa, where New Democrat Colleen Twomey finished a distant third with 22.6 percent of the vote, and Cambridge, where New Democrat Gary Gibson took just 19.4 percent of the vote. In these ridings, the logic of the OEN's campaign was completely undermined by the fact that it backed the wrong "strategic" candidate. In contrast, in the fourteen ridings where the OEN endorsed Liberals, the party lost vote share in just two of them (both at the expense of the Conservatives).[93]

Despite strong evidence that the union's strategy had not worked to elect its endorsed NDP candidates, Hargrove argued that if just a few thousand more voters had bought into strategic voting, the Liberals would have defeated the Tories, and "we would have had a minority government with our party [the NDP] in control of the agenda."[94] The results in Windsor–St. Clair, Oshawa, and Cambridge, however, not only cast doubt on the union's ability to deliver votes to its strategically backed candidates but also suggested that the NDP's fortunes did not really hinge on the CAW's electoral efforts. As Geoff Bickerton argues in *Canadian Dimension,*

> In 1995, the Party brass somehow convinced themselves that it was Buzz, the CAW and the public-sector unions that were responsible

for the NDP vote declining from 39 per cent to 21 per cent. Forget the social contract, the denial of collective bargaining rights for half of the province's workers, forget the broken promises concerning auto insurance, Sunday shopping and casinos. Ignore the fact that Bob Rae was sounding more and more like Conrad Black. Just blame it on Buzz and the public-sector unions. Convinced that the source of the political disaster lay with Hargrove and public-sector unionists, the NDP leadership and moderate trade leaders banded together to elect Howard Hampton, an unrepentant Bob Rae supporter, as its new leader. Here we are in 1999 and the vote has collapsed to 12 per cent. The explanation? Why, it's none other than Buzz Hargrove who the party establishment once again has identified as the villain. This time, his crime was to have actively advocated "strategic voting," whereby voters would be encouraged to support the candidate most able to defeat a Conservative.[95]

This perspective, however, cuts both ways for the CAW. Did its endorsement really matter? And if not, what would that mean for both the party and the union?

In any case, CAW-NDP relations went from bad to worse in the aftermath of the 1999 election campaign. Hampton declined an invitation to speak at the June 1999 CAW Council meeting, telling the *Toronto Star* that "it would be even beyond theatre of the absurd for me to be spending time on a podium with someone who spent the better part of the past two years trashing me and trashing the party."[96] Hargrove was unimpressed. "Whether you like us or not, we are an important organization in this province and we've historically played a role in the politics of the province, and the fact that he doesn't understand that or ignores that, or it's the arrogance of just saying I don't give a damn, it doesn't bode well for the future of our party," he shot back.[97]

In an August 1999 meeting with reporters at Queen's Park, Hampton raised the possibility of having Hargrove kicked out of the party. Although he did not mention the CAW leader by name, his reference to someone "who claims to be a New Democrat, but spends the better part of three years either attacking the party or attacking the leader of the party every chance they get," was unmistakeable.[98] Hampton's comments raised the ire of Local 444 president Ken Lewenza, who told the *Windsor Star* that "the NDP has become a weak party. Our union is strong and militant. Maybe Howard Hampton should take a look at us, then work to build up a party that could be supported by labour."[99]

Like Hampton, many party activists were furious with Hargrove. The September 1999 NDP Provincial Council meeting was dominated by a discussion of whether the CAW leader's party membership should be revoked. In the end, delegates adopted a resolution that condemned strategic voting in general but did not single out specific party members for discipline.[100] In response to the resolution, Hargrove told the *Toronto Star*, "As long as we're wasting time on this kind of resolution, we're not getting at the real issues. How we build a strong left party in Ontario and Canada should be the (focus of) debate."[101]

Clearly disappointed with the ideological direction of the party, Hargrove went on to call for a re-examination of the union's relationship with the NDP at both the provincial and federal levels. He made headlines in August 1999 when he threatened to quit the party in response to Alexa McDonough's drive to push the federal NDP to the political centre. Inspired by Tony Blair's electoral victory in the 1997 UK elections, many social democratic parties around the world, the NDP included, sought to embrace a "third way" politics that involved jettisoning core social democratic values in order to become more electorally viable in the face of a rising tide of neoliberal politics.[102]

For his part, Hargrove saw the party's ideological drift as an electoral dead end. "The 'third way' is simply the centre of the political spectrum, which has been captured by the Liberals. It is about being another Liberal Party. There is not enough room in our Canadian political system for another centrist party like the Liberals," he argued. However, rather than organizing to defeat any "third way" policy proposals at the federal NDP's upcoming convention, Hargrove indicated that the union would instead simply distance itself further from the party, noting that the CAW would send only half of its typical 125 delegates to the convention.[103]

Saskatchewan NDP member of Parliament (MP) Lorne Nystrom told the media that there was "no ideological consistency" between Hargrove's support for strategic voting in Ontario and his criticisms of the federal NDP's perceived shift to the centre.[104] Many NDP partisans agreed with

Nystrom's observation that one could not campaign for Ontario Liberals who opposed anti-scab legislation and then turn around and accuse the NDP of not being left enough, even though the NDP was clearly to the left of the provincial Liberals by almost any measure.

After the federal NDP's 1999 policy convention, where McDonough's efforts to move the party to the centre were partially successful even in the face of opposition from the CAW, she politely reminded the media that the policy convention was an exercise in democracy and that Hargrove did not speak for the broader labour movement. "Hargrove is a very, very outspoken, strong leader with a very high profile and is an excellent communicator, but he's not the labour movement," she said.[105] Ontario NDP leader Howard Hampton, however, was less kind in his assessment of Hargrove:

> It's hard to figure out where Mr. Hargrove is coming from. It all seems so contradictory. He says the NDP is abandoning its roots because we've said we should have a strategy for talking to business, and two days later, what happens? It's Mr. Hargrove doing exactly that, wining and dining Air Canada's CEO Robert Milton and Gerry Schwartz. You just shake your head and say "Hello?"[106]

Schwartz, a financier and CEO of Onyx Corporation, made headlines along with Hargrove in November 1999 when the latter endorsed a bid by the former to take over and restructure Air Canada and Canadian Airlines. The move by Hargrove was viewed as a betrayal by many airline workers.[107]

Hargrove's CAW was a thorn in the side of not just the NDP. The union also proved a persistent irritant to elements of the labour leadership in Ontario. After defeating the CAW's Paul Forder to win the presidency of the OFL in 1997, Wayne Samuelson faced another CAW challenge in 1999, this time from Local 1256 activist Willie Lambert. Although the CAW's leadership officially supported Lambert's bid, "I was not the toast of the national union," Lambert recalls, pointing out that the union had mobilized much greater resources in support of Forder's bid two years earlier. Lambert's run was more spontaneous and emerged in response to the feeling that Samuelson's divisive decision to wind down the Days of Action should not go unchallenged. Despite spending just $1,800 on his campaign,

Lambert won 45 percent of the vote.[108] The result sent a clear message of dissatisfaction best understood as a protest vote against Samuelson, reflecting the deep and lingering divisions between Pink Paper and other unions in the province. Many of these divisions revolved around how unions should engage in political action and elections.

THE CAW TASK FORCE ON WORKING CLASS POLITICS IN THE TWENTY-FIRST CENTURY

Hargrove's call for the union to re-examine its relationship with the NDP and its approach to political action more generally took form as the Task Force on Working Class Politics in the Twenty-First Century. Launched at the CAW Council meeting in December 1999, the task force would tour the country seeking input from members concerning the role of the union in politics.[109] The task force was Sam Gindin's brainchild and was structured as a "listening device" rather than an exercise in having members simply validate the dominant view of the union's leadership.[110] As then secretary-treasurer Jim O'Neill explains, "These were rank and file workers who were pulled out of a lottery of each local, they weren't hand-picked. We didn't know one day to the next who would show up, and it was a good opportunity to hear what people had to say on political elections."[111]

Gindin was looking to get two things out of the task force. First, he hoped and expected that members would indicate their preference for having the union remain involved in political action broadly speaking and would convey an understanding that the union could not avoid politics. Second, Gindin "wanted to see a confirmation of an interest in a more radical politics." This interest meant embracing a political orientation to the left of the NDP. Gindin always thought that "the NDP was a barrier to a serious left politics, that the NDP was a progressive party that had no interest in social transformation ... It didn't believe workers could transform the world, and it didn't believe that the world could be transformed. It was awed by capitalist power. It wasn't going to challenge it." Gindin believed that "the trick was to go beyond the NDP to recognize that we had to have a different kind of politics that was rooted in seriously thinking about class formation and developing the kind of a working class that understood capitalism and that was committed to a long-term project of changing it."[112] The task force, in his view, could kick-start that process. However, Gindin suffered a heart attack shortly after the task force was launched, and others in the union with different ideas and allegiances were tapped to take over.

Peggy Nash, who eventually oversaw the task force, describes it as "a way to engage the membership and listen to the membership and help build class consciousness among the membership." She approached the work differently from Gindin, taking inspiration from the idea that the union could learn from the political approach of Quebec's labour movement, which favoured developing a list of demands or proposals and then "shop[ping] them around to different parties to see who bit." Nash thought that this was "a better approach than just saying, 'Well, a few crumbs here are better than no crumbs there or whatever' ... I was hoping that we would get to a situation where people would say, 'Listen, here are our priorities.' It was in that vein that we conducted our outreach, our consultation with the members in the task force," she explains.[113]

THE 2000 FEDERAL ELECTION AND RISING UNION-PARTY TENSIONS

While the task force toured the country consulting with members, the CAW continued to make waves in the labour movement. When the US-based Service Employees International Union (SEIU) merged its Canadian locals without their consent, eight of the SEIU's local leaders in Canada came together in February 2000 to propose that their 30,000 members leave the union to join the CAW. Hargrove framed the move as a response to "dictatorial leadership from Washington, poor service, and a fundamental lack of control over their Canadian affairs."[114] In response, the SEIU accused the CAW of raiding in contravention of the CLC's constitution – a charge that was upheld by the CLC. Undeterred, the CAW continued to court SEIU members, which in turn led to sanctions being imposed and the CAW's ouster from the CLC on July 1, 2000.[115] The raiding allegations further polarized the CAW's relationships with other unions and reinforced party-union tensions given that New Democrats were unwilling to support the union as they had in 1987, when the Newfoundland Fishermen, Food and Allied Workers Union had broken away from the United Food and Commercial Workers to join the newly formed CAW.[116]

For the first time in its history, the CAW declined to endorse the federal NDP in the November 2000 election, although it did donate an estimated $1 million in "cash, goods and services" to the NDP campaign.[117] This support included a $300,000 loan guarantee, a $150,000 contribution to the party's pre-election coffers, another $150,000 during the campaign itself, and twenty-five members or staff booked off to work on riding-level campaigns.[118] The union chose to endorse only nine NDP candidates, all with ties to the CAW.[119] Curiously, strategic voting did not figure into the endorsements.[120] On election night, Jean Chrétien's Liberals secured their third straight majority government, and the NDP held onto fourth place with just thirteen seats. The NDP saw its vote share drop from 11 to 8.5 percent, and only two of the nine candidates endorsed by the CAW were elected.[121]

In the wake of the federal NDP's disappointing election result, the CAW leadership continued its criticisms of NDP leader Alexa McDonough's efforts to bring the party closer to the political centre, and Hargrove's ongoing feud with Ontario NDP leader Howard Hampton did not encourage rapprochement. Hargrove called for the establishment of a task force on the future of the NDP: "I believe it is now time for us to get back, as a party, to our roots, to move away from the centre of the road and get back to defining ourselves as a democratic socialist party of Canada with the people's agenda, not an agenda for the elite and the wealthy in this country."[122] But Ontario NDP leader Howard Hampton argued that a "navel-gazing" exercise was the last thing that the party needed. "At every opportunity [Hargrove] either tries to embarrass, to criticize or to undermine, so people have to start asking, what is Mr. Hargrove's real agenda?" asked Hampton at a year-end session with reporters.[123] "From the party's perspective, Mr. Hargrove has basically no credibility anymore," he added. In response, Hargrove told the *Toronto Star*, "Howard finds it easier to blame me for the problems of the provincial NDP than to come to grips with the real problems." He pointed to a "lack of leadership" in Ontario and at the federal level.[124]

A few months after the election, Hargrove called on McDonough to resign within a year and signalled that the union might permanently sever its relationship with the NDP. "I believe now it very well may be time for us to end any kind of formal relationship, any kind of funding to the NDP," said Hargrove.[125] Some New Democrats, like Hampton, seemed more than happy for Hargrove to make his exit, but others, like Windsor MP Joe Comartin, cautioned that a formal split would have severe repercussions in terms of party funding, noting that the CAW was among the unions that had guaranteed the $3 million loan that the party had used to fund its $7 million national campaign the previous year. What "would probably be the most serious impact," said Comartin, "is the loss of the loan guarantees they have given us in the past, which has enabled us to conduct a campaign at a much more sophisticated level."[126]

Although party-union tensions were most evident in Ontario and at the federal level, they also emerged in places like Manitoba, where Gary Doer's newly elected NDP government was forced to deal with the fallout over a labour dispute between CAW Local 2224 and John Buhler, the owner of the Versatile tractor factory in Winnipeg. After using a loan from the federal government to purchase the factory, Buhler immediately set out to bust the union. Local 2224 struck in November 2000 in the face of extreme concessionary demands. In response, Buhler threatened to move the operation to the United States and eventually made good on his promise.[127] The union criticized the Doer government for its unwillingness to get involved in the dispute and for its refusal to nationalize the factory.[128] In March 2001, Hargrove charged,

> If the government of Manitoba, an NDP government dismisses this out of hand, they can be assured they've lost the support of our union locally and nationally. If that's what an NDP government means for working people, then there's not much reason for us to support the NDP ... If the NDP can't step in there, then there's absolutely no question I will recommend across the country that we withdraw our support completely from the NDP.[129]

Looking back on the ordeal, Doer – a former labour leader himself – argues,

> We could not have taken over the plant on the basis of a strike. If a dispute hits the rocks, you have to have incentives for both sides to come to a settlement. The worst time to walk into a takeover is on the basis of a labour management dispute. We cannot go around nationalizing every company when there is a dispute that does not go the right way.[130]

THE AUTO PACT, THE NEW POLITICS INITIATIVE, AND THE 2003 FEDERAL NDP LEADERSHIP RACE

The CAW-NDP relationship was clearly on the ropes, but other external crises were arguably more pressing for the union's leadership. The World Trade Organization declared the Auto Pact illegal in October 2000 and struck it down in February 2001.[131] This development meant that US automakers would no longer be required to manufacture a vehicle in Canada for each one sold in the country. The death of the Auto Pact, the expansion of free trade, and increased competition from low-cost international labour markets meant that Canada had lost much of its competitive advantage, leading the Big Three and many parts suppliers to scale back production.[132] This development dealt a severe blow to the CAW and stripped the union of leverage at the bargaining table.[133] In response to General Motors' decision to close its only Quebec-based auto plant in Sainte-Thérèse in September 2001, the CAW launched a press tour to denounce plant closures and to advocate for job guarantees in exchange for government support of the automotive industry.[134] However, this strategy partly played into the hands of the Big Three automakers. "The insecurity of workers has been skilfully adapted and exploited by private capital as a sort of 'veto power' over workers' bargaining demands," explains Euan Gibb, a Local 707 member who has chronicled the shifting power dynamic at Ford's Oakville plants. Gibb argues that Ford successfully demanded that the union agree to changes to work rules and local operating practices in exchange for potential new investments.[135] The fear of losing out on investments to other jurisdictions prompted the union to shift its approach. Gibb writes, "The historic rhetoric of temporary accommodation to management's goals and 'no concessions' has been abandoned ... The rhetoric is now more conservative and it emphasizes the competitive advantages of some workers over others."[136] This shift in the union's approach did not happen overnight. Labour studies scholar Don Wells has documented how, over the course of the 1990s, increased competition and job insecurity gradually compelled the union to adopt a more "complex, cooperativist orientation to labour-management relations."[137] The demise of the Auto Pact in 2001 only accelerated this tendency.

The loss of the Auto Pact also helped to reinforce the anti-globalization movement, which had been intensifying since the World Trade Organization's meetings in Seattle in December 1999. The rise of an anti-capitalist and anti-globalization movement sharply contrasted with the NDP's shift to the political centre.[138] The changing political landscape provided an opening to push for a new kind of politics on the left. The surge in extra-parliamentary anti-globalization youth activism combined with a string of bruising NDP defeats in Ontario, British Columbia, and federally between 1999 and 2001 to spark the formation of the New Politics Initiative (NPI), an informal grouping committed to exploring the possibility of launching a new grassroots left-wing party to replace the NDP.[139] CAW chief economist Jim Stanford emerged as a key spokesperson for the group, which also included NDP MPs Libby Davies and Svend Robinson and political activist Judy Rebick. Although the NPI was not "union-driven," its national coordinating committee included influential union staffers like Stanford and Morna Ballantyne of CUPE.[140]

Widely perceived by party loyalists as wanting to take over the NDP, the architects of the NPI viewed it as a grassroots attempt to radically democratize the party and strengthen its ties both to social movements and to the unions that had embraced extra-parliamentary politics since the mid-1990s. In the end, the NPI proposal was defeated at the federal NDP's November 2001 convention, with 37 percent of delegates in favour and 63 percent opposed. Union delegates were split over the resolution, with the CAW, CUPE, the Canadian Union of Postal Workers, and the Public Service Alliance of Canada in support and the United Steelworkers, United Food and Commercial Workers, and Communications, Energy and Paperworkers Union (CEP) opposed. Notably, the same groupings of unions found themselves on opposite sides over the OFL's 1993 resolution about withdrawing support from the Ontario NDP, with the former group in favour and the latter group opposed.

Interviewees offer contradictory accounts of the CAW's role in the NPI. According to Gindin, the NPI was a project of the CAW, but he argues that it was more a half-hearted attempt by Hargrove to rebuild his influence in the party than a serious effort to build a new party of the left.[141] Stanford, in contrast, claims that "the CAW was not organizationally involved in the NPI," although he did liaise with the union's central leadership team about his work with the NPI.[142] Despite Hargrove's support for the NPI, Stanford concedes that there "wasn't a big mobilization effort to get delegates to the convention."[143] According to Hargrove, the CAW supported the NPI "because we wanted to keep a burr under the NDP's ass."[144] He wanted to keep the NDP true to democratic-socialist ideals. Asked whether it was ideologically consistent to actively push the NDP to the left through the NPI while also actively helping to elect Liberals through strategic voting, Hargrove says, "Had we been successful pushing the NDP to left with the NPI or other things, like the Days of Action ... then there would have been no reason to do strategic voting, and supporting the NDP would have made sense because they would have had an opportunity to form government."[145] Sam Gindin, however, does not buy Hargrove's theory or explanation: "The point of Hargrove's support for the NPI wasn't to challenge the NDP. The point was to bureaucratically challenge them so they would take Buzz Hargrove seriously ... He wanted to be a player."[146] Peggy Nash is even less generous in her interpretation of Hargrove's position: "I think it was a diversion. It's like saying, 'I'm to the left of the NDP' when really he was moving to the Liberals. It's a diversion."[147]

Several interviewees argue that Hargrove's move to the political centre during this period was partly precipitated by the 9/11 terrorist attacks. In the wake of the attacks, Hargrove urged CLC president Ken Georgetti to pressure the International Confederation of Free Trade Unions to suspend worldwide anti-free-trade demonstrations planned for November 9, 2001, "as a symbolic act to signify our movement's outrage and our condemnation of terrorist acts as well as all senseless acts of violence against any of the world's people." Hargrove went on to argue that calling off the demonstrations "would be an important statement of our anger and our movement's commitment to the rights of political protest free of violence."[148] Hargrove's intervention did not sit well with key staff members, who felt that he was conflating senseless acts of violence with the democratic right to protest and engage in civil disobedience. Carol Phillips, for example, says that "Buzz thought I was crazy for wanting to pursue anti-globalization work in the union post-9/11," asserting that the CAW leader "took the wind out of a movement that had been poised to grow."[149] Earlier that year, the union withdrew financial support for the militant and anti-capitalist Ontario Coalition against Poverty after members of the group trashed Ontario finance minister Jim Flaherty's office.[150] Echoing many of the comments made by former CAW staffers like Phillips, Nash, and Rosenfeld concerning the union's trajectory during this period, academics Scott Aquanno and Toba Bryant argue that Hargrove's "approach changed in the early 2000s as downsizing continued, and the 2001 attack on the World Trade Centre threatened continental trade and seemed to close space for anti-establishment politics." They further argue that "Hargrove's repudiation of working-class militancy (revolutionary or not) and shift to the centre reflected his trajectory towards a narrow approach to the politics of the union, promoting short-term perspectives and narrow cost-benefit calculations."[151] Hargrove, however, rejects this view, insisting that neither his politics nor his perspectives wavered in the face of 9/11 or any other external factor.[152]

Even though the NPI resolution was defeated at the November 2001 federal NDP convention, Alexa McDonough did ultimately decide to step down as leader in June 2002. Just a few days after her announcement, McDonough took aim at Hargrove in an interview with CBC Radio's *The House,* referring to Hargrove's politics as "theatre" and dismissing him as a "gutless and destructive force" who had done more harm than good in the labour movement.[153] Later that month, in advance of Big Three contract negotiations, Hargrove told the media that he would consider running for the NDP leadership to replace McDonough if no "credible" left-leaning candidates emerged. "Quite frankly, I think I could win the leadership," he said.[154] Many NDP partisans collectively rolled their eyes at this suggestion. The idea that Hargrove could win the leadership race seemed highly implausible given his support for strategic voting and his very public spats with McDonough and Hampton over the years. By the end of the summer, Hargrove had apparently reached this conclusion himself. Although he very much thought that the "NDP needs someone to lead the party, the same way that I lead this union," he acknowledged in a press release that "there was a notable lack of enthusiasm for my potential candidacy from the party hierarchy, and from the leadership of the rest of the labour movement. This caused me to seriously reflect on what I could achieve in the party, even if I were to win the leadership." Hargrove ultimately "came to the conclusion that it would take several years, largely wasted years, to pull the party together behind my leadership."[155]

During the actual leadership campaign, Hargrove was uncharacteristically reserved. He eventually endorsed Windsor NDP MP Joe

Comartin, a long-time labour lawyer with ties to the CAW who pledged to take the party to the left.[156] However, there is no evidence that the union marshalled much support for Comartin. Hargrove's endorsement of Comartin was even viewed as a negative by some party members. For example, Dee Chisholm, president of the Brant NDP Riding Association, told the local newspaper, "Frankly, I don't care what Buzz Hargrove says. He gets far more press than he deserves and he's mostly negative."[157] In the end, Comartin captured just 7.5 percent of member and 8.3 percent of labour votes in the weighted vote contest, finishing a distant fourth place overall. Most union affiliates supported the eventual winner, Toronto city councillor Jack Layton, who also enjoyed strong backing from NPI supporters.[158] Although the NPI was wound down in the wake of Layton's win, union support for strategic voting was about to take off in unprecedented ways.

CONCLUSION

The CAW's decision to shift gears politically in an effort to confront the challenge of the Common Sense Revolution and broader macroeconomic changes was fraught with struggles and seeming contradictions over what the union stood for and how best to re-establish union power. Initially, the Days of Action demonstrated that unions had the capacity to engage in a sustained politics beyond the strict confines of the electoral arena. The emphasis that organizers placed on mobilization, cross-union solidarity, labour-community alliances, and popular education shifted the left's centre of gravity toward the labour movement and away from the NDP. Ultimately, however, the protests failed to stop the Harris government's agenda. In the words of Sam Gindin, "the demoralization of having done everything possible and still failing set the stage for even greater defeats."[159] Ontario's PC government was re-elected despite the fact that an unprecedented number of unions, the CAW included, pragmatically backed strategic voting in a bid to defeat the government. These dynamics further strained relations between the CAW and the NDP. The union's influence in the party, both federally and in Ontario, clearly declined during this period, as evidenced by the fact that the union found itself on the losing side of key party leadership contests and policy debates. Moreover, Hargrove's support for the Days of Action and the

NPI appeared to stand in stark ideological contrast to his embrace of strategic voting, indicating a lack of coherence in the union's approach to politics. Although Hargrove routinely chastised the NDP for moving to the right during this period, there is evidence that the union itself was headed in the same direction, a process that appeared to be accelerated in the wake of 9/11 and in the face of the demise of the Auto Pact.

CHAPTER 5

A FORK IN THE ROAD
The CAW Turns to Economic and Political Defensiveness, 2003–12

Despite myriad challenges, the Canadian Auto Workers (CAW) witnessed significant growth between 1985 and 2002, adding an average of 6,471 new members per year during this period and making it one of the fastest growing unions in North America.[1] However, the CAW's impressive growth trajectory, the product of both mergers and new organizing, was about to take a dramatic U-turn. Major macroeconomic shifts would result in significant job losses and downward pressure on wages and benefits in the manufacturing sector. This reality, in turn, helped to shape the union's political trajectory.

After the CAW's attempt to build a politics to the left of the New Democratic Party (NDP) failed and the post-9/11 climate put a chill on strategies of militant confrontation, the union adopted a decidedly more defensive posture. On the economic front, the union forged closer relationships with employers as it struggled to protect jobs and to help secure investments. On the political front, the CAW's attention shifted back to the electoral arena and to blocking the election of anti-union Conservative candidates. With each election, strategic voting seemingly became less controversial within the union despite mixed evidence about the strategy's success. Defending the use of strategic voting initially as a form of electoral harm reduction, the union gradually used the cover of strategic voting to forge relationships with key Liberal politicians in an effort to advance the union's interests both politically and economically.

FINAL REPORT OF THE CAW TASK FORCE ON WORKING CLASS POLITICS IN THE TWENTY-FIRST CENTURY

In August 2003, the union's task force on working-class politics wrapped up its work with the presentation of a policy paper that ultimately validated the union's move to a more independent approach to politics. The paper called for the establishment of Union in Politics Committees in each local to replace existing Political Action Committees, whose work traditionally centred on building support for the NDP. In contrast, the Union in Politics Committees' "central goal will not be to promote awareness of, and support for, the NDP during election campaigns (or the PQ [Parti Québécois] in Quebec). Rather, our goal is to develop a long-run, more well rounded, and consistent level of political awareness and action among our rank-and-file members."[2] This outcome was presaged at the CAW Council meeting in December 2002, when the union voted to retool its strategic-voting strategy, pairing it with an issue-oriented campaign focused on anti-scab legislation and turmoil in the auto industry.[3] The task force's policy paper affirmed that "in English Canada the NDP remains the most progressive political party, and it still makes sense for our union to offer its support to the NDP and to NDP candidates in particular circumstances." However, it rejected "trying to rebuild our union's political activism on the basis of group affiliations" and instead called for "politically active members to join a progressive political party of their choice on an individual basis."[4] In other words, the union would not be returning to the NDP fold, at least not as a formal partner.

Leaders in the union interpreted the task force's findings in different ways. In a *Globe and Mail* editorial, CAW chief economist Jim Stanford claimed that "rank-and-file members confirmed that they supported union involvement in broader political debates, but on two strict conditions: The issues the union took on must reflect members' concrete concerns. And members did not want their union to tell them how to vote." The conclusion he drew from these conditions was that "unions need a more independent and flexible approach to politics: rooted in identifying members' hopes and fears, then mobilizing the union's collective strength in support of those goals." The union's interventions, he argued, "must be conducted in the name of the union, not on behalf of any party."[5] Similarly, in recounting the work of the task force, CAW secretary-treasurer Jim O'Neil explains the view of members as follows:

> "You can give us some advice but at the end of the day don't tell us who to vote for, we'll vote for who we think is the best candidate." And I think from that day forward, we've changed a lot of things we've done in our political campaigns. Ultimately, the results of the Task Force have taken us in the direction of strategic voting, and issue-based election campaigns, letting our members decide who's the best, and what's best for their community.[6]

Former CAW president Ken Lewenza also sees the task force as "the stepping stone" that validated strategic voting.[7] Many of the union members and officials interviewed for this book, including long-time CAW president Buzz Hargrove, make similar claims, emphasizing that the task force's work justified strategic voting as a tactic and that members did not want to be told how to vote.

However, in promoting strategic voting, the union was not moving away from endorsing candidates. It may no longer have been telling members to vote NDP across the board, but it was certainly still telling members how to (or how not to) cast their ballots. In this sense, long-time assistant to the president Hemi Mitic retrospectively calls the task force a "charade, a diversion tactic" for Hargrove to move the union toward the Liberals.[8] Even though she penned the task force's final report, Peggy Nash more or less concurs with Mitic's assessment of how the leadership interpreted the task force's findings, suggesting that Hargrove "was really wanting to move away from the NDP, I think for good."[9] Sam Gindin, who served as Hargrove's advisor when the task force was initially launched, reinforces this view:

> The most important thing was that Buzz got to define how [the report] was interpreted ... Peggy wrote the report, which I thought was a good report. But the real point was that Buzz got to interpret it ... Buzz manipulated the report to confirm what he wanted ... He used what I initiated. I was used ... to make an argument for the fact that, yeah, people want politics, but the NDP's irrelevant.[10]

Carol Phillips, another long-time assistant to the CAW president, hints at Gindin's role and intentions in launching the task force: "Some on the left believed that this was a very exciting development, that this opened up the opportunity for the left to become stronger, for us to move away from social democracy." She adds, "What I was afraid would happen ... with a working class that sometimes doesn't have a class analysis, is we were losing an anchor that anchored us further to the left than we could have been had we not in fact endorsed the party." Ultimately, Phillips argues, "what happened was, politically, the union did not move to the left. It's quite obvious." Instead, she says, the move away from the NDP provided cover to fully embrace strategic voting and to develop closer ties to the Liberals.[11] "I take some responsibility for that," acknowledges Gindin.[12]

MCGUINTY COMES TO POWER: ONTARIO'S 2003 PROVINCIAL ELECTION

In the run-up to the Ontario provincial election on October 2, 2003, the CAW joined forces with building and construction trades unions and teachers' unions to launch a major third-party anti-Conservative ad campaign.[13] The newly formed Working Families Coalition officially registered as a third party with Elections Ontario and amassed an impressive war chest to help defeat the Progressive Conservatives (PCs), now led by former finance minister Ernie Eves.

"We're going to do everything humanly possible in this election to defeat the Tories," Hargrove announced at the CAW Constitutional Convention in August 2003.[14] In advocating for strategic voting, however, he made clear that the union was expecting concrete public policy in return for its support. For example, he told delegates that the union would "pin down the Liberals and the New Democratic Party on where they're at. We want anti-scab legislation back to defend the interests of working people in this province."[15] Whereas the NDP answered the union's call for anti-scab legislation, the Liberals did not. However, this distinction did not stop Hargrove from forging ahead with his plan for strategic voting – a plan that ultimately benefited the Liberals as the most viable electoral alternative to the PCs.

Notably, the CAW did not contribute a penny directly to the Liberals, instead reserving its contributions for the NDP and several of its candidates.[16]

Funding Liberals was viewed as a bridge too far, especially given that the Liberals were not actually meeting the union's primary public-policy demands. Thus the CAW's major contributions to the Liberals came exclusively through participation in the Working Families Coalition.

Riding a wave of anti-PC sentiment, Dalton McGuinty's Liberals handily won the 2003 election. New Democrats, once again, lost official party status in the process. Strategic voting was both credited for the result by unions associated with the Working Families Coalition and blamed for the result by many NDP activists and union allies opposed to the tactic.[17] Hargrove considered the outcome a victory. For the CAW, the 2003 election, like the preceding election, was all about dumping the Tories and less about securing a particular policy objective. Although a weakened NDP was arguably bad for the overall public-policy terrain from a labour movement perspective, the CAW's association with the Working Families Coalition meant that it now had access to the new Liberal government. Access was important for the CAW because the PC's open hostility to labour meant that unions were largely excluded from consultations. The CAW could credibly argue that they had helped to elect McGuinty as premier and could claim something in return from the new government. At the same time, the CAW's continued ties to the NDP meant that Hargrove could rely on the party to raise issues important to the union and could push the government to enact labour-backed reforms that were not a priority for the new premier. This delicate balancing act managed to pacify different elements of the union. Hargrove could point to the overall result and declare victory because the PCs had been defeated. Even though the NDP lost official party status, Hargrove could also point to the union's financial backing and tactical support of a good number of NDP candidates to dull criticism from partisan-aligned CAW activists that the union had "betrayed" the party.

THE 2004 FEDERAL ELECTION:
THE POLITICS OF MINORITY GOVERNMENT

The CAW's embrace of strategic voting in Ontario did not immediately transfer over to federal politics. In Ottawa, the record of Jean Chrétien's government on everything from unemployment insurance to the Auto Pact rendered the Liberals unsupportable in the eyes of the CAW leadership. The party's decision to hand the reins to former finance minister Paul Martin in November 2003 had many on the left asserting that the Liberals would drift even further from a progressive policy orientation.[18] Although delegates to the CAW's Constitutional Convention in August 2003 had approved a new, less partisan approach to politics, they had also warmly received newly elected federal NDP leader Jack Layton's speech.[19] Under Layton, the party was making overt efforts to connect with labour and social movement partners on a range of issues, including democratic reform, peace and international development, sustainability, community investment, health, and diversity. The party's Fly Our Flag campaign, which sought to embarrass Martin for flying flags of convenience from countries in the Global South on his company's steamships to avoid taxes, dovetailed perfectly with the CAW's own nationalist impulses.[20] The CAW leadership's attitude toward the federal NDP was reflected in the fact that the union remained among the top donors to the party in 2003. In anticipation of campaign finance reforms that would soon severely curb corporate and union donations, the CAW and other unions helped the NDP to purchase a three-storey building in downtown Ottawa that it could use as collateral to secure loans for future election campaigns.[21]

Not only did the CAW seem to be extending an olive branch to the federal NDP, but it was also strengthening links to the Bloc Québécois (BQ). Speaking to a reporter in May 2004 about the decision of the union's Quebec wing to endorse the entire slate of BQ candidates, CAW Quebec director, Luc Desnoyers, commented, "Buzz has never hidden the fact that he would meet with the Bloc Québécois, that he had the support of the Bloc. So for him, it's one of the parties that can help us bring files to the floor of the House of Commons, just like the NDP has done."[22] Desnoyers and an unidentified Bloc member of Parliament (MP) also in attendance at the meeting conveyed Hargrove's view that "in Quebec, it's the Bloc and in the rest of the country, it's the NDP."[23] BQ leader Gilles Duceppe was subsequently invited to address delegates to the 2004 CAW-TCA (Travailleurs canadiens de l'automobile) Joint Council in Montreal.[24] The BQ had been climbing in the polls ever since the auditor general had reported in February 2004 that tens of millions of dollars in federal sponsorship money had been awarded to Liberal-friendly ad agencies in return for little or no work. The whole ordeal was particularly damaging to the federal government in

Quebec and threatened the Liberal Party's dominant position at the federal level. Meanwhile, at the CAW's April 2004 Canadian Council meeting, Hargrove recommended that the union "double its efforts to elect as many New Democrats as possible," as the party's standing in public opinion polls was steadily improving.[25]

Despite the sponsorship scandal and a spirited campaign by the newly reformulated Conservative Party of Canada, the Liberals managed to hang on to a minority government in the 2004 election, thanks in part to a last-minute plea by Paul Martin for NDP voters to flock to the Liberals to block the Conservatives from forming government.[26] The Liberals still lost nearly three dozen seats, and Canadians elected their first minority government since 1979. Although a united Conservative Party had eroded much Liberal support on the right, the CAW spun the election results as a political shift to the left, pointing to increased seat totals for both the NDP and the BQ, which, when combined, held the balance of power in the new minority Parliament. According to Hargrove, "The election of a Liberal minority government was not an endorsement of the Liberal record, but a rejection of the regressive policies of Stephen Harper and the Conservatives."[27]

Layton's first election as leader yielded the party nineteen seats and 15.7 percent of the popular vote. The party made its biggest inroads in Ontario, capturing six new seats, but the party's dismal result in Quebec (4.6 percent and no seats) became Hargrove's focus. The CAW president made headlines in August 2004 when he suggested that the NDP abandon fielding candidates in Quebec, arguing that a party like the NDP, so deeply rooted in English Canada, could never make significant inroads in a francophone province. He instead advocated that the NDP form a parliamentary alliance with the BQ. According to Hargrove, the partnership would be based on a common progressive vision of social policy, labour rights, and international affairs. The strategy, outlined in a policy paper titled "Canadian Politics after the Election: Seizing the Opportunity," was adopted unanimously by delegates at a CAW-TCA Joint Council meeting in Montreal in August 2004.[28] Unsurprisingly, neither party was willing to commit to such an alliance.[29]

Despite its criticisms of the federal Liberals, the CAW saw in the new minority government an opportunity to advance its political agenda. Anti-scab legislation and worker-friendly changes to bankruptcy legislation topped the CAW's list of priorities.[30] Although the labour movement made uneven headway on the public-policy front, the CAW did gain greater access to the prime minister. In December 2004, Martin met with the CAW's National Executive Board (NEB) to discuss the union's legislative priorities. The next month, Jim Stanford was appointed by the House Finance Committee to review the federal government's budget projections.[31] Several years later, Hargrove told a reporter that "Paul Martin was the only prime minister we had in the past 30 years who met regularly with the labour movement," adding that "a lot of people found him better to deal with than Bob Rae."[32]

The labour movement certainly had greater influence with Martin's minority government than with the preceding governments of Jean Chrétien and Brian Mulroney. However, this influence was not because the Liberals aligned ideologically with union goals. Rather, it reflected the dynamic of a party working diligently to stay afloat in a precarious minority-government situation. By fulfilling the NDP's priorities on the social-spending front, the Liberals gambled that they could, at best, win strategic support from labour and social movements and, at worst, drive these movements to pressure the NDP into propping up the government.

In April 2005, the Martin Liberals reached a deal with Layton's NDP to pass a budget that included a commitment to increase social spending and foreign aid by $4.6 billion over two years, along with deferred tax cuts for large corporations. The widely touted "NDP budget" suddenly re-established the NDP as a major player in federal politics. "This agreement is fiscally responsible. It is progressive. We agreed to it because we want Parliament to work," Martin told reporters.[33]

The new progressive shine on the federal Liberals certainly caught the attention of the labour movement. After at least a decade of austerity, labour finally had a government responding positively to its calls for social invest-ments. But although the CAW enjoyed improved political access to the federal government during Martin's tenure as prime minister, the union was also experiencing an extraordinary economic crisis. A combination of improved import sales in North America, the strength of the Canadian dollar, and the rising price of oil provided challenges for the Big Three automakers and, in turn, for the CAW. At the April 2005 CAW Council meeting, "Hargrove noted that in the first three months of 2005 and for the first time in GM history, its sales have dropped below 25 per cent of the US market."[34] Hargrove predicted that, if the trend continued, the impact on jobs and investment would be devastating. Along with automotive manufacturers, he urged the federal government to act. Federal government investments in the automotive sector beginning in 2004 were designed to address mounting job losses. The Martin government's Automotive Innovation Fund, operational between 2004 and 2008, provided auto manufacturers with low-interest loans to incentivize investment in Canada. Other initiatives by both the Ontario and federal governments during this period provided multimillion-dollar subsidies in return for promised reinvestments in existing facilities.[35]

In the 2005 round of Big Three bargaining, Hargrove was praised by auto industry insiders for his unprecedented decision to double-target Ford and DaimlerChrysler, picking the former as the pattern target and the latter as the strike target. "Hargrove's strategy appears to be securing a wage pattern from Ford, with which it has the best relationship, and then striking against Chrysler's demands for outsourcing," explained a media report at the time.[36] Hargrove was shrewdly playing defence, recognizing that concessions would be on the table across the board given declining market share. Although the deal that the CAW inked with Ford contained wage increases of 1.4, 0.9, and 0.9 percent over three years and modest benefit and pension improvements, it also resulted in the expected elimination of 1,100 jobs.[37] To avoid a strike, Chrysler dropped its outsourcing demands and matched the compensation deal that the union had negotiated with Ford.[38] Up next, General Motors (GM), which had stressed for months that it could not afford the pattern, did in the end accept the same monetary terms as Ford and Chrysler, albeit with the union's understanding that involuntary layoffs in the range of 1,000 should be expected. GM workers ratified the contract in October 2005, with 79.6 percent in favour.[39]

Despite having previously accepted $450 million in government subsidies to preserve jobs, the company announced that 3,000 more jobs were on the chopping block only weeks after the deal between GM and the CAW was ratified. For some, the union's response to this shocking announcement was unusually muted. "Where was the union's anger or sense of betrayal? Where was any challenge to the neoliberal promise that competitiveness brought job security?" asked Gindin.[40] Jim Stanford defended the CAW's role in securing government subsidies, arguing that the membership "overwhelmingly supported" the direction and pointing out that the subsidy agreements included provisions to force automakers to repay them if they did not adhere to minimum employment levels.[41]

In addition to auto industry investments, the CAW credited Martin's minority government with new investments in housing and culture, progress on Aboriginal land claims, bankruptcy protection for workers, and same-sex marriage rights. According to Hargrove, "Pressed by the labour movement and social advocates from outside Parliament, and by the NDP and BQ inside, the Liberals were finally forced to start acting liberal – to the clear benefit of Canadian families and communities."[42] However, on Parliament Hill, sinking poll numbers for the governing Liberals (due largely to the daily revelations of the public inquiry into the sponsorship scandal) convinced NDP strategists that it was the right time to withdraw support from the minority government. The NDP leadership's electoral calculation was that it could not afford to be seen as propping up a scandal-plagued Liberal government and that dwindling support for the Liberals would likely translate into more votes and seats for the NDP.

According to Stanford, the NDP's decision to withdraw support for the Martin government "was made over the explicit objection of many progressive movements ... Aboriginal leaders, urban advocates, the child care constituency, and labour leaders (not just Buzz Hargrove, but others – including CLC President Ken Georgetti) all wanted the election later, not sooner."[43] Stanford argued that, despite its shortcomings, the Martin minority government had shown an unprecedented openness to progressive movements and that a Conservative victory in an election would represent a step backward for organized labour and its allies. Andrew Jackson confirms that the Canadian Labour Congress (CLC) was opposed to Layton pulling the plug on Martin. The Liberals "were kind of offering us everything on a platter ... child care ... Indigenous rights ... the Kelowna Accord ... They had signed child care agreements with four or five provinces." The labour movement was unwilling to sacrifice all the policy progress that it had made to help the NDP to gain a bigger footprint in Parliament, he argues.[44]

Despite the objections of the CAW, the CLC, and other key stakeholders, on November 24, 2005, the NDP voted with the Conservatives and BQ to topple the Liberal minority government. The next day, a federal election was called for January 23, 2006. Political scientist Alan Whitehorn outlined Layton's strategy in the 2006 election campaign as follows:

> One possible solution was to inoculate NDP supporters by making the Liberal Party seem so unappealing to social democrats that the gulf between the Liberal Party and the NDP would widen. To accomplish this, NDP ads targeted the Liberals and were more negative. The other side of the strategy was to lessen the fear of the Conservative Party and its Alberta-based leader. In order to achieve this, the NDP had to resist the temptation to portray the Conservatives as extremely right-wing and their leader as a scary man with a hidden agenda. Instead, the Conservative Party would be characterized as simply being wrong on policies and not congruent with most Canadians' values.[45]

This strategy irked many labour movement activists who saw the Harper Tories as the clear and present danger. They worried not only that Harper would do away with all the progressive policy and spending commitments that unions had helped to secure from the Liberals but also that the Tories would wreak havoc for unions on the labour relations front, just as PC governments had done provincially.[46] NDP partisans, like former NDP caucus research and communications director Jamey Heath, offered a different perspective: "If we'd like a government that reflects our values, we'll need to see beyond what the Liberal Party wants us to. And chart our own course, based on a progressive – not Liberal – map."[47] Heath maintained that "fear of angering a party destined for hegemony caused the CLC and NDP to interpret politics' new rules differently, as the mirage keeps getting in the way of lefties punishing governments that don't do what we want."[48] Heath, who argued that the Liberals had ignored every big labour movement priority for the past decade, was unapologetic about the NDP's decision to target the Liberals, even if the end result was a Conservative victory in 2006: "No question, stopping Harper is a worthy goal, but how we replace him matters as well, and with the Liberals down anyway, it's time to break hegemony ... One look at the corroded, directionless hulk of the Liberal Party is surely incentive to ponder – even briefly – if we could do better."[49]

Peggy Nash, who successfully defeated a Liberal MP to pick up a seat for the NDP in Parkdale–High Park in 2006, also defends the federal NDP's strategic approach: "I think demonizing Conservatives paves the way for Liberals ... They're clearly not identical ... I think the Conservatives are a measure worse, but I also think the Liberals are measurably worse than New Democrats. Obviously, a lot of people disagree."[50] Buzz Hargrove turned out to be one of these people.

PAUL MARTIN AND THE CAW JACKET: THE 2006 FEDERAL ELECTION

On December 2, 2005, less than two weeks into the federal election campaign, Hargrove dropped a political bombshell by embracing Martin at a CAW Council meeting in Toronto and presenting him with a CAW jacket. His actions infuriated NDP activists both inside and outside the union. Despite their tense relationship with Hargrove, they had never imagined that he would so boldly endorse a Liberal prime minister. Martin encouraged CAW members to vote strategically, reminding them that "the wrong government could put it all at risk ... It matters who Canadians choose to lead the country."[51] Windsor–Tecumseh NDP MP Joe Comartin, who also spoke at the council meeting, reminded delegates of the differences between his party and the Liberals, focusing on the issues of anti-scab legislation and corporate tax cuts. However, Comartin's plea to stick exclusively with the NDP was unsuccessful. Instead, CAW members overwhelmingly endorsed Hargrove's plan for a strategic-voting campaign aimed at "ensuring a Liberal minority with an NDP balance of power, and stopping a Conservative victory."[52] The resolution on strategic voting called on the union to "endorse the sitting NDP Members of Parliament, and individual NDP candidates in potentially winnable ridings."[53] In other ridings, the resolution called on the CAW to "not endorse any specific candidates; rather, individual voters will need to decide what best contributes to electing a Liberal minority with NDP balance of power, and stopping the Conservatives."[54] In effect, the CAW was calling on Canadians to vote Liberal in the vast majority of ridings across Canada.

Strategists running the NDP war room scrambled to formulate a response to Hargrove's decision to back Martin, emphasizing that although Hargrove was entitled to his opinion, it was ill-considered given the Liberal record.[55] The media, however, ignored this spin and instead framed the incident as a devastating blow to NDP fortunes.[56] Sure enough, pollsters detected a slide in NDP support following Hargrove's endorsement of Martin, and at least one attributed the NDP's drop in the polls to Hargrove's call for strategic voting. "Hargrove has sown the seeds and legitimized for NDP voters to strategically vote to block the Conservatives. He's normalizing it," argued SES Research president Nik Nanos.[57]

Giving Martin a CAW jacket was "one of the defining moments for the union," according to Hemi Mitic. Hargrove got a "hell of a round of boos" from the rank and file, he adds.[58] Wayne Gates, a Local 199 member who was running for the NDP in Niagara Falls, concurs: "It was a split room ... There were a lot of brothers and sisters that were upset that he put a jacket on Paul Martin."[59] Chief among them were members of CAW retiree chapters. According to former CAW staffer Jenny Ahn, retiree chapters were much more committed to the NDP than were other segments of the union.[60] Gindin explains that there was a generation of NDP stalwarts in the union, now retirees, who received their political education in the heyday of relations between the United Auto Workers (UAW)/CAW and the NDP: "They really internalized the NDP because they had to go into the workplace and sell the NDP to people who didn't like the NDP. And they had to sacrifice to do it and they did it. So there's a cadre of solid NDPers who really resented the turn to the Liberals later on."[61]

In the debate on Hargrove's strategic voting recommendation that followed Martin's speech, delegates lined up to have their say. The same familiar arguments for and against strategic voting were put forward. In a bit of a twist, Local 199 delegate Malcolm Allen spoke against the recommendation, accusing the CAW president of "breaking covenant" with the union's commitment to equality by asking local unions to "strategically" back some Liberal MPs who had actively opposed same-sex marriage.[62] Allen's intervention raised an important question about what differentiated the Liberals and New Democrats and about what, if any, criteria the union might use to weed out unacceptable Liberal candidates, even if they were the logical strategic vehicle to defeat a Conservative.

Allen estimates that, in the end, 25 to 30 percent of council delegates opposed Hargrove's recommendation. Resistance to Hargrove had become increasingly futile, he argues. According to Allen, it was not so much that people had been convinced by the logic of strategic voting. Rather, the result was a "fait accompli" based on Hargrove's centralized control of the union.[63] Although a strong majority of delegates went along with Hargrove's plan for strategic voting, Gindin says that behind closed doors Hargrove's decision to give Martin the jacket "was universally condemned. And Buzz didn't care." Gindin adds, "There is an arrogance that comes with power when there's no opposition. And part of the reason there was no opposition was because the union had developed its credibility historically and lived off of it ... It is kind of amazing when you see in practice how undemocratic it is."[64]

A week after the jacket kerfuffle, Hargrove and Martin shared a stage once again, this time in Windsor. The two joined McGuinty at a DaimlerChrysler event to announce a $768 million investment in plant upgrades. Hargrove joked with the assembled executives and politicians that they should not expect a warm embrace. "I've been forewarned though, Paul, that we have two NDP members of Parliament in this city and I've been instructed ahead of time not to hug you today, even though I feel like hugging you based on this wonderful announcement," he said. Later, when quizzed by reporters, the CAW leader was unrepentant about the union's support for the prime minister. He explained, "We've had more meetings with Paul Martin in his 17 months in power than we had with Jean Chrétien and Brian Mulroney in their entire time."[65]

Joe Comartin criticized Hargrove for "going off on a tangent" and for sowing the seeds of confusion over his strategic support for Liberals.[66] Although a call to back the local candidate best positioned to defeat a Conservative sounded straightforward enough, Hargrove's interventions in the campaign demonstrated that there were several complicating factors that confused the matter. A week after the CAW Council meeting, in an opinion piece titled "Making the Most of Opportunity," Hargrove argued that "the best the left can now hope for is a re-creation of another Liberal minority – hopefully, this time, with the NDP holding a clearer balance of power, and the two parties negotiating a more stable and lasting way of working together." Hargrove went on to argue that "if the Liberals lose Quebec seats to the BQ, then the math favours a Conservative minority (supported by the BQ). A marriage of convenience between the Conservatives' anti-statist, decentralizing inclinations and the BQ's separatism could quickly destroy all the good that's been done in the past 17 months, and then some."[67]

Hargrove made a similar argument at a Liberal campaign event outside of London, Ontario. His views were interpreted as questioning the patriotism of Conservative leader Stephen Harper.[68] Reporters also picked up on the fact that Hargrove's suggestion that the BQ would do more harm than good seemingly contradicted his previous statements concerning the BQ's progressive policy orientation, not to mention that the CAW's Quebec section was endorsing the entire slate of BQ candidates.[69] According to Jonathan Rose, Hargrove's intervention "meant Martin was knocked off his message to mop up the damage left by someone else. In Hargrove's case it meant that Martin's sound bite that day was an endorsement of Stephen Harper's patriotism."[70] Martin quickly distanced himself from Hargrove's remarks, and the CAW leader did not appear alongside the prime minister for the rest of the campaign.

Even the CAW's Quebec wing held an event designed to distance itself from Hargrove's endorsement of Martin. In late December, the union's Quebec director, Luc Desnoyers, appeared at a campaign event alongside Gilles Duceppe and a hundred CAW members in Longueuil. Desnoyers dramatically draped the BQ leader in a CAW jacket in order to underscore the point that, in Quebec, the CAW was firmly in the BQ's camp.[71]

In January 2006, the CAW released its list of recommended candidates. The union endorsed forty-three NDP candidates in English Canada who were either incumbents or considered competitive. In other ridings in English Canada, the CAW urged people to vote for the candidate with the best chance of defeating the Conservative candidate.

Although the CAW resolution called for the union to "endorse the sitting NDP Members of Parliament, and individual NDP candidates in potentially winnable ridings (to be determined following consultation with our local leaders and activists)" and mandated that "in other ridings, the CAW not endorse any specific candidates,"[72] Hargrove did not hesitate to personally endorse high-profile Liberal candidates with ties to the automotive industry, like Magna executive and former Conservative leadership contestant Belinda Stronach in the riding of Newmarket–Aurora and Toyota Canada's assistant general manager Greig Mordue, running for the Liberals in Oxford.[73] The CAW's endorsements of NDP candidates, in contrast, went virtually unnoticed in the mainstream media.

On January 14, 2006, worried that the CAW's strategic-voting campaign was sending union members the wrong message, a group of unions loyal to the federal NDP helped to organize a rally in downtown Toronto as a show of support for the party. Speakers took turns denouncing the CAW's strategy, and union activists handed out buttons that read, "Buzz off. I'm voting NDP."[74] Referring to Hargrove's public endorsement of Martin a month earlier, Ontario Public Service Employees Union (OPSEU) president Leah Casselman told the rally, "The boss does not become the friend of working people just by putting on a union jacket ... The boss is the boss is the boss."[75]

Despite Hargrove's prominence in the push for strategic voting, the CAW was not the only union endorsing the tactic. It was also the preferred strategy of the Public Service Alliance of Canada, the largest union representing federal public-service workers, who endorsed NDP, Liberal, and BQ candidates in and around the national capital region.[76] Despite some unions' efforts to prop up Martin's government through strategic voting, both the effects of the sponsorship scandal and a lacklustre performance in the election campaign proved impossible to overcome. On January 23, 2006, the Liberals were replaced by a Conservative minority government led by Stephen Harper, with no one opposition party holding the balance of power.

A week after the election, Jim Stanford blasted the NDP in a *Globe and Mail* column for having precipitated the election and by extension helping to produce a Liberal defeat and the Harper minority.[77] Jamey Heath later retorted that the CAW had "long demanded the [NDP] lurch further left and punished it for refusing, but shies away from punishing Liberals because it doesn't believe the NDP is viable enough." He described this Catch-22 as "a cyclical loop, which unless broken will keep us stuck with the Liberal Party being the not-Tory governing option forever."[78]

Despite the election's outcome, proponents of strategic voting were quick to defend their approach. Hargrove claimed that Decima Research's post-election poll and analysis of the 2006 federal election results demonstrated that the CAW's strategic-voting campaign was crucial in preventing a Conservative majority.[79] A closer look at the Decima results revealed a different story, namely that the strategy's impact on the election was mixed. Decima reported that although 65 percent of the electorate was aware of

Hargrove's call for strategic voting, only 5 percent of voters were thus more likely to cast ballots for Liberal or NDP candidates.[80] Decima further reported that 17 percent of electors (and only 15 percent of electors in Ontario) voted strategically in the 2006 federal election.[81] Among strategic voters, 22 percent reported that they were more likely to vote Liberal as a result of the CAW's call for strategic voting, 9 percent indicated that they were more likely to vote Conservative, and 9 percent indicated that they were more likely to vote NDP.[82]

In Ontario, strategic voting primarily benefited the Liberals. Among strategic voters, 36 percent cast ballots for the Liberals, 30 percent opted for the NDP, and 23 percent voted Conservative. In Quebec, however, strategic voting overwhelmingly benefited the Conservatives. Among strategic voters, 45 percent cast ballots for the Conservatives, 19 percent for the BQ, 13 percent for the NDP, and just 12 percent for the Liberals. Overall, the majority of self-identified strategic voters, at 58 percent, wanted a Conservative majority or minority government, and only 34 percent of strategic voters wanted the Liberal majority or minority government that the CAW was promoting.[83]

Duncan Mavin of the *National Post* claimed that Hargrove's stature had been severely tarnished by his support for the Liberals in the federal election campaign:

> The move simultaneously allied Mr. Hargrove with the only national party to lose seats and alienated labour movement leaders and allies in the NDP. Meanwhile, personal attacks on prime minister-designate Stephen Harper will hardly help smooth relations with the new political regime in Ottawa. Meanwhile, there's not much evidence the views Mr. Hargrove expressed in the election run-up are in tune with voters either, even in areas with a large proportion of autoworkers. In Oshawa, home to thousands of GM employees and retirees, the local CAW membership publicly rejected their leader's support for outgoing Liberal Prime Minister [Paul Martin] in favour of the NDP campaign. The riding then returned Conservative candidate Colin Carrie with an increased majority. In Elgin-Middlesex-London, home to a Ford plant that will lose more than 1,000 jobs after Monday's announced restructuring, voters re-elected Conservative Joe Preston.[84]

OUT OF THE FRYING PAN AND INTO THE FIRE: THE NDP
EXPELS HARGROVE AMID A CRISIS IN THE AUTO SECTOR

In the wake of the 2006 federal election, the state of Canada's automotive industry went from bad to worse. While Canadians were busy electing a new government on January 23, 2006, Ford unexpectedly announced that 30,000 autoworker jobs would be cut across North America, including an anticipated 1,100 jobs in Windsor and 1,200 jobs in St. Thomas.[85] The CAW was reeling; its preferred prime minister was defeated and replaced by Stephen Harper, who harboured no sympathy for organized labour.

On February 11, 2006, still seething over Hargrove's very public promotion of strategic voting, the provincial executive of the Ontario NDP voted to suspend his party membership. Subsequently, this decision was "overwhelmingly" endorsed by the NDP's Provincial Council in March 2006 with a proviso that Hargrove could rejoin if he promised, in writing, that he would not endorse candidates from opposing parties in future elections.[86] Hargrove refused, and in response, the CAW's NEB recommended that CAW locals disaffiliate from the NDP. Hargrove argued that "the NDP's arrogant decision says that organizations affiliated to the NDP cannot make independent decisions on political strategy. Our union cannot remain under these circumstances."[87] Even NDP partisans within the union were sympathetic to this argument. Malcolm Allen, who was a delegate to the meeting of the NDP's Provincial Council where Hargrove's ouster was debated and approved, thinks that the party made a strategic error in turfing the CAW leader because it "exacerbated the rift, cemented it … It forced CAW members to choose between the president of their union or the party."[88] Joe Comartin also opposed the decision to oust Hargrove, arguing that the party should have adopted a policy that would have allowed labour leaders "more flexibility without the party having to take action against them."[89]

For context, it is noteworthy that although Toronto mayor and NDP luminary David Miller also backed a Liberal candidate, John Godfrey, against a New Democrat in a Toronto riding in 2006, he faced little to no backlash, let alone expulsion.[90] Admittedly, Hargrove's overt support for the tactic and his decision to actively and publicly campaign for the Liberals were brazen in comparison. However, the contradiction perceived in the difference between Miller's treatment and Hargrove's dismissal was exploited by the union to paint the CAW and its leader as unfairly targeted victims. As Hargrove explains, "I never got notice that I was going to be thrown out, and I never got an opportunity to make my case to the party hierarchy, about why I shouldn't be thrown out."[91]

Whether he held a membership card or not, Hargrove's support for distancing the union from the party had been in evidence for some time and had only accelerated based on his interpretation of the findings of the CAW Task Force on Working Class Politics in the Twenty-First Century. In March 2006, he told a group of university students, "If we simply go to our members today and tell them – as we did for decades – 'We recommend the NDP, and if they get elected, everything will be OK,' they will laugh at us ... We've learned the hard way that electing the NDP does not solve all our problems."[92]

In the run-up to the April 2006 CAW Council meeting, the union leadership organized an open meeting for members in southern Ontario to address the state of the party-union relationship and to build support for the NEB's position in favour of disaffiliation from the NDP. Ritch Whyman, then a member of CAW Local 303, showed up to the meeting with a one-page handout appealing to CAW activists to resist efforts to disaffiliate from the NDP without a concrete plan to build an alternative left politics in concert with the broader labour movement. Whyman's intention was to link up with like-minded members and to generate support for a challenge to what he perceived as the union leadership's stealth attempt to shift the union to the right using the language of the left. The break with the NDP was "painted red to be a left break, but it's really Liberal red," explains Whyman. "The pitch was not done by Hargrove. The pitch was not done by the right. The pitch around leaving the NDP was completely sold as a progressive maneuver by Jim Stanford." In Whyman's view, Stanford used "full-blown left credentials" to justify the decision to leave the NDP, but he "would never answer the question: Where does this leave us? Who are our allies? What other unions are we engaged in discussions with? ... Where does this leave us, but in the arms of the Liberals?"[93]

For people like Whyman, a critique of the traditional party-union relationship had the potential to breathe new life into the idea of building a radical independent labour politics in Canada – to move beyond the NDP – but he thinks that in practice the CAW's political orientation was clearly morphing into a defensive Gomperism focused on convincing Liberal governments to invest in sectors where the union had a presence.[94]

In April 2006, delegates to the CAW Council meeting endorsed the NEB's call to withdraw support for the NDP. Most, although not all, locals took their cue from the resolution and disaffiliated from the party. In Nova Scotia, many CAW locals remained affiliated after the provincial NDP adopted a resolution in May 2006 urging "the federal party and provincial and territorial party organizations to amend NDP constitutions to accept and respect that labour leaders and others will act in accordance with the democratic decisions made by their unions or organizations."[95] In Ontario, Local 199 in Niagara was one of the few CAW locals to remain affiliated. The local had a long history of association with the party, and many of its activists had run for the NDP both federally and provincially.[96] Local 199's then president, Wayne Gates, had run unsuccessfully for the federal NDP in the Niagara Falls riding in 2004 and 2006. He spoke against the resolution to cut ties at the April 2006 CAW Council meeting and recalls arguing that the "NDP was the only party that really stood up for workers ... Instead of leaving the NDP, we should take over the party, get involved in riding associations, bring resolutions forward to NDP councils." His plea, however, was ignored. "I was on an island by myself that day speaking against the establishment ... Buzz had all his national reps that would run to the mic and make sure whatever they want, it would get passed."[97] Although the union's centralized structure no doubt contributed to this outcome, it did not help that NDP bases of CAW support in communities like St. Catharines and Kitchener had been hollowed out through years of deindustrialization and job loss. The union was transforming, and the attachments that many autoworker retirees had to the NDP were fading in importance.

Looking back on this period, Jim Stanford considers the break with the NDP an "inevitable and relatively minor consequence" of moving toward a more independent, or what he calls "syndicalist," approach to politics. Stanford is careful, however, to differentiate between independence and partisanship: "Being independent doesn't mean being nonpartisan. I don't see those as synonymous at all. It means not being beholden to a party. It doesn't mean we stay out of party politics. What it means is that we will make up our own mind on party politics."[98]

Jenny Ahn, who headed up political action for the CAW from 2009 to 2013, emphasizes that even after Hargrove was expelled from the party, the union continued to work with the NDP and even had strong relations with various leaders and MPs. Where strategically advantageous and legally permissible, the union continued to fund both the party and select candidates. The union would "still continue to work with any and all political parties that would take on our issues," she argues.[99] In other words, the loosening of formal partisan ties did not mean that there was not an ongoing relationship with the NDP. The nature of the relationship, however, was different. According to long-time CAW education staffer Herman Rosenfeld, the "relationship with the NDP became transactional" rather than being based on ideological commitments once the formal partisan partnership was severed.[100]

This direction was confirmed in August 2006 at the 8th CAW Constitutional Convention in Vancouver when delegates adopted a position paper that justified the CAW's unprecedented push for strategic voting, criticized the NDP for putting "its own short-term electoral interests ahead of the longer-run priority of fighting for progressive change," and rationalized the union's decision to sever ties with the party.[101] The union affirmed that, going forward, its

> intervention in elections will be flexible and independent. We may endorse particular candidates where that is seen to advance workers' interests, or even entire slates of candidates ... In each case, we will make an independent judgement of what strategy will be most effective in advancing the interests of our members, their families and communities, and the broader progressive and working-class movements.[102]

Although the CAW's decision to endorse specific Liberal candidates gave the impression that the union was moving away from the NDP and toward a more Gomperist and transactional approach to electoral politics, the union's position paper concluded with a seemingly contradictory "statement of principles on working class politics," which argued that "the opportunities for Canadian working people to bring about change are enhanced when progressive parties, accountable to the labour and progressive social movements, are stronger."[103] Given the CAW's unprecedented support for the Liberal Party's election efforts, even more paradoxical was the union's newly restated goal of "replacing capitalism with socialism."[104] In 2010, CAW Quebec director, Jean-Pierre Fortin, argued that there was no contradiction in the union's approach. "It is possible that, if the parties we traditionally support shift too far to the right and if we can't live with that, as happened at the national level, then we'll decide to vote strategically by backing the candidates who support our union's demands," he said. "But in no way does this compromise our political commitment. On the contrary, it reinforces the influence that we can have both on individual Members of Parliament and on the party as a whole," he argued.[105]

HARGROVE CHALLENGED FOR THE PRESIDENCY

Although the union's leadership framed the CAW's move away from the NDP as a left-wing break, it was difficult to sustain this rhetoric in the face of strengthening ties to the Liberal Party, dissipating militancy vis-à-vis employers, and a decline in the union's fightback culture more generally. The union was still involved in significant mobilizations, as was the case in Windsor in an effort to reverse the decline of manufacturing jobs, but these mobilizations were increasingly being carried out in tune with the demands of employers for government aid, not in opposition to them.[106] Thus the union's adversarial orientation vis-à-vis employers was also in flux, pointing to increased collaboration with capital in an effort to preserve employment for members.

This turn in the union's political approach prompted CAW Local 1256 chair Willie Lambert to announce that he would challenge Hargrove for the national presidency at the August 2006 convention. In launching his campaign in April 2006, Lambert specifically criticized Hargrove's support for strategic voting and his willingness to accept concessions at Ford and General Motors.[107] According to Lambert, if the union was going to preserve its capacity to act as a countervailing force against what he saw as the corporate agenda, "you had to do something better than dance with Belinda Stronach or become Gerry Schwartz's drinking buddy."[108] Lambert also called on the union to democratize its structures. Instead of the established practice of having convention delegates vote to elect the national president, "it should be one member, one vote, and a lot less space between the union leadership and the rank-and-file," he told the *Ottawa Citizen*.[109]

Lambert's challenge to Hargrove was newsworthy insofar as the union had never experienced a contested election for its presidency. However, his campaign was short-lived. Lambert claims that he was contacted by one of Hargrove's assistants and encouraged to abandon his bid.[110] "Buzz says he welcomes the debate and the challenge, but there's been quite a bit of pressure exerted from the administration to shut me out wherever possible. Even in my own local it's been a problem for me," Lambert told the media at the time.[111] Although Lambert refused to back down, his intended nominators were not as resilient. Lambert says that there was a "real fear factor" around the election contest and that his nominators "turned tail" in response to internal pressures. Because of "the kind of intimidation that existed ... it was not something anybody was prepared to do," he recalls.[112] David Camfield has explored the culture of intimidation and fear in the CAW in a series of interviews with dissident activist members. Local 707 activist Euan Gibb told Camfield that members who get involved in the CAW learn "that they better shut up with the criticism or they are not going to have time out of the plant" to attend educational courses, councils, or conventions. As a result, Gibb said that there is a lot of "self-censoring out of fear for the consequences."[113] Local 199 activist Bruce Allen told Camfield that the union leadership "bully the shit out of people ... They publicly embarrass people and they never want to speak out again. They hammer people."[114] The level of hostility to Lambert's challenge to Hargrove was so intense that it was disorienting for him. "It's almost as if I was doing something anti-union, when I felt Buzz was taking us down a dead-end street," Lambert says.[115]

No one interviewed for this book considered Lambert's candidacy a serious threat to Hargrove. If it was not a threat, how do we account for the level of effort that was seemingly poured into derailing Lambert's campaign? Whyman believes that the union's leadership fiercely resisted internal left challenges because it did not want its own "left veneer removed."[116] In other words, in the absence of an organized internal left, the leadership could claim the mantle of the left and thus a sort of moral high ground and legitimacy that might otherwise have been difficult to maintain if left challenges had gained visibility.

CONSOLIDATING A TRANSACTIONAL POLITICS:
THE 2007 ONTARIO ELECTION

The massive job loss experienced by CAW members throughout 2006 prompted the union to launch a Made in Canada Matters campaign in order to bring attention to the loss of manufacturing jobs and to the wider importance of such jobs to the communities where they were located.[117] The campaign called on governments to commit to local procurement policies and to initiatives aimed at protecting manufacturing jobs. The campaign also aligned the union with the manufacturers that employed its members as part of a joint effort to secure government support. This cooperation with employers represented an important shift in the union's strategic approach to job loss, pivoting away from direct actions like plant occupations and toward labour-management alliances to protect jobs and investments.

Plant occupations were not abandoned altogether. An occupation at the Scarborough auto parts facility Collins & Aikman was launched in late March 2007 to prevent the company from taking the equipment that it needed to shift production elsewhere. Local 303's occupation ended when Chrysler agreed to pay a significant portion of the severance pay owed to the workers.[118] However, the union's appetite for the tactic of occupation was clearly in decline, as depicted in a 2009 *Fifth Estate* episode that catalogues how officials at various levels of the union struggled over what to do when German-owned Edscha of Canada decided to close its Niagara Falls plant and to withhold severance pay from the CAW members it employed. The documentary showcases Jerry Dias, an assistant to the president, explaining that Dias was dispatched to corral Brian Nicholl, described by the *Fifth Estate* as the "idealistic plant steward, ready to fight for every penny owed the workers."[119] In the end, the union opted against any type of direct action and settled for much less than what the company owed displaced workers.

The militant fightback culture that had defined the union in the 1980s and 1990s was gradually and unevenly being replaced by a less adversarial approach that swapped conflict for cooperation as the union's primary modus operandi. However, on the public-policy front, the union's lobbying efforts delivered decidedly mixed results, as the McGuinty Liberals overturned only some of the previous PC government's anti-union reforms.[120] In a speech to the 2005 National Collective Bargaining and Political Action Convention in Toronto, Hargrove acknowledged that the union was "not quite successful in trying to get a card check for all sectors of the economy," but he did strike a conciliatory tone when he went on "to compliment the Ontario government for the support they have shown for the auto and the aerospace industries."[121] Increasingly, the union sought local political alliances with key provincial Liberal Cabinet ministers to shore up support for its priorities. "Politics is local," reflects Hargrove, who argues that fostering relationships with Liberals Sandra Pupatello and Dwight Duncan helped to secure auto investments in Windsor.[122]

As evidence of this increasingly sectionalist and transactional brand of politics, Hargrove nominated Pupatello at her 2007 nomination meeting in Windsor West.[123] Ken Lewenza, who was then Local 444 president and accompanied Hargrove to the meeting, acknowledges that their support for Pupatello "was controversial" because "strategic voting never applied in that riding." He justifies the endorsement by reasoning that "it was a signal that we appreciated the Liberal government's support of the many programs that we needed during that particular time." For Lewenza, it was all about "keeping your foot in the door in the interest of our members." He does not regret the union's support for Pupatello and Duncan, even though anti-Conservative strategic voting did not make sense in these particular ridings: "You had to find that balance ... having NDP tattooed on my forehead at those particular times wouldn't advance the needs of our members, and quite frankly you have to build some credibility when there are common causes," Lewenza argues.[124] Hargrove is also unapologetic. By abandoning an exclusive relationship with the NDP, he reasons, the union broadened its potential tent of political allies. As a result, the CAW gained the attention of politicians who otherwise may not have been responsive to the union. In Hargrove's estimation, all parties now had to compete for CAW support – and that was a good thing.[125] The union leadership's endorsement of Liberal members of the provincial Parliament in Windsor highlighted just how quickly electoral strategy had evolved within the CAW. Just a few years earlier, at the CAW Council meeting in December 2002, Hargrove had beat back opposition to strategic voting within the union by insisting that the CAW would always back New Democrats in races where the Conservatives were not a factor. "In Windsor you could support all three NDP candidates. You got a race between the NDP and the Liberals; we'll always support the NDP," he asserted.[126] By 2007, however, the union leadership appeared willing to use the cover of anti-Conservative strategic voting to justify partnerships with and endorsements of key Liberal politicians who could help to advance the union's agenda.

In advance of the 2007 Ontario election, Hargrove doubled down on this direction and invited McGuinty to address the April 2007 CAW Council meeting. Hargrove was setting the stage for a planned endorsement of McGuinty's Liberals, but these plans were complicated when a group of CAW retirees got up, turned their backs, and walked out on the premier during his address.[127] A full press endorsement did not sit well with Hargrove's advisors, who did not want to see a repeat of the divisive CAW jacket debacle involving Paul Martin. Mitic explains that they convinced him to dial back a full-fledged endorsement of the Ontario Liberals and instead to "recommend that the CAW endorse strategic voting in the October Ontario provincial election to prevent the Conservatives from forming a government. This too would be coupled with our own issue-oriented campaign in order to elect those candidates who best represent the interests of our members."[128] The staff recommendation was judged to be more palatable on the basis that excluding reference to the Liberals left a theoretical opening for the NDP to be the strategic vote to block a Conservative win. It would also commit the union to an issues-based campaign that would more clearly define differences between the parties. The recommendation was eventually presented to and approved by council delegates without much opposition.[129]

The resolution may have been watered down at the behest of his advisors, but Hargrove went out of his way to play up McGuinty, telling the *Toronto Star* that the premier "is the only political leader in the province or in the country who understands the importance of the manufacturing sector, especially the auto industry."[130] Specifically, Hargrove credited the Ontario Liberal government with a $500 million investment to encourage plant expansions in the province. Once the provincial election was officially underway in the fall, Hargrove came out even more forcefully in favour of the Liberals, this time at the direct expense of the NDP.

Despite the union's official policy of anti-Conservative strategic voting, Hargrove also launched a blistering attack on Ontario NDP leader Howard

Hampton. He told the *Toronto Star* that the Ontario New Democrats "are worse than they've ever been. I see absolutely no reason to vote NDP." Hargrove went on to complain that the New Democrats under Hampton have "lost complete touch" and "don't understand economics." In contrast, Hargrove made the dubious claim that McGuinty's "Liberals have been more left than the NDP over the last four years."[131] Campaigning for select Liberals was one thing, but Hargrove's decision to overtly attack the NDP mid-campaign was unprecedented. Although there was no love lost between Hargrove and Hampton – the two men had been taking shots at one another for many years – the CAW leader's intervention came across as personal, vindictive, and outside the scope of the union's formal strategic-voting election policy.

In the minds of many voters, strategic voting became synonymous with voting Liberal in the 2007 campaign. This was the case not only because the Liberal Party was polling much better than the NDP but also because the nearly $1.1 million third-party anti-PC ad campaign financed by the Working Families Coalition reinforced this notion by dovetailing perfectly with Liberal campaign themes.[132] The CAW contributed roughly $300,000 to a coalition ad campaign that trumpeted the McGuinty government's achievements and warned voters not to turn back to the PCs.[133] Although union support for the Ontario Liberals was far from unanimous, the unions associated with the coalition easily outspent the partisan unions still loyal to the NDP. For example, teachers' unions and building and construction trades unions, the labour organizations that constituted the core of the coalition and the backbone of union support for the Liberals, were responsible for roughly two-thirds of all union donations to political parties in the 2007 election campaign, with the bulk of this money, nearly $800,000, going into Liberal Party coffers.[134] The United Steelworkers, Canadian Union of Public Employees (CUPE), Service Employees International Union (SEIU), United Food and Commercial Workers (UFCW), and Communications, Energy and Paperworkers Union (CEP) backed the New Democrats, whereas OPSEU endorsed an equal number of Liberals and NDP candidates.[135]

The McGuinty government proved a willing partner in a reciprocal political relationship with the major unions associated with the Working Families Coalition. For example, the Liberals locked down ongoing support from teachers' unions by achieving labour peace in the education sector. Building and construction trades unions, the key actors in the coalition, were rewarded with the restoration of card-based union certification on construction sites.[136] The CAW, for its part, did not make much headway on the public policy front but did manage to secure provincial government subsidies for the automotive sector.

In the absence of the Auto Pact, the burden of securing investments had shifted from automotive manufacturers to governments and unions, who were now required to meet the standard of competitiveness and profitability required by individual manufacturers for them to continue operations in Canada.[137] To do so, the union had to work in much closer collaboration with the Big Three automakers. Key to the union's strategy was not to target employers as the source of the problem. Rather, the lack of a manufacturing strategy was identified as the problem – and subsidies were offered as the answer.[138] In April 2004, the McGuinty government answered the union's call by announcing a $500 million incentive to "support auto sector investments worth more than $300 million or that create or retain more than 300 jobs."[139] Hargrove praised the move, telling the media that McGuinty "has listened to us and this strategy is going to be good for Ontarians."[140] In the following years, the CAW also managed to secure investments from the province for job-retraining programs and for initiatives to help members coping with job loss to transition to new careers.[141]

The Liberals easily cruised to victory in the election held on October 10, 2007, capturing seventy-one seats and 46.5 percent of the popular vote. The win came after the PCs fumbled badly during the campaign with an ill-fated promise to extend public funding to private religious schools.[142] The PCs took twenty-six seats and 31.6 percent of the vote, and the NDP won ten seats and 16.8 percent of the vote. Hargrove celebrated the result, but for others like Carol Phillips, the union's intervention in the campaign further demonstrated that it was moving "towards Gomperism, towards the type of politics where you reward your friends and punish your enemies."[143]

FRAMEWORK OF FAIRNESS

On October 15, 2007, less than a week after the Ontario election, the CAW's leadership announced that it had negotiated a neutrality agreement called the Framework of Fairness with global auto parts supplier Magna International that would open the door to unionization for the company's 28,000 workers across forty-five plants in Canada. The agreement, which had been in the works since 2005, was designed to address the rapid decline in union density in the auto parts sector. Most controversially, it committed the company to card-check neutrality in exchange for a union commitment to give up the right to strike for ten years, during which disputes would be settled by binding interest arbitration. It also replaced the traditional shop steward system with "employee advocates" who enjoyed less autonomy vis-à-vis management.[144] In some cases, workplace referendums would provide a mechanism for co-workers to determine whether a disciplined worker would be discharged or reinstated as an alternative to traditional grievance arbitration.[145]

Magna had long operated with an exclusively nonunion model of worker representation. As labour studies scholars Wayne Lewchuk and Donald Wells explain, the Magna model, which promoted a firm-as-family ideology, was based on the idea that "communication, worker voice, and consultation policies help defuse labour-management conflicts while encouraging workers to consider themselves to be key players in the company's success." This dynamic of interest interdependence was rendered possible by several external factors and through material incentives like profit-sharing schemes that linked "management and worker goals together in ways that workers internalize."[146]

The CAW had long struggled to gain a foothold at Magna but to no avail.[147] Hargrove's leadership team saw in the Framework of Fairness an innovative and mutually beneficial agreement that could both boost union membership and provide stability for Magna in a turbulent automotive industry. Hargrove framed the deal as "a new way of working together" and asserted that it would "strengthen the CAW's ability to support auto-parts workers at an incredibly challenging time, but in a way that also strengthens Canada's auto industry."[148] This framing was a clear departure from the CAW's principled opposition in the 1980s to competitiveness strategies rooted in partnerships with employers.[149] Although Andrew Jackson notes that, in practice, the CAW had "tried to push employers to invest and to train, and lobbied governments to subsidize new investments" throughout the 1990s and 2000s, the Framework of Fairness announcement made its pro-partnership rhetoric more public and explicit.[150]

For critics of the Framework of Fairness, temporarily giving up the right to strike in order to secure new members was a bridge too far. As Sam Gindin wrote, "the CAW's abandonment of the right to strike at Magna has enormous implications in terms of the labour movement's struggles (including in the CAW) to win this democratic right." Gindin argued that "it doesn't make much sense to kill the patient to cure the disease; the union is better off without Magna than with getting Magna but giving up what the union stands for." For Gindin, the CAW's willingness to abandon the right to strike at Magna "mindlessly undermines those workers who never had this right or have seen it eroded as governments expanded the scope of 'essential services,' or introduced back to work legislation."[151] In trying to make sense of the CAW leadership's decision to pursue the Framework of Fairness, Gindin opined, "Perhaps this is not surprising from a CAW president who personally campaigned for the Ontario Liberal government that ignored labour movement pressure to remove the barriers to unionization the Harris government introduced and to follow other provinces in introducing anti-scab legislation."[152]

Condemnation of the Framework of Fairness was widespread both inside and outside the union. Gerry Michaud, former president of Local 199, called the agreement "a travesty" and said, "It makes me sick to my stomach."[153] Former president of the Ontario Federation of Labour (OFL) and CAW education director Gord Wilson told the media, "This is the first time in my life on an emotional level, I feel ashamed of my union," adding that "what my union now needs more than new members at Magna is new leaders that haven't forgotten union principles."[154] Keith Osborne, chairperson of Local 222 at General Motors in Oshawa, linked the union's decision to pursue a partnership with Magna to a shift in the union's approach to politics more generally. "We used to say the NDP had lost its way but we (the CAW) must be on another planet with this (Magna deal)," he argued.[155] Local 222 president Chris Buckley penned a letter in opposition to the agreement, fearing what the framework would mean for Oshawa autoworkers already facing demands to weaken existing labour rights.[156] "Suppliers employing my members completely lose any playing field if the right to strike becomes a factor in the competition's favour," he argued.[157] Buckley, however, was the lone dissenter on the CAW's NEB.[158]

Criticism from the broader labour movement was also pointed. Wayne Fraser, the Ontario-Atlantic director of the United Steelworkers, accused

Hargrove of "creating CAW-employer associations."[159] Echoing criticisms voiced by Buckley, he asked, "What's to stop other employers, especially Magna competitors, from rightfully asking the CAW for the same no-strike right?"[160] Former NDP leader Ed Broadbent wrote an editorial in the *Globe and Mail* accusing Hargrove of "attacking the very foundations of an independent union. He has proposed an agreement with Magna International that denies workers exactly those powers that underpin the right of collective bargaining, namely the right to strike and to elect their own shop stewards."[161] The OFL convention in November 2007 condemned the Framework of Fairness agreement, with president Wayne Samuelson urging delegates to "send a clear message" to employers that the labour movement would not support such deals.[162] CUPE Ontario president Sid Ryan went so far as to accuse Hargrove of "playing footsie in the backroom with the boss."[163] The allusion to Hargrove's friendship with Belinda Stronach was unmistakable.

In response to criticism of the deal, former CAW president Bob White defended the agreement in his own editorial in the *Toronto Star,* lashing out at "armchair critics or academics" and arguing that a union facing the continued erosion of private sector union density must "keep finding new strategies and innovations to make a positive difference in workers' lives."[164] On October 31, 2007, Ken Lewenza wrote to White, Hargrove, Gindin, and former national secretary-treasurer Bob Nickerson pleading for a ceasefire. "I believe the average rank and file expects more of us and the infighting can destroy what each of you has played such a huge role in building," he argued. Lewenza also used the opportunity to express his personal support for the Framework of Fairness. "I know the history of our Magna organizing attempts as well as anybody as it relates to Windsor/Essex and I don't think anybody in their heart of hearts believes we can organize these workplaces in the traditional way. Getting our foot in the door is not a bad start," he wrote.[165]

A few days later, Chrysler announced that it would be cutting 1,100 jobs in Brampton. This was on top of the 13,000 North American job losses that it had announced in February 2007.[166] The rising Canadian dollar also contributed to fears that the manufacturing sector was poised for even greater job losses.[167] These developments contributed to a greater sense of urgency around the need to protect and expand the union's membership base.

For his part, Hargrove was dismissive of critics. "I hear people saying: 'Oh my god, you're giving up the right to strike.' The Magna workers don't have a union. They don't have a grievance procedure. They don't have any rights except what the employer gives them. So how do you give up something you don't have?"[168] In an interview with Steve Paikin, Hargrove took another swipe at his critics when he argued, "Not many workers are coming up, knocking on the door, calling Buzz Hargrove saying, 'we'd like to join your union so we can strike our employers.' They're saying, 'we'd like to join your union to change the conditions in our workplace.'"[169] Although it is true that most workers do not join unions in order to strike, Hargrove's detractors replied that strong strike mandates were key to delivering the goods in collective bargaining and thus in actually changing workplace conditions.[170]

Some CAW members opposed to the agreement organized under the banner of CAW Members for Real Fairness to challenge the leadership's promotion of the Magna deal,[171] but the internal mobilization was not enough to derail the agreement, which was later overwhelmingly ratified by delegates at a CAW Council meeting in December 2007. According to the union, only 25 of the 800 delegates in attendance opposed the agreement.[172] This outcome was helped, in part, by the fact that workers at Windsor Modules, who negotiated a first contract under the Framework of Fairness agreement, had secured a wage increase of $3 per hour, even if some have questioned the framework's contribution to this gain.[173] Malcolm Allen was one of the delegates who spoke out against the agreement at the December 2007 council meeting. From Allen's perspective, the framework agreement with Magna epitomized the union's new pragmatic transactional direction.[174]

Once endorsed, the Framework of Fairness enjoyed very limited success from an organizing perspective, securing hundreds rather than thousands of new members, with workers at most Magna properties in Ontario ultimately rejecting the deal.[175] Analysis of the deal's implications by labour studies scholars has been generally negative. Although the CAW did manage to gain a toehold at Magna by temporarily giving up the right to strike, Charlotte Yates argued at the time that the price was too high for the CAW and the labour movement as a whole and that the deal was therefore likely to undermine the very goals of union revitalization sought by the CAW.[176] Several years after its implementation, David Camfield panned the agreement and its impact on organizing, asserting that it "flopped even on its own terms."[177]

But Hemi Mitic rejects this view, pointing to a handful of break-throughs, including a bargaining unit in Windsor organized under the Framework of Fairness that struck after the agreement's ten years of mandated binding arbitration expired. "They are good local unions," he insists.[178] Mitic organized four units under the framework in London, Windsor, and Brampton. The CAW's Bill Murnighan and Jim Stanford have also defended the framework, arguing in 2013 that "the wage improvements provided under the contract (which have averaged over 2 percent per year since the new framework was implemented in 2007) have been the best in the sector, and a welcome contrast to the wage freezes which prevailed in most other unionized auto parts work-places."[179] Although Magna workers' favourable wages, working condi-tions, and access to profit sharing did not naturally predispose them to unionization, Mitic makes the case that the union's failure to secure a bigger breakthrough came as a result of persistent internal opposition and external critics who gave both Magna and its employees a reason to believe that they could not trust the CAW.[180]

For Mitic, the Framework of Fairness was a missed opportunity for the union. Although he acknowledges that the initial agreement curbed the right to strike by mandating ten years of binding arbitration, Mitic argues that the union could have used this time to mould the newly organized units into real unions. He also dismisses criticism from other labour leaders concerning the right to strike, pointing out that these unions were not even exercising the very right that they claimed was sacred – a point certainly backed up by Canada's declining strike rate. Finally, Mitic argues that the strike weapon was relatively ineffective in the auto parts sector because the Big Three would simply have found alternate suppliers if workers had struck. The real power, he claims, rested with the union members in the Big Three since they could help to shape the terms and conditions of work in auto parts production more easily if the workers were all part of the same union. "[Frank] Stronach was a big thinker. He wanted to avoid potential supply chain issues," argues Mitic.[181] But for David Camfield, the Framework of Fair-ness was a symptom of a broader trend that saw the CAW "cozying up" to employers in response to increased competition for the Big Three from nonunion competitors.[182]

UNION DEMOCRACY AND THE ADMINISTRATION CAUCUS: LEWENZA BECOMES CAW PRESIDENT

Because the CAW constitution included a clause mandating retirement at age sixty-five for elected officers, Hargrove was set to retire by 2009. A successor would need to be chosen. The stakes were very high given the turmoil in the union's manufacturing base. The opportunity to choose a new president would also present the union with a strategic choice: continue with Hargrove's approach to electoral politics, government relations, and employer cooperation or forge a new direction? Behind the scenes, several people in the union signalled interest in replacing Hargrove, including Hemi Mitic and Tom Collins, a Hargrove assistant who came out of the Retail Wholesale Department Store Union, which had merged with the CAW in 1999. Hargrove, however, made it known through staff channels that his preferred successor was Ken Lewenza, with Peter Kennedy as secretary-treasurer, and he expected the union's Administration caucus to confirm this direction in the name of unity.[183]

In its internal political life, the CAW operated like a one-party state run by the Administration caucus and led by the president. Although there had been a Left caucus in the UAW's Canadian section, there were no rival caucuses at the national level in the CAW. The Administration caucus had no formal standing in the union and no written rules or membership requirements. It was ostensibly open to anyone with the expectation that, if you joined the caucus, you were committing to backing the candidates that it endorsed. The caucus would vote on a slate recommendation from the NEB, which voted on a recommendation from the president. From the perspective of a local union leader, Wayne Gates describes the Administration caucus as "the face of the CAW" that does all the "legwork before you actually get into the room of the convention."[184] Formally, conventions elect people to leadership positions, but according to Gates, "the reality is that by the time the election came to the floor, it was already decided who was going to get the positions." In the words of long-time Fishermen, Food and Allied Workers Union/CAW president Earle McCurdy, "The goose was pretty much cooked before the convention."[185] From time to time, members would run from the floor against caucus-endorsed candidates "but not very many, and certainly not successfully," says Gates. This self-disciplining was an acknowledgment of the caucus's control over mobility within the union leadership and staff. "People understand that the Administration caucus is their ticket to climb the ladder of the union," says Gates.[186] Malcolm Allen agrees, describing the Administration caucus as more of an "information meeting" with a very "top-down" structure. Allen explains that "the president and a close coterie of advisors ... would make the decisions and the NEB would endorse it."[187] In 2008, Gindin described the power dynamic as follows: "Though formally elected by union delegates, the NEB had never, a few secondary issues aside, demonstrated any collective autonomy from the CAW President."[188] Outside of local elections, no one in the union's history had ever successfully defeated a caucus-endorsed candidate for any significant position in the union, although the caucus had on rare occasions opted for candidates not recommended by the NEB.[189]

The union operated in this way for decades without any major internal resistance.[190] According to Gindin, however, the changing economic land-scape and tougher bargaining environment of the early 2000s left a growing number of CAW activists "frustrated and restless."[191] For these leaders and activists, Hargrove's looming retirement was an opportunity to debate the union's direction and priorities against the backdrop of a crisis in manufacturing.

Mitic and Carol Phillips were among the most prominent voices calling for change. Both had grown increasingly concerned with Hargrove's leader-ship style, and tensions were high. In fact, Mitic had delivered Hargrove an ultimatum: step down and support his bid to become president or face a challenge.[192] This was a controversial move because, in the words of Jim Reid, former president of Local 27, there had "always been a cultural or organizational acceptance of the outgoing President selecting his successor."[193]

Mitic's challenge was somewhat ironic given that he had been a loyal foot soldier to Hargrove and had played a leading role in torpedoing Willie Lam-bert's attempted run at the presidency in 2006. Mitic had been a welder in the Lear auto parts plant in Kitchener and was elected president of Local 1524 before joining the UAW staff in 1981. Mitic was appointed the CAW's director of organizing by Bob White in 1986 and assumed the role of Hargrove's assist-ant in 1992. Described by various other interviewees as an effective "fixer" and "enforcer," Mitic understood the union and its culture very well. He had grown increasingly uncomfortable with how Hargrove was running the CAW and seized the opportunity to do something about it.

Mitic's challenge to Hargrove, however, was not exactly a challenge to the caucus system itself. As Gindin explained, "Mitic's intention was to run *within* the caucus, which would have allowed staff members to vote for him there. He was thus intending to use one aspect of caucus tradition to challenge another, i.e., to open the possibility of a free caucus choice among the candidates."[194] Mitic posed a credible threat because of his extensive network throughout the country, his background in organizing, and his ties to influential staff representatives. He had also managed to garner the strategically significant support of Quebec director Jean-Pierre Fortin.[195]

Hargrove, however, viewed Mitic's manoeuvre as a betrayal. In response, he lined up Ken Lewenza (president of the CAW Council and the popular president of Local 444) as his preferred candidate for president and Peter Kennedy (assistant to Secretary-Treasurer Jim O'Neil) as his preferred candidate for secretary-treasurer. The internal turmoil spilled into the open when Phillips, who was interested in the secretary-treasurer position, told the *Toronto Star* that Hargrove was pressuring the union's leadership to fall in behind his preferred candidates. She "was expected to endorse the team before we've had any discussion or debate in the union," Phillips complained. "If you don't, you're portrayed as someone who doesn't play the game and is disloyal. This isn't any way to run a union."[196] In the face of these now-public tensions, Hargrove organized a special meeting of the NEB on July 8, 2008, where the Administration caucus's picks for president and secretary-treasurer would be decided (thereby conflating the NEB and the Administration caucus). "I want to avoid any splits," Hargrove told the *Toronto Star* in response to Phillips. "Our focus should be on helping our members, not on politics."[197]

In a tactical move before the meeting, Hargrove announced that he would retire earlier than expected, which some argued was done in order to foreclose the possibility of a long campaign period.[198] He also convinced Fortin to withdraw his support for Mitic and to back Lewenza instead, despite Fortin's confession at the meeting to having worried that "this step was a bit too high for Ken."[199] The fact that Mitic lost the support of the Quebec director "was amplified because it potentially weakened the resolve of others both at the Board and on staff," argued Gindin.[200] Hargrove's manoeuvres succeeded in locking down the NEB's support for Lewenza and Kennedy. Recalling these events, Hargrove does not want to get into his reasons for choosing Lewenza over Mitic, but he offers that union politics is a "cutthroat business, and you better be up to the challenge."[201] Gindin's assessment at the time was that Hargrove "seemed more concerned with ensuring executive control over the presidential succession and especially determined not to open debates it could not control and risk commitments that might hold future leaders accountable."[202] Phillips more or less agrees, arguing that Hargrove "was fairly confident that he could continue to influence Ken." But she also feels that "Buzz had this romantic view that the president needed to come from auto and that, more specifically, for whatever reason, he wanted to hand the mantle over to somebody from Windsor."[203]

According to the minutes of this meeting, Phillips's decision to speak to the media had clearly struck a nerve. She was roundly condemned by Hargrove and others for having criticized the union's caucus system. However, it was also clear from the minutes that many on the NEB were not sure exactly how the caucus system worked, what role staff played vis-à-vis the caucus, and who ultimately got to make the decisions about endorsements. For her part, Phillips called for changes to the caucus system, arguing that the process should be democratized by allowing for a campaign period culminating in an opportunity to address the national caucus in advance of the convention. However, her arguments were largely ignored, with her detractors accusing her of a double standard – that of voicing opposition to the caucus structure only when it did not benefit her personally.

Hargrove explained the caucus system's origins to members of the NEB as follows:

> The international [UAW] executive board decided in every region who was going to be the administration candidate, and that was carried out by the staff. The staff in that region would go out and work to make sure the administration caucus selection got elected. Why? Because the staff were part of the administration caucus. They were the vehicle that carried out the mandate of the administration caucus, and that worked very well. Our union didn't happen by chance ... it wasn't ordained to be a great union. It's a great union because of the people and the processes that made it a great union, and people adhered to that.[204]

Hargrove went on to argue that the Administration caucus was essential to ensuring balanced regional representation on the NEB and to preventing the Ontario majority from swamping smaller groups of members across the country. "If we just throw it open, as some people are suggesting, and have secret ballot votes in caucuses ... Ontario could have every position on the board. That's the reality. You can't elect people from the west or the east based on the size of the membership."[205] Hargrove appealed to the NEB to "defend and protect your structure. That's what makes us who we are. That's what makes us strong. That's what gives us the ability to do what we do, and do it better than anyone else."[206]

Phillips challenged Hargrove's appeals to loyalty and tradition, drawing a parallel between her decision to call for changes to the caucus system and the union's decision to break away from the UAW:

> If we insist that the union has to continue to function on the basis of past traditions and practices, if what we're saying here today is our past has to dictate our future, you know, we would still be the United Auto Workers ... The old UAW way did not work any longer. It wasn't helpful, and when something needs to change, when it becomes part of the problem rather than part of the solution, we do need to change it. There should be no sacred cows in this union. We are stronger than that. The arguments that were made when we broke away from the UAW are very similar to some of the arguments that are happening here. Bob White, Bob Nickerson, Buzz Hargrove, they were told that they were being divisive, disloyal, wanting to destroy the UAW.[207]

Phillips, however, was also not interested in eliminating the caucus system altogether. She agreed that the slate-making process for the NEB was key to ensuring regional diversity.[208] However, she called for the caucus system to be reformed in order to provide greater opportunity for democratic debate and discussion:

> You can't inspire leadership to feel more optimistic about the future with a process that feels fixed or with a campaign that is dirty ... I'm running because I think I have some very important ideas to put forward for consideration, and I'll take my chances in terms of whether those

ideas are accepted or not ... So, my appeal is let's just agree that there are good candidates, serious candidates, a tribute to the union that is there, and if we're talking about the presidency right now over the next 30 days or so, let's have a short, sharp campaign where those good candidates put forward their ideas. Let's have that campaign. Let's make it positive ... Let's make it about going forward into the future stronger and then let's let our leadership decide based on that. I can't accept this process. I cannot accept this process that has gone forward, and I won't be withdrawing my candidacy, although I'm not quite sure what that means, since there is no rule book on any of this.[209]

The NEB ultimately confirmed Hargrove's recommendations. Mitic accepted the outcome and withdrew his candidacy, as did Collins, clearing the way for Lewenza to become CAW president on September 6, 2008. Phillips did not immediately withdraw her candidacy for secretary-treasurer, declaring that she intended to run against Kennedy at the convention. In the end, she did not go through with the campaign and instead left the union for the Ontario Labour Relations Board in 2009.[210]

Two weeks after the NEB special meeting, Hargrove sent the minutes to all national staff representatives with a memo reminding them that "when we join the staff of the union everyone knows or should have known that you are giving up your political rights to campaign against the administration of the union as an appointed person who does not face election. Your cooperation is anticipated and appreciated." The message was clear: staff could not campaign against the Administration caucus's preferred NEB candidates but were expected to work in support of these candidates or to remain neutral.[211] This mandate complicated things for Phillips, who was a staff member herself and had many supporters within staff ranks. "I was absolutely determined. I was going to run, and then, of course, I had to go back to the office, and then it was the constant intimidation, the constant threats. They tried to demote me. Then they started picking off my allies," she recalls. "Eventually, they wore me down. Some of my supporters were coming to me and saying, 'Please bow out because they're killing us.'"[212]

Phillips argues that her candidacy and the larger succession issue were related to a disagreement over the union's overall direction: "Strategic voting and the way the decision was made, and the reasons behind the decision, were a symptom of broader changes and direction and move towards business unionism."[213] Mitic more or less agrees, arguing that under Hargrove the "leadership of the union lost its moral compass."[214] Given the direction of the national union, Malcolm Allen says that he was "disheartened" when Mitic's and Phillips's candidacies fell apart. "'I make the decisions and you carry them out' was the attitude that prevailed. That's not to say the union wasn't centralized under White, but it was exacerbated under Buzz," he argues.[215]

In the wake of the succession dispute, a group of nearly two dozen CAW local leaders in Quebec wrote a joint letter to Hargrove registering their "profound discomfort" with the NEB's process in recommending his successor, arguing that it "eliminates the possibility of other candidates running for president and the chance for delegates to choose the best successor. We consider this approach to be undemocratic."[216] However, if so many influential leaders within the CAW were opposed to the Administration caucus, Hargrove's leadership style, and the union's overall direction, why did the NEB fall in line behind Hargrove when presented with an unprecedented opportunity to challenge his decision-making authority? Part of the answer lies in the fact that it lacked true autonomy from the president. This lack of autonomy was rooted in the president's ability to command loyalty from members of the NEB through the promise of staff appointments.

The national president was responsible for appointing staff representatives, which accounts in part for why NEB members interested in staff appointments were reluctant to publicly oppose Hargrove. "There has hardly been a National Executive Board member ... who didn't eventually become a staff rep," Phillips claims.[217] Many interviewees echo this perspective, pointing out that the prospect of obtaining a relatively lucrative staff position became an important incentive for NEB members to fall in line behind the president. Some interviewees who preferred not to have their views attributed described the NEB as a "room of bobble heads" or "the waiting room for staff." Jenny Ahn, who herself was a former member turned union staffer, rejects this characterization of the union's NEB: "Just because we came out as a solid front, didn't mean that there wasn't a lot of discussion and debate and dissent."[218] "There are checks and balances," acknowledges Peggy Nash. "Any president or leadership team can't go against the wishes of the major locals. That would be foolish. So you have to be in sync with them." However, Nash argues that "things became more and more centralized over time. I mean, Buzz talked to a lot of people, but I think he tended to consolidate power."[219] Malcolm Allen agrees that the union became more centralized over time: "The old maxim was you got up and opposed them, and they bought you off by bringing you onto staff." But this practice ended in the 1980s. Under Hargrove, "you towed the line, and you had a shot at a getting a job," says Allen.[220] Phillips agrees, arguing that under Hargrove's leadership the prevailing attitude was "you're with us or against us ... That very much became the culture."[221] This attitude also extended to the realm of staff-leadership dynamics. According to one long-serving staff member who did not want their views attributed, "You were either in favour or you're out of favour. If you're out of favour, you get more work, crappy assignments, and your life isn't as pleasant."

Hargrove's legacy as president is certainly contested. "Depending on whom you ask, Hargrove is either a great leader who has carried his union through the greatest challenges in its history, or a self-serving turncoat. To some, he's a bit of both," wrote journalist Craig Saunders shortly after Hargrove's retirement.[222] Hargrove, for his part, had no regrets. "We've changed the face of the union. I leave it, I think, the most open, progressive, democratic union that I've experienced around the world," he told Saunders.[223]

"ANYBODY BUT CONSERVATIVE": THE 2008 FEDERAL ELECTION

Ken Lewenza took over as CAW president at a time of economic turmoil and political contention. In the run-up to the 2008 federal election, the CAW engaged in what Gindin called a round of "panic bargaining" with Ford, during which the union agreed to a base salary freeze (in exchange for a lump-sum payment and marginal benefit improvements) and gave up cost-of-living allowances for the next five years. The union also negotiated a cap on long-term health care, a freeze on the base pension of existing retirees, and the cancellation of the first of three annual cost-of-living allowances for retirees.[224] The union's acceptance of concessions was predicated on the hope that it would help to stimulate investment and to create jobs. However, as Gindin noted at the time,

Concessions don't guarantee jobs. Jobs depend on so much else beyond the control of workers – from the economy, trade policy, exchange rates and the chaos in financial markets, to the age of plants, technologies used, and especially the models placed in the showrooms. Currently, jobs also depend on the extent to which the new vehicles are sensitive to the implications of escalating oil prices and environmental concerns. What concessions *do* guarantee is more of the same.[225]

Gindin also likened the CAW's decision to accept concessions to its approach to electoral politics: "That same reorientation from taking on power, to accommodating to it, was reflected in the union moving from strategic voting – once voiced as a criticism of the NDP's lack of resistance to corporate pressures – to supporting the business-backed Liberal Party."[226]

Perhaps proving Gindin's argument that concessions do not secure jobs, despite having just concluded a collective agreement with the union on June 3, 2008, which guaranteed that its truck plant in Oshawa would remain open in exchange for a deal "loaded with concessions" and that saved the company $300 million, GM announced the closure of the truck plant.[227] Furious CAW members responded by blockading GM's headquarters, demonstrating that in times of crisis a syndicalist reflex was still very much part of the CAW's culture, even if this impulse had been worn down in recent years. In the end, however, the union's blockade did not prevent the plant closure.[228]

The union's already tense relationship with Stephen Harper's government became even more strained in the wake of the plant closure, given that Conservative finance minister Jim Flaherty represented an Oshawa-area riding. The CAW felt that Flaherty was disinterested in doing anything to reverse the tide of manufacturing job loss and, in response, called on workers to "Give Flaherty the boot."[229] On October 6, 2008, the union collected thousands of old work boots and dumped them in front of Flaherty's constituency office in Whitby.

The action was part of a broader strategic-voting campaign to oust the Harper Tories, as the CAW geared up for another election campaign inspired by an "Anybody but Conservative" (ABC) logic. Hargrove was even touted as a potential challenger to Flaherty.[230] In his autobiography, Hargrove claims that Liberal leader Stéphane Dion contacted him twice to ask that he run for the Liberals.[231] He considered it seriously, meeting with Liberal senator David Smith to discuss potential ridings, but ultimately ruled out a run.[232]

The union developed a two-pronged strategy combining third-party advertising with support for particular candidates. According to records filed with Elections Canada, the CAW spent $39,721.28 on a national advertising campaign in support of strategic voting in the October 2008 federal election.[233] The union also targeted forty "slim win" ridings during the campaign where it believed that strategic voting could help prevent a Conservative victory. The CAW directly endorsed ten Liberal candidates, nine NDP candidates, and Green Party leader Elizabeth May. In the remaining twenty "slim win" ridings, the union urged people to vote for the candidate with the best chance of defeating the Conservative candidate.[234] In virtually every case, that meant voting Liberal. In addition, the CAW endorsed twenty-six "safe" NDP incumbents, and the CAW's Quebec section once again endorsed the entire slate of BQ candidates.

Between September 23 and October 6, newly installed CAW president Ken Lewenza visited Oshawa, Welland, Windsor, Oakville, Kitchener, and London to speak at CAW rallies in support of the union's strategic-voting campaign. In Oakville, Lewenza announced that in the Greater Toronto Area, the union was encouraging its members to vote for the candidates best able to defeat the Conservatives in all ridings with the exception of Parkdale–High Park, where former CAW staffer and NDP MP Peggy Nash was running for re-election.[235] In Windsor, Lewenza endorsed NDP incumbents Joe Comartin (running in Windsor–Tecumseh) and Brian Masse (running in Windsor West).[236] In Oshawa, Lewenza endorsed CAW member and NDP candidate Mike Shields but noted that CAW members should vote strategically in surrounding ridings, where the NDP had little chance of winning.[237] Similarly, in Welland, Lewenza endorsed CAW member and NDP candidate Malcolm Allen but argued that strategic voting should be employed to defeat Conservative incumbents in surrounding ridings.[238] In London, Lewenza endorsed NDP incumbent Irene Mathyssen (running in London–Fanshawe), Liberal incumbent Sue Barnes (running in London West), and Liberal candidate Glen Pearson (running in London–North Centre).[239] In Kitchener, Lewenza exclusively endorsed Liberal candidates.[240]

Once Lewenza's tour wrapped up, the union officially released its list of forty "slim win" ridings. In half the ridings, the union directly endorsed a

Liberal, New Democrat, or Green Party candidate. In the other half, the union simply endorsed an "Anybody but Conservative" candidate. In the vast majority of cases, the logical ABC candidate was a Liberal.

Despite the union's ambitious effort, the opposition parties eked out very few "slim wins." In Welland, CAW member Malcolm Allen managed to win by just 300 votes over a Conservative, with the Liberal incumbent finishing not too far behind in third. Although Lewenza had technically endorsed Allen, the NDP candidate argued that the ABC framing of the CAW's message had undermined his campaign by confusing union members and the public. Allen recalls that at the Welland rally on October 1, 2008, OFL president Wayne Samuelson gave a "full-throated speech in support of the NDP." Lewenza, in contrast, emphasized the importance of strategic voting. Allen was unimpressed, and local union activists were angry because they thought that Lewenza had "sent the wrong message" given that Welland's incumbent MP was a Liberal. According to Allen, the ABC siren call signalled to local voters they should support Liberal incumbents.[241]

Overall, in the CAW's forty targeted ridings, the Conservatives won thirty-two seats, the NDP took five, and the Liberals carried just three. No Conservative incumbents were defeated, and the party lost only one seat that it had previously held – St. John's East. This seat flipped to the NDP column, largely because of Premier Danny Williams's much more successful ABC campaign in Newfoundland and Labrador.[242] However, a Conservative victory in the Vancouver Island North riding over an NDP incumbent meant that the NDP did not win any net new seats from the Tories. Overall, in the forty "slim win" ridings, the Conservatives saw a net increase of ten seats, the NDP saw a net increase of one seat (at the expense of the Liberals), the Liberals saw a net loss of twelve seats, and the Greens lost their only seat.

Of the ten Liberal candidates endorsed directly by the CAW, four were incumbent MPs, all of whom had voted against a third reading of Bill C-257, an Act to Amend the Canada Labour Code, which was an anti-scab law and a legislative priority for the CAW.[243] Curiously, the CAW did not directly endorse any of the several dozen Liberal incumbents who had voted in favour of the anti-scab law. All ten of the Liberal candidates directly endorsed by the CAW were defeated by Conservatives.

Despite the fact that the CAW's strategic-voting campaign relied heavily on direct and indirect endorsements of Liberal candidates, not a single CAW member ran under the Liberal Party banner in 2008. In addition to Malcolm Allen in Welland, CAW member Peter Stoffer won re-election as the NDP member for Sackville–Eastern Shore, and former CAW Quebec director Luc Desnoyers won election as a BQ candidate in Rivière-des-Mille-Îles. Peggy Nash, an NDP incumbent, was defeated by the Liberals in Parkdale–High Park, CAW member Mike Shields, also running for the NDP, lost a close contest in Oshawa to the Tories, and CAW member Ryan Dolby finished third as the NDP candidate in Elgin–Middlesex–London. Another CAW member, Jeff Watson, won re-election as a Conservative in the riding of Essex, even though his union was encouraging strategic voting to defeat him.

In both 2006 and 2008, the CAW leadership was critical of Jack Layton's campaign strategy, particularly the party's decision to focus attacks on the Liberals rather than on the Conservatives.[244] The union pointed to the NDP's prioritization of partisan advantage over what it saw as the political result most likely to produce good policy for the labour movement. According to Hargrove, the "logic is simple: the NDP takes votes from Liberals, not Conservatives. This might help the party win more seats ... but it can do grave damage to the country if it makes it easier for people like Harper to get a foot in the door."[245] Indeed, the CAW and other labour organizations played a key role in supporting the ultimately unsuccessful effort to pull together a Liberal-NDP-BQ coalition to topple the re-elected Harper minority in December 2008. The coalition effort fell apart when the Liberals got cold feet.[246]

FINANCIAL CRISIS AND THE GREAT RECESSION

The CAW leadership continued working very closely with Dalton McGuinty's government on the auto-sector file, partly because an anti-subsidy Conservative government at the federal level meant that the Ontario Liberals were the union's only willing dance partner. This dynamic worked to the mutual political advantage of the union and McGuinty because it allowed the Liberals to use manufacturing job loss as a wedge issue to criticize the Harper government. For example, in January 2008,

McGuinty floated the idea of imposing provincial tariffs to block imports of South Korean vehicles if free trade talks between the federal government and South Korea failed to produce an agreement guaranteeing that Canadian-made cars had access to the South Korean market. The union applauded the premier's move, and Hargrove used the opportunity to name and shame the Harper Conservatives. "It just angers me that the federal government wouldn't pick up the mantle here and carry it, be the champion of the Canadian industry," he argued.[247] With the onset of the 2008 global financial crisis and a deep recession that threatened to bankrupt the Big Three automakers, the CAW's relationship with the Harper government went from bad to worse.

Precipitated by the collapse of a housing bubble south of the border, the 2008–09 Great Recession forced General Motors and Chrysler into bankruptcy protection. Although the Big Three's market share had been declining for several decades, sales plummeted with the onset of the recession.[248] GM and Chrysler relied on government intervention in the form of emergency loans to stay afloat – albeit with significant strings attached. The automakers were required to develop restructuring plans as a condition of government support, prompting both the UAW and the CAW to agree to reopen recently negotiated union contracts and to bargain significant concessions. In the case of GM, these concessions included a freeze on wages and pension benefits, reduced vacation time, and the loss of an annual bonus.[249] The concessions amounted to a savings of $7.25 per worker per hour in labour costs.[250] Chrysler demanded even deeper concessions, prompting outrage and a protracted fight with the union. However, without any real leverage to resist Chrysler's demands, which were reinforced by conditions laid down by the Harper and McGuinty governments, the union reluctantly agreed to a deal that reduced labour costs by $19 per worker per hour.[251] A week later, the company filed for bankruptcy protection.

Emboldened by Chrysler's deal and under the imminent threat of bankruptcy, GM returned to the bargaining table to demand even more from the union at the behest of the federal and Ontario governments. The CAW initially resisted, but in the end it accepted concessions amounting to $22 per worker per hour, which the membership ratified with 86 percent in favour.[252] As a result, GM Canada locked down $10.5 billion in government aid.[253] In return, the federal and Ontario governments acquired millions of shares in the company.[254]

The CAW's Bill Murnighan and Jim Stanford argued that the union had successfully managed to ward off the worst of the concessionary demands in the 2009 round of bargaining.[255] They also pointed to the union's successful mobilization to pressure the McGuinty government into reversing its position on pension funding as part of the restructuring deal with GM.[256] But this silver-lining analysis unquestionably carried a cloud. In the midst of the crisis, *This Magazine* asked Lewenza, "If you went to a high school career day what would you say to someone who asked if they should become an assembly-line autoworker?" Lewenza responded, "I'd tell them to avoid the auto industry. [Years ago] I told them it was hard work, boring work, but you could earn a good living and support your family. I wouldn't say that now."[257]

Although the CAW viewed both the Harper and the McGuinty governments' interventions in the bailout process as hostile to union interests, Lewenza saw these two governments as cut from very different cloths. Whereas Lewenza argues that Harper and the Conservatives were "full of disdain," he credits McGuinty's government for funding retraining programs and worker-adjustment centres, providing subsidies to employers in exchange for investments, and being willing to listen and change course. In Lewenza's words, the union did not "jump in bed with the provincial Liberals" but formed a "respectful relationship" with the McGuinty government, specifically around tackling the problem of job loss in the manufacturing sector. "McGuinty argued aggressively about what the auto industry meant to the province of Ontario ... McGuinty was very approachable ... and programs that were implemented by the provincial government, I can tell you first-hand, literally helped thousands of people get retrained and move on," Lewenza argues.[258]

Although the Ontario Liberal government worked closely with the CAW on investments in retraining and manufacturing, McGuinty had little interest in the union-friendly labour law reforms also being promoted by the CAW and by the rest of the labour movement. Indeed, Lewenza offered the lack of progress on labour law reform as the primary reason for the CAW's decision to rejoin the OFL in June 2010. "I thought we would be in a better position to influence government with a united labour movement," said Lewenza, explaining that issues like anti-scab legislation and card-based union certification could be won only if unions came together with a common political purpose.[259] With Wayne Samuelson replaced by former CUPE Ontario leader Sid Ryan as OFL president in November 2009, there was hope that old grudges stretching back to the Social Contract Act and to the Days of Action could be set aside and that the renewal of the OFL could become a real possibility. However, there was still no consensus within the labour movement over political strategy. Strategic voting was the preferred tactic for significant segments of the movement, and NDP-union relations remained strained as a result. The movement was fragmented along partisan lines, and Ryan's leadership style polarized affiliates in ways that amplified tensions and complicated long-standing divisions.[260] The province's union movement was arguably more divided than ever – as partly reflected in the divergent political strategies adopted by key labour organizations.

THE 2011 FEDERAL ELECTION: CONSERVATIVE MAJORITY

In the 2011 federal election, the CAW backed candidates from no less than four parties as part of its largest strategic voting effort yet. Several prominent CAW members offered themselves up to run as NDP candidates. MPs Malcolm Allen and Peter Stoffer announced their intentions to seek re-election. Peggy Nash would attempt a comeback in Parkdale–High Park, Local 222 president Chris Buckley challenged a Conservative incumbent in Oshawa, and CAW Local 2168 president Ryan Dolby was announced as the NDP candidate for Elgin–Middlesex–London. Days after the writ was dropped – with the NDP polling in third, at just below 18 percent – Dolby captured national headlines when he announced that he was abandoning his campaign and throwing his support behind the local Liberal candidate in an effort to avoid vote splitting and defeat the riding's Conservative incumbent.[261]

Despite accumulating evidence that its strategic-voting campaigns had failed to defeat many Conservative candidates, the CAW continued to promote the strategy as the key to defeating Harper. In the 2011 federal election, the CAW targeted fifty priority ridings that it believed would determine the outcome of the election. In these races, the CAW explicitly identified thirty-four Liberals, fifteen New Democrats, and Green Party leader Elizabeth May as the union's "preferred" candidates. The CAW also compiled a separate list of twenty-nine additional NDP incumbent ridings where the union backed New Democrat candidates. The union did decline, however, to endorse the NDP's only Quebec MP, Thomas Mulcair, in deference to the CAW's Quebec section, which, once again, endorsed the entire slate of BQ candidates, including former CAW Quebec director Luc Desnoyers. The BQ endorsement had been set in motion a year earlier, in August 2010, when Gilles Duceppe was invited to address delegates at the CAW-TCA Joint Council in Montreal, although it was hardly unexpected given that the union had endorsed the BQ in every election since 1993.[262]

Once endorsements were locked in, something unexpected happened. Jack Layton's appearance on a popular Quebec television talk show resulted in an immediate spike in popularity for the NDP leader in Quebec.[263] Layton's performance in the English leaders' debate, particularly his stinging critique of Liberal leader Michael Ignatieff's attendance record in the House of Commons, propelled the NDP even higher in the polls, eventually supplanting the Liberals as the main challenger to Harper's Conservatives.[264]

Not having anticipated the NDP surge and corresponding decline of Liberal and BQ fortunes, the CAW's strategic-voting campaign was thrown into disarray. Based on riding-by-riding results, it was a failure by any measure. Whereas New Democrats outside Quebec were elected or re-elected in all but one of the twenty-nine NDP incumbent ridings where the CAW endorsed candidates, the union-backed BQ was virtually wiped out by the NDP, which captured fifty-nine of seventy-five seats in the province. Declining support for sovereignty, relative calm over linguistic divisions, and the desire for a social democratic alternative all undermined support for the Bloc and boosted NDP fortunes.[265]

In the CAW's fifty priority ridings in the rest of Canada, the union's preferred candidates managed to win only ten seats. The Tories won thirty-eight contests, the NDP carried six ridings, the Liberals were victorious in five, and Green Party leader Elizabeth May won her BC riding. In seven ridings, the CAW's endorsed candidate actually finished in third place, thus undermining the entire logic of the union's campaign. The NDP's unexpected surge in the second half of the campaign dramatically changed the dynamic in many ridings across the country, but the CAW made no public attempt to revise its strategic priorities. In the end, in the CAW's fifty priority ridings, the Tories saw a net increase of twelve seats, whereas the Liberals witnessed a net decrease of seventeen seats. The CAW's strategic-voting campaign had failed, and the Harper Conservatives had their coveted majority.

In terms of CAW-affiliated candidates, Stoffer and Allen won re-election as incumbents, and Peggy Nash made a successful comeback. Chris Buckley, however, failed to win a seat in Oshawa, and CAW Local 2168 activist Fred Sinclair was unable to topple the Tory incumbent in Elgin–Middlesex–London – although he managed to finish second ahead of the Liberal candidate endorsed by NDP defector Ryan Dolby. The BQ's Luc Desnoyers was swept away as part of the NDP's "Orange Wave" in Quebec, losing his Rivière-des-Mille-Îles riding north of Montreal by nearly 11,000 votes to twenty-year-old Laurin Liu, a McGill University student.

2011 ONTARIO ELECTION: TRANSACTIONAL POLITICS

For the CAW, years of hard bargaining and trauma associated with plant closures meant that resistance to concessions became more difficult. As a result, the union's focus shifted toward negotiating buyouts to minimize the damage to those members least able to transition either to retirement or to other sectors in the labour market. In this context, partnership strategies with employers and willing governments were further amplified, particularly as governments were central to providing supports for workers in the form of retraining programs (like Second Career in Ontario) and labour adjustment centres, known as Action Centres in the CAW's lexicon.[266] This embrace of collaboration was likely best exhibited by Lewenza's decision to personally campaign alongside McGuinty in the 2011 provincial election campaign. The fact that Andrea Horwath had replaced Howard Hampton as Ontario NDP leader in 2009 gave hope in NDP circles that, with new leaders at the helm of both the CAW and the party, there was a prospect of turning the page on the acrimonious relationship between Hargrove and Hampton. These hopes were dashed, however, when Lewenza appeared on the hustings with McGuinty.[267]

Lewenza acknowledges that he "took a fair amount of criticism" for attending a campaign event with the premier in Thunder Bay.[268] The choice of location was odd given that the union's stated policy of anti-PC strategic voting did not seem to apply to either of the Thunder Bay ridings, one of which the NDP had lost by only fifty votes to the Liberals in the previous election.[269] Although the Tories were not a serious threat in the Thunder Bay ridings, Lewenza was more focused on the overall outcome of the election. His support for McGuinty was driven primarily by the government's willingness to invest in the province's automotive and manufacturing sectors. To this end, aggressively supporting the Liberals "was not always comfortable ... but at the same time, the alternative was the Conservatives. The alternative was not the New Democratic Party," according to Lewenza.[270]

Even in retirement, Hargrove did not hold back in voicing his views on the state of the party-union relationship. "The party's gone too far to the right," he told the media in relation to the Ontario NDP. "It's very discouraging. I don't belong to any political party today ... I may not even vote."[271] In the end, the McGuinty Liberals were reduced to a minority, losing seventeen seats – seven of which were won by the NDP. The NDP caucus grew from ten to seventeen seats and, more importantly, now held the balance of power.

Jenny Ahn argues that the union under Lewenza was focused on tailoring its political strategy to the broader political and economic landscape.[272] For Lewenza, that meant working with a government that could deliver concrete results for his members. McGuinty, he argues, was willing to play ball.[273] However, the minority government made the NDP more important as a lever for the labour movement to shape government policy. To this end, Lewenza met with Horwath after the 2011 campaign "trying to build up the relationship" with the understanding that the CAW would never go back to "writing blank cheques." However, according to Lewenza, things fell apart when Horwath met with a group of labour leaders during budget talks to consult on priorities. Lewenza was convinced that she had already made up her mind, arguing that Horwath ignored their requests to prioritize minimum-wage increases and labour law reforms, opting instead to emphasize freezing auto insurance rates. Lewenza left the meeting in "a solemn mood" and "disillusioned." That meeting also reinforced Lewenza's commitment to strategic voting.[274]

DECLINING UNION POWER

The defensive nature of the CAW's strategies in the electoral arena were also evident at the bargaining table. The union was increasingly operating from a position of weakness, attempting to shield itself from the worst possible political or economic outcomes. However, the union had not given up on militancy or direct action altogether. Electro-Motive Diesel, a London, Ontario, subsidiary of US multinational Caterpillar, locked out members of CAW Local 27 on January 1, 2012, after the union rejected the company's demand for a 50 percent wage cut. In response, the union mounted a boycott campaign of Caterpillar-branded products and organized secondary pickets across the country at a dozen outlets selling Caterpillar equipment.[275] More dramatically, members of Locals 27 and 88 blockaded a company-owned locomotive that was being moved out of the plant, eventually destined for Brazil. Although the union lifted the blockade after a week, Caterpillar announced two days later that it would permanently close the London plant. The union threatened to occupy the plant in retaliation, but in the end it agreed to a closure agreement that provided three weeks' pay for each year that unionized workers had been on the job, a ratification bonus worth $1,500, limited company-paid health care benefits, full funding of the workers' pension trust, and $350,000 to settle outstanding grievances and to establish an adjustment program.[276] The closure agreement also required the union to "cease any picketing, pamphleting, leafleting, posting of signs or other activity" and to agree that "there shall be no boycott related to the operations or products of the Company or its associated or affiliated corporations."[277] In effect, in the words of Stephanie Ross and labour historian Jason Russell, "the closure agreement was contingent upon the union leadership demobilizing not only the picket lines but also the community allies leading the boycott initiatives."[278]

Things went from bad to worse for the CAW when Ford entered the 2012 round of bargaining with concessionary demands similar to those that it had tabled in 2009. The union balked, threatening a strike, but in the end the CAW and the Big Three agreed to a pattern deal that provided signing bonuses and annual lump-sum cost-of-living payments instead of wage increases, cut starting wages for new employees, and extended the length of the two-tier wage structure for new employees from six years to ten.[279] Gindin bemoaned the "culture of concessions" that had seemingly gripped the CAW, leading to the loss of roughly 49,000 autoworker union members since the late 1970s.[280] The union was in crisis, but its political and economic response to the crisis reflected a culture of defensiveness that hindered a clear vision for progress.

2012 FEDERAL NDP LEADERSHIP RACE

Despite the federal NDP's unprecedented electoral breakthrough in the 2011 election, there appeared to be little appetite among CAW leaders to re-establish partisan ties. In fact, in September 2011, just months after the NDP formed the Official Opposition and weeks after the untimely death of Jack Layton in August 2011, Lewenza publicly called for the party to merge or to create an electoral alliance with the Liberals in order to defeat the Conservatives in the next election.[281]

However, Lewenza's position was subsequently complicated when his former assistant, MP Peggy Nash, decided to join the NDP leadership race to replace Layton. Even though BC MP Nathan Cullen emerged as the only federal NDP leadership contestant to campaign in support of an electoral alliance with the Liberals and Greens, Lewenza opted to rejoin the NDP and instead to endorse Nash, who opposed any sort of electoral pact with other parties. When *Maclean's* reached out to Lewenza to explain this seemingly contradictory position, a CAW spokesperson provided a confusing response that read, in part,

> I don't know that a possible merger between the Liberal Party and the NDP is still an issue ... Peggy Nash's position is that of moving to a proportional representation system, which would deal with the problem of a lack of appropriate representation based on votes cast. The CAW has firmly endorsed independent politics and strategic voting. This means we are committed to support candidates that champion the interests of working Canadians. Ken's endorsement of Peggy doesn't imply that the CAW strategic vision of politics changes. But it does recognize that no politician, in the country, is better fit to champion the interests of working Canadians than Peggy.[282]

From a strategic perspective, Lewenza's endorsement seemed driven more by personal allegiance than by logic, especially given that all NDP leadership candidates were supportive of proportional representation, whereas only Cullen shared Lewenza's support for an electoral pact with the Liberals. Even so, it is unclear what impact Lewenza's endorsement had on Nash's campaign. There is certainly no evidence that the union launched any significant mobilization to sign up members to back her candidacy in the one-member–one-vote contest. In the end, Nash finished fourth behind Cullen, party insider Brian Topp, and the eventual winner, Thomas Mulcair. The fact that Mulcair was fluently bilingual and had political experience in government as a former provincial Liberal Cabinet minister in Quebec made him the most electable candidate in the eyes of many New Democrats. After decades of sitting on the opposition benches, NDP activists appeared willing to cast off the last vestiges of the party's perceived ideological baggage and vie for power by voting to remove reference to "socialism" from the NDP constitution at its April 2013 policy convention.[283]

Notwithstanding this ideological repositioning, for Lewenza, as a political strategy, returning the union en masse to the NDP simply could not be justified. Pointing to Premier Gary Doer's three consecutive NDP majorities in Manitoba, Lewenza argues that "the right to organize was just as tough under an NDP government as it is in a conservative environment."[284]

CONCLUSION

Between 1986 and 2005, the CAW's membership grew from 136,480 to 241,381.[285] However, by 2012, this number had dwindled to barely 200,000 as a result of massive job loss in the automotive and manufacturing sectors.[286] In this context, the CAW adopted a more defensive posture in relation to political action. The CAW leadership, however, was adamant that its embrace of strategic voting and closer ties to the Liberals should not be interpreted as a deradicalization of the union's approach to politics. In the weeks leading up to the 2006 federal election, Hargrove argued,

> Politics is not about abstract ideals, it's about power – just like bargaining. We have an obligation to our members, and to the communities where they live, to make the most of our current opportunity. An opportunity to deliver more of the policies we've seen in the last 17 months, and to prevent the social destruction that would accompany a Conservative victory.[287]

Hargrove explained that "by endorsing a Liberal minority with an NDP balance of power, the CAW is not 'drifting' toward Liberal views. Indeed, my opinions (on everything from free trade to public ownership to gun control) clearly place me to the left of the NDP hierarchy."[288] Gindin agreed that the NDP had indeed moved to the political centre. But for Gindin, "the irony is that in leaving the NDP, the CAW leadership was hardly breaking new ground on the left, but rather *also* moving, in its own way, to the center."[289]

The CAW's political reorientation toward the Liberal Party coincided with a deepening economic crisis in Canada's automotive industry. The union struggled with workforce downsizing, the growing market share of nonunionized automotive companies, and declining union influence over wages and benefits throughout this period. These economic pressures, combined with a global crisis in social democratic politics, nudged the CAW into embracing a defensive Gomperist political orientation in an effort to shield itself from the worst of neoliberal globalization. By aligning itself more closely with the Liberal Party, the union took the gamble that it would be better positioned to lobby for government subsidies in support of Canada's automotive industry. By aligning itself more closely with automotive industry employers, the union hoped that cooperation, rather than conflict, would help to protect autoworker jobs and investment.

However, on balance, there is little consensus over whether a closer relationship with the Liberal Party or with major automotive industry employers yielded positive results for the CAW. Indeed, according to labour studies scholar John Peters, "What CAW members are learning the hard way is that their recent embrace of concessions, labour-management co-operation, and political lobbying for subsidies and competitive business supports does not add up to a winning approach for working people."[290]

CHAPTER 6

MERGE AHEAD

The Birth of Unifor and the Consolidation of Transactional Politics, 2013–21

The merger of the Canadian Auto Workers (CAW) and the Communications, Energy and Paperworkers Union (CEP) to create Unifor in 2013 was presented by its architects as a game changer for the Canadian labour movement. The new union, now the largest private-sector union in the country, held the promise of greater power for working-class people at both the bargaining table and the ballot box. However, in the case of the former, the new union struggled to maintain jobs, organize new members, and secure bargaining breakthroughs in the face of economic restructuring and hostile employers. Unifor's capacity to influence political power holders was put to the test in a series of key provincial and federal elections. Although the question of political strategy was initially sidestepped in the 2013 process of merging the CAW with the CEP, which was affiliated to the New Democratic Party (NDP), it did not take long for the new union to resolve this question in favour of anti-Conservative strategic voting. This political direction helped to consolidate Unifor's transactional relationship with Liberal governments in Ontario and Ottawa as the union worked to save jobs and to secure investments in key sectors.

THE LEAD-UP TO THE MERGER

Unifor's genesis can be traced to a May 2011 Canadian Labour Congress (CLC) executive meeting at which Ken Lewenza sat beside Dave Coles, head of the CEP. As Coles would recall, the two listened to labour leader after labour leader share "one horror story after another." The CAW's membership had shrunk by 25 percent since 2005, and the CEP was reeling from the loss of 30,000 members over the course of the previous five years due to severe job cuts at Nortel and across the forestry industry. Coles reportedly leaned over to Lewenza and whispered, "This just doesn't work. We've got to be able to respond in a better way." Lewenza replied that the two "should have a conversation about how we strengthen the labour movement."[1] A few days later, the two union leaders met at a steak house and agreed, in principle, on a plan to join forces in an effort to reverse their respective unions' fading fortunes.

This meeting led to "small group meetings of top elected leadership of both unions" in November 2011 and to the adoption by the CEP and CAW National Executive Boards of a joint protocol "to develop and agree upon the main principles of a new Canadian union, with a new identity and structure" in January 2012.[2] The joint protocol was heavily influenced by a seven-page document titled "A Moment of Truth for Canadian Labour," co-authored by the CEP's Fred Wilson and the CAW's Jim Stanford.[3] The document reviewed the elements of the crisis in the Canadian labour movement that now called for urgent attention, including the continued erosion of private-sector union density, the failure of organizing initiatives to keep pace with plant closures and labour market growth, the decline in labour's share of the national wealth, new levels of political hostility and growing negative public opinion toward unions, aggressive attacks by employers, dramatic generational change within unions, and the paralysis and dysfunction of some union centrals.

Peter Kennedy (CAW) and Gaétan Ménard (CEP), second-in-command in their respective unions, joined Wilson and Stanford at the helm of the "new union project." Although neither union was new to mergers, this coming together would be unprecedented given the size and scope of the undertaking. The joint committees formed to build the new union had to contend with significant organizational, personal, and cultural barriers. For example, Wilson describes heated debates concerning the perceived benefits of the CAW's centralized versus the CEP's decentralized structure. Architects of the new union argued about whether the preservation of regional vice-president positions (a holdover from the CEP) would encourage the development of competing fiefdoms. They sparred over the rights of retirees to participate in the new union and the proper role of the Quebec director. Committee members overseeing the merger also went back and forth about how to balance representation and delegate allocation at union conventions and debated dues structures and the administration of strike pay. In short, there were lots of details to sort out and many obstacles to overcome. According to Wilson, in the end, the architects of the new union settled on a "balance between democratic centralism and autonomous regional, sectoral and equity structures to ensure diversity and encourage local initiative and innovation."[4]

Before the new union could be formed, delegates at both the CAW and CEP national conventions would have to endorse its creation. At the CAW Constitutional Convention in August 2012, leaders worked hard to frame the creation of the new union as a bold and exciting initiative rather than an act of desperation designed to save two unions in decline.[5] Delegates voted unanimously to approve the new union proposal.[6] CEP delegates also voted to move forward with the merger at their October 2012 convention. One local union president in attendance estimated the vote carried with 85 to 90 percent of delegates in favour.[7] According to Wilson, internal opposition to the creation of the new union was rooted in concerns that the CEP would be swallowed up by a larger union, reticence to work with the CAW specifically, and protest votes against Coles's leadership.[8]

At the Unifor founding convention in August 2013, using a weighted per-capita voting system, delegates voted almost 96 percent in favour of adopting a new constitution.[9] The constitution mandates the creation of a twenty-five-member National Executive Board consisting of the three national officers (i.e., president, secretary-treasurer, and Quebec director), three regional directors from Atlantic Canada, Ontario, and western Canada, five elected chairpersons from the regional councils (i.e., Ontario, Atlantic, Prairies, BC, and Quebec), one representative from skilled trades, one representative of racialized and Indigenous workers, one representative of retirees, and eleven representatives from the union's industry councils to provide a voice for sectoral interests. The constitution requires that the number of women on the board be at least equal to the proportion of women who are members of Unifor. To avoid regional domination, the constitution also provides that members from a single region cannot hold the majority of board seats. In the years between the union's triennial conventions, the constitution stipulates that a Canadian Council must meet annually, bringing together all Unifor locals. Industry councils also meet annually, often in conjunction with the Canadian Council. Regional councils are required to meet at least once a year – more often in Quebec – and are responsible for electing their own chairpersons, executives, and standing committees.

Demographically, Unifor's composition has not changed dramatically since its founding. In 2013, 51 percent of the union's members were based in Ontario, followed by 17 percent in Quebec, 13 percent on the Prairies, 9 percent in Atlantic Canada, 9 percent in British Columbia, and less than 1 percent in the North. Sectorally, 31 percent of the membership worked in manufacturing, 25 percent in services, 17 percent in resources, 13 percent in communications, and 14 percent in transportation. The largest subsectors were auto assembly and parts (13 percent), telecommunications (9 percent), health and social services (9 percent), and forestry (7 percent).[10] As of 2022, the share of Ontario-based membership was 52 percent, followed by 16 percent from Quebec, 13 percent from the Prairies, 10 percent from Atlantic Canada, 9 percent from British Columbia, and less than 1 percent from the North. Sectorally, 28 percent of the membership was based in manufacturing, 27 percent in services, 17 percent in resources, 16 percent in transportation, and 12 percent in communications. The largest subsectors were auto assembly and parts (13 percent), health and social services (9 percent), forestry (7 percent), and road transportation (7 percent). Public-sector workers accounted for 17 percent of the union's membership in 2022, and women accounted for 28 percent.[11]

Given Unifor's significant membership diversity, the union has been confronted with having to preserve unity in pursuit of a common vision. To this end, Unifor's founding constitution contains a unifying statement of principles similar to that of the CAW:

> Our goal is transformative. To reassert common interest over private interest. Our goal is to change our workplace and our world. Our vision is compelling. It is to fundamentally change the economy, with equality and social justice, restore and strengthen our democracy and achieve an environmentally sustainable future. This is the basis of

social unionism – a strong and progressive union culture and a commitment to work in cause with other progressives in Canada and around the world.[12]

The merger was premised on the power of consolidation to challenge the fragmentation, duplication, competition, and inability to cooperate that has often characterized much of Canada's labour movement. The merger also signalled an explicit embrace of general unionism, meaning that the union would accept members from any sector of the economy. Although both unions had been moving in the direction of general unionism for some time, the adoption of a new name that eschewed a sectoral identity allowed Unifor to claim a broader identity than either of its predecessors. In pursuit of this goal, the new union made a commitment at its founding convention to dedicate 10 percent of its annual budget to new organizing and touted a potentially radical new model of union membership called community chapters. These chapters were designed to extend membership in Unifor to those unable to establish a pro-union majority in their workplace, to laid-off workers, or to young workers or contract workers for whom unions were simply out of reach.[13]

Despite repeated claims by leaders that the CEP and the CAW were creating a new union rather than merging, the size imbalance between the two unions led some to speculate that the CAW was simply absorbing the CEP under a new name. Fred Wilson rejects this view, arguing that the creation of Unifor was neither a takeover nor a merger but rather the building of an entirely new union.[14] The CEP did, however, concede that the first president of Unifor would come from the CAW. Although everyone expected this person to be Lewenza, his decision to retire paved the way for Jerry Dias, a long-time assistant to both Buzz Hargrove and Lewenza, to assume the presidency. "They'd been training Jerry for that role in CAW circles for a long time," explains Wilson.[15]

Dias came out of the aerospace sector and was the son of a United Auto Workers staff rep. His only challenge for the presidency came from Lindsay Hinshelwood, a CAW Local 707 activist who ran from the convention floor and captured 17.49 percent of the vote.[16] Her run was significant because it represented the first contested presidential election in CAW/Unifor history. It also demonstrated the enduring strength of the CAW's Administration caucus, reformulated as the Unity Team, to ensure that the positions on the new union's National Executive Board would be filled by those selected in advance by the leadership of the two unions.

The new union's founding created much fanfare, but from the very start, there were doubts about Unifor's ability to carry out its ambitious mandate. Although the merger made Unifor into Canada's largest private-sector union, it did not immediately generate any new union members. Rather, Unifor simply combined CAW and CEP members into a single union. As a result, pre-existing identities, whether sector- or workplace-based, did not wither away, and it would take time for the new union to forge a unique identity.

The need for unity in part explained why Unifor deferred the decision on political affiliation to the NDP for a year after the merger. As Stanford explains, the decision to delay was "strategic" because it was going to be a "controversial decision" in some quarters of the CEP.[17] That union had been NDP-aligned for many years, even siding with the Pink Paper unions in support of Bob Rae's government in the dispute over the Social Contract Act in the early 1990s. Wilson acknowledges the CEP's partisan relationship with the NDP but stresses that it "was not in the same unconditional way that you found in a lot of other industrial unions like the Steelworkers and United Food and Commercial Workers." He explains that although different components of the union had different levels of allegiance to the party and that CEP activists had strong relations with Jack Layton, the union as a whole was growing increasingly concerned with the party's tendency to put its electoral ambitions ahead of the labour movement's legislative priorities.[18] In other words, the perceived gulf between the CAW and the CEP on the question of the NDP was not as wide as it appeared. Nevertheless, then CAW Local 199 president Bruce Allen described the distinct CEP and CAW approaches to the NDP as "oil and water" and predicted that "one position will prevail and the other is going to be discarded, meaning that the political legacy of the union whose political direction does not prevail will disappear into an Orwellian-like memory hole."[19] He was seemingly proven right, as Dias rallied the union around anti-Conservative strategic voting in advance of the 2014 Ontario provincial election, just as the broader labour movement also appeared to be embracing the tactic in an unprecedented way.

STOP HUDAK: THE 2014 ONTARIO ELECTION

Reduced to a minority after the 2011 provincial election and still reeling from the economic impact of the recession, Dalton McGuinty's Liberals turned their attention to the findings of the Commission on the Reform of Ontario's Public Services. Headed by former Toronto-Dominion Bank chief economist Donald Drummond, the commission had been mandated by McGuinty to figure out how to eliminate Ontario's mounting provincial deficit. Drummond's final report called for massive cuts in public spending and public services.[20] Unsurprisingly, the recommendations were universally panned by the labour movement. According to an analysis by the Ontario Confederation of University Faculty Associations, "Drummond's model of labour relations consists primarily of hard bargaining on the part of broader public sector (BPS) employers, with government ... supporting the employer when the going gets tough."[21] The analysis further observed that Drummond "is counting on the devastating size of his cuts to the funding of public services to force the parties to bargain concessionary agreements, eliminate jobs, and find 'efficiencies,' which obviously can only translate into dramatically higher workloads for the remaining public sector workers."[22]

With the commission's findings in hand, the Liberals shifted gears on the education front, teaming up with the Conservatives to pass Bill 115, the Putting Students First Act, in August 2012. The new law implemented a wage freeze, clawed back sick days, and extinguished meaningful collective bargaining rights for those education workers who refused to follow the lead of the Catholic and French-language teachers' unions in negotiating concessionary agreements with the provincial government.[23] Like the CAW, teachers' unions had been reliable allies of the McGuinty Liberals since the late 1990s, but his government's attack on collective bargaining rights in the education sector changed the party-union dynamic overnight. After convincing long-serving Progressive Conservative (PC) member of provincial Parliament (MPP) Elizabeth Witmer to resign her seat with the offer of a patronage appointment, McGuinty hoped that his party would win her vacated Kitchener–Waterloo riding and regain a Liberal majority. However, in an unexpected twist, the NDP managed to effectively tap into the anger of teachers and other unionized public-sector workers.[24] The

NDP's stunning and decisive by-election victory in September 2012, combined with mounting teacher protest and several constitutional challenges to Bill 115,[25] convinced the Liberals to re-evaluate their strategy. In the wake of this turmoil, McGuinty announced his resignation, providing the Liberals with an opportunity to recalibrate and potentially to repair its damaged relationship with teachers and other groups of unionized workers.

By the end of McGuinty's tenure as premier, he had fallen out of favour not only with teachers' unions but also with former labour movement allies like Buzz Hargrove. In an interview with the *Windsor Star,* Hargrove took a shot at McGuinty while expressing support for former Windsor MPP Sandra Pupatello's leadership bid. "She's the one with experience and she knows how to work with people," Hargrove said. "She's not a left politician, but (Pupatello) also knows in order to make a province like Ontario work you have to be working with the labour movement, not slapping it in the face as Mr. (Conservative Leader Tim) Hudak is guaranteed to, or as Mr. (Premier Dalton) McGuinty did to the teachers," he added.[26] Pupatello, however, was unsuccessful. Instead, Liberals opted for Toronto MPP and left-leaning former education minister Kathleen Wynne to replace McGuinty as premier.

In the days leading up to the Liberal leadership vote, the government tried to dampen growing opposition to the party by hastily announcing that it would repeal Bill 115. The tactic was an olive branch of sorts designed to allow the new premier to start with a clean slate. In the weeks and months that followed, the Wynne government was able to achieve labour peace and even to convince Ontario Secondary School Teachers' Federation president Ken Coran to run as a Liberal in an August 2013 by-election in the Liberal-held riding of London West. However, on election day, the NDP candidate again unexpectedly scored a decisive victory after locking in endorsements from a wide range of labour organizations, including teachers' unions whose members viewed Coran's candidacy as both opportunistic and unprincipled. That same night, the NDP easily picked up a second seat from the Liberals in a Windsor–Tecumseh by-election – a result that *Toronto Star* reporter Richard J. Brennan credited to "a combination of Liberal scandals, nagging unemployment, and general voter discontent."[27] Earlier in the campaign, CAW Local 444 president Dino Chiodo had expressed doubts that his members would head to the polls for the

Liberals as they had in previous elections.[28] The NDP's winning streak continued with a stunning February 2014 by-election win in Niagara Falls, when Unifor Local 199 president and Niagara Falls city councillor Wayne Gates scored a narrow victory over former PC MPP Bart Maves to pick up yet another seat from the beleaguered Liberals.

Gates's win was historic for the union because it was the first time that a member of Unifor had been elected to provincial or federal office. Oddly, however, Gates says that the union's national leadership tried to dissuade him from running for fear of splitting the vote in what the leadership considered a traditional Liberal riding. "In the by-election, they said we couldn't win," Gates recounts.[29] He ignored the union's advice and ran anyway, and the labour movement eventually consolidated around his winning campaign. "I don't think I would have been elected without the support of the labour movement, particularly around finances," says Gates.[30] The episode revealed that, despite its new configuration, Unifor was as committed to anti-PC strategic voting as its CAW predecessor. Unifor was not alone in this thinking, as soon became evident when a provincial election was triggered by the Ontario NDP's withdrawal of support for the Liberal minority government in May 2014.

Although the NDP was riding high on a string of impressive by-election victories, its decision to provoke a general election badly backfired. The decision proved wildly unpopular in labour movement circles, and support for the party declined. Dias was furious, publicly criticizing NDP leader Andrea Horwath for precipitating the election and calling Wynne's budget "a win-win for working class people." "When politics is more important than direction then I have to start to second guess," he said, referring to the NDP's decision to turn down the budget in favour of an election.[31] Despite her government's flaws, union leaders saw progressive potential in Kathleen Wynne and, more importantly, feared that defeating her government would open the door to a PC majority and to the introduction of right-to-work legislation, an idea that had been floated by PC leader Tim Hudak in a 2012 policy paper.[32] Determined to defeat the PCs and unconvinced that the NDP could form government, the Ontario Federation of Labour (OFL), led by former Canadian Union of Public Employees (CUPE) Ontario president Sid Ryan, mounted the well-financed #StopHudak campaign, which asked union members to vote for whichever candidate was best positioned to defeat the PCs at the riding level. The NDP's electoral ambitions had, in effect, driven many unions further into the arms of the Ontario Liberals.[33]

Hobbled out of the gate, Horwath suffered another blow mid-campaign when a group of thirty-four long-time and influential NDP activists complained in an open letter that she was "running to the right of the Liberals in an attempt to win Conservative votes."[34] The activists had a point. Horwath's campaign bizarrely declared that an NDP government would appoint a minister responsible for cutting red tape, irking public-sector union leaders who for years had been fending off attacks from the right over the size of the public sector.[35] With the NDP campaign failing to take off, the Liberals regained the lead over the PCs when Hudak faltered badly after making an ill-advised commitment to cut 100,000 public-sector jobs. The announcement fed directly into the labour movement's portrayal of Hudak as anti-labour, and the issue of job cuts became a focal point of the election. The OFL's #StopHudak campaign was backed by resources to key ridings where unions thought that they could influence the outcome. Given public opinion polls, that meant supporting Liberals in most ridings, although NDP incumbents also enjoyed support.

The 2014 provincial election also saw a sharp increase in the labour movement's use of third-party advertising, largely in response to the urgency of defeating Hudak's overtly anti-union campaign. Of the thirty-seven registered third parties in the 2014 campaign, twenty-six were unions or union centrals. Virtually all the largest unions in Ontario, including Unifor, registered as third parties. Moreover, the union-backed Working Families Coalition was active for its fourth consecutive election campaign. The coalition enjoyed its broadest base of union support yet, gathering contributions from fifty separate unions (up from nineteen in 2011) and spending nearly $2.5 million on anti-PC advertising, with Unifor pitching in $300,000.[36]

On election day, the Liberals secured a majority, capturing 38.7 percent of the vote and fifty-eight seats. The PCs fell to twenty-eight seats and 31.2 percent of the vote. The NDP treaded water, winning twenty-one seats and 23.75 percent of the vote. On election night, Jerry Dias was one of the first people to congratulate Wynne, appearing in person at the Liberal victory party in Toronto. Meanwhile, in Niagara Falls, New Democrat Wayne Gates was re-elected by a convincing margin. He was the only candidate associated with the union to secure election to the provincial legislature.

In the wake of Wynne's victory, Ontario Public Service Employees (OPSEU) president Smokey Thomas charged that union leaders who backed the Liberals had been "played" and had "sold their souls."[37] OPSEU had been one of the few unions to support the NDP's decision to trigger the election over wage freezes and cuts in the Liberal budget. Dias responded with a counterattack against Thomas, defending the decision to promote strategic voting and expressing confidence in the Wynne government's ability to treat public-sector workers fairly. "Frankly, it is because of Unifor and other labour organizations that thousands of OPSEU members still have jobs," Dias shot back in a Unifor press release. "No wonder, so many public service workers have thanked Unifor for our leadership," he added.[38]

Not everyone thanked Unifor for its election efforts. In Windsor West, newly elected NDP MPP Lisa Gretzky narrowly defeated Unifor-backed Liberal Cabinet minister Teresa Piruzza. The contest was further complicated by the fact that Gretzky's husband was a Unifor member. The showdown in Windsor West highlighted some of the contradictions in Unifor's approach to strategic voting. Four weeks before the election, Unifor Local 444 president Dino Chiodo endorsed Piruzza. "To get rid of a cabinet minister at the Liberal level that can do so much about talking about the issues that are important to us so we can potentially have a person that carries no voice and lose the cabinet minister in this riding is absolutely wrong," he explained to a gathering of union retirees.[39] Given that the PCs had historically not been competitive in the riding, backing a Liberal over a competitive New Democrat on the basis of anti-Conservative strategic voting did not make much sense. Instead, Chiodo made a pitch for preserving a voice in Cabinet – the same argument that Lewenza had made to justify supporting Liberals in two-way races with New Democrats in previous campaigns in Windsor and Thunder Bay. In other words, there was more to the union's strategy than stopping Conservatives. The union was also interested in building and preserving relationships with those in positions of power. Nevertheless, the "Anybody but Conservative" frame remained dominant in the union's own political discourse and certainly carried over into the 2015 federal election, which saw Unifor gunning to defeat Stephen Harper's government.

STOP HARPER: THE 2015 FEDERAL ELECTION

In September 2014, federal NDP Official Opposition leader Thomas Mulcair was invited to Vancouver to deliver a speech to Unifor's very first Canadian Council meeting. As part of his address, Mulcair cast the Liberals as fair-weather friends to labour. As a result of his speech, "[Dias's] nose was a little out of joint," recalls Mulcair.[40] Fred Wilson's assessment is that Mulcair came to the council meeting to "score points" on Unifor. He argues that the NDP leader's condemnation of strategic voting was a "colossal mistake" and says that Unifor's "leadership was furious."[41]

It is not too difficult to understand why Unifor's leaders were angry at Mulcair. At the very same gathering, Canadian Council delegates were being asked to approve a policy and discussion paper titled "Politics for Workers: Unifor's Political Project" and a related recommendation from Dias to support strategic voting in the next federal election. The wide-ranging policy and discussion paper acknowledged the labour movement's historic relationship with the NDP but outlined Unifor's differences with the party over electoral strategy:

> Unifor cautioned against provoking elections federally and in Ontario and warned against the consequences of electing the Harper Conservatives and the Hudak Conservatives in Ontario. However the NDP chose instead to risk the interests of labour in a partisan competition with Liberals over incremental gains. This disagreement will continue with the NDP, or any party, if the worst outcome for labour is accepted as the better outcome for the party.[42]

The policy section of the document stated that "Unifor participates in the labour movement's relationship with the NDP, based on the involvement and affiliation of Unifor members who have voluntarily joined the NDP," and that "Unifor's independent relationship with the NDP is based on mutually shared goals but is shaped by our own analysis, policies and strategies which may differ from the party." Consistent with the CEP and CAW approaches that preceded Unifor, the document also committed the union to recognizing "the distinct political relationships of the union in Quebec and the decisions of the Quebec labour movement to develop political tactics for each election, including endorsements of PQ and Bloc Quebecois candidates."[43]

In terms of electoral policy, the union reserved the right to make recommendations to its members in advance of federal and provincial elections and made a commitment to ensure that "any electoral recommendation shall be debated by the appropriate Unifor Council or the National Executive Board." The union further outlined that "electoral recommendations for a party or individual should be specific to a particular election" and that such recommendations would not "tell members who to vote for." Perhaps most significantly, Unifor asserted that the union would be "guided by the ultimate reality that we can never 'contract out' our politics to any other party or structure. Our political goals will only be achieved through the organized strength of the labour movement and by Unifor's own independent analysis and strategic directions."[44] This latter point underscored the independent nature of the union's stated approach.

At the time of Unifor's 2014 Canadian Council meeting, Justin Trudeau's Liberals were leading in public opinion polls, with the NDP trailing in third. Recall also that the union had deferred making a decision about affiliation to the NDP until a year after its founding convention. In Stanford's words, "It turned out to be a nonevent."[45] Members overwhelmingly eschewed affiliation to the NDP in favour of an independent approach to elections. Tim Hudak's defeat in the Ontario provincial election appeared to validate the leadership's preference for an independent approach centred on strategic voting. Delegates thus strongly endorsed Dias's recommendation to pursue strategic voting in order to defeat the Harper Conservatives in 2015. In addition to backing the NDP's ninety-five incumbent members of Parliament (MPs), the union would support individual Liberal, Green, Bloc Québécois (BQ), and New Democrat candidates best positioned to prevent the election or re-election of Conservatives at the riding level.[46] Although Dias openly acknowledged that the labour movement and the NDP were most closely aligned ideologically, he reasoned that in ridings where the party was not competitive, endorsing a New Democrat "doesn't make a stitch of sense."[47]

The news that Unifor would not offer the NDP a full-throated endorsement was disappointing but not altogether surprising for NDP MPs with long-standing ties to the union. Like the CAW before it, Unifor had clearly tied itself to strategic voting as its primary electoral strategy despite the NDP's Official Opposition status. However, Unifor's continued support for strategic voting did cause new tensions within the recently merged union. Citing irreconcilable differences over electoral strategy, Unifor parted ways with the parliamentary staff of the federal NDP caucus in Ottawa, for whom it held bargaining rights.[48] The NDP staffers objected to their union dues being used to help Liberals and other electoral opponents in future election campaigns – a direct threat to their own job security. Dias refused to end the union's commitment to strategic voting, and the NDP's staff opted to become members of the NDP-aligned United Food and Commercial Workers (UFCW) instead. Mulcair recalls, "It was very clear to us that this guy [Dias] was not an ally, but it didn't stop me from trying to work to get the guy on side. I did whatever I could to boost that relationship after, but yeah ... it was unpleasant."[49]

Dias was not the only labour leader to butt heads with Mulcair. According to long-time CLC political action director Danny Mallett, there were also tensions between Mulcair and Hassan Yussuff, a Unifor member who served as secretary-treasurer and then president of the CLC during Mulcair's tenure as NDP leader. In his capacity as CLC secretary-treasurer, Yussuff also served (by tradition) as a vice-president of the federal NDP. Yussuff, however, was not a dyed-in-the-wool New Democrat like some of his predecessors in leadership positions at the CLC.[50] He had supported the CAW's embrace of strategic voting. Moreover, during his time at the CLC, the organization had pursued a less partisan and more lobby-oriented approach to political advocacy – an environment in which he thrived.[51] As a result, his loyalty to the party always seemed to be in question. Preferring not to be identified, one interviewee with intimate knowledge of the party's executive explains, "He would walk in the room, and eyeballs would roll."

Yussuff's presumed partisan allegiances were not the only source of tension. The CLC's participation in NDP caucus meetings also became a point of contention. In an effort to strengthen ties and lines of communication between labour and the party, a representative from the CLC was invited to sit and participate in caucus meetings during Ed Broadbent's tenure as leader.[52] The practice continued for several decades before the CLC lost its voice and was relegated to observer status at caucus meetings during Mulcair's tenure as leader.[53] The move was viewed as a signal that organized labour no longer warranted special status as a key electoral partner. In Mallett's words, the CLC was "frozen out of caucus." In response, the CLC stopped sending a representative altogether.[54]

Thanks to the strong financial and organizational backing of Unifor,[55] Yussuff was elected as CLC president in May 2014. Shortly thereafter, Mulcair met with him and Mallett to debrief the provincial election results in Ontario. Mallett recounts that he and Yussuff took the view that Horwath had to go. However, Mulcair "didn't trust Hassan. He thought he was a Liberal," explains Mallett, adding that Mulcair told Yussuff that he'd need to "prove himself" to demonstrate that he was a true New Democrat.[56] The meeting set the tone for what would prove a very tense relationship between Yussuff and Mulcair. "Mr. Yussuff played a very active role in trying to undermine my leadership," Mulcair explains.[57] Yussuff chooses not to address his relationship with Mulcair directly, but he describes his relationship with Mulcair's predecessor, Jack Layton, as amicable. "The individual leader of a party does make a difference," he explains. "[Layton] wanted to have good relationships with people." When asked about Mulcair's relationship to labour leaders, Peggy Nash remarks, "My observation is Tom really liked credentials. If you were a lawyer, if you had those kinds of credentials, I think he appreciated that because he had credentials. A lot of us who came out of the labour movement didn't have the same credentials."[58] NDP-turned-CLC staffer James Pratt is more blunt: "Tom alienated a bunch of union folks ... He lacked some of that political acumen to make people feel like they were important."[59]

Union leaders, however, could forgive Mulcair for his perceived interpersonal shortcomings if he could deliver a win. Although this outcome seemed unlikely in 2014, the stunning and unexpected election of Rachel Notley's NDP to a majority provincial government in Alberta on May 5, 2015, changed the dynamic overnight. Notley's win gave a boost to federal NDP fortunes as the party climbed into first place in public opinion polls over the summer of 2015. Mulcair entered the 2015 federal campaign as the presumptive front runner, and union leaders began coalescing around his campaign.

During the first half of the campaign, when the NDP was still leading in the polls, Mulcair claims that even Dias reached out and offered to address a party rally in Vancouver on August 9, 2015. However, as Mulcair explains, he declined the offer: "My campaign director, she was adamant that he would not speak, that he was not trustworthy. We would have no way to control what he would say, and it was just too dangerous to have him up on the stage."[60] In retrospect, the NDP had good reason to be apprehensive given how Unifor would figure into the unfolding federal election campaign.

The union and the party soon butted heads publicly over a $15 billion deal with a company in London, Ontario, to supply armoured vehicles to Saudi Arabia. The company employed Unifor members, but the deal raised serious international human rights issues. When Mulcair questioned Harper about the deal during the leaders' debate on September 28, 2015, a staff representative for Unifor, concerned about the potential for job loss, told the media that the union had "asked the NDP to not make this an issue, that it be kept under wraps."[61] London NDP MP Irene Mathyssen was quickly dispatched to mend the party-union rift, insisting that an NDP government would not cancel the contract but would commit to "more transparency."[62] The union issued a tweet indicating that its staff rep "spoke extraordinarily out of turn, damaging our union and putting the NDP in a very bad position."[63]

However, by this point in the campaign, the Liberals had overtaken the NDP in the polls, as the anti-Harper vote had begun to consolidate around Trudeau. Mulcair's principled position in support of a woman's right to wear a niqab at citizenship ceremonies severely damaged the party's fortunes in Quebec, and the party was in free fall.[64] "Once the polls started to show that the Liberals had taken over as the party to beat Harper, we were cooked. It shows that our campaign was a little bit out of sync with the population because we were still holding up signs in the final week of the campaign that said 'stop Harper,'" Mulcair argues.[65] The NDP campaign was also heavily criticized by union activists for being outflanked on the left by Trudeau's Liberals. Mulcair's campaign commitments to pursue tax breaks for small businesses and to balance the budget through public-spending cuts stood in stark contrast to Trudeau's call for public investments and higher taxes for the ultra-wealthy.[66] "I actually remember when Mulcair came out and said that one of his priorities is balancing the budget, it made my head explode," recalls Alberta Federation of Labour president and Unifor member Gil McGowan, who was running for the NDP in Edmonton Centre.[67]

Sensing the changing mood and worried about what impact it might have on the race in Parkdale–High Park, Peggy Nash got in touch with Dias:

> I called him up, and I said, "Jerry, I think I'm in trouble here, and I'd really like some help from the union." And he said, "Well, come on into the board and make the case," which I did. But then somebody came up to me after the board meeting and said, "You know that Justin Trudeau and Gerry Butts [a senior political advisor to Trudeau] were in here yesterday evening, meeting with the board. And so, I think that maybe we're already thinking of going in a different direction."[68]

Unifor and the Quebec Federation of Labour emerged as the strongest proponents of strategic voting in the 2015 federal election.[69] Both organizations asserted that their approaches would be much more targeted than in previous elections by focusing resources in ridings where Conservatives were vulnerable to defeat and where unions claimed a significant number of members. The "Stop Harper" effort was informed by a combination of riding-specific polling and focus groups.[70] Unifor abandoned the CAW's previous tactic of making publicly available its lists of preferred candidates. Instead, the union financed a mass mailing to its 310,000 members with a generic message urging them to vote out the Harper Conservatives using strategic voting.[71] Key to the union's strategy was door-to-door member canvassing where Unifor members talked to their co-workers and other members about the importance of defeating Harper.

However, despite these refinements, the polling data that the union used to select its target ridings proved counterproductive in more than a few cases. For example, two weeks before the election, Unifor was organizing member canvasses in support of NDP candidates in Edmonton Centre, Toronto Centre, and University–Rosedale.[72] By then, the surging Liberals were polling far ahead of the fading NDP campaign in both Alberta and Ontario. On election day in Edmonton Centre, the Liberal candidate edged out the Conservative by just over 2 percent of the vote, and Gil McGowan finished a distant third for the NDP. In this case, Unifor's decision to back one of its own helped to splinter the anti-Conservative vote in a way that almost allowed the Conservatives to retain the seat despite the Liberal surge. In University–Rosedale and Toronto Centre, Liberal candidates cruised to victory, besting their second place NDP rivals by over 20 points in each case. Conservatives were not a factor in either riding and had not held either seat for over twenty years. How these seats became strategic targets for Unifor in its quest to defeat Harper is therefore quite puzzling.

Unifor's concentrated boots-on-the-ground approach appeared to have paid off in the riding of Essex, where Unifor member Tracey Ramsey bucked the trend by growing the NDP vote share and besting a Conservative incumbent. However, Essex was the exception rather than the rule. The 2015 Liberal surge that defeated dozens of Conservative incumbents also managed to wipe out over half of the Unifor-backed NDP incumbents, including former CAW/Unifor members Malcolm Allen in Welland, Peggy Nash in Parkdale–High Park, and long-time MP Peter Stoffer in Sackville–Preston–Chezzetcook.[73] Still, Unifor touted the outcome as a victory.[74]

Six weeks later, Earle McCurdy, former president of the Fishermen, Food and Allied Workers Union/Unifor, led the Newfoundland and Labrador NDP in that province's 2015 provincial election campaign. The party held onto just two seats and lost more than half its vote share from the 2011 campaign. McCurdy himself failed to win a seat in the legislature, finishing a distant second in St. John's West. The result – an overwhelming Liberal majority – was not surprising, he argues. He knew that the provincial party was "going down the drain" when, weeks earlier, popular NDP MP Jack Harris, who had won his St. John's seat in 2011 by a margin of over 22,000 votes, went down to defeat. McCurdy, in part, blames Mulcair's lacklustre performance in the federal election for the disappointing result and credits Justin Trudeau's Liberals for helping to put wind in the sails of the provincial Liberals.[75]

UNIFOR, JUSTIN TRUDEAU, AND THOMAS MULCAIR

In the wake of the 2015 campaign, former CLC president Ken Georgetti blasted Dias and others in the labour movement who backed strategic voting. "With part-time friends and sometime supporters like these, the NDP needs no enemies. Telling NDP members to vote for other parties will never make a solid roadbed we can pave to power," he argued.[76] But

Dias strongly defended his union's approach to the campaign: "As a trade unionist and a progressive, I understand the importance of defeating conservatives. If our labour movement is compromised by legislation, then all workers and our entire country is at risk."[77]

Dias had an ally in Georgetti's successor, Hassan Yussuff. As previously noted, Yussuff owed his election to Unifor and was very much committed to building the independent capacity of the labour movement to act politically. In other words, he did not think that the CLC should rely on the direction of the federal NDP's leader.[78] In the election's aftermath, Yussuff emerged as an outspoken critic of Mulcair and a cautious ally of Trudeau.

On April 10, 2016, delegates at the federal NDP convention in Edmonton voted 52 percent in favour of a leadership race to replace Mulcair. Yussuff was one of Mulcair's harshest critics ahead of the vote, breaking with most other labour leaders, including Dias,[79] who expressed support for the NDP leader to stay on.[80] Despite not having lived up to expectations, Mulcair was fluently bilingual, stood out as leader of the Official Opposition and in parliamentary debates, and had led the party to its second highest seat total ever. Most labour leaders worried that there was no heir apparent waiting in the wings who could have done any better and felt that Mulcair deserved a reprieve and an opportunity to turn things around.[81] Yussuff was unconvinced. "The election was a devastating loss and I don't really understand what (Mulcair) will offer from what I heard so far," Yussuff told the press before the vote. "All I've heard him say is that he takes responsibility for what happened and he never elaborates."[82] Yussuff was not alone among labour leaders opposed to Mulcair's continued leadership. Fellow Unifor member and Alberta Federation of Labour president Gil McGowan and Public Service Alliance of Canada president Robyn Benson also came out against Mulcair at the convention.[83] McGowan explains his support for new leadership as follows:

[Mulcair] snatched defeat out of the jaws of victory ... and he did it by moving to the right, contrary to the values of our party. So I think it was entirely appropriate for people in the labour movement and people in the party more generally to question his leadership and say, "Is this the guy we want us to lead us into the twenty-first century?[84]

It did not help that Mulcair's pitch to delegates was sandwiched between keynote speeches by party heavyweights Rachel Notley and Stephen Lewis. Notley, the only NDP premier, and Lewis, an iconic elder statesman, diminished Mulcair in the eyes of delegates.[85] To make matters worse for Mulcair, both Notley and Lewis offered compelling, yet very different, visions for the party. Mulcair appeared unable to reconcile these diverging visions in his address and thus gave delegates on both the left and right wings of the party a reason to oppose him.[86] Some of his own MPs noted that Mulcair's own presence at the convention was marginal. "People didn't see Tom all weekend," Ontario NDP MP Charlie Angus told the *Globe and Mail*. "By Saturday, people were starting to think he wasn't all that interested … The one person who really needed to be there wasn't."[87]

The eventual result took delegates and political observers by surprise. Although some predicted that Mulcair might secure less than 70 percent support from the convention, which would render his continued leadership untenable, none thought that Mulcair would lose the vote outright. But even after his defeat, Mulcair did not step down immediately, pledging to stay on as leader until a successor could be chosen. This decision to stick around until October 2017 annoyed some members of caucus and labour movement leaders, who complained that the party could not effectively fundraise and dig itself out of debt with a lame duck leader. In September 2016, for example, Dias told *CTV News* that Mulcair should have "stepped down yesterday."[88] Undeterred by the pressure to resign, Mulcair stayed put, even fending off an internal challenge in June 2017 orchestrated by James Pratt, the former NDP operative turned CLC staffer.[89]

The ordeal further complicated the already tense relationship between Mulcair and Yussuff and provided the Liberals with an unprecedented opportunity to build links with the labour movement. "Justin Trudeau's Liberals did an excellent job of realizing that opportunity and the personal rift that was there," says CLC staffer Brent Farrington.[90] By opening the door to the labour movement in unprecedented ways, the Liberals won over important segments of organized labour. For example, Trudeau was the first prime minister in over fifty years to address a CLC meeting[91] and won friends by making good on his commitments to scrap Harper's anti-union Bills C-377 and C-525.[92] In sharp contrast to Harper's Conservatives, who mostly shut unions out of policy-development processes, the Liberals provided labour movement leaders with access to people in power and engaged in meaningful consultation.[93] Unifor was more than willing to play ball with Trudeau, and delegates to the union's August 2016 convention in Ottawa warmly greeted the prime minister with a standing ovation when he appeared as a keynote speaker.[94] Of course, the Liberals did not move on every labour movement priority, leading some left-leaning critics to cast figures like Yussuff and Dias as sell-outs.[95]

Yussuff categorically rejects this characterization of his relationship with the Liberals, dismissing charges that he was too cozy with the government as baseless "chicken-shit politics."[96] Instead, he draws parallels between how unions engage with governments and how unions engage with employers, noting that unions still have to work with them even if they don't like how they're being treated. "They are the government. They are the people who are governing the country and we have to talk to them. We have to build a relationship with them, no different than what we do with an employer," argues Yussuff.[97] Recalling the "ten-year drought under the Harper regime," Yussuff says,

> Affiliates collectively recognized when Harper got defeated and Justin Trudeau got elected as prime minister [that] this was a moment for us to see whether we could cut a different path because there was so much for a decade that either got taken away or was lost because of this nasty political regime. We tried different tactics. Affiliates didn't resist because it yielded results. The Liberals wanted to engage with the labour movement.[98]

According to Yussuff, the CLC's approach delivered several policy victories, including improved pension and collective bargaining legislation, card-based union certification in federally regulated industries, improved pay equity, and the asbestos ban.[99]

When asked to describe Yussuff's political orientation, Mallett refers to him as "more of a Gomperist than anything else ... He's a trade unionist first. Some people are New Democrats first."[100] Yussuff prefers the term "pragmatic" to describe his approach to political action. "It's not a dirty word," he asserts.[101] However, some of his former colleagues have expressed doubt about what a strictly transactional approach to politics could achieve over the long term. Peggy Nash, for example, offers the following view:

> I think that pragmatism is helpful. You can't just say, "Well, I hate Conservatives, I'm never going to deal with a Conservative government." If you have a labour dispute or a health and safety issue or a pension issue, you have to deal with people. So you have to form those relationships. But I think it is a strategic mistake to think that those relationships should determine your vision for where you want to go as a labour movement. You have to have a bigger political vision.[102]

For Nash, this vision includes building a social democratic left – a political project that she contends was undermined by settling for tactical or transactional partnerships with Liberals.[103] NDP critics of strategic voting often complain that settling for Liberals on the basis that they are not Conservatives makes it impossible to build a genuine left-wing political alternative.[104] Farrington contends that Yussuff did hold the federal Liberals "to a much lower standard" than he did the NDP but suggests that the dynamic was more complicated than Yussuff's detractors are prepared to admit: "The same strategy [Yussuff] would apply to the Liberals, he would not apply to the NDP because he held the NDP in a higher regard in terms of what their agenda should be." According to Farrington, Yussuff's view was that "Tom Mulcair should not be a Liberal leader; he should be a New Democrat leader … Tom would be doing a disservice to working people if the head of the political party of working people wasn't fighting for working people."[105] Given the lower bar, the Liberals could easily clear it in the eyes of the labour leadership through modest and progressive policy reforms. Although this double standard drove partisan New Democrats batty, most union leaders appeared content with the policy results.

Interestingly, unlike Lewenza, neither Yussuff nor Dias called for the NDP to merge with the Liberals. When asked by *CTV News*, Dias questioned the viability of such a merger but more importantly argued that the NDP had an essential role to play as a political force in pushing or keeping the Liberals in the progressive lane. Without the NDP, the Liberals would have less pressure to deliver on progressive policies.[106] Dias's influence within the party, however, was clearly in decline. His decision to invite Trudeau to address the Unifor convention, his continued support for strategic voting, and the shocking revelation in November 2016 that he had made a personal donation to Kellie Leitch's Conservative leadership campaign increasingly rendered him an unpredictable and unreliable outsider in NDP and labour movement circles.[107] Yet all of these political machinations were overshadowed by significant challenges on the collective bargaining front.

THE POLITICS OF PRESERVING
JOBS AND GROWING THE UNION

The 2016 round of bargaining with General Motors (GM) was strategically significant because the company's commitment to maintaining at least 16 percent of its production in Canada (a condition of the 2008 government bailout of GM) was set to expire. Rumours swirled that the company intended to wind down production at its Oshawa plant by 2019, prompting the union to commission a study highlighting what the plant closure would mean for the province's economy and local community: a loss of 30,000 jobs and over $5 billion in provincial GDP by 2017.[108]

Because GM would not commit to maintaining operations at its Oshawa facility in the run-up to bargaining, the union launched a campaign called GM Oshawa Matters to pressure the company to preserve production jobs and investments in the city. The campaign involved demonstrations, an online petition, and deputations to politicians.[109] "We bailed out GM, members and retirees were hit hard and we're not gonna stand for it," a union spokesperson told the crowd at a union news conference held in Oshawa to launch the campaign in June 2016.[110] Labour studies researcher Chris Fairweather describes the campaign as "wholly protectionist."[111] Earlier campaigns to save Canadian jobs and investments had seen "the union carefully toe a line, attempting to protect their jobs from foreign competition while framing their Mexican counterparts not as threats but as victims of the same villain," Fairweather says. In contrast, during the GM Oshawa Matters campaign, "the very notion of raising standards in Mexico to protect Canadians from job loss was completely absent from any of the campaign materials."[112]

The union regarded the campaign as a success when it reached a tentative agreement with GM in September 2016. It was later ratified with 64.7 percent support from local union members in Oshawa, St. Catharines, and Woodstock.[113] "I am proud to say today that we have secured a bright future, one that includes good full-time jobs with benefits and wage increases for future generations, and a solid economic base for our communities and all our members," declared Unifor-GM Master Bargaining Committee chair Greg Moffatt of Local 222.[114] In particular, the union touted the additional work that GM agreed to bring to the Oshawa plant as part of the deal. Members, however, were more skeptical. For example, GM retiree Russ Rak, interviewed by local media at the ratification meeting, characterized the deal as "not good" and cast doubt on the ability of the union to enforce any sort of commitment from GM to invest in Oshawa. "Is there concrete language in there to stop GM from changing its mind two years down the road if the truck's not selling?" he asked presciently.[115] The union also faced criticism for agreeing to a concession that allowed GM to switch new hires to a defined-contribution pension plan, creating a two-tier pension structure in the bargaining unit. But Dias defended the decision. "Was it worth it to get new employees the opportunity to get jobs at our wages, at our security level, and give up the [defined-benefit] plan for new starts? The answer is yes," he said.[116]

Not only did the union work hard to preserve jobs, but it also sought to organize new members. After all, one of the primary justifications for creating Unifor was that private-sector union density had reached dangerously low levels and that this trend needed to be reversed in order to re-establish working-class power. Thus the new union invested significant resources in union-certification drives designed to organize the unorganized. But some of Unifor's largest organizing targets, like Toyota and the casinos in Niagara Falls, remained nonunion after several failed certification campaigns. Unifor's most ambitious goal – to become "a union for everyone" – proved even less successful. Its community-chapters program, designed to extend union membership to nonunion workers, never really took off, and five years after its founding, Unifor had only a couple hundred members organized into just two chapters. Arguably, Unifor's community-chapters project was stillborn upon the new union's founding. The rights and responsibilities of such chapters was a major point of contention in merger discussions. Ultimately, community-chapter members were relegated to second-class standing within the new union, without equal democratic rights, because architects of the merger struggled with how to see beyond the traditional model of union citizenship.[117] Over its first decade, Unifor's membership grew by just 3 percent from 305,000 to 315,000. Given the union's ambitious investments and targets in terms of organizing population growth and campaigns, this number should be interpreted as a failure.

Against the backdrop of disappointing progress on the organizing front, Unifor's leadership looked to grow the union through raiding. In February 2017, Unifor ignited a firestorm when it tried to induce members of Local 113 of the Amalgamated Transit Union (ATU), a local representing Toronto Transit Commission workers, to defect and join Unifor. The move raised the ire of ATU members and their US-based parent union, which accused Unifor of colluding with the renegade president of Local 113 to raid the ATU's largest Canadian local. The ATU placed Local 113 under trusteeship, and its president, Bob Kinnear, resigned amid the controversy.[118]

The ATU argued that Dias had been cooking up a secret deal with Kinnear to secure authorization from the CLC for Local 113 members to move to Unifor under Article 4 of the CLC's constitution – the provision that governs disputes between affiliates and provides for a pathway for workers to switch unions. Dias denied the allegations and, in reaction to the trusteeship, convinced CLC president Hassan Yussuff to temporarily suspend Article 4, thus paving the way for ATU members to shift unions. However, Yussuff's move triggered a series of complaints from other CLC affiliates that he was siding with Dias on the basis of their shared membership in Unifor.[119] According to Sam Gindin and Herman Rosenfeld,

> Suspending Article 4 formally allowed Unifor to raid Local 113, but with a trusteeship in place and no signs of serious membership support, a raid was clearly not on. The affiliates' anger reflected a deeper concern: setting a dangerous precedent. Trusteeships are not uncommon in many Canadian unions; in condemning the ATU trusteeship and linking this to suspending protection against raiding, it seemed that raiding in cases of trusteeship was being endorsed. The strong reaction against this promptly led the CLC to reverse its position and reinstate Article 4.[120]

Many unions were unhappy with the way that the CLC handled the situation as the arbiter of disputes between affiliates. Unifor also expressed disappointment with the way that the CLC ultimately applied and interpreted Article 4 of its constitution. Unifor and its predecessor unions had long been critics of international unions and had a history of providing a home for discontented Canadian sections of international unions concerned about their lack of autonomy. Unifor's critics, however, argued that the union's appeals to nationalism and democracy were selectively applied and that they ultimately served to undermine unity and solidarity in the labour movement.[121]

Nearly a year after the ATU debacle, on January 17, 2018, Unifor announced that it was leaving the CLC, effective immediately, after its national executive board unanimously approved the decision a day earlier. The decision sent shockwaves through the labour movement for two important reasons. First, the CLC's president, Hassan Yussuff, was himself a member of Unifor, making for personal political intrigue. Second, Unifor was a major power broker in the CLC, making up roughly 10 percent of the organization's affiliated membership. Its decision to disaffiliate would thus have severe financial repercussions for the broader Canadian labour movement.[122]

On January 18, 2018, the union released a statement indicating that its decision to disaffiliate was related to "the governance of the Canadian Labour Congress and its failure to prevent attacks on workers from their US-based unions."[123] The union pointed specifically to the CLC's application and interpretation of Article 4 of its constitution. Although this very issue had been at the centre of the Unifor-ATU dispute a year earlier, it now returned in relation to the breakaway attempt by UNITE HERE Local 75 in Toronto. A local of the international union representing hotel and hospitality workers across North America, Local 75's leadership was working to leave UNITE HERE and join Unifor. Because this attempt to shift members from one union to another would no doubt be frustrated by Article 4 of the CLC's constitution, Unifor's leadership disaffiliated in order to allow the union to raid UNITE HERE without fear of reprisal or sanction from the CLC. Nevertheless, the overwhelming majority of hotel workers targeted by Unifor opted to remain members of UNITE HERE.[124] Unifor's decision to leave the CLC "was very painful for me on a personal level," recounts Yussuff. "I think the split was really a fundamental disagreement about how workers can leave their union when they're part of an international union," he argues. It had nothing to do, he asserts, with political direction.[125] This is a reasonable take given that Yussuff and Dias were quite aligned on questions of political action and advocacy. However, organizational tensions always carry with them political dimensions, and the CLC's lingering partisan ties to the NDP, reconfirmed at the 2021 CLC convention, were clearly at odds with both Yussuff's own views and Unifor's new direction.[126]

DOUG FORD AND THE 2018 ONTARIO ELECTION

With Ontario facing another provincial election in 2018, political divisions between unions were once again front and centre at the OFL's November 2017 convention in Toronto. Delegates narrowly endorsed an amendment to the OFL's Action Plan committing the OFL to mobilize 1 million union members in support of the Ontario NDP in advance of the election.[127] Unifor leaders spearheaded an unsuccessful attempt to defeat the amendment with the support of the Ontario English Catholic Teachers' Association and the Ontario Secondary School Teachers' Federation.[128] Delegates from these unions framed their opposition to the amendment around the uncertain implications of new campaign finance legislation banning corporate and union donations. However, it was lost on no one that these same unions were among the strongest proponents of strategic voting. It was also no surprise when these unions geared up to pursue strategic-voting campaigns independent of the OFL's Action Plan. However, over the next seven months, the political dynamic complicated matters for strategic-voting unions. The Liberals sagged in the polls, and the NDP gained momentum thanks, in part, to a solid performance by NDP leader Andrea Horwath in the first of three leaders' debates.[129]

Eclipsed in the polls by a rejuvenated NDP, the Wynne Liberals conceded defeat mid-campaign and turned their sights on Horwath, warning of endless strikes and a government controlled by union leaders.[130] This move destroyed any remaining goodwill between the Liberals and the labour movement. Even the strategic-voting unions completely abandoned the Liberals and backed the NDP.[131] But combined attacks from the Liberals and

PCs halted the NDP's growing popularity, and Doug Ford's Conservatives cruised to victory on election day. The Tories won seventy-six seats and 40.5 percent of the vote. The NDP formed the Official Opposition, winning forty seats and 33.6 percent of the vote. And the Liberals held onto just seven seats and 19.6 percent of the vote, losing official party status in the process. NDP MPP Wayne Gates, re-elected in Niagara Falls, was the only Unifor member who secured a seat, although Unifor staffer Niki Lundquist placed a respectable second place running as a New Democrat in Whitby.[132]

The province's labour movement feared the worst from Ford, who was purposely tight-lipped during the campaign about what his party would do in government. The Tories wasted no time cancelling a scheduled minimum-wage increase and repealing the two permanent paid sick days introduced by the Wynne government. Ontario's labour movement was clearly much weaker than it had been during the years of Mike Harris. Disappointing turnouts at anti-government demonstrations underlined this point, and lingering internal divisions did not help. Unifor's disinterest in mending fences with the CLC and the OFL further complicated the movement's fightback strategy. This disunity in the labour movement would later be exploited by the Ford government to pursue a divide and conquer strategy on the labour relations front.[133]

THE GM OSHAWA PLANT CLOSURE AND THE 2019 FEDERAL ELECTION

With the PCs back in power in Ontario and Unifor cutting ties to both the CLC and the OFL, the union had withdrawn from the labour movement at a time when it could ill afford to be isolated. This became apparent in the wake of GM's November 2018 announcement that it would close its Oshawa assembly plant by the end of 2019.[134] The union stood to lose thousands of members in one fell swoop. In protest, Unifor Local 222 orchestrated walkouts and sit-ins, and on January 23, 2019, it erected a barricade of the GM Canada headquarters in Oshawa to pressure the company to reverse the decision.[135] The blockade ended two days later, but Unifor announced a boycott of Mexican-made GM vehicles. Dias declared, "GM is making a choice to increase manufacturing in Mexico while it abandons communities that have supported it for generations, but make no mistake Canadian and American consumers also have a choice."[136] According to Scott Aquanno and Toba Bryant, the union's predicament was the product of a gradual shift away from working-class militancy and social unionism. They argue that "the union attempted to manage competitive pressures and got caught in the political dead end of embracing corporate investment goals."[137] They go on to argue that, like the union's embrace of competitiveness strategies, its associated drift toward "business unionism stands out less because it dramatically extended concessions and failed to save the plant, but rather because it fragmented and demoralized workers, combined their interests with those of General Motors, and taught them that fighting for an alternative future was futile."[138]

When the Oshawa closure was announced, Doug Ford accused Dias of selling "false hope" that he could successfully keep the plant open – a barb that ignited a war of words between the premier and Unifor's president, culminating in Dias telling Ford "F*** you" in a televised speech to autoworkers on December 1, 2018.[139] While battling it out with Premier Ford, Dias drew closer to Trudeau's Liberals. In August 2019, Unifor featured Trudeau and Foreign Affairs Minister Chrystia Freeland as speakers at the union's national convention in Quebec City. "The labour movement deserves fairness, not a government that sees it as an enemy," Trudeau told delegates in a speech designed to consolidate support for his party through opposition to new Conservative leader Andrew Scheer.[140] Freeland used her speech to trumpet Dias's role in the renegotiation of the North American Free Trade Agreement in 2019. "When it comes to defending workers' rights and supporting the middle class, one thing is certain. No political force is more essential or more effective than strong unions," Freeland told delegates.[141]

When asked by the media about Unifor's approach to the pending federal election, Dias said, "I lived, and we lived, 10 years of Harper. We've now lived over a year of Doug Ford. Our politics as a union are pretty straightforward. It's anybody but Conservative. We will support any politician in any riding who's best positioned to defeat a Conservative."[142] Dias also argued that the Liberal Party's ideological composition had shifted, making it a far more palatable option for the union movement:

When I was growing up, you had the Conservatives as the far-right party. You had the Liberals which were the small-c conservative party.

And then you had the New Democrats. If you take a look at the Kathleen Wynne government or the Trudeau government, I think it's clear these Liberals are much different than the Liberals of old. The Liberals have tacked more centre-left. I think Kathleen Wynne was one of the most progressive leaders we've ever had in this country. I take a look at the last federal campaign, where Tom Mulcair ran on a platform of balanced budgets. That's taken right out of the Conservative playbook. That's why I don't have any blind loyalty.[143]

This position did not mean that New Democrats would not receive any support from Unifor. As in the past, the union supported NDP incumbents and NDP candidates considered best positioned to knock off Conservatives. In Quebec, the union mounted an anti-Scheer ad campaign, warning voters that he would govern even further to the right than unpopular Conservative governments in Ontario and Alberta.[144] The union endorsed at least one BQ candidate and a dozen NDP incumbents, but only one New Democrat, Alexandre Boulerice in Rosemont–La Petite-Patrie, managed to hold onto a seat.[145] By recapturing a dozen ridings previously held by the NDP, the BQ regained official party status and overtook the NDP as the third largest party in the House of Commons.

In a way, Unifor's strategic support for select New Democrat candidates across Canada was undermined by Dias's vocal opposition to the party's position on oil pipelines. "I've got a lot of time for the NDP. But I also have concerns. I have members that work in Fort McMurray in the oilsands. I have members that build pipelines. I'm a pipeline guy. So many of my members will disagree with the position the NDP has taken on oil and energy," Dias told *CBC News.*[146] In contrast, although he acknowledged that his union did not agree with the prime minister on everything, Dias heaped praise on the Trudeau government for its reversal of the Harper government's anti-union reforms and for its proposed changes to Old Age Security eligibility. He also credited the government for being open to meet, discuss, and consult with unions on a wide variety of issues, including trade.[147] In this way, like Yussuff at the CLC, Dias used different standards to judge NDP and Liberal commitments to the union's priorities.

Unifor's endorsement of at least one Liberal incumbent, in a Nova Scotia riding where the Conservatives were not competitive but where New

Democrats had a credible shot at winning, raised eyebrows in union circles. In Halifax, in a riding that the Conservatives had not won since 1984, Unifor backed rookie Liberal MP Andy Fillmore over NDP challenger and Unifor Local 567 member Christine Saulnier, director of the Canadian Centre for Policy Alternatives in Nova Scotia.[148] In the 2015 election, the Conservative candidate in Halifax placed a distant third, with just 8.6 percent of the popular vote. The NDP, in contrast, had held the seat between 1997 and 2015 and had secured 36.1 percent of the popular vote in the previous election. Even though the Liberal incumbent had voted against a bill to ban scab labour in 2016 and in favour of back-to-work legislation for striking members of the Canadian Union of Postal Workers in 2018, Unifor broke ranks with the rest of the labour movement and endorsed Fillmore over his NDP challenger.[149] It is unclear whether the federal Liberal government's pre-election blitz of spending announcements played a role in the union's decision. Although Fillmore denied that his government's spending announcements were politically motivated, they included a $500 million contract for the Irving Shipyard, where Unifor represents workers.[150] On election day, Fillmore was re-elected, finishing 12 points ahead of his NDP rival. The Conservative candidate placed fourth, garnering 11.6 percent of the popular vote.

Similarly, in Windsor–Tecumseh, a riding that the New Democrats had held since 2000, Unifor declined to endorse NDP incumbent Cheryl Hardcastle. Instead, Dave Cassidy, the president of Unifor Local 444, sang the praises of Hardcastle's Liberal challenger Irek Kusmierczyk in the union's newsletter.[151] Hardcastle lost to Kusmierczyk by just over 600 votes. Recall, it was not the first time that the local had snubbed a Windsor New Democrat in a two-way race between the Liberals and the NDP. These actions in Windsor and Halifax provided more evidence that there was more at play in the union's electoral strategy than strict anti-Conservative strategic voting. In these cases, Unifor was apparently looking to strengthen ties to the governing party by using the cover of anti-Conservative strategic voting to deflect criticism for what might otherwise be viewed as a crass attempt to buy political access and influence.

In the end, the Liberals held onto government but were reduced to a minority, losing seats to both the Conservatives (who actually won the popular vote) and the BQ. The NDP held onto just twenty-four seats and fell to fourth place, securing 16 percent of the vote. In a press release, Unifor touted its role in the election outcome, claiming to have defeated Conservatives in 72 percent of the sixty-nine ridings that it had targeted. The union, however, never released a list that could be independently verified.[152] Although the Conservatives had been defeated, a much bigger threat to the union was just around the corner.

THE POLITICS OF THE COVID-19 PANDEMIC

The rapid spread of COVID-19 in Canada, which began in early 2020 and had led to shutdowns of economic and social activity by mid-March of that year, resulted in thousands of workers losing their jobs. The unemployment rate more than doubled in a matter of months, from 5.6 percent in February 2020 to 13.7 percent in May 2020.[153] Physical-distancing requirements and restrictions on indoor events meant that workplaces in many sectors were forced to close. Travel restrictions designed to interrupt the virus's spread had an immediate and devastating impact on transportation and hospitality workers represented by Unifor.[154] But the pandemic also offered the union a silver lining: GM announced in November 2020 that it would reopen the Oshawa facility.[155] This strategic corporate decision was made in part because the company needed to expand its production capacity in Canada due to pandemic-related shortages in the United States.[156] "The pandemic has thrown a curve into the auto industry, so they are looking for opportunities to maximize the capacity," explained Dias.[157] However, the union also credited its long-wrapped-up Save Oshawa GM campaign for the decision.[158] Critics inside the union refuted this interpretation and pointed out that GM was making no long-term commitment to Oshawa, casting doubt on Dias's claim that GM's announcement constituted a "home run."[159] "In effect, GM will open a brand new plant inside the shell of the old plant – with an almost entirely new workforce, an inferior wage scale, fewer benefits, and no job security," argued Local 222 members Tony Leah and Rebecca Keetch.[160]

In a political twist, the ongoing economic insecurity felt by autoworkers in Oshawa was finally being acknowledged and seemingly taken seriously by a federal Conservative politician. Oshawa-area MP Erin O'Toole won the leadership of the federal Conservative Party in September 2020 and immediately grabbed headlines by taking aim at "corporate and financial power brokers" and at "bad trade deals" for Canada's ailing manufacturing sector.[161] After having run as a "True Blue" candidate during the Conservative leadership campaign, O'Toole pivoted almost immediately upon becoming leader, making overt efforts to appeal to segments of the labour movement and to the blue-collar working class more generally.[162]

However, O'Toole's overt efforts to win over union and working-class voters did not resonate with the union leadership.[163] Dias and other union leaders had been granted unprecedented access to the Trudeau government. With the pandemic, they saw an opening to push the Liberals even further left and focused most of their energy on working with a government with whom they had grown comfortable. NDP activists in the labour movement argued that Yussuff and Dias had become too close to the Liberals,[164] but this partisan lens overlooked the fact that these union leaders were also working closely with British Columbia's NDP government. In other words, their allegiance was not to a particular party but to those in positions of power with a sympathetic ear. This political approach had become dominant at Unifor.

Nevertheless, Yussuff was widely considered a fixer for the Trudeau government, working behind the scenes to help resolve public-sector labour disputes.[165] He is "a political operator. He is one of the smartest people I've ever seen on the Hill, and I've seen a lot of people on the Hill. He is excellent at building relationships and maintaining those relationships and peddling influence through them," argues Brent Farrington, who credits Yussuff and the CLC with successfully securing Canada Emergency Response Benefit funding and a bailout for municipalities from the Liberals in the early days of the COVID-19 pandemic.[166] Labour studies scholar Adam D.K. King views these relationships and outcomes differently, arguing that Yussuff's "cozy" partnership with the Liberals and business leaders during the pandemic was counterproductive for working people and arguably undermined the independent "organization and development of working-class power."[167] According to James Pratt, Yussuff eventually overplayed his hand by endorsing Trudeau's finance minister, Bill Morneau, for secretary-general of the Organisation for Economic Co-operation and Development (OECD) without the approval of the CLC's Canadian Council. He explains,

> I got my ass kicked coast to coast to coast over this ... not just because he hadn't consulted but because of who Bill Morneau is. You know,

to say that Bill Morneau is a friend to working people is garbage. But I do believe that Hassan saw an opportunity to further ingratiate himself with the government of the day.[168]

CLC affiliates complained that Yussuff had acted unilaterally in endorsing Morneau's candidacy, and in a stunning rebuke, the CLC executive met in December 2020 to rescind the endorsement.[169] Morneau later withdrew his candidacy to lead the OECD, and Yussuff announced that he would not seek re-election as CLC president.[170]

Some CLC affiliates saw Yussuff's departure as an opportunity to officially reassert the organization's support for the NDP. The debate over the party-union relationship at the June 2021 CLC convention took an unexpected turn when Lionel Railton, the Canadian regional director for the International Union of Operating Engineers, questioned whether an endorsement of the NDP was congruent with the CLC's constitution, which states that the CLC shall not be beholden to any political party or organization. The intervention was odd given that the CLC had been a founding partner of the NDP and had regularly endorsed the party for decades. Shockingly, Yussuff intervened in support of Railton's position, arguing that the CLC should not endorse the party because that would contravene the CLC's constitution. "I found it not only bizarre, but it was almost like it was orchestrated," says former CLC staffer Michael MacIsaac.[171] After all, Yussuff had served as a CLC officer for years and had even filled the role of vice-president of the federal NDP by virtue of his position at the CLC. Why raise the constitutional validity of an endorsement now, right before Yussuff's retirement? In the end, delegates did not heed Yussuff's warnings and followed through with the NDP endorsement by a vote of 1,491 to 1,098.[172]

Shortly after the CLC convention wrapped up, Trudeau announced Yussuff's appointment to the Senate as an Independent senator. Yussuff's detractors held up the appointment as proof that he had used his position at the CLC for personal gain. But this view was not universal. Former CLC chief economist Andrew Jackson, for example, argues, "I don't think [Yussuff] woke up one day and wanted to become a Liberal senator ... He thought you could make gains for the labour movement on our agenda by working the backrooms."[173] In this way, Yussuff was a quintessential pragmatist, building relationships to extract whatever gains he could from whomever he could. The Liberals, however, clearly saw him as an asset, and his appointment to the Senate likely reflected a broader strategy to carve into the NDP vote and to bring unions into the Liberal tent.

Since the turn of the century, the federal Liberals have recruited more than a handful of federal and provincial New Democrats to run as Liberals. For example, former NDP provincial premiers Bob Rae and Ujjal Dosanjh were recruited to run for the federal Liberals in 2008 and 2004 respectively. Both secured seats, with Dosanjh serving as a Liberal Cabinet minister and Rae serving as interim federal Liberal leader in the transition from Michael Ignatieff to Justin Trudeau. Former Manitoba NDP Cabinet minister MaryAnn Mihychuk ran and secured election as a Liberal in the 2015 federal election and was later appointed as minister of employment, workforce and labour. Former Nova Scotia NDP member of the Legislative Assembly Lenore Zann won a seat for the federal Liberals in 2019. Rookie NDP MP Lise St-Denis crossed the floor to join the federal Liberal caucus in 2012. Former three-term Saskatchewan NDP MP Chris Axworthy ran unsuccessfully as a Liberal in the 2004 and 2006 federal elections. Former Saskatchewan NDP Cabinet minister Joan Beatty ran unsuccessfully for the Liberals in a 2008 by-election. More recently, former NDP MP Rathika Sitsabaiesan unsuccessfully contested the Ontario Liberal Party nomination for a 2016 by-election in Scarborough–Rouge River, and Sudbury NDP MP Glenn Thibeault resigned his seat and went on to win the provincial riding of Sudbury as a Liberal candidate in a 2015 by-election. The list of federal and provincial Liberals subsequently running for the NDP is considerably shorter. NDP defections to the Liberals helped contribute to the sense that the two parties were becoming indistinguishable. "The line between the Liberals and the NDP became increasingly blurred in Ontario and federally as the Liberals moved somewhat left and the NDP became more 'moderate,'" argues Jackson.[174] This dynamic would complicate things for the NDP heading into the 2021 federal election.

TRUDEAU HOLDS ON TO A MINORITY GOVERNMENT: THE 2021 FEDERAL ELECTION

With a significant lead in public opinion polls, the Trudeau Liberals triggered an election for September 20, 2021. Incumbent premiers had performed very well in pandemic elections, and the Liberals saw their opportunity to regain a majority. However, Trudeau's decision was very unpopular, and the opposition parties pounced on the prime minister for his perceived political opportunism. The Liberal Party's standing in the polls took a hit, and O'Toole's Conservatives took the lead mid-campaign.

O'Toole positioned himself as a moderate in the run-up to the campaign and made several overtures to win over union and working-class votes. In a speech to the Canadian Club in October 2020, he made a case for unions, arguing that a high level of private-sector union density "was an essential part of the balance between what was good for business and what was good for employees. Today, that balance is dangerously disappearing. Too much power is in the hands of a few corporate and financial elites who have been only too happy to outsource jobs abroad."[175] These remarks, uncharacteristic of a Conservative leader, prompted *Globe and Mail* columnist Robyn Urback to joke that O'Toole sounded as though he was running in the 1989 NDP leadership race.[176] The Conservative strategy was designed to appeal to workers experiencing real economic insecurity, often as a result of economic restructuring, who did not see their material concerns being taken up concretely by other parties.[177] O'Toole doubled down on this strategy with his announcement during the 2021 federal election campaign that a Conservative government would require all federally regulated corporations with over 1,000 employees or $100 million in annual revenue to include worker representation on their boards of directors.[178]

The Liberals rallied, however, when Trudeau attacked O'Toole over his refusal to support compulsory vaccinations for federal public servants and travellers. The polarizing issue swayed the overwhelmingly pro-vaccine electorate back to the Liberals, and the party managed to keep its minority government with no real change in party standings. As in 2019, the Conservatives won the popular vote but lost the election.

Unifor had pumped millions into third-party ads attacking O'Toole.[179] This effort primarily benefited the governing Liberals, with whom the union worked closely on a range of issues related to pandemic supports and recovery. Unifor claimed electoral success in 75 percent of its unnamed "battleground ridings."[180] A union communication indicated that "member organizers knocked on 25,210 doors and connected directly with 3,549 members either on the phone or face-to-face. On the day before Election

Day, a small group of organizers and volunteers pulled off an extensive get-out-the-vote campaign by texting 22,917 members in 77 ridings across the country."[181] The union referred to its member-to-member campaign as "non-partisan" despite the fact that Unifor endorsed a number of Liberal and NDP candidates and spent millions warning its members and the broader public not to vote Conservative.[182] According to Unifor, it organized member canvasses in eighteen ridings across the country,[183] and its preferred candidate was successful in two-thirds of them. Curiously, the union organized canvasses in ridings like Hamilton Mountain, St. John's East, and Winnipeg Centre, where Conservatives posed no credible threat in what were Liberal-NDP races.[184] In half of the eighteen ridings targeted for member canvasses, the union backed Liberal candidates, and in the other half, it backed New Democrats. With the exception of King–Vaughan, Liberals prevailed in each riding where the union had organized a member canvas in support of the local Liberal candidate. Unifor-backed NDP candidates did not fare as well, winning just four contests. Counterintuitively, Liberals managed to defeat Unifor-endorsed NDP candidates in the NDP-held targeted ridings of Hamilton Mountain and St. John's East. Former NDP MPs Tracey Ramsey and Malcolm Allen were among the Unifor-backed candidates associated with the union who went down to defeat.

In Quebec, the campaign took on a different tone because of a shifting political landscape. Although the BQ had managed an impressive comeback in 2019, the province's labour movement was uncomfortable with how the party had reoriented itself as an ally of Premier François Legault's right-wing Coalition avenir Québec government.[185] Unifor's Quebec director, Renaud Gagné, reported in November 2021 that the union's efforts consisted of encouraging *all* parties to take up the priorities outlined in Unifor's Build Back Better Covid-19 recovery plan.[186] Although Unifor's Quebec section did not appear to formally endorse any candidates during the campaign, an official from the union spoke at a campaign stop in Saguenay region, appearing alongside BQ leader Yves-François Blanchet.[187] The Bloc's seat count of thirty-two did not change between 2019 and 2021.

The Liberals won 160 seats across Canada, an increase of five over their 2019 result. The NDP, meanwhile, increased its seat total from twenty-four to twenty-five. This result handed the party and its new leader, former Ontario NDP MPP Jagmeet Singh, the balance of power in the minority

Parliament. On September 22, 2021, Dias wrote to both Trudeau and Singh seeking a joint meeting to figure out a way for both parties to work together and to deliver on progressive policy initiatives.[188] The joint meeting never took place, but the Liberals and the New Democrats signed a confidence-and-supply agreement on March 22, 2022, that would keep the minority Trudeau government in power in exchange for a commitment to prioritize, among other things, the introduction of a national pharmacare program, ten permanent paid sick days for workers in federally regulated industries, and anti-scab legislation – a long-standing legislative priority for Unifor.[189] However, as discussed in the next chapter, the news of the confidence-and-supply agreement was overshadowed by an unfolding scandal that would rock the union for months to come.

CONCLUSION

In his book reflecting on Unifor's first five years, Fred Wilson argues that Unifor was conceived as a change agent and that it had managed to shake up the labour movement and to force power holders to take notice. Our assessment is more mixed. Organizationally, the CAW-CEP merger was heralded by its architects as an opportunity to build an entirely new union. But even with a new structure, the merger that created Unifor appeared to gradually displace the CEP's internal culture, thus allowing the CAW's top-down, leader-focused culture to win out. Nevertheless, Unifor's executive structure did break new ground in terms of equity. On the organizing front, despite the significant commitment made at Unifor's founding convention to dedicate resources to organizing new workers, the creation of Unifor has neither significantly boosted new membership nor reversed the decline in private-sector union density. The new union's controversial raiding efforts were arguably even less successful, if not counterproductive.

On the political front, Wilson boldly claims, "Unifor, and the labour politics it unleashed, was a material factor in defeating labour's worst political adversaries in critical provincial and federal elections, and it established a political influence for Canadian labour unseen in recent history."[190] Although the Harper government went down to defeat in 2015, Unifor's role in delivering this outcome is difficult to measure. At the provincial level, the electoral ledger swung strongly toward Conservative parties during Unifor's first decade despite the union's sustained support for anti-Conservative strategic voting. In the years that followed, the union's electoral interventions morphed beyond strict anti-Conservative strategic voting, as they had during the later CAW years, by taking on more transactional dimensions that were designed to develop stronger ties to influential Liberal politicians. Although this approach seemingly ensured that Dias had the ear of key provincial and federal politicians, just how much influence he had is unclear given Unifor's mixed record of legislative victories.

CHAPTER 7

HEAD-ON COLLISION
The Fall of Jerry Dias and the Future of Unifor

Jerry Dias's leadership of Unifor was unquestionably controversial. As president, he did not hesitate to forge his own path. Dias put his stamp on the union both at the bargaining table and in the political arena, often in ways that raised the ire of the broader labour movement. His power and influence, however, evaporated in the wake of a kickback scandal that prompted his early retirement and a police investigation. The unfolding scandal plunged Unifor into a deep crisis that was further complicated by tensions related to leadership succession. The subsequent campaign for the union's presidency exposed deep divisions within Unifor, and the August 2022 convention turned into a referendum of sorts on Dias and his legacy.

CONTROVERSY AND SCANDAL ROCK UNIFOR

Jerry Dias's decision to speak and stand alongside Ontario premier Doug Ford at a November 2021 press conference to announce an increase in the provincial minimum wage proved incredibly controversial.[1] After all, this was the same Progressive Conservative (PC) premier who had previously scrapped a scheduled minimum-wage increase, eliminated paid sick days, and capped the wages of health care and other public-sector workers. Just a few years earlier, Dias had told Ford "F*** you" over the General Motors (GM) Oshawa closure and had mobilized Unifor members to defeat him in the 2018 election.[2] Nevertheless, Dias was unrepentant about appearing alongside the premier, telling the *Toronto Star* that he didn't "give a rat's a–" what his critics thought. However, many union activists were uncomfortable with what he had done.[3] "I would say there was discomfort, not just outside of Unifor, but inside of it," admits his eventual successor, Lana Payne.[4] "I think it was an excessive form of pragmatism," explains Fred Wilson, Unifor's former director of strategic planning. "It certainly did not meet the standard, in my opinion, of our political policy, which calls on the leadership to keep in mind not just short-term issues but also more long-range political goals," he says.[5] "For the life of me, I don't know what Jerry was trying to accomplish," says former Canadian Auto Workers (CAW) president Buzz Hargrove, who himself had played a key role in redefining the boundaries of political action within the union. When Dias "stood next to the premier and complimented him on bringing back some of the things ... he took away from the labour movement, that showed me that he's closer to the Tories than the NDP [New Democratic Party]," he adds.[6] Former CAW president Ken Lewenza is equally frank: "I don't think Ford deserved our presence ... For us to stand behind Ford, I think that was a strategic mistake by both Jerry and Smokey [Thomas]," president of the Ontario Public Service Employees Union (OPSEU). Recalling a conversation with Dias after the press conference, Lewenza conveys that "Jerry felt obligated in the sense that 'How can I tell them to go to hell when, in fact, he did what we asked him to do?'"[7] Others are more harsh in their assessment. "Whatever happened to ABC?" asks former NDP member of Parliament (MP) and CAW activist Malcolm Allen – in reference to the "Anybody But Conservative" strategy that Dias had long championed. "To see [Dias] stand beside a Conservative premier, who is no friend of workers ... he gave credibility to a guy who doesn't deserve any ... It was crass politics at its zenith."[8] Shortly after Allen's interview for this book, Ford appointed Dias to head the province's auto task force in December 2021.[9]

Dias's political dalliance with Ford proved short-lived when his legacy as Unifor's first president began to implode in the face of a serious internal complaint against him. On January 26, 2022, one of Dias's assistants, Chris MacDonald, filed a complaint alleging that Dias had inappropriately accepted $50,000 from a supplier of COVID-19 rapid test kits. Dias had been promoting the use of the kits among employers of Unifor members in December 2021 and January 2022. On January 20, 2022, Dias gave half the money to

MacDonald, who lodged the complaint with the union's secretary-treasurer, Lana Payne, a few days later. Upon receiving the complaint, Payne commissioned an independent investigator, Catherine Milne of Turnpenney Milne LLP, to investigate the matter under Article 4 of the union's constitution, which provides for enforcement of the Unifor Code of Ethics.[10] This move required that Dias be informed of a complaint being lodged against him. Almost immediately after MacDonald and Dias were notified of the investigation on January 29, 2022, MacDonald "received calls and text messages from Dias [and] then texts and calls from [Dias's other assistant, Scott] Doherty, which he did not answer. Those messages asked MacDonald to call Doherty immediately."[11] MacDonald would not answer, and he texted Doherty only to tell him that he could not talk about it. Doherty also called MacDonald's wife in an attempt to reach him and showed up at his father-in-law's residence.[12]

Meanwhile, as this storm was brewing, Dias recommended that Doherty receive the support of the National Executive Board (NEB) to be his successor as national president. The NEB voted unanimously to endorse Doherty on February 1, 2022.[13] However, two members of the NEB were conspicuously absent: Lana Payne and Ontario regional director Naureen Rizvi. Unbeknownst to most NEB members, Payne had recently received the complaint from MacDonald, and Rizvi had accompanied MacDonald to his meeting with Payne. Although Dias knew that he was facing an investigation, he proceeded with the endorsement process anyway despite repeated attempts to dissuade him from doing so.[14]

Dias was asked to participate in the investigation but declined. He went on medical leave on February 6, 2022, and on March 11 notified the NEB of his immediate retirement. The union made public Dias's retirement on March 13 and a day later confirmed that he was under investigation.[15]

On March 23, 2022, the union announced at a press conference that Dias was charged with contravening Article 4 of the constitution. The independent investigator had determined that Dias breached his obligations to the union by accepting money from an unnamed third-party supplier of COVID-19 rapid test kits.[16] The charges were announced after someone from within the union leaked an email to the *Globe and Mail,* forcing the union to issue a public statement.[17]

The source of the complaint against Dias was initially kept confidential, but Chris MacDonald was quickly revealed as the whistleblower. Media pointed out that MacDonald had been passed over to succeed Dias as president in favour of Scott Doherty.[18] As reported by the *Toronto Star*, a leaked psychiatric assessment of Dias revealed that he "was under 'significant stress' after being forced to choose between two 'close friends' to endorse as his successor, [and] was consuming heavy amounts of drugs and alcohol when he allegedly took $50,000 from a COVID-19 rapid test supplier that he promoted to Unifor employers."[19] Dias also reportedly entered a rehabilitation facility to deal with substance abuse issues.[20] The *Globe and Mail* later revealed that Doherty was interviewed as part of the investigation into Dias because, in the days after MacDonald received the $25,000, Doherty "called and visited Mr. MacDonald multiple times about the interaction with Mr. Dias."[21] The investigator also found that Dias completely ignored instructions not to contact MacDonald and that both Dias and Doherty had pressured MacDonald to drop the complaint. Doherty had deleted his text messages, but MacDonald's records disclosure to the investigator contained plenty of evidence that he was being pressured, including memes about loyalty sent to him by both Dias and Doherty.[22] Unifor handed over the money to Toronto Police, and on April 5, 2022, a police spokesperson confirmed that its financial crimes unit was investigating Dias.[23]

These events set in motion an unprecedented political shake-up in the union, leading to a lengthy and competitive election campaign for national president. A week later, Payne announced that she would be seeking the presidency of Unifor.[24] Her entry into the race prompted Doherty to preemptively ask the NEB to withdraw its endorsement of his candidacy. According to media reports, he wanted to avoid "undue strain" on NEB members who wished to back Payne.[25] The election campaign was a three-way race between Payne, Doherty, and Local 444 president Dave Cassidy, a long-time member of the NEB and national chair of the union's Skilled Trades Council, who publicly declared his intention to run in February 2022 after the NEB had endorsed Doherty.[26]

Cassidy mounted a populist campaign aimed at delivering decision-making power to rank-and-file members and to reorienting the priorities of the national union to focus on bread-and-butter issues. His campaign website read,

He understands that political and social involvement are essential but that it must never come before the MEMBERS, their JOBS and JOB

SECURITY. The Union does not need to participate, debate or casually throw money at ideas that will not benefit our members, their jobs or enhance job security. We must stay in our lane and refocus our time and energy on what is the main thing ... our members.[27]

Cassidy had a reputation inside the union as a bit of an iconoclast, having run against and defeated Administration caucus candidates in Local 444 not once but twice during his union career.[28]

In addition to having served as an assistant to Dias, Scott Doherty was a former national representative, a former local president in the Communications, Energy and Paperworkers Union (CEP), and a CAW member from British Columbia. Because he was Dias's preferred successor, the scandal rubbed off on his campaign. Once Payne entered the race, Doherty shifted gears to champion a host of reforms and priorities designed to frame himself as a change agent. He touted his bargaining experience, and his platform included commitments to lead on equity, to ensure a just transition, and to reform reporting structures in order "to address concerns and perceptions about concentration of power in the National President's Office."[29] Whereas Cassidy was viewed as a long shot, Doherty was considered a real contender going into the convention, even if his candidacy was no longer the juggernaut that it had once been.

His main challenge would come from Lana Payne, the union's secretary-treasurer, who had previously served as both Atlantic regional director of Unifor and president of the Newfoundland and Labrador Federation of Labour. She joined the union in 1991 via a staff position with the Fishermen, Food and Allied Workers Union/CAW. As the face of the union during the investigation that led to Dias's resignation, Payne positioned herself as a principled leader with integrity who was uniquely capable of navigating a crisis and rebuilding trust.[30]

A UNION DIVIDED

Payne's candidacy emerged out of the turmoil of an internally divided union leadership confronted with a damning investigator's report and a looming crisis of legitimacy. At the NEB meetings on March 21, 2022, where members received details of the complaint and the investigator's report, the sense of anger, fear, and betrayal was palpable. The investigator's summary report, attached to the minutes, found that on a balance of probabilities, "Dias' conduct was in breach of the Code of Ethics in that he accepted personal gifts/profit in connection with his role as President of Unifor and further that his actions during the investigation were in breach of his obligation to maintain confidentiality and not to impede or interfere."[31] The report further concluded that

Dias breached his obligation to cooperate in a fair and impartial investigation process, including breaching confidentiality repeatedly and pressuring MacDonald on multiple occasions for weeks to drop his complaint ... The investigator finds that Dias' actions were calculated and driven by his own self-interest and preservation, and not by a desire to uphold Unifor's Constitution.[32]

Payne told NEB members that, before the investigator's report was even received, Dias had proposed terms of settlement in February 2022 that were

challenging to accept. For example, he proposed a restriction on information that could be released by Unifor to its members or the public. All that Unifor could state was an acknowledgement of his retirement and contribution, and that Unifor wished him well. Regardless of what was ever leaked or released in the future, Unifor could say no more, that the allegations would, in that effect, be completely covered up, and that Unifor would never disclose or confirm anything about this.[33]

The union's leadership team rejected Dias's terms. On March 13, 2022, an email from Dias's doctor was forwarded to the investigator indicating that participation in the investigation could worsen his condition.[34] The investigator delivered her report two days later.

Outgoing Quebec director Renaud Gagné told NEB members, "You should understand that this report is really devastating. I'm sick to my stomach."[35] Doherty also expressed disappointment but with somewhat more optimism that the report's findings were not fatal for the organization: "I wish that Jerry would have done the right things. I wish he would have made different decisions. He didn't. He's a personal friend of mine. He is doing things that he shouldn't be doing on a regular basis. It's unfortunate, but we will get through this as an organization."[36]

Not everyone shared Doherty's view about the union's ability to move forward, particularly with him at the helm. After Doherty left the meeting because of his status as a potential hearing witness, NEB members discussed his role in the affair and what appeared to be discrepancies between the findings of the investigator and what he had told the NEB about his involvement.[37] The question of reconsidering the NEB's endorsement of Doherty was front and centre. Forestry Council chair Yves Guérette argued, "Scott and Jerry, they're practically interchangeable. And if we want to be above board, we have to find somebody else to be President of Unifor because this will not be accepted by the members ... We have to clean house."[38] Doherty's allies shot back that it was not Dias who had installed Doherty as his preferred successor but rather members of the NEB in a unanimous decision.[39] Other NEB members argued that their endorsement of Doherty had been made under false pretences. Telecommunications sector chair Marc Rousseau argued that he and other NEB members had been "manipulated without having all this information. This is all linked. I voted for someone. I gave my support to someone without knowing the whole picture."[40]

Doherty's supporters raised other doubts about the motivations of those bringing forward the complaint against Dias and implicating Doherty by association. Tullio DiPonti, the NEB's Industry Council representative for the health care sector and an ally of Doherty, questioned MacDonald's motive in lodging the complaint in the first place, arguing that "this is all political, but we all know there's a few people who are looking to seek the presidency job and Chris is one of them. He's made it clear to me."[41] This mention of "a few people" was intended to raise doubts about whether the investigation was primarily motivated by individuals' personal political ambitions within the union.

However, the larger implications of not investigating also weighed heavily on NEB members. Western regional director Gavin McGarrigle's overall assessment was that "the organization is in peril."[42] Quebec Council chair Benoît Lapointe concurred, telling NEB members, "Really, it could sink us what's happening now. And I think that the only way of getting out of this is to prove that our organization is not a corrupt one."[43] Jennifer Moreau, the NEB's Industry Council representative for the media sector, also agreed: "Our members will likely forgive a mistake, but they won't forgive a cover up ... And the best way to do that, to rebuild trust, is through complete transparency."[44]

Although most NEB members seemed to support this approach, Auto Council chair John D'Agnolo wanted to hear from Dias directly, arguing that a transparent process was not necessarily in the union's best interest:

> I'm disturbed at the fact that here we are today, we're discussing a major issue, and we don't do this on the floor. We go to HR; we deal with this issue with the individual. And when a decision is made, good or bad, he's been told, we know it, we let people say he's been punished if it's severe, and that's it. We don't go on the floor and tell everybody this is what he did, this is how he did it. We don't do that. We've never done that, but we're having a debate on that and that scares me. I've never been taught that way.[45]

Meeting participants feared that public scrutiny would reflect very poorly on the union and give its opponents ammunition. Shane Wark, another assistant to the president, warned, "We've got right-wing groups, we've got employers, we've got right-wing individuals, everybody is looking at us like we're the Titanic that hit the iceberg and they all want to take Unifor down."[46] Renaud Gagné issued a similar warning: "I'm thinking of the Conservatives and Harper who must be laughing out loud saying we're going to take advantage of this."[47]

If any intervention summed up the collective feeling in the room, it may have been Marc Rousseau's observation: "I feel betrayed. I feel hurt because this is someone I respected and I'm surely not the only one to feel this. We all respected him, and it always hurts more when you're betrayed by someone you love."[48] However, Rousseau insisted, "We have to come clean. We have to lay our cards on the table. We have to inform the membership of our locals."[49]

The next day, on March 22, 2022, the NEB met again to review the report in its entirety and to plan next steps. "We either get in front of this train or it's going to roll us over, and it's not going to be good," Lana Payne argued.[50] After NEB members had read the full investigator's report, attention returned to the role of Scott Doherty in the affair, an important question given the NEB's previous endorsement of him as the next national president.

The investigator found that Doherty was "not a particularly cooperative witness."[51] She further found that it was "likely that Doherty deleted *some* of his texts and Signal messages, or just those that might somehow implicate Dias or show that Doherty and Dias were in communication about the complaint when Dias was specifically told not to be, and that Dias was using Doherty to exert pressure on MacDonald on Dias' behalf."[52] The investigator also pointed to Signal messages in a group chat called "The Big Three" provided to her by MacDonald. The group consisted of Dias, Doherty, and MacDonald, and the former two posted memes about loyalty after MacDonald lodged his complaint.[53] When MacDonald rebuffed Doherty's efforts to mediate a solution without an investigation, Doherty texted him, "If he retires today and we ensure you are exonerated what else is needed."[54] The investigator wrote that "MacDonald stated that he continued to be under intense pressure to drop the complaint noting that Doherty had spent the better part of the previous day doing Dias' bidding and trying to get him to withdraw his complaint."[55] She further noted that, "on March 14, 2022, MacDonald shared a Signal message from Dias sent only to MacDonald which read: 'The Globe and Mail is running the story. Article comes out this afternoon. Was it really worth it to destroy my life. Honestly, you were family. Everyone gets hammered now.'"[56] MacDonald also disclosed to the investigator that on February 6, 2022, Dias had sent the union's table officers and his assistants, including MacDonald, a photo of his wife with a message attached that read, "She is all I have left, please do not take her away from me."[57] According to the investigator, Rizvi viewed the message as "an attempt by Dias to get the team to exert further pressure on MacDonald and Unifor to drop the Investigation."[58]

The full report's revelations immediately put Doherty on the defensive. "I never once asked Chris MacDonald to withdraw his complaint," he told NEB members.[59] "I've never once tried to cover up for Jerry Dias," he said, insisting that he was simply trying to mitigate damage to the union and to mediate a solution.[60] But his explanation was met with resistance from those concerned that the report seemed to suggest that he had not fully cooperated with the investigation. Yves Guérette argued that the report read as though Doherty was "harassing Chris ... You continued to ask

Chris to drop the complaint, and I have a hard time with that."[61] As Doherty defended his role in trying to mediate a solution, Payne interjected, "I explained to Jerry and Scott ... that they had no authority to discuss the investigation. Neither of them had any authority to mediate any kind of settlement, and that that needed to stop right away because this investigation would have carried on whether the complaint disappeared or not."[62]

Amid this turmoil, the NEB voted unanimously to ask that candidates for national officer positions pause their campaigns.[63] The next day, on March 23, 2022, Payne led a press conference to publicly announce the charges.[64] Then, on April 4, as a result of Dias's resignation, Payne asked the NEB for approval to call a special convention in accordance with the Unifor constitution. The motion was approved, although not unanimously.[65]

A week later, on April 11, Payne announced her candidacy for the presidency of Unifor shortly before the day's scheduled NEB meeting. "I had no intention of doing this, running for president ... but these last three months changed everything for me to a point where I felt there were some who were not taking this serious enough and I can't get over that," Payne told NEB members.[66] Payne also explained that she was not seeking an NEB endorsement.[67]

Reactions to Payne's announcement were mixed. Some were relieved that Payne was providing an alternative to Doherty, whose potential leadership they now viewed as tainted. Gavin McGarrigle welcomed Payne's candidacy. "They said he was an uncooperative witness," he noted in reference to the investigator's characterization of Doherty. "It's all there, folks. It's all there. So, if you want to defend that, go right ahead. Go right ahead. I won't."[68] Quebec-based NEB members also rallied to support Payne's candidacy.

Others expressed their opposition to Payne's decision, raising a variety of arguments for why the NEB should stick with Doherty. Atlantic regional director Linda MacNeil said that Payne's email announcement felt "like somebody punched me in the gut."[69] Some focused on the personal ambitions at play in the decision. Tullio DiPonti insisted that "Scott should not be prosecuted for what Jerry did."[70] John D'Agnolo accused Payne and McGarrigle of "taking advantage of a situation that's wrong and you're going to go after another individual and you're going to do what you can to be at the top."[71]

Other opponents raised larger questions about the threat posed to the union's political traditions by Payne's decision to run. NEB members Shinade

Allder and Naureen Rizvi asserted that the decision threatened the union's caucus system, which they argued was key to ensuring that candidates from equity-seeking groups would be represented in leadership positions.[72] Others had criticisms of Payne's own leadership style and organizational decisions. Both Shane Wark and Katha Fortier complained that Payne had frozen assistants to the president out of senior leadership meetings, and the former charged that politics was getting in the way of unity. "That was the way through this ... We have demonstrated the exact opposite, not because of the Jerry issue, in my mind, because of politics," explained Wark, who pledged his continued support for Doherty.[73] Payne shot back that, if anything, it was the assistants to the president who were putting "the politics of the union ... ahead of the crisis," noting that the group had been focusing on fundraising among staff for Doherty's election bid.[74]

Doherty, for his part, was reeling as he continued to face questions about his role in the scandal. "I'm all over the map, you guys, and I'm really sorry. It's been a really tough four weeks while I've had my name run through the mud. I've had NEB members say that I'm going to lose the endorsement," he said.[75] Unifor leaders in Quebec had indeed called for his NEB endorsement to be pulled.[76] The labour movement in that province had been rocked by a corruption scandal a decade earlier that continued to weigh on union leaders and made them very sensitive to any hint of union wrongdoing.[77] Doherty insisted, however, that he was an innocent bystander simply caught in the crossfire. "I'm guilty by association ... I wear the stain of what Jerry Dias did simply because I worked with him for eight-and-a-half years," Doherty complained.[78]

This framing did not go uncontested. The temperature in the room heated up as members began hurling insults and accusations at one another. Keith Sullivan, president of the Fishermen, Food and Allied Workers Union, implied that the NEB's February 1 endorsement of Doherty was illegitimate, arguing, "We just got bullshitted ... things were jammed down our throats."[79] D'Agnolo, however, challenged the legitimacy of the investigator's report, arguing that "there's a lot of holes" and casting doubt on the findings.[80] This prompted Jennifer Moreau to jump in and assert, "It's not a conspiracy."[81]

Part of what cast doubt on the investigator's findings was Chris Mac-Donald's repeated insistence to NEB members that "Scott Doherty didn't ask me to cover it up."[82] In retrospect, and despite the evidence in the report that he himself provided, MacDonald framed his friend Doherty as someone who was trying to help rather than interfere. Notably, MacDonald had also publicly endorsed Doherty's candidacy for president. Payne was clearly exasperated by MacDonald's interventions. "I can't believe I've got to explain this again. You guys don't get to make it go away. I had to protect the union here. There's a lot of reinvention going on right now at the moment in terms of what happened," she told the NEB.[83]

The next morning, Payne opened the April 12 NEB meeting by encouraging members not to allow MacDonald to reinterpret for them what had happened between January 20 and February 2, 2022. The investigator's report and the text messages between Doherty, Dias, and MacDonald were clear, she argued.[84] "I had one job, one, to protect this union from grave harm because the wrongdoing was one thing, but any attempt to cover that up would have ruined our union forever," said Payne.[85] "Friendships have been lost, I've lost a few, but I don't regret any of it, not one second, because someone had to put the union first at that moment, and that was my job," she added.[86]

The mood of the meeting was very tense as Gavin McGarrigle moved a motion "to withdraw the endorsement of Scott Doherty as the National Executive Board candidate for presidency."[87] The motion, however, was pre-empted by Doherty, who intervened to say, "I'm going to continue my campaign without the endorsement of the National Executive Board."[88] Presumably, Doherty had read the room and realized that the NEB's endorsement could potentially be lost if put to a vote. However, Doherty asserted, "I didn't cover anything up. You guys can run whatever you want and say whatever you want, but I did not try and cover anything up ... Technically I interfered by involving myself in discussions with Chris MacDonald. I'll admit to that."[89] Because Payne was not seeking the NEB's endorsement and because Doherty asked that his endorsement be withdrawn, the union's caucus system appeared to be marginalized for the first time in the selection of the union's national leadership.

THE 2022 ONTARIO ELECTION

As the campaign to replace Jerry Dias as president of Unifor heated up, so too did the Ontario provincial election campaign. Amid this severe internal turbulence, Unifor had to sort out and implement a coherent election strategy. In some ways, the union's approach reflected both the disarray in the national office and deeper divisions in an increasingly diverse membership with different relationships to the provincial Conservative government. Given Unifor's long-standing commitment to oppose the election of Conservative politicians, it was unsurprising that on March 9–10, 2022, the union's Ontario Regional Council resolved to "commit to do everything necessary to elect progressive politicians and end the conservative majority" in the upcoming Ontario election.[90] However, the apparent rapprochement between Dias and Ford a few months earlier stood in sharp contrast to this position. To understand this apparent contradiction, one needs to unpack not only the internal tensions within the union, particularly between its various sectors, but also the Ford Conservatives' strategy regarding different segments of working-class voters.

In the run-up to the 2022 Ontario provincial election, Premier Ford broke with the past by making a conscious decision not to campaign on austerity, at least overtly. Rather, Ford's Conservatives promised to invest millions in infrastructure projects and job-creation initiatives as part of a "working for workers" agenda.[91] Dubbed the PC "labour charm offensive" by the media, this overture to union voters was not limited to blue-collar unions. In the fall of 2021, Ford's labour minister, Monte McNaughton, initiated legislation guaranteeing the "right to disconnect" and the extension of some rights to app-based gig workers, although these measures were criticized as more symbolic than substantive.[92]

Some union leaders were open to the idea that the PCs were genuinely willing to turn the page on the party's demonization of organized labour. Given that Ford held power, it would be foolish not to engage, they reasoned. This line of thinking had seemingly convinced Dias and OPSEU president Smokey Thomas to appear alongside Ford to announce the government's minimum-wage increase in November 2021. However, Ford had been tilling the soil before that, and his overtures included working diligently to cultivate blue-collar support in the automotive sector. Unifor Local 444 president Dave Cassidy indicated in an interview that Ford had even asked him to consider running for the PCs in the NDP-held Windsor-area riding of Essex.[93] Cassidy turned him down, but at a meeting with Ford on October 18, 2021, to discuss the future of the Stellantis Windsor Assembly Plant, the premier made a commitment to help the company and the union to bring additional investments to the city.[94] "If Ford didn't support the people that I represent, I wouldn't even talk to him … but he's brought investment to manufacturing," states Cassidy.[95] Even though the national union was backing NDP candidates in Windsor-area ridings, Cassidy did not actively campaign for any candidates, PC or otherwise, during the provincial election campaign. Cassidy was partly preoccupied with his own presidential campaign, but he also acknowledges a political disconnect between the direction of the national union and Local 444 on campaign strategy and focus. Cassidy's praise of Ford should not be confused with an ideological embrace of conservatism. He claims to have never personally voted for a Conservative, and he speaks glowingly about Windsor West NDP MP Brian Masse. Expressing disdain for federal Conservative leader Pierre Poilievre, Cassidy also points out that he campaigned for Windsor–Tecumseh's Liberal MP Irek Kusmierczyk in the 2021 federal election. In other words, he has no partisan allegiance but feels that he could not ignore Ford's overtures. "I don't care what party you're from. If you're going to support the members that I represent, I'm with you," argues Cassidy.[96]

Most unions were not seduced by Ford's strategic moves, reasoning that a leopard never changes its spots. After all, this was the same government that had imposed wage restraint on most of the public sector through Bill 124, the Protecting a Sustainable Public Sector for Future Generations Act, and a few years earlier McNaughton had championed US-style union-busting right-to-work legislation as a member of the Opposition.[97] Conservative wage-restraint legislation was imposing austerity on some segments of the working class and was incredibly unpopular with Unifor's health care membership. This sector fed a persistent "Anybody but Conservative" politics in the union that led to the Ontario Regional Council's vote.

A day before the writ dropped to officially kick off the provincial election campaign, Ford appeared to make good on his promise to Ontario autoworkers. On May 2, 2022, Stellantis announced a $3.6 billion investment in its Windsor and Brampton plants. The province's news release trumpeted the Ford government's role in securing the investments for plant modernization to make electric vehicles.[98] The press release also contained glowing quotes from local Unifor leaders. Unifor Local 1285 president Danny Price stated, "Today's announcement shows how important it is that unions, governments and industry come together to protect automotive manufacturing jobs and keep Canadian manufacturing strong."[99] Dave Cassidy argued, "Ontario is well placed to play an essential role in the new motoring revolution. I want to thank Stellantis and the federal and provincial governments for recognizing the value in our Unifor members and their families."[100]

However, the union had to walk a tightrope with Ford, offering public support for targeted policy commitments or investments, like increasing the minimum wage or government support for the automotive industry, while opposing his health care agenda and treatment of front-line workers. Although Cassidy and Price congratulated the provincial government, the national union was actively promoting its new anti-Ford election website, www.fordfailedus.ca, to counter the narrative that Ford was a champion for workers.[101] Therefore, the union's ad campaign, approved as a result of the Ontario Regional Council's resolution, revolved almost entirely around the plight of front-line health care workers.[102] Meanwhile, some leaders downplayed the union's opposition to Ford with regard to the auto industry. For example, Shane Wark appeared on CBC Radio's *Ontario Today* during the campaign, soft-pedalling the union's opposition to Ford and arguing that his government took a "number of really positive steps for workers" in the automotive industry.[103]

Unifor's electoral intervention sent mixed messages to members. Representatives from the automotive sector were softly supportive of the Ford government's initiatives in the sector, whereas front-line Unifor members in health care and other sectors were appalled by Ford's wage-restraint legislation and refusal to implement permanent paid sick days. The idea at the centre of the merger that created Unifor – that a bigger and more diverse union would deliver more political clout – seemed to be undermined by the fact that different segments of the union had very different political priorities. The internal turmoil within Unifor at the time further overshadowed the union's electoral political strategy, thus potentially contributing to the mixed messaging.

Meanwhile, Ford managed to secure endorsements from eight construction unions – an unprecedented show of union support for an Ontario PC premier. Although these unions together represented less than 5 percent of the province's union membership, the symbolic value of their endorsement of Ford helped to validate the government's "working for workers" narrative, and the endorsements received much more media attention than did the much broader and larger union endorsement earned by the opposition New Democrats.

Unifor, as always, refrained from offering a blanket endorsement of any party and instead pursued strategic voting and an issue-based campaign. The union organized several member canvasses in targeted ridings, although it did not release any data on its record of electoral success in 2022. However, a look at the election results and the ridings targeted through the Unifor Votes website suggests that the union's campaign was unsuccessful overall. Not only did Ford win more seats and a larger share of the popular vote, but he also picked up seats in Windsor and Brampton ridings where Unifor had endorsed NDP candidates.

Unifor appeared to target seventeen ridings with organized member canvasses, but its preferred candidates won in only seven of these races. On election night, the opposition New Democrats and the Liberals split the anti-PC vote right down the middle. Ford secured 40.8 percent of the popular vote and increased his majority by seven seats over 2018. The party picked up seats from the NDP in blue-collar ridings like Windsor–Tecumseh, Essex, Brampton East, Timmins, and Hamilton East–Stoney Creek. The NDP lost nine seats and saw its vote share drop by almost 10 points to 23.7 percent but managed to retain Official Opposition status. Former Unifor Local 199 president Wayne Gates was once again re-elected for the NDP in Niagara Falls, even though Unifor had not included his riding in its targets. The Liberals increased their vote share to 23.9 percent but managed to win only one additional seat, falling short of official party status for the second election in a row. In all five ridings where Unifor assisted Liberal candidates, the local Conservative prevailed – in most cases, by over 10 points.[104] In many ways, however, Unifor's effort in the provincial election campaign was overshadowed by the internal campaign for the leadership of the union, which by July was heating up.

THE CAMPAIGN FOR THE PRESIDENCY AND THE AUGUST 2022 CONVENTION

On July 19, 2022, a few weeks before the August 2022 convention to select a new president, four of Unifor's original architects – Peter Kennedy, Gaétan

Ménard, Fred Wilson, and Jim Stanford – penned an open letter endorsing Lana Payne. The four argued,

> By leading the initial investigation of the former president's actions, against the wishes of those who preferred the issue to remain hidden, Lana demonstrated her commitment to accountability and democratic practice. The credibility she built through these actions will be essential for the difficult task of completing the investigations of past wrongdoing, and establishing better structures of audit, financial control, transparency, and collective leadership to prevent this type of abuse from occurring again.[105]

The release of the open letter roughly coincided with the release to locals of NEB meeting transcripts related to the Dias controversy, including a copy of the investigator's report, the details of which are discussed above. The NEB voted on June 29, 2022, to release these normally confidential meeting transcripts in the name of transparency, but the decision proved controversial, with five members of the NEB aligned with Doherty's campaign abstaining from voting on the motion to release them.[106] The documents provided a much clearer picture of what had transpired before and during the investigation and how individual officers and staff members had attempted to manage the crisis. They would also have an impact on the course of the campaign for national president.

Once the NEB meeting transcripts were released and posted online in July 2022, Doherty's team worked to overcome allegations and rumours that he had attempted to impede the investigation against Dias, whereas Payne had to contend with accusations that she had weaponized the investigation and leaked expense reports to bolster her own candidacy for Unifor president.[107] Doherty implied that Payne's office had leaked his confidential expense reports to the media in order to undermine his candidacy as part of a "smear campaign."[108] Over a four-year period ending in 2021, Doherty had claimed much higher expenses than any other officer or staff person, with the exception of Dias.[109] He asserted no wrongdoing. "Not once in the past three years were my expenses cited or returned by Unifor's finance department which is overseen by the National Secretary-Treasurer," he told the *Globe and Mail*.[110] However, Payne responded that although the secretary-treasurer is generally responsible for approving staff expenses, assistants to the president had their expenses directly approved by Dias.[111] "While others may have sought to influence the investigation, avoid accountability, or spread misinformation to their own personal or political advantage, I have not," she told the *Toronto Star* in response to the allegations.[112] Her campaign included a commitment to introduce new oversight mechanisms in relation to expense accounts.[113]

Payne also faced internal attacks from four NEB members – John D'Agnolo, Tullio DiPonti, Doug Carter, and Tammy Moore – who accused her of a conflict of interest in relation to the NEB's decision to rescind its motion to hold a special convention to replace Dias in accordance with the union's constitution.[114] Members of several locals made similar allegations. The NEB reviewed these charges at its meeting on June 29, 2022. Gavin McGarrigle argued that the charges were neither proper nor timely and that they were politically motivated.[115] Payne vigorously defended herself: "I'm not going to apologize for believing that a better union is possible, and I'm certainly not going to apologize for the actions that I have taken as secretary-treasurer. We are defined not by what we do when things are easy, but what we do when circumstances are hard."[116] After a spirited debate, the NEB ultimately moved to dismiss the charges against Payne and to send the matter to the union's Public Review Board by a vote of thirteen to seven.[117]

On August 8, 2022, the Unifor national convention opened at the Metro Toronto Convention Centre. Much was at stake for the union and its membership. The winner of the presidency would take over a union still reeling from a crisis and be tasked with charting a course forward. The loser would almost certainly be marginalized along with their key staff supporters. Going into the convention, there was no clear heir apparent, although Payne appeared to have a slight advantage according to publicly announced local endorsements. Payne's strongest regional bases of support came from Quebec and Atlantic Canada, whereas Doherty drew the greatest levels of support from western Canada and Ontario. Most locals, however, did not publicly endorse any candidate, leading to a sense of uncertainty and a heightened level of excitement at the convention.[118]

On the first day of the convention, Payne delivered an update on the constitutional breach. The report precipitated an emotional debate about

Dias, his legacy, and how the union had handled the fallout from the scandal. In a surreal moment, Chris MacDonald himself took to the microphone to tell delegates that he had never been pressured to cover up what happened, contrary to what the investigator's report concluded. "Scott Doherty is one of the most caring individuals I have ever met and he never suggested that this be swept under the carpet," MacDonald asserted.[119] The reaction from the convention speakers was mixed. Unifor Local 8300 president Kathleen Brooks followed MacDonald in the discussion and challenged his framing of the issue, pointing out that the investigator's report contradicted his assertion. She thanked Payne "for taking the hard road and doing what she needed to do."[120] The convention then heard from a delegate representing Local 29-X, who referenced Dias's substance abuse problem, asking if any members of the NEB had thought to bring Dias "to rehab long before this because you couldn't talk to him from 4 o'clock on."[121] The discussion became more and more heated as delegates expressed their concerns and frustrations. Some delegates used the forum to promote their preferred candidate for president, and others complained that the publicity around the scandal and release of information had hurt the union. Most delegates, however, expressed support for the leadership's decision to embrace transparency about the constitutional breach.

On August 10, 2022, delegates elected Lana Payne as president on the second ballot with a weighted vote share of 60.8 percent versus 39.2 percent for Doherty. Cassidy had been dropped from the ballot after finishing third with 17.9 percent in the first round of voting. The vast majority of his votes had migrated to Payne, pushing her campaign over the top. Despite Doherty's best efforts to position himself as a change agent rather than the continuity candidate, most delegates viewed his association with Dias and his proximity to the scandal as a liability. Dias's endorsement, once the key to victory, had become Doherty's kryptonite. In contrast, Payne's campaign managed to successfully portray her as the principled steady hand who was best positioned to right the ship and move past a very dark chapter in the union's history. The other members of Payne's Forward Together slate were easily elected to the union's top officer positions except for Dayle Steadman, who narrowly lost to incumbent Ontario regional director Naureen Rizvi, a member of Doherty's Stronger United slate. Nevertheless, Payne's victory was decisive, and the near-unanimous election of her slate meant that her team's reform mandate was clear.

Payne was the first woman elected to the union's top post. But perhaps equally notable is the fact that she was the first candidate elected president without the official backing of the NEB. Her victory did not rely on the caucus system. "I think it's almost as exciting as when we left the UAW [United Auto Workers]," comments Carol Phillips.[122] Doherty and Mac-Donald left Unifor soon after Payne took over the presidency. Both took positions in human-resource management for private-sector employers. "Isn't that interesting?" asks Dave Cassidy, who describes MacDonald as "the little rat who exposed all of this because he never got his way."[123]

CONCLUSION

Jerry Dias was a polarizing figure both within and beyond the ranks of his union. Former CAW Quebec director Sylvain Martin describes Dias as a "bulldozer" inside the union, a leader who did not shy away from confrontation and who knew how to aggressively drive his agenda.[124] Dias "did a lot of good things for Unifor," argues Dave Cassidy, "but I think Jerry stayed three years too long." Notably, Cassidy is one of the few interviewees who is not critical of Dias's decision to stand alongside Ford at the premier's press conference on the minimum wage in November 2021, describing the move as evidence that "we can work with anyone we need to work with."[125] Flavio Volpe, head of the Automotive Parts Manu-facturers Association in Canada, told the *Toronto Star* that Dias had redefined what it meant to be a labour leader. "He had strong predeces-sors, but he surpassed them," said Volpe.[126] Professor Dimitry Anastakis credited Dias with playing an instrumental role in the promotion of electric-vehicle production in Ontario and in fighting for workers to receive pandemic supports.[127]

Former NDP strategist Robin Sears chided Dias's detractors in the wake of the scandal, complaining that "Dias's enemies in his union, in parts of the media, and among social media hysterics, seem determined that this should be his end." Sears argued that Dias's legacy deserved better. "Surely some of those with whom he worked so hard, some of the members whose lives were made better by the victories they won together will stand up and offer a less cruel and balanced assessment of a life devoted" to the labour movement and working-class struggles.[128]

But others who knew him throughout his union career could hardly contain their disdain. "Jerry Dias was an old school business unionist, and I don't think he ever changed the entire time all the way up," says former staffer Carol Phillips, who came out of the same workplace as Dias.[129] She was a member of Local 673 and worked in the office at De Havilland in Toronto, and Dias was a member of Local 112 and worked on the shop floor. Phillips likens Dias to an "irresponsible teenager" who "never quite matured." She says Dias "fed into the stereotypes of trade unionists that a lot of people hold out there – people who aren't friendly to the union movement." In Phillips's view, "his ending was sad and inevitable ... I really think it was inevitable. That it would end with some petty little kickback was not a surprise to me."[130]

Although a police investigation concluded that no criminal charges would be laid against Dias, the union maintained its finding that Dias had violated the Unifor Code of Ethics.[131] "I am a lot of things but crooked is not one of them," Dias told the *Globe and Mail*. "The police finished their investigation and aren't proceeding. There is nothing there. All you need to know is that I never took a dime," he added. In response, Payne asserted that the "findings of the investigator speak for themselves ... It was never an option for Unifor to sweep such serious allegations under the rug."[132] Whatever Dias's legacy, it was clearly tarnished by the scandal that precipitated his early retirement. The existential crisis that emerged from the scandal not only took down Dias but also seems to have displaced the importance of the caucus system. According to Wilson, Unifor's architects did not intend to replicate the CAW's Administration caucus. Rather, he argues that the Unity Team was designed to play a transitional role in ensuring balanced representation from the former CAW and CEP in the structures of the new union. However, Wilson acknowledges that, over time, "a culture had developed around the role of the assistants" that very much resembled the CAW's Administration caucus.[133] This culture had clearly become entrenched under Dias.

Payne's successful challenge of Doherty effectively upended the caucus system and led to a genuine race for the presidency and other leadership positions in the union via competitive slates headed by Doherty and Payne respectively. Whether the caucus system will re-emerge under Payne's leadership is unclear, but several decades of experience with the caucus system point to serious potential pitfalls related to its continued use. As the head of the caucus, the president always wielded tremendous power. The highly centralized nature of the union and a culture of deference to the president, reinforced by the latter's unilateral role in appointing members to staff positions, meant that loyalty had become the most important currency in the union. Of course, the caucus also played a key role in reinforcing discipline and in ensuring that the leadership of the union spoke with a unified voice. These objectives are worthwhile so long as the president adheres to democratic ideals and principles. However, in the absence of accountability to these principles, a command-and-control structure becomes open to abuse and exploitation in the service of private interests and can bring the entire organization into disrepute.

Dias's dalliance with Ontario premier Doug Ford is a good example of the risks of a centralized decision-making system with few counterweights. This move clearly stirred controversy within Unifor, but the level of centralization in the union and the concentration of power in the president's office muted any internal opposition, leading to a seemingly disjointed and ultimately unsuccessful campaign to defeat the Ford government in the 2022 provincial election. More generally, the Dias scandal put a spotlight on the union's culture of deference to the president and on the need for more meaningful checks and balances.

CHAPTER 8

THE ROAD AHEAD
Unifor and the Changing Landscape of Working-Class Politics

There is strong support among union leaders for the idea that the job of a union is to build the power of its members and, by extension, of the broader working class. How unions go about building political power, however, is the subject of great debate. The aim of this book has been to analyze and explain the reasons why Unifor, like its primary predecessor union, the Canadian Auto Workers (CAW), shifted gears in terms of its approach to building political power. Structure and agency play equally important roles in making sense of the union's shifting political strategies in the workplace, at the ballot box, and in the streets. Drawing on union records, media reports, and interviews with two dozen key informants, we use an integrated theoretical approach to make the case that the union's strong commitment to, and exercise of, a social unionist politics has, over time, played a diminished role in its politics. Specifically, we argued that social unionism has increasingly taken a back seat to political frames and repertoires traditionally associated with a sectionalist and economistic brand of transactional politics.

The landscape of labour and working-class politics in Canada is constantly changing, reflecting a diversity of strategies and tactics that gain or lose steam based on the political-economic context and on the political objectives of key leaders. Given the size and influence of CAW/Unifor, the union's political shifts have resulted in labour movement waves, not ripples. Indeed, they help to shape how political parties, employers, and social movements understand labour politics and its relationship to Canadian politics more broadly.

Historically, the union's political playbook has included a full range of political strategies, including community-union alliances contesting unfair trade deals and other societal injustices, partisan ties to the New Democratic Party (NDP), electoral mobilizations to support or oppose particular parties, parliamentary lobbying, and mass demonstrations to pressure governments and employers. These strategic repertoires have always coexisted in the politics of CAW/Unifor, framed by the union's core commitment to social unionism. But as the political-economic landscape has shifted, so too have the political perspectives of the union's leaders charged with advancing the interests of union members, leading to a significant reordering of political strategies.

SHIFTING PARTY-UNION RELATIONS

The union's traditional partisan alignment with the NDP always involved tensions, but until the early 2000s, there was never any question that CAW leaders saw the NDP as *their* party. Over time, however, once the relationship broke down and was eventually severed by the CAW in 2006, the union moved in a more independent direction that Unifor has since embraced, crafting ad hoc political alliances to defend against the worst electoral outcomes and building purely transactional relationships with power holders in pursuit of union-supported public-policy outcomes and investments.

Importantly, neither Unifor nor the CAW ever framed its own political transformation in this way. Both unions offered strong critiques of the NDP and its policy directions and claimed that severing the formal partisan link with the party gave the union space to move to the left in pursuit of a more progressive worker-centred agenda. In practice, however, the union shifted toward sectionalism, increasingly relying on Gomperist political strategies that enraged NDP activists and their labour movement allies, who argued that the union had lost its ideological moral compass.

Historically, the CAW's support for the NDP was rooted in its commitment to social unionism, but this relationship required both the party and the union to identify with a common set of goals and principles, namely addressing economic inequality through wealth redistribution and expansion of the welfare state and through the promotion of labour and human rights both at home and abroad. This relationship proved increasingly tricky to maintain, especially when the party saw these shared principles as potentially interfering with its electoral fortunes. But it was not only the party that faced pressure to moderate its politics amid the rise of neoliberalism. The union, too, faced pressure to tone down its militancy at the bargaining table and to seek political strategies that would help to prevent the worst electoral outcomes, even if that meant compromising its own political values. In this way, the union's commitment to social unionism was tested by wave after wave of plant closures and layoffs in the 1990s and 2000s that forced the union to reassess its priorities and ultimately led to a more inward, sectionalist orientation.

The union's *official* commitment to social unionism as a guiding principle has outlasted any sort of formal party-union relationship or round of economic restructuring and was preserved through the transition to Unifor. However, social unionism has also become a catch-all term that includes everything from extra-parliamentary direct action to fundraising for local charities.[1] The fact that virtually every union in Canada now embraces the social unionist label has undermined this label's explanatory value for social scientists and political activists. As a result, it is more helpful to focus on what Unifor does politically rather than on what is says about its political approach.

"Unifor is nonpartisan," asserts Unifor president Lana Payne. "We have to make it toxic for any political party to attack union rights ... If I only talk to [the NDP], I can't change minds," she explains. According to Payne, engaging with all parties helps the union to "shift the needle" politically. She argues that this is "better for the NDP because they are now operating in an environment where they can also up the ante."[2] Unifor's former economist and policy director Jim Stanford argues that one of the union's distinguishing features is that its "capacity to advocate for its members and its issues is enhanced when it is seen as an independent force rather than as an arm of the NDP."[3] This approach means that the NDP cannot take Unifor's support for granted and allows the union to keep better lines of communication open with all parties. Stanford, however, rejects the notion that Unifor has drifted toward a Gomperist brand of transactional politics, arguing that a narrow focus on the party-union relationship is misplaced. He argues that to be an effective and progressive countervailing political force, unions should not limit themselves to the electoral arena and to one particular party. When you tell union members to "vote for a particular party and things will change, you're narrowing your scope of action to a kind of endorsement every few years. You're also narrowing how your members conceive of politics," Stanford says.[4]

Stanford's critics do not disagree with his assertion that "democracy has to be more than voting every four years."[5] However, they take issue with his characterization of how the union's politics have shifted. For example, former CAW activist Ritch Whyman argues that "far from the promised left-wing shift that Stanford told us we were going to get, it's clearly produced, ideologically, a right-wing pull inside the union."[6] This analysis is compelling. Although loosening ties with the NDP theoretically held the promise of creating space for a more radical working-class politics, neither the CAW nor Unifor moved in this direction. Rather, the embrace of a formally independent labour politics led to a partisan break with the NDP and strengthened Gomperist electoral impulses. These impulses sometimes helped the NDP in specific places or campaigns where the party was a real contender for power,[7] but they generally undermined the NDP's overall electoral prospects and led to ad hoc electoral alliances with Liberals. The union's new approach meant that endorsements and resources could not be taken for granted by any party and needed to be earned on a case-by-case basis. To paraphrase Samuel Gompers himself, the union sought to punish its enemies and to reward its friends.

TRANSACTIONAL POLITICS

Carol Phillips, a former assistant to the CAW president, believes that the influence of the labour movement, in general, has moved "behind closed doors." According to Philips, "there is not the visibility of the trade union movement in everyday life that there was."[8] Former NDP member of Parliament (MP) and CAW activist Malcolm Allen sums up Unifor's approach to politics with one word: "transactional."[9] However, the trend toward a more explicitly transactional brand of politics is not unique to Unifor. Ottawa Centre NDP member of the provincial Parliament (MPP) Joel Harden, a former labour movement staffer, remarks that when he was at the Canadian Labour Congress (CLC), union leaders "would look at political parties like they look at employers. Why would I commit to one? I'm negotiating. I'm going to get the best thing I can from the person who will be in power."[10]

This tendency to view relationships with parties and governments in transactional terms is not dependent on direct campaign contributions either. In fact, this brand of labour politics grew in popularity *after* campaign finance changes gradually banned union donations to parties at the federal level between 2004 and 2006. Former CLC president Hassan Yussuff argues that the campaign finance reforms "exposed the movement for its weakness. If you couldn't give money, what are you going to do to involve and engage your membership in the political world that was so fundamentally important to the movement?"[11] Without the capacity to write cheques, unions could not farm out their politics to the NDP, prompting serious reflection on the part of the union movement. "There was a growing perception that just yelling at members to vote NDP had not been particularly effective," explains former CLC chief economist Andrew Jackson.[12] Unifor Local 444 president Dave Cassidy agrees, describing the NDP partisans in his union as "purists." He argues that Unifor should continue to embrace a more pragmatic approach to elections and political parties. "I think we need to be engaged with every single [party] and leverage what we can accordingly."[13] Cassidy's political prescription is quintessentially Gomperist, an approach that has seemingly gained steam within the union's ranks despite how uncomfortably it sits alongside social unionism as a core political principle.

STRATEGIC VOTING

In response to the rise of neoliberalism and the associated crisis in social democratic electoralism, anti-Conservative strategic voting proved a particularly popular alternative to partisan political allegiance to the NDP. The CAW and Unifor have been among the strongest proponents of strategic voting. Beginning in 1999, anti-Conservative strategic voting gradually became the union's dominant electoral strategy, first in Ontario and eventually in federal politics. Given the union's long-standing partisan ties to the NDP, strategic voting was initially controversial, but internal opposition to the practice gradually fell by the wayside. In this way, strategic voting evolved in a manner that mirrored the union's more general political shift away from searching for left-wing alternatives and toward a transactional politics rooted in sectionalism.

Hassan Yussuff was an early proponent of strategic voting. "I think unions are very pragmatic about what is a winning hand at election time," he explains. "I think that, increasingly, the hostility from the right is not like what it used to be ... They really see the labour movement as their enemy, and I think people are quite rightfully fearful of how far this is going to go and of course, preventing them from achieving power is ultimately the objective," he argues.[14] Others have more mixed views. "I think [strategic voting] has some merit but only if you can deliver the vote," argues long-time CAW staffer Hemi Mitic, adding that union-backed strategic voting has often lacked leadership and strategic thinking.[15] Thinking about the bigger picture, Mitic argues that abandoning exclusive party-union relationships in the short term can "get you a sprinkling of success, but if you look at the long-term strategy, you've got disarray all over the place."[16]

Former local leader Willie Lambert points to the CAW's embrace of strategic voting as evidence of its retreat as a militant union. Sold by the leadership as a way to take down Conservatives, the tactic simply brought the union closer to the Liberals in Ontario and federally, he argues.[17] This sentiment is widely shared by NDP activists in the union. "Strategic voting weakens us and hurts our ability to have governments support all workers and not allow them to pick us off one union at a time," argues Wayne Gates, the Unifor local president turned Ontario NDP MPP. Gates expresses the importance of unions acting as a unified movement and argues that the NDP is the best political vehicle to achieve gains for working-class people and their communities, even if the party is not always best positioned to win.[18]

Andrew Jackson offers a more nuanced view of the party-union relationship, emphasizing the factors pushing unions away from the NDP. "It's very hard for me to accept that the NDP should operate solely on the basis of political logic. Winning five or six extra seats ... at the cost of bringing in a right-wing government is a pretty high price to pay," he argues.[19] Whereas the NDP's success is primarily viewed as a means to an end for the labour movement, it is an end in itself for the party. Placing the party's electoral fortunes ahead of the labour movement's policy goals has increased tensions in the party-union relationship. As we have seen, in several moments over the 2000s, CAW/Unifor leaders were frustrated by NDP decisions to pull the plug on minority Liberal governments even when the labour movement's policy priorities were being delivered or despite the real risk of an anti-labour Conservative government being elected. Nevertheless, Jackson contends that New Democrats anchor Canadian politics on the left. "A weak NDP ultimately favours the right since it ceases to put electoral pressure on centrist and even right-wing Liberals to respect labour rights and to invest in social programs and public services," he argues.[20]

Reflecting on the CAW's decision to pursue strategic voting back in 1999, former CAW research director Sam Gindin argues,

> I think it's fair to say, in retrospect, given how it evolved, that actually [strategic voting] was dangerous ... But the reality was that it was very dangerous because there wasn't a left to take advantage of it ... Unions are not going to move to the left without an organized left force ... I was looking for an opening ... and even if I thought the odds were against it, it was still kind of a chance. At some point, the NDP had to be challenged that way. And so, yeah, it was dangerous. And it did lead to something worse, although sticking to the NDP isn't like it would have been so wonderful.[21]

Unsurprisingly, NDP partisans have been outspoken in their opposition to strategic voting. In general, union-backed strategic-voting campaigns appear to have had only a modest effect on voting intentions, but in some cases they backfired spectacularly.[22] As a result, the electoral tactic proved very divisive and unquestionably drove a wedge between the NDP and the CAW. One reason why party activists were so annoyed with the union's leadership was the double standard that they perceived in its scrutiny of the NDP. Liberals could lock down union endorsements without any substantive pro-labour policies simply by virtue of not being Conservatives, whereas nonincumbent New Democrats were dismissed as unelectable despite being aligned most closely with the union's policy agenda. Liberal governments also seemed to get a free pass pursuing austerity agendas, with unions like CAW/Unifor more concerned about which government might replace them. In short, strategic voting and ad hoc alliances with Liberals were less about realizing the union's political and economic policy objectives and more about blocking the possibility of worse outcomes.[23] This mitigation strategy eventually morphed into an effort to cultivate support from Liberal powerbrokers. Political-economic push and pull factors help us to explain this transition. The crisis of social democratic electoralism in the face of neoliberal restructuring pushed the CAW away from the NDP over time, and the pull of sectionalism and the promise of transactional benefits in the context of a worsening economic crisis for workers, especially in the auto sector, kept the union invested in strategic voting as a tactic, despite the mixed results that it produced.

It must be emphasized, however, that the CAW never abandoned the NDP altogether. Rather, its relationship with the party took on a different character based on the jurisdiction and particular electoral contest. This dynamic continued after the creation of Unifor. "We always support New Democrat incumbents. That's a given," explains Payne.[24] Yet rhetorically, "Anybody but Conservative" has been the rallying call, and in practice Unifor has suffered from what the union's retired director of strategic planning, Fred Wilson, calls the "inconsistent application of good policy."[25] Federally and in Ontario, the union has sometimes endorsed Liberals in races where NDP candidates are competitive but the Conservatives are not. Other times, the union has poured resources into local NDP campaigns where Conservatives pose no threat whatsoever. In provincial elections in British Columbia and Alberta, Wilson argues that Unifor has offered support to the NDP without reciprocal commitments to pursue significant pro-labour reforms. According to Wilson, NDP provincial governments in these provinces "have been quite prepared to preside over a continuous decline in private-sector union density in the interest of so-called labour neutrality."[26] He makes an excellent point, one reinforced by CLC political action director Brent Farrington's observation that "the NDP is always worried about making the wrong decision or looking like they're too progressive or undercutting their long-term viability."[27] Wilson argues that if the NDP's timidity points to the limits of social democratic electoralism, "it also has to be seen as an abject failure of labour politics that we set the bar so low for our support, and we don't have the power needed to change that."[28]

POLITICAL INFLUENCE

The union's use of strategic voting shifted over time in important ways that demonstrated a greater desire for proactive political influence with sitting governments. Initially pitched as a tactical necessity to block the re-election of anti-union Conservatives, strategic voting morphed into a long-term imperative for key leaders and staff of the union. No longer an ad hoc reaction to a crisis, strategic voting instead has become the conventional wisdom for how the union should participate in election campaigns. Although early strategic-voting campaigns were framed as key to stopping Conservatives, with Liberals in power, strategic voting was also viewed by some union leaders as an opportunity to use support as leverage for pro-union public policy and investments.

However, CAW/Unifor's ability to win such outcomes from governments has been mixed at best, especially when measured in relation to the time, money, and effort that the union has put into election campaigns. Although some may point to policy outcomes like government subsidies for electric-vehicle and battery production, there have been few breakthroughs on key labour relations issues like anti-scab legislation or improved union-certification rules. Here, *access* to government should not be confused with *influence*. As Sam Gindin recounts,

> I had a worker from Newfoundland who said, "We loved joining the union because when we joined the union, all of a sudden, we had access to the Cabinet. We'd have a problem and call Buzz [Hargrove], and he'd say, 'Okay I'll set up a meeting.'" A few meetings later, he said, "We discovered that that's what you get – meetings with the Cabinet, [but] nothing happens."[29]

In Gindin's view, union leaders themselves "are made to feel important when Cabinet ministers return their calls and the prime minister speaks at their conventions. It's not so much that union leaders wield real influence but that they are seen to wield influence."[30] In short, although Unifor's more independent approach to politics has undoubtedly granted its leadership more access to the halls of power, there is little evidence that the union has increased working-class power in the ambitious way that it laid out in its

2014 policy and discussion paper "Politics for Workers: Unifor's Political Project." Stanford points to the union's capacity to save jobs, secure investments, and extract public-policy concessions from governments despite a hostile economic and political environment,[31] but these largely rearguard victories have more or less helped the union to tread water rather than to advance its interests in path-breaking ways.

THE WORKPLACE AS POLITICAL TERRAIN

Given unions' relationship with the workplace, the economic context is key to understanding the shifting landscape of labour politics. After all, unions do face real and changing constraints and must make the best deals that they can in difficult circumstances. In the case of CAW/Unifor, the union's political drift had important workplace and labour relations dimensions that reflected and reinforced the union's decision to shift gears on the electoral front. There is no question that the CAW under Bob White was a force to be reckoned with. The union's membership grew under his leadership and made major gains on the collective bargaining front by negotiating indexed pensions and a child care fund with the Big Three automakers in 1987.[32] The union also played a key role in fostering union alliances with social movements in the fight against free trade. Its connection to social unionism was rooted in an activist and progressive political and collective bargaining agenda. In contrast, by the time the CAW merged with the Communications, Energy and Paperworkers Union to create Unifor, concessions had become normalized, and the union's historically militant fightback culture was clearly in decline.

According to Willie Lambert, who ultimately failed in his challenge for the union's presidency back in 2006, Hargrove's and Stanford's focus on partnerships with capital amounted to an argument for "never-ending extortion that the automakers would enjoy from provincial and federal governments."[33] Lambert says that he no longer recognized his own union, asserting that historically it had "argued against corporate welfare. We argued against corporations not paying their fair share. What Stanford did, and I know he was directed to do it, he basically pulled our sharpest teeth and our claws right out of us ... and we've become this really docile animal compared to what we once were."[34] The union had indeed aligned itself more closely with the interests of employers in hopes that cooperation rather than conflict would help to grow and protect investments and to secure union jobs. This alignment was evident in the controversial Framework of Fairness arrangement with Magna and in the way that the union increasingly allied itself with employers to lobby for subsidies. Occupations, barricades, and mass demonstrations were not altogether sidelined, but they were used with less regularity and rarely produced the desired result. The changing political-economic context contributed to this shift in political strategy, but so too did the choices that the union's leadership made in response. Part of its response was to put a greater emphasis on sectionalism at the expense of broader notions of class solidarity and social justice. That said, there is no question that the union's focus on social justice was more difficult to maintain given the immediate battle to fend off concessions and job loss. As Peggy Nash relays, "I remember [Bob White] saying you can only do things like that when you're making progress for the workers, for the members. If you come back and say, 'Guess what folks, we got a pay cut, but the important news is we've got a social justice fund,' you're going to get run out of town."[35] In short, not only is sectionalism politically expedient, but it also becomes difficult to resist when the union is on the defensive.

Sectionalism can also drive unions closer to employers. In Ritch Whyman's view, CAW/Unifor's decision to develop links with corporations, embrace industry "handouts," and tout productivity arguments as the basis for encouraging investments fostered an organizational logic that said, "The entity is what you must save, not the objective of the entity."[36] In other words, preserving the union and its membership, at the expense of its core principles and values, became the overriding concern.

WHAT ARE THE ALTERNATIVES?

One need look no further than the beleaguered labour movement in the United States to see the limitations of Gomperism as a political orientation. Although a sectionalist approach may deliver benefits to individual unions with a direct stake in a particular public-policy outcome, this orientation rarely delivers the goods to the labour movement more broadly. Labour relations scholar Elaine Bernard warns that a Gomperist approach further reduces unions to the status of special-interest groups and "condemns labor to being forever on the outside."[37] Moreover, a sectionalist brand of politics is ultimately a dead-end strategy because the politics of self-preservation in a context of declining union density risks widening the gap between union members and other working-class people, thus fostering resentment and disunity.[38]

That said, although Unifor's approach to electoral politics has important contradictions and limitations, the alternatives are not so evident. Once the union's trusted electoral vehicle, the NDP has proven to be a fair-weather friend, especially when in government. CAW/Unifor's long-standing grievances with the party in both federal and provincial politics have been well documented in this book. But even if relationships could be repaired with different sets of leaders, there appears to be little appetite in either the party or the union to return to a 1960s-style partisan relationship. Both organized labour and the NDP are generally satisfied with the loosening of formal ties.[39] For its part, the NDP is no longer expected to go out of its way to orient itself to unions, especially when doing so would cost it support in the polls. As for unions, they are no longer expected to stick with the NDP through thick and thin, and they have more freedom to criticize the party when it adopts positions that are contrary to the aims and objectives of individual unions. Thus it is fanciful to think that Unifor should or even could uncritically flock back to the party in an effort to fashion the NDP into the political arm of labour. In the words of Jim Stanford, "I can't see any rationale for returning to a situation where we're going to be allied to a political party and we're going to be there for them in every election."[40] Even NDP activists like Peggy Nash recognize the real barriers to rebuilding a partisan union-party relationship:

> I think there's tension on both sides. I think there were some MPs and some people within the party who were disdainful of the labour movement, who thought that they're too conservative ... And then there's tension on the other side, where people in labour felt like the NDP don't understand what working people are facing every day. [People in labour argued,] "They're just interested in their own narrow electoral interests, they don't get who we are, they don't respect us as thinking activists. They see us as a source of money and a source of campaign workers."[41]

These latter concerns reflected long-standing grievances by CAW members dating back to at least the 1970s that were exacerbated as the union gradually lost influence within the NDP.[42] Even in the face of policy disputes and arguments about strategy, the union always considered the NDP to be *its* party. This approach, however, gradually eroded during Buzz Hargrove's tenure as president, ultimately leading to a severing of the partisan relationship in 2006. Although political and economic circumstances drove the party and union apart, interpersonal relationships also played a significant role. McDermott and White had significant influence in the party and played important roles in delivering NDP leadership wins to David Lewis, Ed Broadbent, Bob Rae, and Audrey McLaughlin, whereas Hargrove backed losing NDP leadership candidates in every single race in Ontario and federally during his tenure as CAW president.[43] This dynamic both weakened the union's influence over the party and, in turn, seemingly validated Hargrove's attempts to distance the CAW from the NDP.

Union-party disputes sometimes generated calls for the creation of a new left-wing workers' party to displace the NDP. But most of these efforts proved half-hearted. Although the New Politics Initiative held promise, its backers underestimated both the NDP's staying power and the lack of union interest in building a new and competitive party of the left. More recently, key segments of the labour movement have gone in the opposite direction, calling on the NDP to merge or to cooperate electorally with the Liberals – a direction that would likely further dilute the party's pro-union ideological orientation.[44]

Ideology aside, the fact that the federal NDP has never formed a national government weakens the instrumental case for a labour party in Canada. But even if the party was electorally viable, as it is in several provinces, a significant portion of union activists view the NDP as an unreliable vehicle to achieve a truly social democratic government. The ghost of Bob Rae looms large here, and the influence that unions affiliated to the NDP lost during the early 1990s has never been fully recovered.

For some on the radical left, the answer lies not in political parties, elections, and government but in anti-power politics. Sociologist John Holloway's call to "change the world without taking power" effectively encapsulates this approach that eschews parties and elections in favour of popular assemblies and other nonstate institutions.[45] However, as labour studies scholar Paul Christopher Gray argues, "disengaging from the state cedes much political space and operational terrain to ruling classes," and a strictly extra-parliamentary approach "has proven to be as unable to challenge capitalism from outside of the state as is any purely party politics from the inside."[46] As Gray notes, and as we have argued elsewhere, unions need not put all of their eggs into one political-action basket. Parliamentary and extra-parliamentary strategies can be reconciled and potentially enhanced by judicial or workplace-based strategies in order to maximize unions' political leverage.[47]

THE FUTURE OF WORKING-CLASS POLITICS

If a lack of confidence in social democratic electoralism has breathed new life into old Gomperist approaches at the expense of a more radical left politics, what does that mean for the future of labour and working-class politics in Canada? Strong and effective left-wing parties arguably require the support of a mobilized and energized labour movement to be electorally competitive. Conversely, the labour movement's interests are best served when left-wing parties have strong political influence. But beyond any sort of labour-left electoral link, working-class politics must be anchored in a broader left project, one that seeks to transform capitalist social relations and the very state that underpins them. When rooted in strong and transformative left projects led by working-class people, unions are better equipped to resist reverting back to sectionalist or Gomperist strategies.

Too much of what today's unions do politically relies on public-relations campaigns and slick television ads rather than on building and activating the membership. "The activist base is too small to achieve our goals," argues Fred Wilson. "To go to the next stage of labour politics, we need a lot more political education, especially for leadership."[48] At a basic level, unions require a better understanding of class politics and how power is wielded. This knowledge is needed to help members make sense of the myriad problems that they face at work and in society more generally. This orientation does not mean abandoning pragmatic political considerations altogether. There is no question that unions need to engage with parties and politicians with whom they do not share much in common ideologically, especially when these parties are in government. The real question is how this engagement happens and whose interests are articulated and ultimately served. Moreover, a union's political effectiveness is based on what forms of power are available in a given period. However, the problem is that some unions are increasingly detached from core left-wing principles. If union strategies are narrowly cast in service of the needs of members in a particular workplace, to the exclusion of others, what implications does this approach have for building broader forms of solidarity among working-class people? Increasingly, movement leaders have abandoned the idea that union power rests with workers or that capitalism is an impediment to workers' progress and eventual emancipation.

Although working-class politics has incredible transformational potential, its character is not necessarily progressive by nature. Historically, left-wing working-class movements and political parties directly mobilized working people into political action at the level of the community and workplace. This mobilization was rooted in challenging income inequalities and social exclusion and succeeded in making working-class politics synonymous with left-wing politics. However, throughout the 1970s and 1980s, social democratic parties around the world increasingly adopted supra-class electoral strategies designed to broaden their appeal to middle-class voters. According to Dennis Pilon and Larry Savage, by pursuing this strategy, "left parties that had initially emerged as vehicles to organize the working class in the electoral arena were now, whether consciously or unconsciously, beginning the work of disorganizing the working class."[49]

When a crisis in social democratic electoralism fractured party-union links in the 1990s, social democratic parties like the NDP further veered to the political centre based on a "mistaken belief that adapting to neoliberal political imperatives was the only viable alternative to traditional social democracy."[50] As these parties lost touch with working-class needs and interests, many working-class voters simply lost faith in the promise of social democratic electoral politics and dropped out or turned to right-wing parties that framed the problem of growing economic insecurity by pointing the finger at immigrants and foreign actors. The lack of a compelling left counternarrative has allowed populist xenophobia and moral traditionalism to gain steam in working-class communities, thus shifting the landscape of working-class politics in Canada.[51]

Given this trend, the political challenges facing unions are significant. They are confronted with the difficult task of marrying the need to protect members' material interests with a commitment to broader social transformation for all workers. All unions are torn between these two faces of their role in capitalist society – "sword of justice and vested interest."[52] All unions must sort out the balance that they will strike between these two faces, particularly as economic and political circumstances change. Given the labour movement's internal divisions and unions' tendency toward sectionalism and economism, this task is not easy. But the challenges are not simply on the union side of the ledger. Social democratic parties have consistently failed to rise to the occasion.

Part of the problem is that the policy prescriptions of the social democratic left over the course of the last four decades have consistently fallen short of delivering on the promise of social and economic justice. Too much time is spent tinkering with commonly accepted neoliberal orthodoxy in an effort to humanize it rather than rejecting neoliberal ideas outright and proposing better ideas that will unite and excite the base, not reinforce cynicism and despair. Reminding activists of the left's glorious victories from decades past will no longer cut it.

A union, however strong and dynamic, cannot substitute for a left-wing political party. After all, unions are and will likely always be primarily focused on improving the terms and conditions of work for their members. Thus the need for a political party to champion and advance broader working-class interests through legislative means is essential. At their best, left-wing parties create spaces where common issues and priorities emerge out of the sectionalist interests of individual union affiliates. In short, they transform the particular into the general. In the case of Unifor, however, the union has formally retreated from both the party and the movement (by leaving the Canadian Labour Congress), thus making it less likely that the union can overcome its own sectionalist impulses and less necessary for Unifor to find common cause with other unions in pursuit of broader working-class interests.

None of this analysis should be interpreted as support for unions' ceding their politics to left-wing parties. Unions should absolutely take charge of their own political thinking and develop their own political program. However, unions cannot naively assume that their ideas and solutions will simply be adopted by sympathetic parties. Rather, labour must consciously fight for these issues to be taken up and prioritized. That requires active involvement in party affairs, even if unions maintain relative autonomy.

Some in Unifor might argue that the union has already embraced this path and that its principles are clearly articulated in the union's own policy documents related to political action.[53] Drawing on the spirit of these policy documents, Lana Payne, for example, asserts that Unifor is a "social union. That means our work doesn't stop at the workplace door. It means we don't see collective bargaining as being transactional. We see it as being transformative, and that is, I think, the crucial difference between how we approach our work at the bargaining table and at the political tables and in the community."[54]

There is no doubt that Unifor continues to promote social unionist campaigns, whether in the form of support for a national child care program, reproductive justice and abortion rights, or queer and trans rights. However, campaigns that emphasize broader social justice have increasingly taken a back seat to those aimed at protecting the immediate workplace interests of Unifor members. In this sense, we might observe not an abandonment of social unionism but a shift in where and how these commitments are integrated within union activity. As Stephanie Ross has argued elsewhere, even unions committed to social unionism vary in how they apply these values. In some unions, "social unionism is what happens 'outside of bargaining' and is counterposed to – or at least separate from – what remains the core of union activity: collective bargaining and the labour-management relationship."[55] The CAW long worked to counter this tendency, to infuse collective bargaining with social unionist elements, and to prioritize political struggles for broader working-class interests. Over time, however, there appears to have been a reordering of priorities and a restructuring of how social unionism figures into both collective bargaining and electoral strategy. Although social unionist campaigns persist in Unifor, its electoral campaigns have become more important and more transactional.

Such a reordering of priorities can give credence to the claim of a widening value-action gap between the union's political commitments and its actual political practice. Words in policy papers are just words. What matters is how these words are acted upon. To make sense of current economic and political circumstances, words in policy documents are sometimes interpreted in ways that blur their original intent or meaning. When Unifor convention delegates were debating their union's political approach, no delegate imagined that independent political action meant that Jerry Dias would be providing political cover for Doug Ford by standing alongside him at a press conference to announce restoration of the minimum-wage increase that his government had previously cancelled. Nor did they imagine that Unifor's former president would be making campaign contributions to Conservative Party leadership candidates. Notably, both events took place without anyone from the union's National Executive Board (NEB) challenging Dias's leadership.

However, Unifor's often contradictory approach to political action must also be understood in the context of the dilemmas that have always faced all unions under capitalism. Rather than reflecting a gap between values and action, these seeming inconsistencies reflect the reality that unions are complex organizations containing multiple constituencies, purposes, and hence approaches to unionism that pull them in different directions. As historian Perry Anderson argues, "trade unions are dialectically both an opposition to capitalism and a component of it. For they both resist the given unequal distribution of income within the society by their wage demands, and ratify the principle of an unequal distribution by their existence, which implies as its complementary opposite that of management."[56] As a result, their relationship to political-economic structures and systems is complicated, and changing circumstances make certain approaches and strategies more or less difficult. Canada's political and economic elites first attempted to contain militant and anti-capitalist working-class currents by more fully integrating labour organizations into the country's labour relations framework in the mid-twentieth century. However, toward the end of the century, once the balance of class forces had shifted to become so unequal that unions were seen as posing no threat to the capitalist order, the business community and its political allies jettisoned any notion that adversarial unions needed to be tolerated, let alone accommodated. Ill-equipped to shield themselves from attacks on workers' hard-won rights and freedoms, unions went into retreat.

In the case of the CAW, an adversarial approach encapsulated in the slogan "Fighting Back Makes a Difference" gave way to closer collaboration with employers and governments in a defensive effort to preserve jobs and secure capital investments. The changing nature of the union's own education programs reflected these shifts. Gindin describes the CAW's early internal education programs as a space where members were free to offer up critiques of the union and its politics, structures, or strategies. "When the union turns, all of a sudden, you can't say that they made a concession and discuss it. You couldn't say it. All of a sudden, you're being censored," he explains. The very same structure that had built up thousands of activists in the union was later "used to co-opt, integrate, and neutralize these terrific leaders, and the lesson is that structures are essential for struggle, but struggle is the key. If you're not in struggle, any structure can be used two ways," Gindin adds.[57] In short, the union was playing a key role in preserving the very economic system that had precipitated the rise of industrial unionism, and internal union education was reoriented to reinforce this role. Moreover, strategies to mitigate job loss, like early-retirement packages, had a significant impact on the union's internal political culture and capacity by wiping out nearly an entire generation of trained activists.

Although the creation of Unifor in 2013 was presented by its architects as a game changer for the labour movement and for labour politics more generally, the union has more or less spun its wheels during its first decade. The threats that precipitated Unifor's formation still hang over Canada's unions. In fact, declining union density, hostile political actors, reduced bargaining power, and division among unions are arguably worse problems than they were a decade ago. A much-touted independent and progressive approach to labour politics has lost ground to a sectionalist and transactional brand of nonpartisanship that sometimes has more in common with the politics of Samuel Gompers than it does with the politics of Walter Reuther. On occasion, Unifor seemingly has closer relations with political power holders and employers than with the rest of the labour movement. These relations have created an environment where the union's values, principles, and capacity to act independently from capital have been compromised. This dynamic is reflected in the union's defence of industry subsidies (even without job guarantees), its trumpeting of competitiveness arguments, and its willingness to play ball with anti-union politicians and governments in the hopes of securing a short-term policy win or investment.

How unions position themselves in relation to dominant economic and political systems plays an important role in shaping workers' understanding of class and the role of workplace conflict and struggle in advancing workers' interests. However, adopting an independent class-based political analysis is not enough. Unions must also look inward to their own structures, cultures, and practices and transform themselves from the inside out with a view to enhancing participation and political education. Although Unifor and former CAW leadership often describe their union as among the most democratic anywhere, there is no shortage of activists and rank-and-file members who reject this notion. In particular, such critics point to the level of centralization in the president's office and the managed democracy of the Administration caucus as key factors undermining rigorous and democratic internal debates and elections. This culture helps to explain why Dias's questionable political alliances were never publicly challenged by leaders from Unifor's NEB. In reference to the broader labour movement, political scientist Bryan Evans and colleagues argue,

> Which precise constitutional mechanisms, democratic forums, and internal structures are technically best in terms of maximizing accountability and democratic decision-making is not the issue here. The point is rather to measure these mechanisms in terms of the contribution they make to developing democratic capacities whereby members overcome deference, leaders pass on expertise rather than hoard it like their personal capital, and more frequent changes of leadership are made possible. Above all, debate needs to be encouraged rather than avoided, even over the most potentially divisive issues.[58]

Indeed, member participation and confidence are key both to building unions' political power and to short-circuiting overtures from right-wing parties seeking to build an alternative working-class politics that positions hard-working members in opposition to the "greedy" and "reckless" so-called "union bosses" who are the source of all the problems. Although this dichotomous framing is clearly designed to unfairly undermine the union leadership, union leaders have to be honest with themselves. Only a small minority of union members are active in most unions. This reality helps to contribute to the idea that unions themselves are abstract institutions separate and apart from workers rather than vessels steered by workers themselves. With such a small layer of union members organized as activists, union mobilizations cannot reach their full potential.[59] As a result, union leaders become more vulnerable to insular and defensive thinking about how to weather the storm in the face of hostile governments and an unmotivated membership.

The solution to this problem seems clear. Unions need a majority of members to be active in order to change the dynamic, and that requires internal organizing. Organizing is key to expanding the base of people who actively participate in the union's political work. In turn, mobilizing an expanded base of activist members gives unions much more clout both at the bargaining table and in the political sphere. It also gives workers themselves greater ownership and a direct stake in the outcome of union struggles, which in turn reinforces and builds workers' capacities to fight, organize, and win. Although these prescriptions are not pie in the sky, they do require a significant commitment on behalf of leaders to help reorient their unions in ways that challenge sectionalist impulses and build capacity to meaningfully organize politically outside the confines of electoral cycles. They also require investments in political education aimed at challenging a purely transactional brand of politics rather than at reinforcing it.

Ultimately, the way forward depends on how we understand what causes change in union politics and strategy. On the one hand, those who focus on the power of people like Bob White, Buzz Hargrove, Jerry Dias, or Lana Payne would say that a union's direction, whether good or bad, comes down to the choices that leaders make. And there is no doubt, as we have shown in this book, that individuals – elected leaders, staff, and activists – make an enormous difference with their choices at key moments. On the other hand, others point out that such choices are shaped by a host of important constraints, including the economic conditions that the union finds itself in, the limited range of political and partisan options, and the powerful organizational and cultural legacies of past union practices. We have also shown here how the weight of these factors explains in part the union's trajectory. But there are risks in overemphasizing either agency or structure in these processes. We prefer to keep our attention on how union leaders and activists make meaningful choices in conditions that they do not control. Although the union finds itself in circumstances that are very different from those of the 1930s or the 1980s, it is worth remembering that the birth of the union in Canada through militant strikes in 1936 and 1937, the triumphant breakaway and birth of the CAW in 1985, and even the formation of Unifor in 2013 were not the products of destiny. They may seem so with the benefit of hindsight, but these conjunctural events were, in fact, risky long shots given the political-economic contexts and the powerful actors involved. Agency, even if constrained, is never completely eclipsed by structure. Taking the political-economic context seriously means recognizing that, although the strategies of the past decade have not always lived up to the union's own stated principles and vision for labour and working-class politics, this shortcoming, too, is not inevitable. Rediscovering these values with the aim of committing to the Herculean task of reorienting the union's politics so that they might live up to Unifor's promise is a possible and necessary step on the path to reasserting working-class power in Canada. The union has shifted gears before, and it can do so again. As Canada's largest private-sector union, Unifor will play a critical role in any reorientation of labour politics through the choices that it makes in the coming years.

NOTES

CHAPTER 1: SHIFTING GEARS

1 Ontario Federation of Labour, "Ontario Federation of Labour Pledges Support for Ontario NDP," https://ofl.ca/ontario-federation-of-labour-pledges-support -for-ontario-ndp/.

2 Robert Benzie, "Flanked by Union Leaders, Doug Ford Raises Ontario's Minimum Wage to $15 an Hour," *Toronto Star,* November 2, 2021, https://www.thestar.com/ politics/provincial/2021/11/02/flanked-by-union-leaders-doug-ford-raises-ontarios -minimum-wage-to-15-an-hour.html.

3 Sara Mojtahedzadeh and Rosa Saba, "Union Leader Leaves Complicated Legacy," *Toronto Star,* March 18, 2022, https://www.pressreader.com/canada/toronto-star/ 20220318/281522229574511.

4 Martin Regg Cohn, "Doug Ford's Temporary Truce with Union Leader Shows the Enemy of My Enemy Is My Friend," *Toronto Star,* December 19, 2021, https://www. thestar.com/politics/political-opinion/doug-ford-s-temporary-truce-with-union -leader-shows-the-enemy-of-my-enemy-is/article_91bfc089-92ab-54ad-bafd -c65c897c52d0.html.

5 UAW Canada, *Solidarity,* Fall 1985, 37.

6 Lorne Slotnick, "Broadbent Vows to Fight Free Trade," *Globe and Mail,* September 7, 1985, 18.

7 Donald Swartz and Rosemary Warskett, "Canadian Labour and the Crisis of Solidarity," in Stephanie Ross and Larry Savage, eds., *Rethinking the Politics of Labour in Canada,* 18–32 (Halifax: Fernwood, 2012); Richard Hyman, *Industrial Relations: A Marxist Introduction* (London: Macmillan, 1975), 42–63.

8 Stephanie Ross, "Business Unionism and Social Unionism in Theory and Practice," in Stephanie Ross and Larry Savage, eds., *Rethinking the Politics of Labour in Canada,* 2nd ed., 29–46 (Halifax: Fernwood, 2021).

9 For more on the formation of the Pulp, Paper and Woodworkers of Canada and the Canadian Paperworkers Union, see Thomas Dunk, "Notes on the Labour Movement

and the Rise and Fall of the Pulp-and-Paper Industry in Anglophone Canada," in Michel S. Beaulieu and Ronald N. Harpelle, eds., *Pulp Friction: Communities and the Forest Industry in a Globalized World*, 70–84 (Thunder Bay, ON: Centre for Northern Studies, Lakehead University, 2012).

10 Canadian Auto Workers, *Twenty Years of Fighting Back: The CAW Makes a Difference* (2005), 37, 43.

11 Unifor, *New Member Kit* (2002), 4, unifor.org/sites/default/files/documents/New%20 Member%20Kit%202022%20EN-Web.pdf.

12 Ibid., 3.

13 See, for example, Walter Korpi, "Power Resources Approach vs. Action and Conflict: On Causal and Intentional Explanations in the Study of Power," *Sociological Theory* 3, 2 (1985): 31–45; and Nicos Poulantzas, "The Problem of the Capitalist State," *New Left Review* 1, 58 (1969): 67–78.

14 Selig Perlman, *A Theory of the Labor Movement* (New York: Macmillan, 1928); Neil Chamberlain, *The Labor Sector* (New York: McGraw-Hill, 1965).

15 James G. March and Johan P. Olsen, "The New Institutionalism: Organizational Factors in Political Life," *American Political Science Review* 78, 3 (1984): 736.

16 Lewis Minkin, *The Contentious Alliance: Trade Unions and the Labour Party* (Edinburgh: Edinburgh University Press, 1991).

17 Scott Aquanno and Toba Bryant, "Workplace Restructuring and Institutional Change: GM Oshawa from 1994 to 2019," *Studies in Political Economy* 102, 1 (2021): 26.

18 Pamela Sugiman, *Labour's Dilemma: The Gender Politics of Auto Workers in Canada, 1937–1979* (Toronto: University of Toronto Press, 1994), 214.

19 For a range of perspectives on the varied history of Canadian labour politics, see Bryan Palmer, *Working Class Experience: Rethinking the History of Canadian Labour, 1800–1991* (Toronto: McClelland and Stewart, 1992); Jacques Rouillard, *Le Syndicalisme québécois: deux siècles d'histoire* (Montreal: Boréal, 2004); Gregory S. Kealey, *Toronto Workers Respond to Industrial Capitalism, 1867–1892* (Toronto: University of Toronto Press, 1980); Craig Heron, "Labourism and the Canadian Working Class," *Labour/Le Travail* 13 (Spring 1984): 45–76; Charles Lipton, *The Trade Union Movement of Canada, 1827–1959*, 3rd ed. (Toronto: NC Press, 1973); Ivan Avakumovic, *The Communist Party of Canada: A History* (Toronto: McClelland and Stewart, 1975); Desmond Morton, *Social Democracy in Canada*, 2nd ed. (Toronto: Samuel Stevens Hakkert and Company, 1977); Joan Sangster, *Dreams of Equality: Women on the Canadian Left, 1920–1950* (Toronto: University of Toronto Press, 1989); and Mark Leier, *Where the Fraser River Flows: The Industrial Workers of the World in British Columbia* (Vancouver: New Star Books, 1990).

20 Martin Robin, *Radical Politics and Canadian Labour, 1880–1930* (Kingston: Industrial Relations Centre, Queen's University, 1968).

21 Robert H. Babcock, *Gompers in Canada: A Study in American Continentalism before the First World War* (Toronto: University of Toronto Press, 1974), 55–71.

22 Robert Hoxie, "Trade Unionism in the United States," *Journal of Political Economy* 22, 3 (1914): 201–17; Louis Reed, *The Labor Philosophy of Samuel Gompers* (Port Washington, NY: Kennikat, 1966).

23 Ross, "Business Unionism," 37.

24 Ibid., 35–38.

25 James Naylor, *The Fate of Labour Socialism: The Co-operative Commonwealth Federation and the Dream of a Working-Class Future* (Toronto: University of Toronto Press, 2016).

26 Keith Archer, *Political Choices and Electoral Consequences: A Study of Organized Labour and the New Democratic Party* (Montreal/Kingston: McGill-Queen's University Press, 1990), 35.

27 Gad Horowitz, *Canadian Labour in Politics* (Toronto: University of Toronto Press, 1968), 107–18.

28 Nelson Wiseman, *Social Democracy in Manitoba: A History of the CCF/NDP* (Winnipeg: University of Manitoba Press, 1983), 80. See Chapter 2 herein for a more in-depth discussion of the political dynamic.

29 Richard Ulric Miller, "Organized Labour and Politics in Canada," in Richard Ulric Miller and Fraser Isbester, eds., *Canadian Labour in Transition* (Toronto: Prentice-Hall, 1971), 210. Although in 1943 the Canadian Congress of Labour adopted a resolution to endorse the CCF as "the political arm of labour in Canada," political scientist Keith Archer explains that the "drive for affiliation was confined mainly to Ontario" and that "there never were significant numbers of unions affiliated with the party." Archer, *Political Choices*, 18.

30 Although the CCF formed a government in Saskatchewan, the party was on life support in most provinces and at the federal level. On the rise and fall of the CCF, see Leo Zakuta, *A Protest Movement Becalmed: A Study of Change in the CCF* (Toronto: University of Toronto Press, 1964); and Walter D. Young, *The Anatomy of a Party: The National CCF 1932–61* (Toronto: University of Toronto Press, 1969).

31 Horowitz, *Canadian Labour in Politics*, 162–97. "New Party" was the placeholder name for what would officially become the New Democratic Party after delegates officially adopted a name for the new political formation at the founding convention.

32 Resolution adopted at the CLC convention held at Winnipeg, April 21–25, 1958, as reprinted in Stanley Knowles, *The New Party* (Toronto: McClelland and Stewart, 1961), 127–28.

33 Miller, "Organized Labour and Politics," 211.

34 Bryan Evans, "The New Democratic Party in the Era of Neoliberalism," in Stephanie Ross and Larry Savage, eds., *Rethinking the Politics of Labour in Canada*, 48–61 (Halifax: Fernwood, 2012); Bryan Evans, "From Protest Movement to Neoliberal Management: Canada's New Democratic Party in the Era of Permanent Austerity," in Bryan Evans and Ingo Schmidt, eds., *Social Democracy after the Cold War*, 45–98 (Edmonton: Athabasca University Press, 2012); Leo Panitch and Donald Swartz, *From Consent to Coercion: The Assault on Trade Union Freedoms* (Toronto: Garamond, 2003); Larry Savage, "Contemporary Party-Union Relations in Canada," *Labor Studies Journal* 35, 1 (2010): 8–26; Larry Savage and Charles Smith, "Public Sector Unions and Electoral Politics in Canada," in Stephanie Ross and Larry Savage, eds., *Public Sector Unions in the Age of Austerity*, 46–56 (Halifax: Fernwood, 2013).

35 Yonatan Reshef and Sandra Rastin, *Unions in the Time of Revolution: Government Restructuring in Alberta and Ontario* (Toronto: University of Toronto Press, 2003); Henry Jacek and Brian Tanguay, "Can Strategic Voting Beat Mike Harris?" *Inroads: A*

Journal of Opinion 10 (2001): 55–65; Tim Fowler, "Coordinated Strategic Voting in the 2008 Federal Election," *American Review of Canadian Studies* 42, 1 (2012): 20–33; Larry Savage, "Organized Labour and the Politics of Strategic Voting," in Stephanie Ross and Larry Savage, eds., *Rethinking the Politics of Labour in Canada*, 75–87 (Halifax: Fernwood, 2012); Brian Tanguay, "Parties, Organized Interests, and Electoral Democracy: The 1999 Ontario Provincial Election," in William Cross, ed., *Political Parties, Representation, and Electoral Democracy in Canada*, 145–60 (Toronto: Oxford University Press, 2001); Larry Savage and Nick Ruhloff-Queiruga, "Organized Labour, Campaign Finance, and the Politics of Strategic Voting in Ontario," *Labour/Le Travail* 80 (Fall 2017): 247–71.

36 Archer, *Political Choices*; Horowitz, *Canadian Labour in Politics*; David McGrane, *The New NDP: Moderation, Modernization, and Political Marketing* (Vancouver: UBC Press, 2019); David Laycock and Linda Erickson, eds., *Reviving Social Democracy: The Near Death and Surprising Rise of the Federal NDP* (Vancouver: UBC Press, 2015); Miller, "Organized Labour and Politics."

37 Keith Archer and Alan Whitehorn, *Political Activists: The NDP in Convention* (Toronto: Oxford University Press, 1997); James Laxer, *In Search of a New Left: Canadian Politics after the Neoconservative Assault* (Toronto: Viking, 1996); Evans, "New Democratic Party."

38 Matthew Polacko, Simon Kiss, and Peter Graefe, "The Changing Nature of Class Voting in Canada, 1965–2019," *Canadian Journal of Political Science* 55, 3 (2022): 1–24.

39 Archer and Whitehorn, *Political Activists*; Janine Brodie and Jane Jenson, *Crisis, Challenge and Change: Party and Class in Canada Revisited* (Ottawa: Carleton University Press, 1988); Neil Bradford, "Ideas, Intellectuals and Social Democracy in Canada," in Alain Gagnon and Brian Tanguay, eds., *Canadian Parties in Transition: Discourse, Organization, Representation*, 83–110 (Toronto: Nelson, 1989); Miller, "Organized Labour and Politics."

40 See Table 3 in Archer, *Political Choices*, 37.

41 NDP majority governments were elected in Manitoba in 1969 and British Columbia in 1972, and the party was returned to power in Saskatchewan in 1971.

42 Morton, *Social Democracy in Canada*, 193; Christo Aivalis, *The Constant Liberal: Pierre Trudeau, Organized Labour, and the Canadian Social Democratic Left* (Vancouver: UBC Press, 2018), 125.

43 James Rinehart, "The Canadian Auto Workers: An Inspirational Story," *Monthly Review* 50, 6 (1998): 58.

44 On the gender politics in the union, see Sugiman, *Labour's Dilemma*.

45 Sam Gindin, *The Canadian Auto Workers: The Birth and Transformation of a Union* (Toronto: Lorimer 1995), 160, 204, 269, 272; Mathieu Brûlé, "The Canadian Auto Workers, Social Unionism and the Abortion Debate," *Active History*, July 3, 2012, https://activehistory.ca/2012/07/the-canadian-auto-workers-social-unionism-and-the-abortion-debate/; Prabha Khosla, *Labour Pride: What Our Unions Have Done For Us* (Toronto: WorldPride Committee of the Toronto and York Region Labour Council, 2014), https://labour150.ca/wp-content/uploads/2021/05/Labour_Pride_2014.pdf.

46 Ross, "Business Unionism," 29–31.

47 Stephanie Ross, "Varieties of Social Unionism: Towards a Framework for Comparison," *Just Labour* 11 (2007): 16–34.

48 James Piazza, "De-linking Labor: Labor Unions and Social Democratic Parties under Globalization," *Party Politics* 7, 4 (2001): 413–35.

49 Dennis Pilon, Stephanie Ross, and Larry Savage, "Solidarity Revisited: Organized Labour and the New Democratic Party," *Canadian Political Science Review* 5, 1 (2011): 29; Leo Panitch, "Globalisation and the State," in Ralph Miliband and Leo Panitch, eds., *The Socialist Register 1994: Between Globalism and Nationalism*, 60–93 (London: Merlin, 1994); John Callaghan, "Social Democracy and Globalisation: The Limits of Social Democracy in Historical Perspective," *British Journal of Politics and International Relations* 4, 3 (2002): 429–51; Gerassimos Moschonas, *In the Name of Social Democracy* (London: Verso, 2002).

50 Geoffrey Garrett and Deborah Mitchell, "Globalization, Government Spending and Taxation in the OECD," *European Journal of Political Research* 39, 2 (2001): 145–77; Axel Dreher, "The Influence of Globalization on Taxes and Social Policy: An Empirical Analysis for OECD Countries," *European Journal of Political Economy* 22, 1 (2006): 179–201; Kees van Kersbergen, "The Politics and Political Economy of Social Democracy," *Acta Politica* 38, 3 (2003): 255–73.

51 Archer, *Political Choices;* Thomas Quinn, "Block Voting in the Labour Party: A Political Exchange Model," *Party Politics* 8, 2 (2002): 207–26.

52 Harold Jansen and Lisa Young, "Solidarity Forever? The NDP, Organized Labour, and the Changing Face of Party Finance in Canada," *Canadian Journal of Political Science* 42, 3 (2009): 659.

53 Ibid., 661.

54 Pilon, Ross, and Savage, "Solidarity Revisited," 23.

55 Katrina Burgess, "Loyalty Dilemmas and Market Reform: Party-Union Alliances under Stress in Mexico, Spain and Venezuela," *World Politics* 52, 1 (1999): 105–34.

56 Larry Savage and Chantal Mancini, "Strategic Electoral Dilemmas and the Politics of Teachers' Unions in Ontario," *Canadian Political Science Review* 16, 1 (2022): 1–21.

57 Charlotte Yates, *From Plant to Politics: The Autoworkers Union in Postwar Canada* (Philadelphia: Temple University Press, 1993), 5.

58 David Camfield, *Canadian Labour in Crisis: Reinventing the Workers' Movement* (Halifax: Fernwood, 2011), 47.

59 Hemi Mitic, personal interview, November 15, 2021.

60 See, for example, comments by Buzz Hargrove on the history of the caucus system in Canadian Auto Workers, National Executive Board, special meeting minutes, July 8, 2008, 13, in possession of the authors.

61 Sugiman, *Labour's Dilemma*, 5.

62 Carmela Patrias and Larry Savage, *Union Power: Solidarity and Struggle in Niagara* (Edmonton: Athabasca University Press), 74–81.

63 Sugiman, *Labour's Dilemma*.

64 Unifor, *Welcome to Unifor* (2022), 4, https://www.unifor.org/sites/default/files/documents/New%20Member%20Kit%202022%20EN-Web.pdf.

65 Ibid., 3; Dave Cassidy, personal interview, January 20, 2023.

66 At the April 2000 CAW Council meeting, for example, CAW president Buzz Hargrove made the point that "the auto industry makes up only a third of the membership of our union today but in terms of resources in the union, well over half comes from the auto sector." Buzz Hargrove, "Address to CAW Council," April 2000, 13, CAW/Unifor archives, Unifor National Office, Toronto.

CHAPTER 2: IN THE DRIVER'S SEAT

1 Bob White, *Hard Bargains: My Life on the Line* (Toronto: McLelland and Stewart, 1987), 15.
2 Walter Reuther, "The Job Ahead," speech delivered to the 11th UAW-CIO Convention, Atlantic City, New Jersey, November 9, 1947, 4–5.
3 Nelson Lichtenstein, *Walter Reuther: The Most Dangerous Man in Detroit* (New York: Basic Books, 1995), 299–326.
4 Bromley L. Armstrong with Sheldon Taylor, *Bromley, Tireless Champion for Just Causes: Memoirs of Bromley L. Armstrong* (Pickering, ON: Vitabu, 2000), 78.
5 Carmela Patrias and Larry Savage, *Union Power: Solidarity and Struggle in Niagara* (Edmonton: Athabasca University Press, 2012), 77.
6 White, *Hard Bargains*, 43.
7 Buzz Hargrove, personal interview, November 17, 2021.
8 Charlotte Yates, *From Plant to Politics: The Autoworkers Union in Postwar Canada* (Philadelphia: Temple University Press, 1993), 31.
9 Gad Horowitz, *Canadian Labour in Politics* (Toronto: University of Toronto Press, 1968), 68.
10 Irving Abella, *Nationalism, Communism and Canadian Labour: The CIO, the Communist Party and the Canadian Congress of Labour, 1935–1956* (Toronto: University of Toronto Press, 1973), 30–33, 147, 163–67.
11 Horowitz, *Canadian Labour in Politics*, 158.
12 Sam Gindin, *The Canadian Auto Workers: The Birth and Transformation of a Union* (Toronto: Lorimer, 1995), 121.
13 Horowitz, *Canadian Labour in Politics*, 68.
14 Donald M. Wells, "Origins of Canada's Wagner Model of Industrial Relations: The United Auto Workers in Canada and the Suppression of 'Rank and File' Unionism, 1936–1953," *Canadian Journal of Sociology* 20, 2 (1995): 198–99, 203. Both Local 200 president Roy England and Local 195 president Alex Parent were Communists.
15 Hemi Mitic, personal interview, November 15, 2021.
16 Horowitz, *Canadian Labour in Politics*, 108.
17 Ibid., 85.
18 Yates, *From Plant to Politics*, 139.
19 Gindin, *Canadian Auto Workers*, 135.
20 Janine Brodie and Jane Jenson, *Crisis, Challenge and Change: Party and Class in Canada Revisited* (Ottawa: Carleton University Press, 1988).
21 Craig Heron, *The Canadian Labour Movement: A Short History*, 3rd ed. (Toronto: Lorimer, 2012), 74; Bryan Palmer, *Working-Class Experience: Rethinking the History of Canadian Labour, 1800–1991* (Toronto: McLelland and Stewart, 1992), 291.

22 Gindin, *Canadian Auto Workers*, 134. Although he had run provincially under the Conservative banner in 1943, Reaume was a pro-labour mayor who supported the Ford strikers in 1945, urging City Council to provide relief for their families, and who led the construction of low-cost working-class housing in the aftermath of the Great Depression. Pat Brode, "The Eight Day Mayor," *Walkerville Times*, n.d., http://www.walkervilletimes.com/39/eightday-mayor.html.

23 Palmer, *Working-Class Experience*, 255.

24 Yates, *From Plant to Politics*, 49–50.

25 Ibid., 105.

26 Sam Gindin, personal interview, August 27, 2021.

27 Gindin, *Canadian Auto Workers*, 135–36.

28 John Barnard, *American Vanguard: The United Auto Workers during the Reuther Years, 1935–1970* (Detroit: Wayne State University Press, 2004), 65.

29 Lichtenstein, *Walter Reuther*, 112–28.

30 Barnard, *American Vanguard*, 65.

31 Lichtenstein, *Walter Reuther*, 261.

32 Roger Keeran, *The Communist Party and the Auto Workers' Union* (Bloomington: Indiana University Press, 1980), 282–84.

33 Horowitz, *Canadian Labour in Politics*, 118.

34 Lichtenstein, *Walter Reuther*, 251.

35 Keeran, *Communist Party*, 284, 285.

36 Lichtenstein, *Walter Reuther*, 279–80.

37 Barnard, *American Vanguard*, 260.

38 Ibid., 252–53.

39 Ibid., 461–63.

40 White, *Hard Bargains*, 93.

41 Yates, *From Plant to Politics*, 171; Gindin, *Canadian Auto Workers*, 68–69.

42 White, *Hard Bargains*, 80.

43 Ibid., 85.

44 Carol Phillips, personal interview, November 22, 2022; Sam Gindin, personal interview, August 27, 2021.

45 Patrias and Savage, *Union Power*, 83–84.

46 Wayne Gates, personal interview, October 8, 2021.

47 Horowitz, *Canadian Labour in Politics*, 233.

48 Yates, *From Plant to Politics*, 133.

49 Ibid., 134.

50 Horowitz, *Canadian Labour in Politics*, 256, calculations based on Table I.

51 Richard Ulric Miller, "Organized Labour and Politics in Canada," in Richard Ulric Miller and Fraser Isbester, eds., *Canadian Labour in Transition* (Toronto: Prentice-Hall, 1971), 235.

52 Horowitz, *Canadian Labour in Politics*, 256, calculations based on Table I.

53 Buzz Hargrove, personal interview, November 17, 2021.

54 Yates, *From Plant to Politics*, 136.

55 Gindin, *Canadian Auto Workers*, 148.

56 Canadian Labour Congress, "Memorial Service for Dennis McDermott." March 5, 2003, https://web.archive.org/web/20070311082630/http://canadianlabour.ca/index.php/march_03/Memorial_Service_for.

57 Gindin, *Canadian Auto Workers*, 158.

58 Yates, *From Plant to Politics*, 167.

59 Ibid.

60 Robert Laxer, *Canada's Unions* (Toronto: Lorimer, 1976), 275; Miller, "Organized Labour and Politics," 236.

61 Buzz Hargrove with Wayne Skene, *Labour of Love: The Fight to Create a More Humane Canada* (Toronto: McFarlane, Walter and Ross, 1998), 97.

62 Dimitry Anastakis, *Auto Pact: Creating a Borderless North American Auto Industry, 1960–1971* (Toronto: University of Toronto Press, 2005), 17.

63 Ibid., 24–26.

64 Ibid., 5, 91.

65 Ibid., 151.

66 Sam Gindin, "Breaking Away: The Formation of the Canadian Auto Workers," *Studies in Political Economy* 29, 1 (1989): 67.

67 Miriam Smith, "The Canadian Labour Congress: From Continentalism to Economic Nationalism," *Studies in Political Economy* 38, 1 (1992): 37.

68 Sam Gindin, personal interview, August 27, 2021.

69 Ibid.

70 White, *Hard Bargains*, 86–87.

71 Ibid., 88.

72 Reg Whitaker, "Introduction: The 20th Anniversary of the Waffle," *Studies in Political Economy* 32, 1 (1990): 168.

73 Waffle, *The Waffle Manifesto: For an Independent Socialist Canada* (1969), Resolution 133, http://www.socialisthistory.ca/Docs/Waffle/WaffleManifesto.htm.

74 Yates, *From Plant to Politics*, 168–70.

75 Dimitry Anastakis, "Between Nationalism and Continentalism: State Auto Industry Policy and the Canadian UAW, 1960–1970," *Labour/Le Travail* 53 (Spring 2004): 94–95.

76 Yates, *From Plant to Politics*, 167.

77 Ibid., 168.

78 Pat Kerwin, personal interview, March 7, 2022. On McDermott's NDP ties, Kerwin notes that "Dennis was a very good personal friend of David Lewis and all the Lewis family."

79 Sam Gindin, personal interview, August 27, 2021.

80 Yates, *From Plant to Politics*, 169–70.

81 Anastakis, "Between Nationalism and Continentalism," 108–11.

82 Sam Gindin, personal interview, August 27, 2021.

83 Smith, "Canadian Labour Congress," 38.

84 Bryan Evans, "The New Democratic Party in the Era of Neoliberalism," in Stephanie Ross and Larry Savage, eds., *Rethinking the Politics of Labour in Canada*, 48–61 (Halifax: Fernwood, 2012).

85 Gindin, *Canadian Auto Workers*, 173.

86 Laxer, *Canada's Unions*, 270.
87 Christo Aivalis, *The Constant Liberal: Pierre Trudeau, Organized Labour, and the Canadian Social Democratic Left* (Vancouver: UBC Press, 2018), 97.
88 Buzz Hargrove, personal interview, November 17, 2021.
89 Laxer, *Canada's Unions*, 263.
90 Buzz Hargrove, personal interview, November 17, 2021. This practice was confirmed in all our interviews for this project, including with Hemi Mitic, Peggy Nash, and Malcolm Allen.
91 Sam Gindin, personal interview, August 27, 2021.
92 Ibid.
93 Gindin, *Canadian Auto Workers*, 136.
94 Sam Gindin, personal interview, August 27, 2021.
95 Andrew Jackson, personal interview, February 7, 2022.
96 Jim Stanford, personal interview, October 4, 2021.
97 Heron, *Canadian Labour Movement*, 93–94; Palmer, *Working-Class Experience*, 315–17.
98 Yates, *From Plant to Politics*, 146.
99 Ibid., 147; Gindin, *Canadian Auto Workers*, 175.
100 Gindin, *Canadian Auto Workers*, 175.
101 Ibid.; Yates, *From Plant to Politics*, 158.
102 Gindin, *Canadian Auto Workers*, 175.
103 Bryan Palmer, *Canada's 1960s: The Ironies of Identity in a Rebellious Era* (Toronto: University of Toronto Press, 2008), 219–21.
104 Dennis McDermott, "AIB Program Unified Unions," *UAW Solidarity Canada*, July–August 1976.
105 Yates, *From Plant to Politics*, 187.
106 Ibid., 170, 187.
107 Aivalis, *Constant Liberal*, 132–33.
108 Laxer, *Canada's Unions*, 274.
109 Desmond Morton, *Social Democracy in Canada*, 2nd ed. (Toronto: Samuel Stevens Hakkert, 1977), 198.
110 Canadian Labour Congress, National Political Education Committee, minutes, Toronto, April 4–5, 1977, 2, in possession of the authors.
111 Yates, *From Plant to Politics*, 188.
112 Bob White and Jane Armstrong, "CAW Union Education: Shaping 'Time,' the Challenge of Change," draft report to the CAW National Executive Board, 2006, 7, CAW/Unifor archives, Unifor National Office, Toronto; Alissa Mazar, "Paid Education Leave Program and Development: The Canadian Auto Workers Case Study," *McGill Sociological Review* 5 (2015): 22.
113 Gindin, *Canadian Auto Workers*, 188.
114 Reuben Roth, "'Kitchen Economics for the Family': Paid Education Leave and the Canadian Autoworkers Union" (MA thesis, Ontario Institute for Studies in Education, 1997).
115 Mazar, "Paid Education Leave," 22.
116 Malcolm Allen, personal interview, November 16, 2021; Sam Gindin, personal interview, August 27, 2021; Herman Rosenfeld, personal interview, September 27, 2021.

117 White and Armstrong, "CAW Union Education," 7.

118 White, *Hard Bargains*, 127.

119 Ibid., 41.

120 Solomon Israel, "Former Canadian Union Leader Bob White Dies," *CBC News*, February 20, 2017, https://www.cbc.ca/news/business/bob-white-dead-1.3991048; White, *Hard Bargains*, 52, 58.

121 Gindin, *Canadian Auto Workers*, 163.

122 Lia Lévesque, "L'ancien ministre péquiste Robert Dean n'est plus," *La Presse*, February 4, 2021, https://www.lapresse.ca/actualites/politique/2021-02-04/l-ancien-ministre-pequiste-robert-dean-n-est-plus.php.

123 Yvon Roberge, *Histoire des TCA Québec* (Montreal: Éditions Fides, 2008), 51; Yates, *From Plant to Politics*, 162.

124 Roberge, *Histoire des TCA Québec*, 55.

125 White, *Hard Bargains*, 116–17.

126 Yates, *From Plant to Politics*, 164.

127 Gindin, "Breaking Away," 70.

128 Roberge, *Histoire des TCA Québec*, 30.

129 Bob White, "Report of the UAW Director for Canada and International Vice-President Robert White," presented to the UAW Canadian Council, September 12 and 13, 1981, Port Elgin, Ontario, 14–15, CAW/Unifor archives, Unifor National Office, Toronto.

130 Roberge, *Histoire des TCA Québec*, 31.

131 Larry Savage, "From Centralization to Sovereignty-Association: The Canadian Labour Congress and the Constitutional Question," *Review of Constitutional Studies* 13, 2 (2007): 67–95.

132 Pat Kerwin, personal interview, March 7, 2022.

133 Yates, *From Plant to Politics*, 194.

134 Desmond Morton, *The New Democrats, 1961–1986: The Politics of Change*, 3rd ed. (Toronto: Copp Clark Pitman, 1986), 194.

135 Hemi Mitic, personal interview, October 5, 2021.

136 Yates, *From Plant to Politics*, 194.

137 Morton, *New Democrats*, 194.

138 Canadian Labour Congress, "Report of the National Political Education Committee," December 3, 1983, 2, in possession of the authors.

139 Yates, *From Plant to Politics*, 196.

140 Ibid., 217.

141 Ibid., 218.

142 Quoted in Judy Steed, *Ed Broadbent: The Pursuit of Power* (Toronto: Penguin, 1988), 271.

143 Daniel Drache and Duncan Cameron, "Introduction," in Daniel Drache and Duncan Cameron, eds., *The Other MacDonald Report: The Consensus on Canada's Future That the Macdonald Commission Left Out* (Toronto: Lorimer, 1985), xi–xii.

144 Ibid., xiii.

145 Ibid., xxxi.

146 United Auto Workers, "Can Canada Compete?" in Daniel Drache and Duncan Cameron, eds., *The Other MacDonald Report: The Consensus on Canada's Future That the Macdonald Commission Left Out* (Toronto: Lorimer, 1985), 30.

147 Ibid., 33.

148 Ibid., 34.

149 Drache and Cameron, "Introduction," xx.

150 Yates, *From Plant to Politics*, 222.

151 Fingerhut Opinion, "Memorandum to Gerry Caplan and Chris Chilton re: Polling Program," February 24, 1984, 1, in possession of the authors.

152 The UAW's Paul Forder finished second as the NDP candidate in Windsor West, increasing the party's share of the vote by 5.25 points over the 1980 result, and Local 199 president Gerry Michaud finished second for the NDP in St. Catharines, netting a record high 30.6 percent of the vote for the party.

153 "How Free Trade Came to Canada: Lessons in Policy Analysis," *Policy Options*, October 1, 2007, https://policyoptions.irpp.org/fr/magazines/free-trade-20/how-free-trade-came-to-canada-lessons-in-policy-analysis/.

154 Jane Jenson and Rianne Mahon, eds., *The Challenge of Restructuring: North American Labor Movements Respond* (Philadelphia: Temple University Press, 1993).

155 Gindin, "Breaking Away," 63.

156 Kim Moody, *An Injury to All: The Decline of American Unionism* (New York: Verso, 1988).

157 Gindin, "Breaking Away," 64.

158 Moody, *Injury to All*, 138, 154, 166–67.

159 Gindin, "Breaking Away," 74.

160 Sam Gindin, personal interview, August 27, 2021.

161 Gindin, "Breaking Away," 69.

162 Ibid., 64.

163 Ibid.

164 Gindin, *Canadian Auto Workers*, 185.

165 Gindin, "Breaking Away," 72.

166 White, *Hard Bargains*, 174.

167 Steven High, "'I'll Wrap the F*** Canadian Flag Around Me': A Nationalist Response to Plant Shutdowns, 1969–1984," *Journal of the Canadian Historical Association* 12, 1 (2001): 216–18; Robert Storey and Wayne Lewchuk, "From Dust to DUST to Dust: Asbestos and the Struggle for Worker Health and Safety at Bendix Automotive," *Labour/Le Travail* 45 (Spring 2000): 130–31.

168 Gindin, *Canadian Auto Workers*, 185.

169 Sam Gindin, personal interview, August 27, 2021.

170 Gindin, "Breaking Away," 75.

171 Yates, *From Plant to Politics*, 211.

172 Ibid., 211.

173 White, *Hard Bargains*, 259; Gindin, "Breaking Away," 76.

174 White, *Hard Bargains*, 259.

175 Ibid., 264.

176 Ibid., 265.

177 Dan Benedict, "The 1984 GM Agreement in Canada: Significance and Consequences," *Relations industrielles/Industrial Relations* 40, 1 (1985): 34.

178 Yates, *From Plant to Politics*, 227.

179 Benedict, "1984 GM Agreement," 30.
180 Yates, *From Plant to Politics*, 227.
181 White, *Hard Bargains*, 289.
182 Ibid., 294.
183 Craig Saunders, "The Buzz about Buzz," *Pique Magazine*, January 16, 2009.
184 Herman Rosenfeld, "Reflections on the Birth of the Canadian Auto Workers," *Labor Notes*, July 31, 2005, https://www.labornotes.org/2005/07/reflections-birth-canadian -auto-workers.
185 White, *Hard Bargains*, 15.
186 Ibid., 15.
187 Canadian Auto Workers, "The Birth of the Union," in *Making History: A Visual Record of the CAW's First 25 Years* (2010), 22.
188 For a discussion of the relationship between union purpose, structure, identity, and ideas of democracy, see Stephanie Ross, "The Making of CUPE: Structure, Democracy, and Class Formation" (PhD diss., York University, 2005).
189 Canadian Auto Workers, "An Interview with Bob White, by Randy Ray," in *Making History: A Visual Record of the CAW's First 25 Years* (2010), 15.
190 Charlotte Yates, "Unity and Diversity: Challenges to an Expanding Canadian Autoworkers' Union," *Canadian Review of Sociology and Anthropology* 35, 1 (1998): 113.
191 Sam Gindin, personal interview, August 27, 2021; Carol Phillips, personal interview, November 22, 2022.
192 Sam Gindin, personal interview, August 27, 2021.
193 Carol Phillips, personal interview, October 5, 2021.
194 Ibid.
195 Carol Phillips, personal interview, November 22, 2022.
196 Ibid.
197 Yates, "Unity and Diversity," 94.
198 Canadian Auto Workers, *Making History: A Visual Record of the CAW's First 25 Years* (2010), 163.
199 Yates, "Unity and Diversity," 97–99, calculated from data presented in Tables 1 and 2.
200 Ibid., 94.
201 Canadian Auto Workers, *Constitution* (2003), 1–2.
202 Canadian Auto Workers, "We're Building a Future Together! United in Collective Bargaining and Political Action," report to the National Collective Bargaining and Legislative Convention, Sheraton Centre, Toronto, April 22–24, 1987, 6.
203 Canadian Auto Workers, "Birth of the Union," 24.
204 Carol Phillips, personal interview, October 5, 2021.
205 White, *Hard Bargains*, 375.
206 Peggy Nash, personal interview, January 31, 2022.
207 White, *Hard Bargains*, 374.
208 Ken Lewenza, personal interview, January 17, 2022.
209 Hemi Mitic, personal interview, October 5, 2021.
210 Malcolm Allen, personal interview, November 16, 2021.
211 Wayne Gates, personal interview, October 8, 2021.
212 Gindin, *Canadian Auto Workers*, 136.

213 Ibid., 207, 266–69.

214 Canadian Auto Workers, "An Interview with Buzz Hargrove, by Randy Ray," in *Making History: A Visual Record of the CAW's First 25 Years* (2010), 64.

215 Hargrove with Skene, *Labour of Love*, 157.

CHAPTER 3: BACK-SEAT DRIVER?

1 Ontario New Democratic Party, "Our Policy Direction: We're on the Threshold," excerpt from Bob Rae's speech to the 1986 Ontario NDP convention, reprinted in *The Ontario New Democrat* 24, 4 (July 1986): 2.

2 "NDP Tops the Polls under Leader Ed Broadbent," *CBC News*, 1987, https://www.cbc.ca/player/play/1774026631.

3 Peter Bleyer, "Cross-Movement Coalitions and Political Agency: The Popular Sector and the Pro-Canada/Action Canada Network" (PhD diss., London School of Economics and Political Science, University of London, 2001).

4 Miriam Smith, "The Canadian Labour Congress: From Continentalism to Economic Nationalism," *Studies in Political Economy* 38, 1 (1992): 54.

5 Maude Barlow, *The Fight of My Life: Confessions of an Unrepentant Canadian* (Toronto: HarperCollins, 1988), 111.

6 In the case of Quebec, many sovereignists reasoned that greater continental trade integration would lessen Quebec's reliance on Canada and improve prospects for independence.

7 Ian McLeod, *Under Siege: The Federal NDP in the Nineties* (Toronto: Lorimer, 1994), 117.

8 Sam Gindin, personal interview, August 27, 2021.

9 Hemi Mitic, personal interview, October 5, 2021.

10 McLeod, *Under Siege*, 117.

11 Andrew Jackson, personal interview, February 7, 2022.

12 Ed Broadbent, personal interview, January 15, 2022.

13 Ibid.

14 Jim Stanford, personal interview, October 4, 2021.

15 James Laxer, *In Search of a New Left: Canadian Politics after the Neoconservative Assault* (Toronto: Penguin, 1996), 132.

16 Ibid.

17 Lynn Gidluck, *Visionaries, Crusaders, and Firebrands: The Idealistic Canadians Who Built the NDP* (Toronto: Lorimer, 2012), 181.

18 Ed Broadbent, personal interview, January 17, 2022.

19 Quoted in Wayne Roberts, "Election Replays of NDP Fumbles," *Now Magazine*, January 19, 1989.

20 Bob White, "Lost Opportunity," letter to NDP officers and executive members, November 28, 1988, 1, in possession of the authors.

21 Ibid., 2.

22 Ibid., 1.

23 Ed Broadbent, personal interview, January 17, 2022.

24 Andrew Jackson, personal interview, February 7, 2022.

25 Ed Broadbent, personal interview, January 17, 2022; Michael MacIsaac, personal interview, November 15, 2021.

26 Sam Gindin, personal interview, August 27, 2021.

27 Ed Broadbent, personal interview, January 17, 2022.

28 Sam Gindin, *The Canadian Auto Workers: The Birth and Transformation on a Union* (Toronto: Lorimer, 1995), 225.

29 Herman Rosenfeld, personal interview, September 27, 2021.

30 Ken Lewenza, personal interview, January 17, 2022.

31 Victor John Paolone, "NDP-Labour Relations: Crises and Challenges in the 1990s" (MA thesis, University of Windsor, 1995), 159. Interestingly, White's assistants were not expected to follow suit – a clear indication that White's endorsement of McLaughlin was tepid at best. The assistants gravitated toward opposing campaigns, with some backing former BC premier Dave Barrett and others lining up behind Windsor MPs Howard McCurdy and Steven Langdon. Hemi Mitic, personal interview, October 5, 2021.

32 Georgette Gagnon and Dan Rath, *Not without Cause: David Peterson's Fall from Grace* (Toronto: Harper Collins, 1991); George Ehring and Wayne Roberts, *Giving away a Miracle: Lost Dreams, Broken Promises and the Ontario NDP* (Oakville, ON: Mosaic, 1993), 267–85.

33 Bob Rae, *From Protest to Power: Personal Reflections on a Life in Politics* (Toronto: Viking, 1996), 126.

34 Ehring and Roberts, *Giving away a Miracle*, 276–79.

35 Ibid., 278.

36 Brian Tanguay, "Radicals, Technocrats and Traditionalists: Interest Aggregation in Two Provincial Social Democratic Parties in Canada," in Kay Lawson and Thomas Poguntke, eds., *How Political Parties Respond: Interest Aggregation Revisited* (New York: Routledge, 2004), 162.

37 Ontario New Democratic Party, "Introducing the New Caucus Members," *Ontario Democrat* 27, 3 (November 1990): 8–10. Hayes, the former CAW national health and safety coordinator, represented Essex–Kent, Dadamo represented Windsor–Sandwich, Hope represented Chatham–Kent, Local 222 member O'Connor represented Durham–York, and Christopherson represented Hamilton Centre.

38 Quoted in Patrick Monahan, *Storming the Pink Palace: The NDP in Power: A Cautionary Tale* (Toronto: Lester, 1995), 103.

39 For an examination of such dynamics in European social democratic governments, see Leo Panitch, *Working-Class Politics in Crisis* (London: Verso, 1986).

40 Monahan, *Storming the Pink Palace*, 46–47.

41 Buzz Hargrove with Wayne Skene, *Labour of Love: The Fight to Create a More Humane Canada* (Toronto: McFarlane, Walter and Ross, 1998), 141.

42 Ibid., 142.

43 Ibid. For an analysis of the CAW's climate politics and their contradictions, see Derek Hrynyshyn and Stephanie Ross, "Canadian Autoworkers, the Climate Crisis, and the Contradictions of Social Unionism," *Labor Studies Journal* 36, 1 (2011): 5–36.

44 Gallup Canada, "Canadian Gallup Poll, October 1990," https://odesi.ca/en/details?id=/odesi/doi__10-5683_SP2_8WSZYF.xml.

45 "Labor Day 1990: A Solemn Celebration," *Windsor Star,* September 1, 1990, A6.

46 Brian Cross, "McLaughlin Urges CLC to Gird for Election Fight," *Windsor Star,* June 10, 1992, A2.

47 Sam Gindin, personal interview, August 27, 2021.

48 Keith Damsell, "Caterpillar Firm on Move; Plant Will Close Despite Occupation, Management Says," *Globe and Mail,* April 29, 1991; Frank Calleja, "Caterpillar Workers Refuse to Budge from Plant," *Toronto Star,* April 26, 1991; Gerald Caplan, "Workers Get Shafted as Firms 'Restructure,'" *Toronto Star,* February 2, 1992.

49 Gerald Caplan, "The Hidden History of Bob Rae's Government in Ontario," *Globe and Mail,* October 8, 2010.

50 Thomas Walkom, *Rae Days: The Rise and Follies of the NDP* (Toronto: Key Porter Books), 98–105.

51 Canadian Auto Workers, "An Interview with Buzz Hargrove, by Randy Ray," in *Making History: A Visual Record of the CAW's First 25 Years* (2010), 63.

52 Peggy Nash, personal interview, September 29, 2021.

53 Quoted in "White's Aide Takes Reins of Labor Body," *Toronto Star,* June 28, 1992, A12.

54 Deirdre McMurdy and Luke Fisher, "Big Bad Buzz," *Maclean's,* December 16, 1996, https://www.thecanadianencyclopedia.ca/en/article/buzz-hargrove-profile.

55 Quoted in Monahan, *Storming the Pink Palace,* 156.

56 Quoted in ibid.

57 Ibid.

58 Rae, *From Protest to Power,* 200, 202.

59 Ibid., 200.

60 Hargrove with Skene, *Labour of Love,* 146.

61 Rae, *From Protest to Power,* 207.

62 Walkom, *Rae Days,* 218.

63 Jay Casey, "Why CAW Local 222 Dumped the NDP," *Canadian Dimension,* May 1, 1993.

64 Ibid.

65 Ibid.

66 Gindin, *Canadian Auto Workers,* 249.

67 Buzz Hargrove, personal interview, November 17, 2021.

68 Casey, "Why CAW Local 222."

69 Walkom, *Rae Days,* 5.

70 Ibid., 100–18.

71 Ibid., 119–20.

72 Environics, "Environics Focus Ontario 1993–1," April 1993, https://odesi.ca/en/details?id=/odesi/doi__10-5683_SP3_KLFJFJ.xml.

73 Leo Panitch and Donald Swartz, *From Consent to Coercion: The Assault on Trade Union Freedoms* (Toronto: Garamond, 2003), 172–81; Buzz Hargrove, *Laying It on the Line: Driving a Hard Bargain in Challenging Times* (Toronto: HarperCollins, 2009), 120.

74 Walkom, *Rae Days,* 140.

75 Buzz Hargrove, "Desperately Seeking the NDP," *Our Times,* March 1993, emphasis in original.

76 Quoted in George Martell, *A New Education Politics: Bob Rae's Legacy and the Response of the Ontario Secondary School Teachers' Federation* (Toronto: Lorimer, 1995), 79, 83.

77 Canadian Auto Workers, "Hard Times, New Times: Fighting for Our Future," report to the National Collective Bargaining and Political Action Convention, Toronto, May 4–7, 1993, 22, CAW/Unifor archives, Unifor National Office, Toronto.

78 Ibid., 26.

79 Walkom, *Rae Days*, 133–37.

80 Sam Gindin, personal interview, August 27, 2021.

81 Hargrove with Skene, *Labour of Love*, 159.

82 Three NDP MPPs voted against the Social Contract Act: Peter Kormos (Welland–Thorold); Mark Morrow (Wentworth East), a member of the United Steelworkers; and Karen Haslam (Perth), a member of the Ontario Secondary School Teachers' Federation, who also resigned from Cabinet over the matter. New Democrat turned Independent Dennis Drainville (Victoria–Haliburton) also opposed the bill.

83 Yonatan Reshef and Sandra Rastin, *Unions in the Time of Revolution: Government Restructuring in Alberta and Ontario* (Toronto: University of Toronto Press, 2003), 135; Walkom, *Rae Days*, 144.

84 Hargrove with Skene, *Labour of Love*, 118.

85 Panitch and Swartz, *From Consent to Coercion*, 166.

86 Stephen McBride, "The Continuing Crisis of Social Democracy: Ontario's Social Contract in Perspective," *Studies in Political Economy* 50, 1 (1996): 79.

87 Ontario Federation of Labour, "Labour's Relationship with the New Democratic Party When the NDP Is in Government," 1993, reprinted in Reshef and Rastin, *Unions in the Time of Revolution*, 136.

88 Reshef and Rastin, *Unions in the Time of Revolution*, 137.

89 Ibid.

90 Hargrove with Skene, *Labour of Love*, 162.

91 Rae, *From Protest to Power*, 210.

92 Quoted in Monahan, *Storming the Pink Palace*, 186.

93 McBride, "Continuing Crisis of Social Democracy," 88.

94 Quoted in Christina Blizzard, *Right Turn: How the Tories Took Ontario* (Toronto: Dundurn, 1995), 163.

95 Environics, "Environics Focus Ontario 1993-3," October 1993, https://odesi.ca/en/details?id=/odesi/doi__10-5683_SP3_MNZR3E.xml.

96 Hargrove with Skene, *Labour of Love*, 204.

97 Ibid., 160.

98 Larry Savage, "Organized Labour and Constitutional Reform under Mulroney," *Labour/Le Travail* 60 (Fall 2007): 137–70.

99 McLeod, *Under Siege*, 63–64.

100 Drainville finished a distant fourth place but still managed to win more votes than his NDP opponent.

101 Larry Savage, "Quebec Labour and the Referendums," *Canadian Journal of Political Science* 41, 4 (2008): 861–87.

102 Canadian Auto Workers, *Making History: A Visual Record of the CAW's First 25 Years* (2010), 20.

103 Ibid., 70.
104 Tony Van Alphen, "Auto Union Divided over Deserting NDP," *Toronto Star*, August 24, 1994, A12, quoted in Paolone, "NDP-Labour Relations," 79n70.
105 Canadian Auto Workers, "Labour and Politics: Rethinking, Redefining, Rebuilding," policy paper submitted to the 4th CAW Constitutional Convention, August 23–26, 1994, 74.
106 Canadian Auto Workers, "Where Are the Changes in Our Union Taking Us?" policy paper submitted to the 4th CAW Constitutional Convention, August 23–26, 1994, 1–6.
107 Walkom, *Rae Days*, 144.
108 Quoted in McLeod, *Under Siege*, 127.
109 Brian Cross, "CAW, NDP Vie over Principles," *Windsor Star*, June 6, 1995, A2.
110 Willie Lambert, personal interview, February 28, 2021.
111 Hargrove with Skene, *Labour of Love*, 161.
112 John Ibbitson, *Promised Land: Inside the Mike Harris Revolution* (Toronto: Prentice Hall, 1997), 221.
113 Blizzard, *Right Turn*, 136–48.
114 Laxer, *In Search of a New Left*, 129.
115 Lisa Wright, "Labor's Love Not Totally Lost NDP Insists," *Toronto Star*, April 15, 1995, B5; Tony Van Alphen, "OFL Faces Showdown at Top," *Toronto Star*, May 20, 1995, A19.
116 Cross, "CAW, NDP Vie over Principles," A2.
117 Daniel Girard, "New Democrat Kormos Misses Rae Appearance," *Toronto Star*, June 1, 1995, A12.
118 Rae, *From Protest to Power*, 263.
119 Gindin, *Canadian Auto Workers*, 250, 252.
120 Hargrove with Skene, *Labour of Love*, 137–38.
121 Ibid., 161.
122 Ibid., 138.
123 Larry Savage, "Quebec Labour and the Referendums," *Canadian Journal of Political Science* 41, 4 (2008): 877–78.
124 Sylvain Martin, personal interview, February 15, 2023.
125 Quoted in Sandro Contenta, "White Urges Respect for Quebec Vote," *Toronto Star*, February 22, 1995, A12.
126 Quoted in ibid.
127 Larry Savage, "Contemporary Union-Party Relations in Canada," *Labor Studies Journal* 35, 1 (2010): 22.
128 André Picard, "Quebec NDP Opts for Autonomy," *Globe and Mail*, May 1, 1989, A1.
129 Geoffrey York, "NDP Breaks Link to Quebec Wing: Alignment with Bloc Quebecois Brings Split with Federal Party," *Globe and Mail*, March 12, 1991, A4.
130 Elizabeth Thompson, "Unions Turn Back on NDP; Support Goes to Bloc Quebecois Candidate," *Montreal Gazette*, August 4, 1990, A3; Tu Thanh Ha, "QFL Backs Bloc; Election '93," *Montreal Gazette*, September 20, 1993, A6.
131 Hargrove with Skene, *Labour of Love*, 187.
132 Jean Chrétien, "Why Destroy Canada?" *Globe and Mail*, October 26, 1996.

133 Alan Whitehorn, "The NDP Election Campaign: Dashed Hopes," in Alan Frizzel, Jon H. Pammett, and Anthony Westell, eds., *The Canadian General Election of 1988* (Ottawa: Carleton University Press, 1989), 51.

134 Gindin, *Canadian Auto Workers*, 250.

CHAPTER 4: WINDING ROAD

1 Pradeep Kumar and John Holmes, "The Impact of NAFTA on the Auto Industry in Canada," in Sidney Weinstraub and Christopher Sands, eds., *The North American Auto Industry under NAFTA* (Washington, DC: Centre for Strategic and International Studies, 1998), 92.

2 Ibid., 93.

3 Ibid.

4 Ibid., 114.

5 Andrew Jackson and Sylvain Schetange, "Solidarity Forever? An Analysis of Changes in Union Density," *Just Labour* 4 (2004): 68–69.

6 Felice Martinello, "Mr. Harris, Mr. Rae and Union Activity in Ontario," *Canadian Public Policy* 26, 1 (2000): 17–33.

7 Herman Rosenfeld, personal interview, September 27, 2021.

8 Jim Stanford, personal interview, October 4, 2021.

9 James Laxer, *In Search of a New Left: Canadian Politics after the Neoconservative Assault* (Toronto: Penguin, 1996), 206.

10 Sam Gindin, *The Canadian Auto Workers: The Birth and Transformation of a Union* (Toronto: Lorimer, 1995), 268.

11 Danny Mallett, personal interview, March 7, 2022.

12 Quoted in Ian McLeod, *Under Siege: The Federal NDP in the Nineties* (Toronto: Lorimer, 1994), 125.

13 Yonatan Reshef and Sandra Rastin, *Unions in the Time of Revolution: Government Restructuring in Alberta and Ontario* (Toronto: University of Toronto Press, 2003), 138.

14 Ibid.

15 Quoted in ibid., 139.

16 Sam Gindin and Jim Stanford, "Canadian Labour and the Political Economy of Transformation," in Wallace Clement and Leah Vosko, eds., *Changing Canada: Political Economy as Transformation* (Montreal/Kingston: McGill-Queen's University Press, 2003), 431.

17 Reshef and Rastin, *Unions in the Time of Revolution*, 138.

18 Stephanie Ross, "Union Political Action in the Era of Neoliberalism," in Greg Albo and Bryan Evans, eds., *Divided Province: Ontario Politics in the Age of Neoliberalism* (Montreal/Kingston: McGill-Queen's University Press, 2018), 533.

19 Marsha Niemeijer, "The Ontario Days of Action: The Beginning of a Redefinition of the Labour Movement's Political Strategy?" unpublished manuscript (2000), 5.

20 Quoted in Reshef and Rastin, *Unions in the Time of Revolution*, 139.

21 Douglas Nesbitt, "Days of Action: Ontario's Extra-parliamentary Opposition to the Common Sense Revolution, 1995–1998" (PhD diss., Queen's University, 2018), 121, 149.

22 Ibid.

23 David Rapaport, *No Justice, No Peace: The 1996 OPSEU Strike against the Harris Government in Ontario* (Montreal/Kingston: McGill-Queen's University Press, 1999).

24 Canadian Auto Workers, *Making History: A Visual Record of the CAW's First 25 Years* (2010), 94.

25 Ibid., 104, 109.

26 Canadian Auto Workers, "False Solutions, Growing Protests: Recapturing the Agenda," theme paper adopted at the National Collective Bargaining and Political Action Convention, Toronto, June 4–7, 1996, 18, emphasis in original, CAW/Unifor archives, Unifor National Office, Toronto.

27 Ibid., 19.

28 Ibid., 21.

29 Larry Savage, *Socialist Cowboy: The Politics of Peter Kormos* (Halifax: Roseway, 2014), 56.

30 Ibid., 61.

31 Ibid., 62.

32 Buzz Hargrove with Wayne Skene, *Labour of Love: The Fight to Create a More Humane Canada* (Toronto: McFarlane, Walter and Ross, 1998), 197; Howard Hampton, "Choosing Social Democracy: Ontario's NDP Leader Responds," *Our Times* 15, 5 (1996): 21–22.

33 John Ibbitson, *Promised Land: Inside the Mike Harris Revolution* (Scarborough, ON: Prentice-Hall Canada, 1997), 218.

34 Rastin and Reshef, *Unions in the Time of Revolution*, 141.

35 Quoted in ibid., 146.

36 Nesbitt, "Days of Action," 328.

37 Sid Ryan, *A Grander Vision: My Life in the Labour Movement* (Toronto: Dundurn, 2019), 210.

38 Buzz Hargrove, personal interview, November 17, 2021.

39 Nesbitt, "Days of Action," 329.

40 Sharon Boase, "'A Dramatic Shift to the Right' for OFL," *Hamilton Spectator*, November 26, 1997.

41 Buzz Hargrove, personal interview, November 17, 2021.

42 Hargrove with Skene, *Labour of Love*, 176.

43 Duncan MacLellan, "Neoliberalism and Ontario Teachers' Unions: A 'Not-So' Common Sense Revolution," *Socialist Studies* 5, 1 (2009): 62.

44 Larry Savage and Chantal Mancini, "Strategic Electoral Dilemmas and the Politics of Teachers' Unions in Ontario," *Canadian Political Science Review* 16, 1 (2022): 8.

45 Leo Panitch and Donald Swartz, *From Consent to Coercion: The Assault on Trade Union Freedoms* (Toronto: Garamond, 2003), 191.

46 Nesbitt, "Days of Action," 334–46.

47 Buzz Hargrove, personal interview, November 17, 2021.

48 Sam Gindin, personal interview, August 27, 2021.

49 Leo Panitch, "Corporatism in Canada?" *Studies in Political Economy* 1, 1 (1979): 43–92.

50 Sam Gindin, personal interview, August 27, 2021.

51 Herman Rosenfeld, personal interview, September 27, 2021.

52 Peggy Nash, personal interview, September 29, 2021.

53 Canadian Auto Workers, *Making History*, 140; Euan Gibb, "Trading Workplace Rules for Potential New Investments" (MA thesis, McMaster University, 2004), 26; Alex Levant, "The Problem of Self-Emancipation: Subjectivity, Organization and the Weight of History" (PhD diss., York University, 2007).

54 Savage and Mancini, "Strategic Electoral Dilemmas," 8.

55 Hargrove with Skene, *Labour of Love*, 186.

56 Ibid., 187.

57 Ibid., 199–200.

58 Environics, "Environics Focus Ontario 1998–3," October 1998, https://odesi.ca/en/details?id=/odesi/doi__10-5683_SP3_JC3XSO.xml.

59 "The CAW in the 1999 Ontario Election," *CAW Contact*, December 20, 1998, http://www.caw.ca/en/4361.htm. *CAW Contact* was the union's national monthly newsletter, which ceased publication after the merger with the CEP in September 2013. With the revamping of their website under Unifor, the CAW's newsletter's archives are no longer available directly from the national union's website. However, it is possible to access the full archives via the Internet Archive Wayback Machine at web.archive.org. The original URLs are provided and can be used on the Internet Archive website to locate the original source by first searching for the URL and then selecting a year and a calendar date that corresponds to a version of the website that was saved after the date of the newsletter's publication.

60 Ibid.

61 Ibid.

62 Ibid.

63 Hargrove with Skene, *Labour of Love*, 120–21.

64 "CAW in the 1999 Ontario Election."

65 Ken Lewenza, personal interview, January 17, 2022.

66 Peggy Nash, personal interview, September 29, 2021.

67 Ken Lewenza, personal interview, January 17, 2022.

68 Jim Stanford, personal interview, October 4, 2021.

69 Sam Gindin, personal interview, August 27, 2021.

70 Herman Rosenfeld, personal interview, September 27, 2021.

71 Sam Gindin, personal interview, August 27, 2021.

72 Willie Lambert, personal interview, February 28, 2022.

73 Sam Gindin, personal interview, August 27, 2021.

74 Hargrove with Skene, *Labour of Love*, 122.

75 Reshef and Rastin, *Unions in the Time of Revolution*, 168.

76 Buzz Hargrove, personal interview, November 17, 2021.

77 Ross McClellan to Buzz Hargrove, December 17, 1998, in possession of the authors.

78 Reshef and Rastin, *Unions in the Time of Revolution*, 176.

79 Robert MacDermid, "Changing Electoral Politics in Ontario: The 1999 Provincial Election," unpublished manuscript (2000), https://www.yorku.ca/mediar/releases_1996_2000/archive/090500.htm.

80 "Ontario Election Campaign Is on TV," *CBC News*, April 26, 1999, https://www.cbc.ca/news/canada/ontario-election-campaign-is-on-tv-1.193888.

81 Environics, "Environics Focus Ontario 1999–1," April 1999, https://odesi.ca/en/details?id=/odesi/doi__10-5683_SP3_TQIP7X.xml; Joel Ruimy, "Hampton: Haunted by Rae," *Toronto Star,* May 9, 1999, 1.

82 "Mcguinty Attacked! – 1999 Debate a Disaster for Liberal," *CBC News,* 1999, https://www. cbc.ca/player/play/1811732082.

83 Rob Milling, "Campaign '99 – Final Thought," report to the Provincial Executive of the Ontario NDP, June 20, 1999, in possession of the authors.

84 "Combined, three teachers' unions (OSSTF, OECTA [Ontario English Catholic Teachers' Association], and ETFO [Elementary Teachers' Federation of Ontario]) spent $3 million to support strategic-voting efforts." Reshef and Rastin, *Unions in the Time of Revolution,* 173.

85 Brian Tanguay, "Parties, Organized Interests, and Electoral Democracy: The 1999 Ontario Provincial Election," in William Cross, ed., *Political Parties, Representation, and Electoral Democracy in Canada* (Toronto: Oxford University Press, 2002), 155.

86 Patrick Monahan, "The Provinces: Was Strategic Voting Really Such a Bust?" *Globe and Mail,* July 14, 1999; John Barber, "The Ontario Election: Toronto's Strategic Voting Sends a Message," *Globe and Mail,* June 4, 1999.

87 Reshef and Rastin, *Unions in the Time of Revolution,* 175.

88 Ibid., 177.

89 Ibid.

90 "Elections and Political Action," *CAW Contact,* June 13, 1999, http://www.caw.ca/en/4295.htm.

91 Gary Rennie, "Vote '99: CAW Plots PC Ouster; the Union May Even Ask Members to Vote Liberal in Close Races," *Windsor Star,* May 11, 1999, A4.

92 Blair Crawford, "Hampton Hammered; Criticizing Hargrove Misguided, NDPers Say," *Windsor Star,* August 18, 1999, A3.

93 Reshef and Rastin, *Unions in the Time of Revolution,* 176.

94 Quoted in "Elections and Political Action."

95 Geoff Bickerton, "Buzz, Battles and Bombs," *Canadian Dimension* 33, 4–5 (1999): 16.

96 Quoted in Caroline Mallan, "Left-Wing Grudge Match Sparks NDP Unity Feud; Hampton and Hargrove Trade Insults," *Toronto Star,* June 10, 1999, 1.

97 Quoted in ibid.

98 Quoted in Crawford, "Hampton Hammered."

99 Quoted in ibid.

100 Theresa Boyle, "NDP Backs Off; Its Council Votes against Disciplining Buzz Hargrove," *Toronto Star,* September 26, 1999, 1.

101 Quoted in ibid.

102 Doug Nesbitt, "Alexa McDonough and the Third Way," *Canadian Dimension,* January 26, 2022, https://canadiandimension.com/articles/view/alexa-mcdonough-and-the-third-way.

103 Quoted in Joel-Denis Bellavance, "CAW Leader Says He May Quit NDP If It Moves to Centre," *National Post,* August 26, 1999, A7.

104 Quoted in Anne Marie Owens, "CAW's Buzz Hargrove Proving an Enigma to Insiders: Union Leader Has Threatened to Leave Federal NDP," *National Post,* August 31, 1999, A7.

105 Quoted in Sarah Hampson, "Why Buzz Won't Behave: Labour Leader Buzz Hargrove Is on a Winning Streak. And the Badder He Is, the Better," *Report on Business Magazine* 16, 5 (November 1999): 27–30.
106 Quoted in ibid.
107 "Buzz Hargrove Timeline," *CBC News,* July 9, 2008, https://www.cbc.ca/news/canada/buzz-hargrove-timeline-1.719077.
108 Willie Lambert, personal interview, February 28, 2022.
109 "CAW Council December 3–5, 1999," *CAW Contact,* December 5, 1999, http://www.caw.ca/en/4314.htm.
110 Sam Gindin, personal interview, August 27, 2021.
111 Canadian Auto Workers, "An Interview with Jim O'Neill, by Randy Ray," in *Making History: A Visual Record of the CAW's First 25 Years* (2010), 68.
112 Sam Gindin, personal interview, August 27, 2021.
113 Peggy Nash, personal interview, September 29, 2021.
114 "Letter from Buzz Hargrove," August 18, 2000, http://www.labournet.net/world/0009/caw8.html.
115 Estanislao Oziewicz, "CAW Refuses to Yield to CLC Tactics," *Globe and Mail,* June 28, 2000, https://www.theglobeandmail.com/news/national/caw-refuses-to-yield-to-clc-tactics/article1040803/.
116 Ed Broadbent, personal interview, January 15, 2022; Charlotte Yates, "Unity and Diversity: Challenges to an Expanding Canadian Autoworkers' Union," *Canadian Review of Sociology and Anthropology* 35, 1 (1998): 107.
117 Justine Hunter, "McDonough Should Resign, Hargrove Says: CAW President Threatens to Stop Backing NDP," *National Post,* March 17, 2001, A6.
118 Canadian Labour Congress, "Report on 2000 Federal Election," Appendix E, in possession of the authors.
119 Although the CAW's national office made campaign contributions to all NDP incumbents, the union officially endorsed only NDP candidates with CAW ties, including two in British Columbia, two in Newfoundland and Labrador, four in Ontario, and one in Nova Scotia. "National Union Endorses CAW Candidates Running in Federal Election," *CAW Contact,* November 19, 2000, http://www.caw.ca/en/4276.htm.
120 Ibid.
121 These two MPs were Joe Comartin in Windsor–St. Clair and Peter Stoffer in Sackville–Eastern Shore.
122 Quoted in "Hargrove Calls on Federal NDP to Strike a Task Force to Define the Future of the Party," *CAW Contact,* December 10, 2000, http://www.caw.ca/en/4279.htm.
123 Quoted in Caroline Mallan, "Hampton Heaps Scorn on Union Leader; Hargrove 'Has No Credibility' and Should Be Ignored," *Toronto Star,* December 22, 2000, A07.
124 Quoted in ibid.
125 Quoted in Justine Hunter, "McDonough Should Resign, Hargrove Says: CAW President Threatens to Stop Backing NDP," *National Post,* March 17, 2001, A6.
126 Quoted in ibid.
127 Doug Smith, *Stickin' to the Union: Local 2224 versus John Buhler* (Halifax: Fernwood, 2004).
128 Ibid., 113–14.

129 Quoted in ibid., 125.

130 Quoted in ibid., 165.

131 "Auto Pact Defunct on Monday," *CBC News*, February 20, 2001, https://www.cbc.ca/news/canada/auto-pact-defunct-monday-1.254724.

132 Greig Mordue and Brendan Sweeney, "The Commoditisation of Automotive Assembly: Canada as a Cautionary Tale," *International Journal of Automotive Technology and Management* 17, 2 (2017): 176.

133 Joey DeLazzari, "Driving through Hard Times: Political Strategies of the Canadian Auto Workers in the Neoliberal Era" (MA major research paper, McMaster University, 2017), 44–46.

134 Canadian Auto Workers, *Making History*, 116.

135 Gibb, "Trading Workplace Rules," 2–3.

136 Ibid., 4.

137 Donald M. Wells, "When Push Comes to Shove: Competitiveness, Job Insecurity and Labour-Management Cooperation in Canada," *Economic and Industrial Democracy* 18, 2 (1997): 167.

138 Chris Watson, "The NDP Is in Big Trouble. So?" in Z. David Berlin and Howard Aster, eds., *What's Left? The New Democratic Party in Renewal*, 114–26 (Oakville ON: Mosaic, 2001); Sam Gindin and Jim Stanford, "Canadian Labour and the Political Economy of Transformation," in Wallace Clement and Leah Vosko, eds., *Changing Canada: Political Economy as Transformation*, 422–42 (Montreal/Kingston: McGill-Queen's University Press, 2003).

139 Reshef and Rastin, *Unions in the Time of Revolution*, 181.

140 Jim Stanford and Svend Robinson, "The New Politics Initiative: Open, Sustainable, Democratic," in Z. David Berlin and Howard Aster, eds., *What's Left? The New Democratic Party in Renewal* (Oakville, ON: Mosaic, 2001), 81.

141 Sam Gindin, personal interview, August 27, 2021.

142 Jim Stanford, personal interview, October 4, 2021.

143 Ibid.

144 Buzz Hargrove, personal interview, November 17, 2021.

145 Ibid.

146 Sam Gindin, personal interview, August 27, 2021.

147 Peggy Nash, personal interview, September 29, 2021.

148 Buzz Hargrove, "Letter to CLC President," *CAW Contact*, September 16, 2001, http://www.caw.ca/en/4214.htm.

149 Carol Phillips, personal interview, October 5, 2021.

150 Buzz Hargrove, personal interview, November 17, 2021; Krista Foss and Allison Lawlor, "Leader Arrested, Police Repulse Demonstrators," *Globe and Mail*, June 16, 2001, https://www.theglobeandmail.com/news/national/leader-arrested-police-repulse-demonstrators/article4149648/.

151 Scott Aquanno and Toba Bryant, "Workplace Restructuring and Institutional Change: GM Oshawa from 1994 to 2019," *Studies in Political Economy* 102, 1 (2021): 40.

152 Buzz Hargrove, personal interview, November 17, 2021.

153 Quoted in Reshef and Rastin, *Unions in the Time of Revolution*, 244.

154 Quoted in Peter Brieger, "CAW May Have to Fill Hargrove's Shoes: No Big Names to Hand If Chief Runs for NDP Leadership," *National Post*, June 7, 2002, FP7.

155 Quoted in Steve Erwin, "CAW President Hargrove Rules Out Run for Leadership of Federal NDP," *Canadian Press*, September 26, 2002.

156 David McGrane, *The New NDP: Moderation, Modernization, and Political Marketing* (Vancouver: UBC Press, 2019), 35.

157 Quoted in "Local NDP Supporters Unsure Who They'll Back for Leader," *Brantford Expositor*, January 15, 2003, A4.

158 McGrane, *New NDP*, 37.

159 Sam Gindin, "Beyond the Impasse of Canadian Labour: Union Renewal, Political Renewal," *Canadian Dimension*, May 21, 2014, https://canadiandimension.com/articles/view/beyond-the-impasse-of-canadian-labour-union-renewal-political-renewal.

CHAPTER 5: A FORK IN THE ROAD

1 Jonathan Eaton and Anil Verma, "Does 'Fighting Back' Make a Difference? The Case of the Canadian Auto Workers Union," *Journal of Labor Research* 27, 2 (2006): 193.

2 Canadian Auto Workers, "The CAW & Politics: Taking the Next Steps," policy paper presented at the 7th CAW Constitutional Convention, "Union Resistance and Union Renewal," Toronto, August 19–22, 2003, 17.

3 CAW Council, minutes, December 2002, Recommendation 6, 73, CAW/Unifor archives, Unifor National Office, Toronto.

4 Canadian Auto Workers, "CAW & Politics," 21.

5 Jim Stanford, "There Are Good Reasons for the CAW and NDP to Split Up," *Globe and Mail*, March 27, 2006, https://www.theglobeandmail.com/news/national/there-are-good-reasons-for-the-caw-and-ndp-to-split-up/article1097051/.

6 Canadian Auto Workers, "An Interview with Jim O'Neill, by Randy Ray," in *Making History: A Visual Record of the CAW's First 25 Years* (2010), 68.

7 Ken Lewenza, personal interview, January 17, 2022.

8 Hemi Mitic, personal interview, October 5, 2021.

9 Peggy Nash, personal interview, September 29, 2021.

10 Sam Gindin, personal interview, August 27, 2021.

11 Carol Phillips, personal interview, October 5, 2021.

12 Sam Gindin, personal interview, August 27, 2021.

13 Brad Walchuk, "Changing Union-Party Relations in Canada: The Rise of the Working Families Coalition," *Labor Studies Journal* 35, 1 (2010): 37–38.

14 Craig Wong, "Canadian Auto Workers Union President Buzz Hargrove Virtually Declared War on Ontario's Conservative Government as the Union Opened Its Constitutional Convention Tuesday," *Canadian Press Newswire*, August 19, 2003.

15 Ibid.

16 In the election period, the CAW donated $56,849.25 to NDP candidates. Ontario, Elections Ontario, "CR-1, CR-3, and CR-4 Financial Statements, Ontario New Democratic Party, 2003 Ontario General Elections," https://www.elections.on.ca/en/political-financingo.html, calculations by the authors.

17 Larry Savage, "Organized Labour and the Politics of Strategic Voting," in Stephanie Ross and Larry Savage, eds., *Rethinking the Politics of Labour in Canada* (Halifax: Fernwood, 2012), 80.

18 "Paul Martin – CEO for Canada," *CAW Contact*, December 21, 2003, http://www.caw.ca/en/3999.htm.

19 "CAW 7th Constitutional Convention, Toronto – August 19–22, 2003," *CAW Contact*, August 31, 2003, http://www.caw.ca/en/3982.htm.

20 Alan Whitehorn, "Jack Layton and the NDP: Gains but No Breakthrough," in Jon H. Pammett and Christopher Dornan, eds., *The Canadian General Election of 2004* (Toronto: Dundurn, 2004), 108.

21 Ibid., 135.

22 Quoted in Bill Curry, "Quebec Wing of CAW to Support Bloc Not NDP in Province during Upcoming Federal Election," *CanWest News*, May 19, 2004, 1.

23 Quoted in ibid.

24 Canadian Auto Workers, *Making History: A Visual Record of the CAW's First 25 Years* (2010), 146.

25 "New Democrats in the Federal Election," *CAW Contact*, April 25, 2004, http://www.caw.ca/en/3900.htm.

26 Stephen Clarkson, "Disaster and Recovery: Paul Martin as Political Lazarus," in Jon H. Pammett and Christopher Dornan, eds., *The Canadian General Election of 2004* (Toronto: Dundurn, 2004), 51.

27 Quoted in "A Minority Government: Liberals Challenged," *CAW Contact*, July 4, 2004, http://www.caw.ca/en/3915.htm.

28 "Canadian Politics, after the Election," *CAW Contact*, September 5, 2004, http://www.caw.ca/en/3922.htm.

29 Séverine Defouni, "Le Bloc refuse de former une alliance avec le NPD," *Radio-Canada*, August 28, 2004, https://ici.radio-canada.ca/nouvelle/196164/duceppe-npd-tca.

30 "Prime Minister Meets with CAW National Executive Board," *CAW Contact*, December 10, 2004, http://www.caw.ca/en/3946.htm.

31 "CAW Economist to Review Federal Budget Projections," *CAW Contact*, January 28, 2005, http://www.caw.ca/en/3815.htm.

32 Quoted in Craig Saunders, "The Buzz about Buzz," *Pique Magazine*, 2009, https://www.piquenewsmagazine.com/cover-stories/the-buzz-about-buzz-2481342.

33 Quoted in "PM Shells Out $4.6B for NDP's Support," *CBC News*, April 26, 2005, https://www.cbc.ca/news/canada/pm-shells-out-4-6b-for-ndp-s-support-1.541632.

34 "Challenges at the Big Three," *CAW Contact*, April 8, 2005, http://www.caw.ca/en/3826.htm.

35 Charlotte Yates and Wayne Lewchuk, "What Shapes Automotive Investment Decisions in a Contemporary Global Economy," *Canadian Public Policy* 43, S1 (2017): S17; Joey DeLazzari, "Driving through Hard Times: Political Strategies of the Canadian Auto Workers in the Neoliberal Era" (MA major research paper, McMaster University, 2017), 48–49.

36 Chris Vander Doelen, "Hargrove Hailed as Labour Genius for CAW's Double-Pronged Contract Tactics," *CanWest News*, September 19, 2005, 1.

37 Alisa Priddle, "CAW Negotiations Framed Future of Canadian Auto Industry," *WardsAuto,* June 28, 2006, https://www.wardsauto.com/news-analysis/caw-negotiations-framed-future-canadian-auto-industry.

38 "CAW and Chrysler Reach Agreement," *Globe and Mail,* September 20, 2005, https://www.theglobeandmail.com/report-on-business/caw-and-chrysler-reach-agreement/article1123806/.

39 Priddle, "CAW Negotiations Framed."

40 Sam Gindin, "The CAW's Direction: Some Questions," *The Bullet,* December 14, 2005, https://socialistproject.ca/2005/12/b10/.

41 Jim Stanford, "CAW Bargaining Reflected Principled Approach," *Labor Notes,* December 1, 2005, https://www.labornotes.org/2005/12/caw-bargaining-reflected-principled-approach.

42 Buzz Hargrove, "Put the Tories on a Short Leash," *CAW Context,* January 25, 2006, http://www.caw.ca/en/4580.htm.

43 Jim Stanford, untitled, *Globe and Mail,* January 30, 2006, https://www.theglobeandmail.com/news/national/jim-stanford/article1094039/.

44 Andrew Jackson, personal interview, February 7, 2022.

45 Alan Whitehorn, "The NDP and the Enigma of Strategic Voting," in Jon H. Pammett and Christopher Dornan, eds., *The Canadian General Election of 2006* (Toronto: Dundurn, 2006), 96–97.

46 Andrew Jackson, *The Fire and the Ashes: Rekindling Democratic Socialism* (Toronto: Between the Lines, 2021), 80–81.

47 Jamey Heath, *Dead Centre: Hope, Possibility, and Unity for Canadian Progressives* (New York: John Wiley and Sons, 2007), 128.

48 Heath, *Dead Centre,* 128.

49 Ibid., 152.

50 Peggy Nash, personal interview, September 29, 2021.

51 Quoted in "Prime Minister Paul Martin Speaks to CAW Council," *CAW Contact,* December 9, 2005, http://www.caw.ca/en/3862.htm.

52 "CAW Delegates Vote in Favour of Federal Election Strategy," *CAW Contact,* December 9, 2005, http://wwwcaw.ca/en/4578.htm.

53 Ibid.

54 Ibid.

55 James S. McLean, *Inside the NDP War Room: Competing for Credibility in a Federal Election* (Montreal/Kingston: McGill-Queen's University Press, 2012), 73.

56 Ibid., 74–75.

57 Quoted in Jack Aubry, "Hargrove Comments Delivered Body Blow to NDP: Pollster," *CanWest News,* December 6, 2005, 1.

58 Hemi Mitic, personal interview, October 5, 2021.

59 Wayne Gates, personal interview, October 8, 2021.

60 Jenny Ahn, personal interview, November 15, 2021.

61 Sam Gindin, personal interview, August 27, 2021.

62 Malcolm Allen, personal interview, November 16, 2021.

63 Ibid.

64 Sam Gindin, personal interview, August 27, 2021.

65 Quoted in Anne Dawson and James Gordon, "PM and CAW Leader Continue to Sing Each Other's Praises," *CanWest News,* December 10, 2005.

66 Quoted in ibid.

67 Buzz Hargrove, "Making the Most of Opportunity," *CAW Context,* December 9, 2005, http://www.caw.ca/en/4578.htm.

68 Buzz Hargrove with Wayne Skene, *Labour of Love: The Fight to Create a More Humane Canada* (Toronto: McFarlane, Walter and Ross, 1998), 128.

69 Buzz Hargrove, personal interview, November 17, 2021; Heath, *Dead Centre,* 109–10.

70 Jonathan Rose, "The Liberals Reap What They Sow: Why Their Negative Ads Failed," *Policy Options,* March 2006, https://policyoptions.irpp.org/wp-content/uploads/sites/2/assets/po/the-prime-minister/rose.pdf.

71 "La campagne deviendra vicieuse," *Le Devoir,* December 23, 2005, https://www.ledevoir.com/politique/canada/98371/la-campagne-deviendra-vicieuse.

72 Les Whittington and Bruce Campion-Smith, "PM Pushes NDP Alliance," *Toronto Star,* December 3, 2005, https://www.ekospolitics.com/articles/TheStar3Dec2005b.pdf.

73 Savage, "Organized Labour and the Politics," 81.

74 Whitehorn, "NDP and the Enigma," 115.

75 Quoted in Andrew Mills, "Layton Energizes Supporters," *Toronto Star,* January 15, 2006.

76 Thomas Collombat and Magali Picard, "Third-Party Activism," in Alex Marland and Thierry Giasson, eds., *Inside the Campaign: Managing Elections in Canada,* 185–95 (Vancouver: UBC Press, 2020).

77 Jim Stanford, "NDP Gains: One Hand Clapping," *Globe and Mail,* January 30, 2006, https://www.theglobeandmail.com/opinion/ndp-gains-one-hand-clapping/article727517/.

78 Heath, *Dead Centre,* 228.

79 Decima Research, for the Canadian Auto Workers, *Strategic Voting in the 2006 General Election* (March 2006). The CAW retained Decima Research to develop a report on strategic voting in the 2006 federal election. Prior to the election, Decima had established a 12,000-member "research panel" of Canadian voters who were polled on seven different occasions during the election campaign.

80 Ibid., 4, 41.

81 Ibid., 8.

82 Ibid., 41.

83 Ibid., 17.

84 Duncan Mavin, "Is Buzz Tarnished Goods? *National Post,* January 28, 2006.

85 "Ford Announcement Is Shocking and Painful Blow," *CAW Contact,* January 25, 2006, http://www.caw.ca/en/3765.htm.

86 "Ontario NDP's Provincial Council Backs Buzz Hargrove's Ouster," *CBC News,* March 4, 2006, https://www.cbc.ca/news/canada/ontario-ndp-s-provincial-council-backs-buzz-hargrove-s-ouster-1.598403.

87 Quoted in "NEB Encourages Withdrawal of Support for NDP," *CAW Contact,* March 24, 2006, http://www.caw.ca/en/3773.htm.

88 Malcolm Allen, personal interview, November 16, 2021.

89 Anne Jarvis, "MP Suggests Policy for Those 'Not Fully Supportive' of NDP," *Windsor Star,* February 24, 2006, 1.

90 Jeff Gray, "Toronto Stands by the Liberals," *Globe and Mail,* January 24, 2006, A12.

91 Buzz Hargrove, personal interview, November 17, 2021.

92 Buzz Hargrove, "The State of the Union Movement in Canada: The Challenges We Face; the Innovations We Must Undertake," Don Wood Lecture, Industrial Relations Centre, Queen's University, Kingston, Ontario, March 2006.

93 Ritch Whyman, personal interview, February 28, 2022.

94 Ibid.

95 "Nova Scotia NDP Recognizes Labour Independence," *CAW Contact,* May 12, 2006, http://www.caw.ca/en/3780.htm.

96 Wayne Gates, Ed Gould, Irene Lowell, and Gerry Michaud had all run for the party in provincial and/or federal elections.

97 Wayne Gates, personal interview, October 8, 2021.

98 Jim Stanford, personal interview, October 4, 2021.

99 Jenny Ahn, personal interview, November 15, 2021.

100 Herman Rosenfeld, personal interview, September 27, 2021.

101 Canadian Auto Workers, "In the Eye of the Storm: The CAW and the Re-making of Canadian Politics," policy paper adopted at the 8th CAW Constitutional Convention, Vancouver, British Columbia, August 2006, 4.

102 Ibid., 9.

103 Ibid., 23.

104 Ibid., 23.

105 Canadian Auto Workers, "An Interview with Jean-Pierre Fortin, by Daniel Drolet," in *Making History: A Visual Record of the CAW's First 25 Years* (2010), 158.

106 Stephanie Ross, "Social Unionism in Hard Times: Union-Community Coalition Politics in the CAW Windsor's *Manufacturing Matters* Campaign," *Labour/Le Travail* 68 (Fall 2011): 94.

107 "Willie vs. Buzz in CAW Showdown," *Burlington Post,* April 21, 2006, https://www.insidehalton.com/news-story/2911694-willie-vs-buzz-in-caw-showdown/.

108 Willie Lambert, personal interview, February 28, 2022.

109 Quoted in Deidre McMurdy, "Challenge for CAW Leadership More Than Long Shot for Perennial Loser," *Ottawa Citizen,* July 25, 2006.

110 Willie Lambert, personal interview, February 28, 2022.

111 Quoted in McMurdy, "Challenge for CAW Leadership."

112 Willie Lambert, personal interview, February 28, 2022.

113 David Camfield, *Canadian Labour in Crisis: Reinventing the Workers' Movement* (Halifax: Fernwood, 2011), 46.

114 Ibid., 47.

115 Willie Lambert, personal interview, February 28, 2022.

116 Ritch Whyman, personal interview, February 28, 2022.

117 Canadian Auto Workers, *Making History,* 105, 139.

118 Ibid., 143; "Work Resumes at Collins & Aikman Scarborough Plant," *Canadian Plastics,* April 2, 2007, https://www.canplastics.com/canplastics/work-resumes-at-collins-aikman-scarborough-plant/1000063119/.

119 "The Education of Brian Nicholl," *Fifth Estate*, 2009, https://curio.ca/en/video/the-education-of-brian-nicholl-967/.

120 Larry Savage, "The Politics of Labour and Labour Relations in Ontario," in Cheryl N. Collier and Jonathan Malloy, eds., *The Politics of Ontario* (Toronto: University of Toronto Press, 2016), 303.

121 Buzz Hargrove, speech to the National Collective Bargaining and Political Action Convention, Sheraton Centre Hotel, Toronto, Ontario. July 12–14, 2005, 9–10.

122 Buzz Hargrove, personal interview, November 17, 2021.

123 Nick Taylor-Vaisey, "The Liberals and NDP Are Both Desperate to Win in This Border City," *Maclean's*, October 2, 2019, https://www.macleans.ca/politics/on-the-front-lines-of-the-ndps-fight-for-relevance-in-this-election/.

124 Ken Lewenza, personal interview, January 17, 2022.

125 Buzz Hargrove, personal interview, November 17, 2021.

126 CAW Council, minutes, December 2002, 77, CAW/Unifor archives, Unifor National Office, Toronto.

127 Hemi Mitic, personal interview, November 15, 2021; Buzz Hargrove, personal interview, November 17, 2021.

128 Hemi Mitic, personal interview, November 15, 2021.

129 Ibid.

130 Quoted in Ian Urquhart, "Premier Creating Buzz with CAW," *Toronto Star*, April 13, 2007, https://www.thestar.com/opinion/columnists/2007/04/13/premier_creating_buzz_with_caw.html.

131 Quoted in Linda Diebel, "Hargrove 'No Reason to Vote NDP'; Canadian Auto Workers President Praises Record of McGuinty's Liberals," *Toronto Star*, October 5, 2007, A12.

132 Rob Ferguson, "Campaign Finance Rules 'Too Loose,' Study Says," *Toronto Star*, October 3, 2011.

133 Ian Urquhart, "Tory Faces Union Ad Campaign," *Toronto Star*, June 15, 2007, https://www.thestar.com/opinion/tory-faces-union-ad-campaign/article_f1661caf-f472-578b-a9f0-911796a60104.html.

134 Larry Savage and Nick Ruhloff-Queiruga, "Organized Labour, Campaign Finance, and the Politics of Strategic Voting in Ontario," *Labour/Le Travail* 80 (Fall 2017): 266–67.

135 Larry Savage, "Contemporary Union-Party Relations in Canada," *Labor Studies Journal* 35, 1 (2010): 15–16.

136 Walchuk, "Changing Union-Party Relations," 39; Savage, "Politics of Labour," 303–4.

137 DeLazzari, "Driving through Hard Times," 51.

138 Ross, "Social Unionism in Hard Times," 100–6.

139 "Ontario to Invest $500 Million in Auto Sector," *CBC News*, April 14, 2004, https://www.cbc.ca/news/business/ontario-to-invest-500-million-in-auto-sector-1.514912.

140 Quoted in ibid.

141 Louise Brown, "Ontario Workers' Access to Training Improves," *Toronto Star*, January 3, 2007, https://www.thestar.com/news/2007/01/03/ontario_workers_access_to_training_improves.html; Ken Lewenza, personal interview, January 17, 2022.

142 Karen Howlett, "Tory Admits Faith-Based Schools Funding Mistake," *Globe and Mail*, October 25, 2007, theglobeandmail.com/news/national/tory-admits-faith-based-schools-funding-mistake/article18147998/.

143 Carol Phillips, personal interview, October 5, 2021.
144 Sam Gindin, "Unions Cannot Afford More Magna-Type Deals," *Toronto Star*, October 26, 2007, https://www.thestar.com/opinion/2007/10/26/unions_cannot_afford_more_magnatype_deals.html; Herman Rosenfeld, "Canadian Auto Workers Surrender Right to Strike, Shop Floor Independence in Magna Agreement," *Labor Notes*, November 26, 2007, https://labornotes.org/2007/11/canadian-auto-workers-surrender-right-strike-shop-floor-independence-magna-agreement.
145 Canadian Auto Workers, "Frequently Asked Questions," in possession of the authors.
146 Wayne Lewchuk and Donald Wells, "Transforming Worker Representation: The Magna Model in Canada and Mexico," *Labour/Le Travail* 60 (Fall 2007): 117.
147 Hemi Mitic, personal interview, November 15, 2021.
148 Quoted in Saunders, "Buzz about Buzz."
149 Canadian Auto Workers, *Statement on the Reorganization of Work* (1989).
150 Jackson, *Fire and the Ashes*, 83.
151 Sam Gindin, "The CAW and Magna: Disorganizing the Working Class," *The Bullet*, October 19, 2007, https://socialistproject.ca/2007/10/b65/.
152 Gindin, "Unions Cannot Afford."
153 Quoted in Tony Van Alphen, "Hargrove Gambles with Magna Deal," *Toronto Star*, October 20, 2007, https://www.thestar.com/business/hargrove-gambles-with-magna-deal/article_4f9b430d-de1e-5c23-9757-f71958326590.html.
154 Quoted in ibid.
155 Quoted in ibid.
156 John Gray, "His Way or the Highway," *Globe and Mail*, March 13, 2009; Tony Van Alphen, "Pact Draws New Foe," *Toronto Star*, November 3, 2007, https://www.thestar.com/business/pact-draws-new-foe/article_f7b30aa6-3881-5d9a-9394-4c52558d3234.html.
157 Quoted in Tony Van Alphen, "Key CAW Leader Opposes Magna Deal," *Toronto Star*, October 29, 2007, https://www.thestar.com/business/key-caw-leader-opposes-magna-deal/article_37fb39cf-6c92-58d0-b9bf-4ca1d9fd31b8.html.
158 Van Alphen, "Pact Draws New Foe."
159 Quoted in Tony Van Alphen, "CAW Shelves Right to Strike," *Toronto Star*, October 16, 2007, https://www.thestar.com/business/caw-shelves-right-to-strike/article_44eb1d7c-054c-58e1-8e43-91246d979fcc.html.
160 Quoted in ibid.
161 Ed Broadbent, "No Place for Phony, Defanged Unions," *Globe and Mail*, October 30, 2007.
162 Quoted in Ian Urquhart, "Labour Condemns CAW Deal," *Toronto Star*, November 27, 2007, https://www.thestar.com/business/labour-condemns-caw-deal/article_a4b8c287-2e1d-5ceb-a188-ca64986c839e.html.
163 Quoted in ibid.
164 Bob White, "Unions Have to Innovate to Better Serve Workers," *Toronto Star*, October 30, 2007, https://www.thestar.com/opinion/2007/10/30/unions_have_to_innovate_to_better_serve_workers.html.
165 Ken Lewenza, "Defending the Union – The Institution," letter to Buzz Hargrove, Bob White, Bob Nickerson, and Sam Gindin, October 31, 2007, 1.

166 Nicolas Van Praet, "Chrysler to Cut 1,100 Jobs in Ontario," *Can West News,* November 2, 2007.

167 "Rising Dollar a Hazard to Canadian Manufacturing Jobs," *CAW Contact,* November 23, 2007, http://www.caw.ca/en/3757.htm.

168 Buzz Hargrove, "Positioning the Union to Best Protect Workers' Gains," speech to Windsor's Labour Appreciation/Charles E. Brooks Award, October 26, 2007, Windsor, Ontario.

169 Hargrove, on *The Agenda with Steve Paikin,* October 30, 2007.

170 CAW Members for Real Fairness, "Q&A on Magna," November 29, 2007, 4–5.

171 Camfield, *Canadian Labour in Crisis,* 129.

172 Canadian Auto Workers, "CAW Council Overwhelmingly Endorses Magna Framework of Fairness," December 7, 2007, in possession of the authors.

173 Rosenfeld, "Canadian Auto Workers Surrender"; Socialist Project Labour Committee, "Windsor Modules: The CAW-Magna Deal Delivers – Or Does it?" *The Bullet,* November 18, 2007, https://socialistproject.ca/2007/11/b74/.

174 Malcolm Allen, personal interview, November 16, 2021.

175 Tony Van Alphen, "Magna Plant Rejects CAW's No-Strike Contract," *Toronto Star,* September 9, 2009, https://www.thestar.com/business/magna-plant-rejects-caws-no-strike-contract/article_68c4c53f-c529-5e38-8de3-a9261b1c33c3.html.

176 Charlotte Yates, "The Magna Framework of Fairness Agreement: Implications for Unions in Canada," Sefton Lecture, Woodsworth House, University of Toronto, March 27, 2008.

177 Camfield, *Canadian Labour in Crisis,* 31.

178 Hemi Mitic, personal interview, November 15, 2021.

179 Bill Murnighan and Jim Stanford, "We Will Fight This Crisis: Auto Workers Resist Industrial Meltdown," in Tim Fowler, ed., *From Crisis to Austerity: Neoliberalism, Organized Labour, and the Canadian State* (Ottawa: Red Quill Books, 2013), 149.

180 Hemi Mitic, personal interview, November 15, 2021.

181 Ibid.

182 Camfield, *Canadian Unions in Crisis,* 116.

183 Tony Van Alphen, "CAW Candidate Slams Hargrove Succession Plan," *Toronto Star,* July 4, 2008, https://www.thestar.com/business/2008/07/04/caw_candidate_slams_hargrove_succession_plan.html.

184 Wayne Gates, personal interview, October 8, 2021.

185 Earle McCurdy, personal interview November 28, 2022.

186 Wayne Gates, personal interview, October 8, 2021.

187 Malcolm Allen, personal interview, November 16, 2021.

188 Sam Gindin, "Democracy: Too Important to Leave to the Members?" *The Bullet,* July 14, 2008, https://socialistproject.ca/2008/07/b124/.

189 Canadian Auto Workers, National Executive Board, special meeting minutes, July 8, 2008, 64, in possession of the authors.

190 Jim Reid, "The Death of the Administration Caucus?" *Workers for Union Renewal,* blog, June 30, 2008, http://workersforunionrenewal.blogspot.com/2008/06/death-of-administration-caucus-by-jim.html.

191 Gindin, "Democracy."

192 Hemi Mitic, personal interview, November 27, 2022; Carol Phillips, personal interview, November 22, 2022.
193 Reid, "Death of the Administration Caucus?"
194 Gindin, "Democracy," emphasis in original.
195 Jean-Pierre Fortin to Hemi Mitic, personal email, July 1, 2008.
196 Quoted in Van Alphen, "CAW Candidate Slams Hargrove."
197 Quoted in ibid.
198 Gindin, "Democracy."
199 Canadian Auto Workers, National Executive Board, special meeting minutes, July 8, 2008, 35, in possession of the authors.
200 Gindin, "Democracy."
201 Buzz Hargrove, personal interview, November 17, 2021.
202 Gindin, "Democracy."
203 Carol Phillips, personal interview, November 22, 2022.
204 Canadian Auto Workers, National Executive Board, special meeting minutes, July 8, 2008, 4, in possession of the authors.
205 Ibid., 13.
206 Ibid., 17.
207 Ibid., 54.
208 Ibid., 54.
209 Ibid., 55.
210 Carol Phillips, personal interview, October 5, 2021.
211 Buzz Hargrove, "Staff Responsibilities to Elected Officers and the NEB," interoffice communication, July 24, 2008, in possession of the authors.
212 Carol Phillips, personal interview, November 22, 2022.
213 Carol Phillips, personal interview, October 5, 2021.
214 Hemi Mitic, personal interview, November 15, 2021.
215 Malcolm Allen, personal interview, November 16, 2021.
216 Claude Patry et al. to Buzz Hargrove, August 28, 2008, in possession of the authors.
217 Carol Phillips, personal interview, October 5, 2021.
218 Jenny Ahn, personal interview, November 15, 2021.
219 Peggy Nash, personal interview, September 29, 2021.
220 Malcolm Allen, personal interview, November 16, 2021.
221 Carol Phillips, personal interview, October 5, 2021.
222 Saunders, "Buzz about Buzz."
223 Quoted in ibid.
224 Sam Gindin, "The CAW and Panic Bargaining: Early Opening at the Big Three," The Bullet, May 6, 2008, https://socialistproject.ca/2008/05/b105/.
225 Ibid., emphasis in original.
226 Ibid.
227 Herman Rosenfeld, "The Oshawa Plant Closing," The Bullet, July 23, 2008, https://socialistproject.ca/2008/07/b128/.
228 "Union Blockades GM Headquarters in Oshawa," CBC News, June 4, 2008, https://www.cbc.ca/news/canada/union-blockades-gm-headquarters-in-oshawa-1.720015.

229 Canadian Press, "CAW Workers Give Flaherty 'the Boot,'" *CTV News*, October 6, 2008, https://toronto.ctvnews.ca/caw-November workers-give-flaherty-the-boot-1.331179.

230 Saunders, "Buzz about Buzz."

231 Hargrove with Skene, *Labour of Love*, 117.

232 Saunders, "Buzz about Buzz."

233 Elections Canada, "Third Party Election Advertising Report: CAW-Canada, October 14, 2008," https://www.elections.ca/fin/oth/thi/advert/tp40/tp-0011.pdf.

234 Canadian Auto Workers, "Slim Wins," [2008], in possession of the authors.

235 Canadian Auto Workers, "CAW President Visits Oakville, Rallies Members for Federal Election," September 29, 2008, http://www.caw.ca/en/3913.htm via web.archive.org.

236 Canadian Auto Workers, "CAW President Rallies Members in Windsor for Federal Election," September 30, 2008, http://www.caw.ca/en/3917.htm via web.archive.org.

237 Canadian Auto Workers, "CAW Rallies Members in Oshawa for Federal Election," September 23, 2008, http://www.caw.ca/en/3731.htm via web.archive.org.

238 Canadian Auto Workers, "CAW President Rallies Members for Federal Election, Endorses Malcolm Allen in Welland," October 1, 2008, http://www.caw.ca/en/3949.htm via web.archive.org.

239 Canadian Auto Workers, "CAW President Visits London to Rally Members for Election, Endorses Candidates," October 6, 2008, http://www.caw.ca/en/4114.htm via web.archive.org.

240 Canadian Auto Workers, "CAW President Visits Kitchener to Rally Members for Federal Election," October 2, 2008, http://www.caw.ca/en/4001.htm via web.archive.org.

241 Malcolm Allen, personal interview, November 16, 2021.

242 Tim Fowler, "Coordinated Strategic Voting in the 2008 Federal Election," *American Review of Canadian Studies* 42, 1 (2012): 20–33.

243 Parliament of Canada, Vote No. 135, 39th Parliament, 1st session, Sitting No. 125, Wednesday, March 21, 2007, https://www.ourcommons.ca/Members/en/votes/39/1/135.

244 Hargrove with Skene, *Labour of Love*, 132.

245 Ibid.

246 See Brian Topp, *How We Almost Gave the Tories the Boot: The Inside Story behind the Coalition* (Toronto: Lorimer, 2010).

247 Canadian Press, "Premier Threatens 'Barriers' to South Korean Cars," *CTV News*, January 22, 2008, https://toronto.ctvnews.ca/premier-threatens-barriers-to-south-korean-cars-1.272372.

248 Murnighan and Stanford, "We Will Fight," 134.

249 Tony Van Alphen, "Auto Union to Freeze Pay in Landmark Deal with GM; Concessions by CAW Will Enable Ailing Firm to Qualify for Loans from Ottawa, Province," *Toronto Star*, March 9, 2009.

250 Ibid.

251 Tony Van Alphen, "Chrysler and CAW Agree on Cost Cuts; Struggling Automaker Meets Goal of Slashing Expenses by $19 an Hour," *Toronto Star*, April 25, 2009.

252 Tony Van Alphen, "GM Workers Vote Yes," *Toronto Star*, May 26, 2009, https://www.thestar.com/business/gm-workers-vote-yes/article_97e77033-3715-537e-b36f-36a6515a7641.html.

253 Nicolas Van Praet and Karen Mazurkewich, "GM to File for Creditor Shelter; Canadian Arm Seeks to Avoid Bankruptcy Filing," *National Post,* June 1, 2009.

254 The stock was later redeemed beginning in 2013. Canadian Press, "Federal, Ontario Governments Sell Off $1.1B in GM Stock," *CBC News,* September 11, 2013, https://www.cbc.ca/news/business/federal-ontario-governments-sell-off-1-1b-in-gm-stock-1.1700255.

255 Murnighan and Stanford, "We Will Fight," 156–57.

256 Ibid., 158.

257 Paul McLaughlin, "Interview: CAW President Ken Lewenza," *This Magazine,* April 27, 2009, https://this.org/2009/04/27/interview-caw-president-ken-lewenza/.

258 Ken Lewenza, personal interview, January 17, 2022.

259 Quoted in Danielle Harder, "CAW and Ontario Federation of Labour Turn New Page," *Canadian HR Reporter,* June 18, 2010, https://www.hrreporter.com/news/hr-news/caw-and-ontario-federation-of-labour-turn-new-page/312965.

260 Tony Van Alphen, "Rights Complaint Exposes Deep Rifts at OFL," *Toronto Star,* August 25, 2011, https://www.thestar.com/news/gta/2011/08/25/rights_complaint_exposes_deep_rifts_at_ofl.html.

261 Sarah Boesveld, "NDP Candidate Drops Out to Avoid Splitting Vote," *National Post,* March 31, 2011.

262 Anabelle Nicoud, "Gilles Duceppe obtient le soutien des TCA Québec," *La Presse,* April 16, 2011, https://www.lapresse.ca/actualites/elections-federales/201104/16/01-4390547-gilles-duceppe-obtient-le-soutien-des-tca-quebec.php.

263 Yves Boisvert, "NPD: l'effet *Tout le monde en parle,*" *La Presse,* May 4, 2011, https://www.lapresse.ca/debats/chroniques/yves-boisvert/201105/03/01-4395874-npd-leffet-tout-le-monde-en-parle.php.

264 Brooke Jeffrey, "The Disappearing Liberals: Caught in the Crossfire," in Jon H. Pammett and Christopher Dornan, eds., *The Canadian General Election of 2011* (Toronto: Dundurn, 2011), 68.

265 Éric Bélanger and Richard Nadeau, "The Bloc Québécois: Capsized by the Orange Wave," in Jon H. Pammett and Christopher Dornan, eds., *The Canadian General Election of 2011* (Toronto: Dundurn, 2011), 127–32.

266 Sam Vrankulj, *CAW Worker Adjustment Tracking Project* (Toronto: Canadian Auto Workers, 2010).

267 Gerry Caplan, "Labour and the NDP: The End of a Beautiful Marriage," *Globe and Mail,* September 23, 2011, https://www.theglobeandmail.com/news/politics/second-reading/labour-and-the-ndp-the-end-of-a-beautiful-marriage/article595258/.

268 Ken Lewenza, personal interview, January 17, 2022.

269 Caplan, "Labour and the NDP."

270 Ken Lewenza, personal interview, January 17, 2022.

271 Quoted in Gary Rennie, "NDP Leader on the Hunt for Candidates; Horwath on City, County Tour," *Windsor Star,* January 11, 2011, A5.

272 Jenny Ahn, personal interview, November 15, 2021.

273 Ken Lewenza, personal interview, January 17, 2022.

274 Ibid.

275 Stephanie Ross and Jason Russell, "'Caterpillar Hates Unions More Than It Loves Profits': The Electro-Motive Closure and the Dilemmas of Union Strategy," *Labour/ Le Travail* 81 (Spring 2018): 74.

276 Canadian Press, "Electro-Motive Workers Ratify Closeout Deal," *CTV News Kitchener,* February 23, 2012, http://kitchener.ctvnews.ca/electro-motive-workers-ratify -closeoutdeal-1.772504.

277 "Closure Agreement between Electro-Motive Canada Co. and National Automobile, Aerospace, Transportation and General Workers Union of Canada (CAW-Canada) and Its Local 27," February 23, 2012, http://www.caw.ca/assets/images/emc_RATIFICA TION_(2).pdf via web.archive.org.

278 Ross and Russell, "'Caterpillar Hates Unions,'" 76.

279 Susan Taylor and Allison Martell, "CAW Wraps Up Detroit 3 Bargaining with Chrysler Deal," *Reuters,* September 27, 2012, https://www.reuters.com/article/cbusiness-us -autos-talks-idCABRE88O0WM20120927.

280 Sam Gindin, "Culture of Concessions Has Gutted Organized Labour," *Toronto Star,* September 25, 2012, https://www.thestar.com/opinion/editorialopinion/2012/09/25/ culture_of_concessions_has_gutted_organized_labour.html.

281 Laura Payton, "NDP-Liberal Merger the Way to Win, CAW Says," *CBC News,* September 2, 2011, https://www.cbc.ca/news/politics/ndp-liberal-merger-the-way-to-win-caw -says-1.1057208.

282 Quoted in Aaron Wherry, "Ken Lewenza's Endorsement," *Maclean's,* February 12, 2012, https://www.macleans.ca/politics/ottawa/ken-lewenzas-endorsement/.

283 Laura Payton, "NDP Votes to Take 'Socialism' out of Party Constitution," *CBC News,* April 14, 2013, https://www.cbc.ca/news/politics/ndp-votes-to-take-socialism-out-of -party-constitution-1.1385171.

284 Ken Lewenza, personal interview, January 17, 2022.

285 Canadian Auto Workers, "History of CAW-Canada Finances 1986–2006," document distributed at the 8th CAW Constitutional Convention, Vancouver, British Columbia, August 2006, 1.

286 Thomas Walkom, "Walkom: From CAW and CEP Comes a New (Old) Idea to Rebuild Unions," *Toronto Star,* May 23, 2012, https://www.thestar.com/news/canada/2012/05/23/ walkom_from_caw_and_cep_comes_a_new_old_idea_to_rebuild_unions.html.

287 Hargrove, "Making the Most of Opportunity."

288 Ibid.

289 Sam Gindin, "Toward a New Politics? After the CAW-NDP Divorce," *The Bullet,* July 14, 2006, https://socialistproject.ca/2006/07/b27/.

290 John Peters, "Too Little Too Late? The State of the Canadian Labour Movement Today," *Briarpatch Magazine,* November 1, 2008, https://briarpatchmagazine.com/articles/ view/too-little-too-late-the-state-of-the-canadian-labour-movement-today.

CHAPTER 6: MERGE AHEAD

1 Both quoted in John Lorinc, "State of the Unions," *The Walrus,* December 19, 2013, https://thewalrus.ca/state-of-the-unions/.

2   Canadian Auto Workers and Communications, Energy and Paperworkers Union, *Towards a New Union: CAW CEP Proposal Committee Final Report* (2012), 14, 3, https://www.unifor.org/sites/default/files/legacy/attachments/final.report.pdf.

3   Fred Wilson and Jim Stanford, "A Moment of Truth for Canadian Labour," CAW-CEP discussion paper, [2012], in possession of the authors; Tony Van Alphen, "Unions Must Change Quickly to Survive, Says Secret Report by CEP/CAW," *Toronto Star,* January 26. 2012, thestar.com/news/gta/2012/01/26/unions_must_change_quickly_to_survive_says_secret_report_by_cepcaw.html.

4   Fred Wilson, *A New Kind of Union: Unifor and the Birth of the Modern Canadian Union* (Toronto: Lorimer, 2019), 71.

5   Tony Van Alphen, "CAW Approves Formation of New Union with CEP," *Toronto Star,* August 22, 2012, https://www.thestar.com/news/gta/2012/08/22/caw_approves_formation_of_new_union_with_cep.html.

6   Canadian Press, "CAW Votes to Merge with CEP," *Globe and Mail,* August 22, 2012, https://www.theglobeandmail.com/report-on-business/caw-votes-to-merge-with-cep-union/article4493949/.

7   "CEP Votes Overwhelmingly in Favour of CAW Merger," *CBC News,* October 15, 2012, https://www.cbc.ca/news/canada/windsor/cep-votes-overwhelmingly-in-favour-of-caw-merger-1.1257904.

8   Fred Wilson, personal interview, December 15, 2022.

9   Wilson, *New Kind of Union,* 147.

10 Canadian Auto Workers and Communications, Energy and Paperworkers Union, "Towards a New Union," 8–9.

11 Unifor, *Welcome to Unifor* (2022), https://www.unifor.org/sites/default/files/documents/New%20Member%20Kit%202022%20EN-Web.pdf. The kit for new members contains a calculation error for Ontario.

12 Unifor's founding constitution, Article 2, https://www.unifor.org/node/7871.

13 Wilson, *New Kind of Union,* 102–3.

14 Fred Wilson, personal interview, December 15, 2022.

15 Ibid.

16 H.G. Watson, "Unifor Officially Takes Shape at Historic Union Convention," *Rabble,* September 1, 2013, https://rabble.ca/labour/unifor-officially-takes-shape-historic-union-convention/.

17 Jim Stanford, personal interview, October 4, 2021.

18 Fred Wilson, personal interview, December 15, 2022.

19 Bruce Allen, "The CAW-CEP Merger: A Political Reflection," *Labour/Le Travail* 70 (Fall 2012): 226.

20 Commission on the Reform of Ontario's Public Services, *Public Services for Ontarians: A Path to Sustainability and Excellence* (Toronto: Queen's Printer for Ontario, 2012), https://www.opsba.org/wp-content/uploads/2021/02/drummondReportFeb1512.pdf.

21 Ontario Confederation of University Faculty Associations, "OCUFA Analysis of the Drummond Report: Long on Cuts, Short on Insight," February 22, 2012, 3, http://ocufa.on.ca/wordpress/assets/OCUFA-Drummond-Report-Analysis-Feb.-22-2012Final.pdf.

22 Ibid.

23 Larry Savage and Chantal Mancini, "Strategic Electoral Dilemmas and the Politics of Teachers' Unions in Ontario," *Canadian Political Science Review* 16, 1 (2022): 13–14.

24 Martin Regg Cohn, "Dalton McGuinty's Decision and Timing Were All Wrong," *Toronto Star*, October 23, 2012, http://www.thestar.com/news/canada/2012/10/23/dalton_mcguintys_decisions_and_timing_were_all_wrong.html.

25 Louise Brown, "Ontario Teachers Have Strong Case in Court Challenge, Legal Expert Says," *Toronto Star*, October 11, 2012, http://www.thestar.com/news/canada/2012/10/11/ontario_teachers_have_strong_case_in_court_challenge_legal_expert_says.html.

26 Quoted in Brian Cross, "Pupatello Leads What Looks Like a Two-Woman Race for Liberal Leader," *Windsor Star*, January 15, 2013, https://windsorstar.com/news/former-caw-president-says-pupatello-his-pick-for-liberal-leader.

27 Richard J. Brennan, "NDP Poised to Win Windsor Byelection," *Toronto Star*, July 12, 2013, https://www.thestar.com/news/queenspark/2013/07/12/ndp_poised_to_win_windsor_byelection.html.

28 "Windsor Labour Leader Says Union Vote Matters," *CBC News*, July 5, 2013, https://www.cbc.ca/news/canada/windsor/windsor-labour-leader-says-union-vote-matters-1.1414628.

29 Wayne Gates, personal interview, October 8, 2021.

30 Ibid.

31 Quoted in Rob Ferguson, "Horwath Defends Decision to Provoke Ontario Election," *Toronto Star*, May 5, 2014, https://www.thestar.com/news/canada/2014/05/05/horwath_defends_decision_to_provoke_ontario_election.html.

32 Tamsin McMahon, "Can Tim Hudak Sell Right-to-Work in Ontario?" *Maclean's*, January 27, 2014, https://www.macleans.ca/economy/economicanalysis/can-tim-hudak-sell-right-to-work-in-ontario/.

33 Larry Savage, "The Politics of Labour and Labour Relations in Ontario," in Cheryl N. Collier and Jonathan Malloy, eds., *The Politics of Ontario* (Toronto: University of Toronto Press, 2016), 306–7.

34 Bruce Campion-Smith, "Andrea Horwath Faces Backlash from Prominent NDP Supporters," *Toronto Star*, May 23, 2014, https://www.thestar.com/politics/provincial-elections/andrea-horwath-faces-backlash-from-prominent-ndp-supporters/article_0ab1db86-83e8-57af-b14a-57c91bcc928b.html.

35 CUPE Ontario, "Horwath Promise to Cut Government Spending Wrongheaded, Says CUPE Ontario President," May 14, 2014, https://cupe.on.ca/archivedoc2667/.

36 Larry Savage and Nick Ruhloff-Queiruga, "Organized Labour, Campaign Finance, and the Politics of Strategic Voting in Ontario," *Labour/Le Travail* 80 (Fall 2017): 263; Ontario, Elections Ontario, "Working Families," 2011 General Election tpar-1 Third Party Election Advertising Report, https://finances.elections.on.ca/en/finances-overview.

37 Rob Ferguson, "Unions That Backed Kathleen Wynne 'Sold Their Souls,' OPSEU President Says," *Hamilton Spectator*, June 20, 2014, https://www.thespec.com/news/2014/06/20/unions-that-backed-kathleen-wynne-sold-their-souls-opseu-president-says.html.

38 Quoted in Unifor, "Unifor Leader Challenges OPSEU's Smokey Thomas," June 20, 2014, https://www.unifor.org/news/all-news/unifor-leader-challenges-opseu-smokey-thomas.

39 Quoted in Sharon Hill, "Vote NDP Except If You're in Windsor West, Suggests Union Leader," *Windsor Star,* May 14, 2014, https://windsorstar.com/news/vote-ndp-except -if-youre-in-windsor-west-suggests-union-leader-with-videos.

40 Thomas Mulcair, personal interview, December 2, 2021.

41 Fred Wilson, personal interview, December 15, 2022.

42 Unifor, "Politics for Workers: Unifor's Political Project," paper presented to the Unifor Canadian Council, Vancouver, September 13–15, 2014, 12.

43 Ibid., 22.

44 Ibid.

45 Jim Stanford, personal interview, October 4, 2021.

46 Joan Bryden, "Unifor Aims to Defeat Harper Tories," *Durham Region,* September 18, 2014, https://www.durhamregion.com/news-story/4869478-unifor-aims-to-defeat -harper-tories/.

47 Quoted in ibid.

48 Parliamentary staff had previously belonged to the CEP before joining Unifor via the merger. Joan Bryden, "Federal NDP Staffers Split with Unifor after Union's Strategic Voting Plea," *Toronto Star,* July 3, 2014, https://www.thestar.com/news/ canada/2014/07/03/federal_ndp_staffers_split_with_unifor_after_unions_strategic_ voting_plea.html.

49 Thomas Mulcair, personal interview, December 2, 2021.

50 Hassan Yussuff, personal interview, October 18, 2021.

51 Danny Mallett, personal interview, March 7, 2022.

52 Ed Broadbent, personal interview, January 24, 2022.

53 Danny Mallett, personal interview, March 7, 2022.

54 Hassan Yussuff, personal interview, October 18, 2021; Danny Mallett, personal inter- view, March 7, 2022.

55 Larry Savage, "How Hassan Yussuff Won the CLC Presidency," *Rabble,* May 14, 2014, https://rabble.ca/labour/how-hassan-yussuff-won-clc-presidency/.

56 Danny Mallett, personal interview, March 7, 2022.

57 Thomas Mulcair, personal interview, December 2, 2021.

58 Peggy Nash, personal interview, January 31, 2022.

59 James Pratt, personal interview, December 7, 2021.

60 Thomas Mulcair, personal interview, December 2, 2021.

61 Quoted in Postmedia Network, "Union Asks NDP to Keep Saudi Armoured Vehicles Deal 'Under Wraps,' Fearing 'Significant' Job Losses," *National Post,* September 30, 2015, https://nationalpost.com/news/politics/union-asks-ndp-to-keep-saudi-armoured -vehicles-deal-under-wraps-fearing-significant-job-losses.

62 Quoted in ibid.

63 Quoted in Ethan Cox, "Unifor Walk Back Criticism of NDP for Raising Saudi Arms Deal in Debate," *Ricochet,* September 30, 2015, https://ricochet.media/en/626/ unifor-walk-back-criticism-of-ndp-for-raising-saudi-arms-deal-in-debate.

64 John Paul Tasker, "NDP Dropped 20 Points in 48 Hours after Supporting Niqab, Tom Mulcair Says," *CBC News,* February 13, 2016, https://www.cbc.ca/news/politics/ thomas-mulcair-accepts-responsibility-1.3446241.

65 Thomas Mulcair, personal interview, December 2, 2021.

66 Mikayla Wronko, "As Mulcair Steps Right, Trudeau Steers Left," *The Queen's Journal*, September 10, 2015, https://www.queensjournal.ca/story/2015-09-09/lifestyle/as-mulcair-steps-right-trudeau-steers-left/.

67 Gil McGowan, personal interview, November 9, 2021.

68 Peggy Nash, personal interview, September 29, 2021.

69 Whereas Unifor, the building trades unions, and the Quebec Federation of Labour pursued strategic-voting campaigns, the United Steelworkers, CUPE, the Elementary Teachers' Federation of Ontario, and the OFL called on voters to back the NDP. Sabrina Nanji, "How Do Unions Affect Elections?" *Canadian Labour Reporter*, September 21, 2015, https://www.hrreporter.com/labour/news/how-do-unions-affect-elections/293278.

70 Giuseppe Valiante, "Labour Unions across Canada Preparing to Launch Major Anti-Harper Offensive," *Global News*, September 6, 2015, https://globalnews.ca/news/2206189/labour-unions-across-canada-preparing-to-launch-major-anti-harper-offensive/.

71 Grace Macaluso, "Unifor Steps Up Anti-Harper Campaign as Advance Polls Set to Open," *Windsor Star*, October 8, 2015, https://windsorstar.com/news/local-news/unifor-steps-up-anti-harper-campaign-as-advance-polls-set-to-open/wcm/d444a25e-52a6-44c9-9650-c9e679cbc7fd/.

72 Unifor, *Echo: Unifor Young Workers*, October 2015, https://www.unifor.org/sites/default/files/documents/newsletter/echo_oct_2015.pdf via web.archive.org.

73 After his defeat, Stoffer called on the NDP and the labour movement to cut their formal ties. Kristy Kirkup, "Former East Coast MP Peter Stoffer Proposes New Name, Other Changes for NDP," *CTV News*, October 26, 2015, https://www.ctvnews.ca/politics/former-east-coast-mp-peter-stoffer-proposes-new-name-other-changes-for-ndp-1.2627848.

74 Unifor, "Unifor Celebrates Defeat of Harper Conservatives," October 19, 2015, https://www.unifor.org/news/all-news/unifor-celebrates-defeat-harper-conservatives.

75 Earle McCurdy, personal interview, November 28, 2022.

76 Ken Georgetti, "Mulcair Didn't Fail NDP, Flaky Strategic Voters Did," *The Tyee*, April 6, 2016, https://thetyee.ca/Opinion/2016/04/06/NDP-Flaky-Strategic-Voters/.

77 Jerry Dias, "Strategic Voting Was the Right Call in 2015: Unifor Head," *The Tyee*, April 8, 2016, https://thetyee.ca/Opinion/2016/04/08/Strategic-Voting-Was-Right/.

78 Danny Mallett, personal interview, March 7, 2022.

79 Laura Stone, "Union Head Says Signs of Mulcair's Ouster Were Clear," *Globe and Mail*, April 11, 2016, https://www.theglobeandmail.com/news/politics/mulcairs-marginal-presence-at-ndp-convention-seals-leadership-fate/article29599525/.

80 Canadian Press, "Mulcair Responds to Labour Congress Statement Predicting NDP Leader Will Get Less Than 60 Per Cent in Review," *National Post*, April 6, 2016, https://nationalpost.com/news/politics/mulcair-responds-to-labour-congress-statement-predicting-ndp-leader-will-get-less-than-60-per-cent-in-review. Unifor sent a delegation of thirty to forty delegates to the convention. Stone, "Union Head Says."

81 Stone, "Union Head Says."

82 Quoted in Canadian Press, "Mulcair Responds to Labour Congress."

83 Stone, "Union Head Says."

84 Gil McGowan, personal interview, November 9, 2021.
85 Brent Farrington, personal interview, January 28, 2022.
86 Gil McGowan, personal interview, November 9, 2021.
87 Quoted in Stone, "Union Head Says."
88 "Unifor President Says Mulcair Should've 'Stepped Down Yesterday,'" *CTV News*, September 11, 2016, https://www.ctvnews.ca/politics/unifor-president-says-mulcair -should-ve-stepped-down-yesterday-1.3067378.
89 Stephen Maher, "Canadian Labour Congress Linked to Failed Attempt to Oust Mulcair," *iPolitics*, June 16, 2017, https://ipolitics.ca/2017/06/16/canadian-labour-congress -linked-to-failed-attempt-to-oust-mulcair/.
90 Brent Farrington, personal interview, January 28, 2022.
91 Canadian Labour Congress, "Prime Minister Addresses National Meeting of the Canadian Labour Congress," November 10, 2015, https://canadianlabour.ca/news -news-archive-prime-minister-addresses-national-meeting-canadian-labour-congress/.
92 Canadian Labour Congress, "Canada's Unions Celebrate Repeal of Controversial Anti-union Legislation," June 14, 2017, https://canadianlabour.ca/news-news-archive -canadas-unions-celebrate-repeal-controversial-anti-union-legislation/.
93 Hassan Yussuff, personal interview, October 18, 2021.
94 Sonia Aslam, "Trudeau Tries to Win the Labour Vote, Makes Speech to Unifor," *CityNews*, August 24, 2016, https://vancouver.citynews.ca/2016/08/24/trudeau-tries -to-win-the-labour-vote-makes-speech-to-unifor/.
95 Doug Nesbitt, "Why Trudeau Is No Friend of Labour," *Canadian Dimension*, August 31, 2016, https://canadiandimension.com/articles/view/why-trudeau-is-no-friend -of-labour.
96 Hassan Yussuff, personal interview, October 18, 2021.
97 Ibid.
98 Ibid.
99 Ibid.
100 Danny Mallett, personal interview, March 7, 2022.
101 Hassan Yussuff, personal interview, October 18, 2021.
102 Peggy Nash, personal interview, September 29, 2021.
103 Ibid.
104 Jamey Heath, *Dead Centre: Hope, Possibility, and Unity for Canadian Progressives* (New York: John Wiley and Sons, 2007).
105 Brent Farrington, personal interview, January 28, 2022.
106 "Unifor President Says Mulcair Should've 'Stepped Down Yesterday,'" *CTV News*, September 11, 2016, https://www.ctvnews.ca/politics/unifor-president-says-mulcair -should-ve-stepped-down-yesterday-1.3067378.
107 BJ Siekierski, "Union Leader Jerry Dias among Donors to Leitch Campaign," *iPolitics*, November 1, 2016, https://ipolitics.ca/news/union-leader-jerry-dias-among-donors -to-leitch-campaign.
108 Chris Fairweather, "'We Can't Just Wrap Ourselves in the Flag': Labour Nationalism, Global Solidarity, and the 2016 Fight to Save GM Oshawa," *Journal of Labor and Society* 25, 3 (2022): 379.
109 Ibid., 379–80.

110 Quoted in "Oshawa General Motors Employees Launch Campaign to Save Plant," *CityNews,* June 21, 2016, https://toronto.citynews.ca/2016/06/21/oshawa-general-motors -employees-launch-campaign-save-plant/.

111 Fairweather, "'We Can't Just Wrap,'" 384.

112 Ibid., 383–84.

113 Chris Hall, "Unifor Members Ratify New Contract with General Motors," *Toronto. com,* September 25, 2016, https://www.toronto.com/news/unifor-members-ratify-new -contract-with-general-motors/article_72488b42-1def-57d3-b58a-6a53e0eb44ae.html.

114 Quoted in ibid.

115 Quoted in ibid.

116 Quoted in Mark Gollom, "Unions Face Challenges in Offsetting Potential Pension Losses," *CBC News,* September 21, 2016, https://www.cbc.ca/news/business/ pension-plans-union-unifor-general-motors-1.3770836.

117 Larry Savage, "The Past, Present and Future of the Canadian Labour Movement: Interrogating Insider Accounts," *Labour/Le Travail* 85 (Spring 2020): 291; Sara Mojta-hedzadeh and Rosa Saba, "'A Fighting Culture': Inside the Controversial Career of Former Unifor Head Jerry Dias," *Toronto Star,* March 18, 2022, https://www.thestar. com/business/a-fighting-culture-inside-the-controversial-career-of-former-unifor -head-jerry-dias/article_6f72f25a-5e0e-5ea3-87c4-dafb5bf2e25c.html.

118 Ben Spurr, "Bob Kinnear Resigns as Head of the TTC Union," *Toronto Star,* March 17, 2017, https://www.thestar.com/news/gta/bob-kinnear-resigns-as-head-of-the-ttc -union/article_22c8ffcc-527c-5b88-8692-8cb790f448b3.html.

119 Sam Gindin and Herman Rosenfeld, "The Crisis in the ATU: Labour Shoots Itself in the Foot," *The Bullet,* March 14, 2017, https://socialistproject.ca/2017/03/b1382/.

120 Ibid.

121 David Bush, Gerard Di Trolio, and Doug Nesbitt, "ATU Trusteeship, Unifor Raid, CLC Crisis," *RankandFile.ca,* February 10, 2017, rankandfile.ca/atu-trusteeship-unifor -raid-clc-crisis/.

122 Larry Savage, "Making Sense of the Unifor-CLC Split," *Briarpatch Magazine,* January 18, 2018, https://briarpatchmagazine.com/articles/view/making-sense-of-the-uniforclc-split.

123 Unifor, "Facts on Unifor's Disaffiliation from the CLC," January 18, 2018, https://www. unifor.org/news/all-news/facts-unifors-disaffiliation-clc.

124 Tara Deschamps, "GTA Hotel Workers Vote to Stay with Union amid Unifor Raiding Attempts," *CTV News,* February 8, 2018, https://toronto.ctvnews.ca/gta-hotel-workers -vote-to-stay-with-union-amid-unifor-raiding-attempts-1.3795068?cache=xvlushbbrzkwk.

125 Hassan Yussuff, personal interview, October 18, 2021.

126 Movement of United Professionals, "2021 Canadian Labour Congress Convention Recap," June 2021, https://moveuptogether.ca/the-latest/2021-canadian-labour -congress-convention-recap/.

127 Sid Ryan, *A Grander Vision: My Life in the Labour Movement* (Toronto: Dundurn, 2019), 274.

128 Ibid., 274.

129 Rebecca Joseph, "The Story of the Ontario NDP's 2018 Election Campaign," *Global News,* June 7, 2018, https://globalnews.ca/news/4255960/ontario-election-ndp -campaign/.

130 John Michael McGrath, "How Kathleen Wynne Became One of Ontario's Most Cynical Politicians," *TVO Today*, June 1, 2018, https://www.tvo.org/article/how-kathleen -wynne-became-one-of-ontarios-most-cynical-politicians.
131 Savage and Mancini, "Strategic Electoral Dilemmas," 15.
132 Unifor, "Unifor Pledges to Continue Building Labour Movement Following Progressive Conservative Win," June 7, 2018, https://www.unifor.org/news/all-news/ unifor-pledges-continue-building-labour-movement-following-progressive -conservative.
133 Larry Savage, "The Shifting Landscape of Party-Union Relationships in Ontario," in Cheryl N. Collier and Jonathan Malloy, eds., *The Politics of Ontario*, 2nd. ed. (Toronto: University of Toronto Press, forthcoming).
134 Emily Jackson, "'More to Come': Why GM Closed Its Oshawa Plant and What It Means for Canada's Auto Sector," *Financial Post*, November 26, 2018, https://financialpost. com/transportation/consumer-demand-and-competitiveness-why-gm-closed-its-oshawa -plant.
135 Reka Szekely, "Unifor Vows to Barricade GM Canada Headquarters Until Company Reverses Plans to Close Oshawa Plant," *Oshawa This Week*, January 23, 2019, https:// www.durhamregion.com/news-story/9139306-update-unifor-vows-to-barricade -gm-canada-headquarters-until-company-reverses-plans-to-close-oshawa-plant/.
136 Quoted in Ian Bickis, "Labour Board Rules Unifor Labour Actions against GM Were Unlawful," *Toronto Star*, February 26, 2019, https://www.thestar.com/business/labour -board-rules-unifor-labour-actions-against-gm-were-unlawful/article_739dc9b3-f75f -51dd-b529-039c81664ecd.html; Unifor, "Unifor Launches Boycott of Mexican-Made GM Vehicles," January 25, 2019, https://www.unifor.org/news/all-news/unifor -launches-boycott-mexican-made-gm-vehicles.
137 Scott Aquanno and Toba Bryant, "Workplace Restructuring and Institutional Change: GM Oshawa from 1994 to 2019," *Studies in Political Economy* 102, 1 (2021): 43.
138 Ibid.
139 Quoted in Shawn Jeffords, "Doug Ford Says Union Leaders, Politicians Selling 'False Hope' on General Motors Closure," *Global News*, November 28, 2018, https://globalnews. ca/news/4709606/doug-ford-general-motors-oshawa/; quoted in Chris Herhalt, "Unifor President Says 'F*** You' to Premier Ford in Televised Speech," *CTV News*, December 1, 2018, https://toronto.ctvnews.ca/unifor-president-says-f-you-to-premier -ford-in-televised-speech-1.4200849.
140 Quoted in Unifor, "Unions Vital to a Strong Society, Trudeau Tells Convention," August 19, 2019, https://www.unifor.org/news/all-news/unions-vital-strong-society-trudeau -tells-convention.
141 Quoted in Unifor, "Strong Unions Needed in Canada, Freeland Tells Convention," August 20, 2019, https://www.unifor.org/news/all-news/strong-unions-needed-canada -freeland-tells-convention.
142 Quoted in Nick Taylor-Vaisey, "Jerry Dias Wants to Make an Enemy out of Andrew Scheer," *Maclean's*, August 22, 2019, https://www.macleans.ca/politics/ottawa/jerry -dias-wants-to-make-an-enemy-out-of-andrew-scheer/.
143 Quoted in ibid.
144 Unifor Quebec, Facebook ad, October 19, 2019.

145 "Unifor donne son appui à Denis Trudel," *Le Courier du Sud,* October 18, 2019, https://www.lecourrierdusud.ca/unifor-donne-son-appui-a-denis-trudel/; "Unifor donne son appui à Karine Trudel," *Radio-Canada,* October 15, 2019, https://ici.radio-canada.ca/nouvelle/1346647/unifor-donne-son-appui-a-karine-trudel; Ashley Burke, "Singh Makes Pitch for Union Support in Montreal, but Faces Competition for Their Votes," *CBC News,* October 10, 2019, https://www.cbc.ca/news/politics/ndp-labour-movement-election-support-1.5315676.

146 Quoted in Burke, "Singh Makes Pitch."

147 Ibid.

148 Andy Fillmore, "Proud to be endorsed ... " *Twitter,* September 14, 2019, 2:04 p.m., https://twitter.com/AndyFillmoreHFX/status/1172949354820382720; Saulnier's local, however, appeared to support her. Unifor Local 567, "Christine Saulnier for Halifax," Facebook post, October 11, 2019.

149 Canadian Union of Public Employees, "CUPE Nova Scotia and CUPE National Endorse Christine Saulnier for Halifax in Federal Election," September 18, 2019, https://cupe.ca/cupe-nova-scotia-and-cupe-national-endorse-christine-saulnier-halifax-federal-election.

150 Elizabeth McSheffrey, "Halifax Ranks Eighth for Federal Spending Commitments in Canada under Trudeau," *Global News,* September 3, 2019, https://globalnews.ca/news/5848826/halifax-ranks-eighth-for-federal-spending-commitments-in-canada-under-trudeau/.

151 Anne Jarvis, "In Windsor–Tecumseh, Says Election Website, It's a Three-Way Race," *Windsor Star,* October 5, 2019, https://windsorstar.com/news/national/election-2019/jarvis-in-Windsor–Tecumseh-its-a-three-way-race/.

152 Unifor, "Unifor Proud of Its Role during the Federal Election," November 5, 2019, https://www.unifor.org/news/all-news/unifor-proud-its-role-during-federal-election.

153 Statistics Canada, "Labour Force Survey, November 2020," *The Daily,* December 4, 2020, https://www150.statcan.gc.ca/n1/daily-quotidien/201204/dq201204a-eng.htm.

154 Stephanie Ross and Larry Savage, "Canadian Labour and COVID-19," in Stephanie Ross and Larry Savage, eds., *Rethinking the Politics of Labour in Canada,* 2nd ed., 14–28 (Halifax: Fernwood, 2021).

155 General Motors, "A Statement from GM Canada President Scott Bell on Unifor Negotiations," November 5, 2020, https://media.gm.ca/media/ca/en/gm/home.detail.html/content/Pages/news/ca/en/2020/Nov/1105_Negotiations.html.

156 William Clavey, "Behind the Scenes of GM's Surprising Return to Oshawa," *Toronto Star,* December 23, 2020, https://www.thestar.com/autos/2020/12/23/behind-the-scenes-of-gms-surprising-return-to-oshawa.html.

157 Quoted in Breana Noble and Kalea Hall, "GM's Decision to Build Trucks in Ontario Concerns UAW Workers," *Detroit News,* November 5, 2020, https://www.detroitnews.com/story/business/autos/general-motors/2020/11/05/general-motors-reaches-tentative-agreement-canadian-lanor-union-unifor/6171915002/.

158 Unifor, "How We Saved Oshawa GM," *YouTube,* November 23, 2020, https://youtu.be/2sWE2J1zBGg.

159 Quoted in Tony Leah and Rebecca Keetch, "General Motors Returns to Oshawa – But Offers Only Second-Tier Jobs in a 'Pop-Up' Plant," *Labor Notes*, November 25, 2020, https://labornotes.org/2020/11/general-motors-returns-oshawa-offers-only-second-tier-jobs-pop-plant.

160 Ibid.

161 Erin O'Toole, "Do you think …?" *Twitter*, September 7, 2020, 10:26 a.m., https://twitter.com/erinotoole/status/1302991683072798721.

162 Rachel Aiello, "Conservatives 'United' O'Toole Says, after MPs Give Themselves the Power to Remove Him," *CTV News*, October 5, 2021, https://www.ctvnews.ca/politics/conservatives-united-o-toole-says-after-mps-give-themselves-the-power-to-remove-him-1.5611285; Larry Savage and Simon Black, "How Erin O'Toole's Strategy to Win Over Union Voters Could Work," *The Conversation*, September 15, 2020, https://the-conversation.com/how-erin-otooles-strategy-to-win-over-union-voters-could-work-146259.

163 Joan Bryden, "Unions Reject O'Toole's Worker-Friendly Pitch, Campaign to Prevent Conservative Win," *CTV News*, September 15, 2021, https://www.ctvnews.ca/politics/federal-election-2021/unions-reject-o-toole-s-worker-friendly-pitch-campaign-to-prevent-conservative-win-1.5585922.

164 David Thurton, "No Apologies: Hassan Yussuff Faces Down His Critics as He Retires as Leader of Canadian Labour Congress," *CBC News*, June 18, 2021, https://www.cbc.ca/news/politics/hassan-yussuff-canadian-labour-congress-1.6070255.

165 Andrew Jackson, personal interview, February 7, 2022.

166 Brent Farrington, personal interview, January 28, 2022.

167 Adam D.K. King, "Hassan Yussuff Showed That Access to Power Is Not Actual Power," *The Maple*, July 9, 2021, https://www.readthemaple.com/hassan-yussuff-showed-that-access-to-power-is-not-actual-power/.

168 James Pratt, personal interview, December 7, 2021.

169 Donald Gray-Donald, "CLC's Yussuff Acted Alone in Controversial Endorsement of Morneau for OECD Role," *The Media Co-Op*, November 14, 2020, https://mediacoop.ca/story/clcs-yussuff-acted-alone-controversial-endorsement/37034.

170 Leila El Shennawy, "Canadian Labour Congress President Hassan Yussuff Set to Retire after Years of Government Deal-Making," *Globe and Mail*, April 25, 2021, https://www.theglobeandmail.com/politics/article-top-labour-leader-set-to-retire-after-years-of-government-deal-making/.

171 Michael MacIsaac, personal interview, November 15, 2021.

172 Larry Savage, "Hassan Yussuff's contention …" *Twitter*, June 18, 2021, 1:42 p.m., https://twitter.com/Prof_Savage/status/1405959103411802114.

173 Andrew Jackson, personal interview, February 7, 2022.

174 Andrew Jackson, *The Fire and the Ashes: Rekindling Democratic Socialism* (Toronto: Between the Lines, 2021), 81.

175 Quoted in John Michael McGrath, "Why the Next Group of Voters Canada's Conservatives Will Chase Is … Unions?" *TVO Today*, November 3, 2020, https://www.tvo.org/article/why-the-next-group-of-voters-canadas-conservatives-will-chase-is-unions.

176   Robyn Urback, "The Main Philosophy of Erin O'Toole's 'Principled Conservatism' Is Winning Elections," *Globe and Mail*, November 11, 2020, https://www.theglobeandmail. com/opinion/article-the-main-philosophy-of-erin-otooles-principled-conservatism-is/.

177   Savage and Black, "How Erin O'Toole's Strategy."

178   Conservative Party of Canada, "Conservative Leader Erin O'Toole to Ensure Canadian Workers Have Their Voices Heard," August 23, 2021, https://www.whhconservativeeda. ca/conservative_leader_erin_o_toole_to_ensure_canadian_workers_have_their_voices_ heard.

179   Unifor, "Unifor Launches TV Ad Cautioning Canadians against Voting for Erin O'Toole," August 2, 2021, https://www.unifor.org/news/all-news/unifor-launches-tv-ad -cautioning-canadians-against-voting-erin-otoole.

180   Unifor, "Unifor Shows the Value of Membership Engagement in Election Campaign," September 22, 2021, https://www.unifor.org/news/all-news/unifor-shows-value -membership-engagement-election-campaign.

181   Ibid.

182   Ibid.

183   Unifor, "Events," Unifor Votes, 2021, https://www.uniforvotes.ca/events.

184   Unifor, "Events."

185   Sylvain Martin, personal interview, February 15, 2023.

186   Unifor-Québec, "Rapport du directeur québécois d'Unifor Renaud Gagné," November 24, 2021, 28–29, https://www.uniforquebec.org/fr/document/rapport-du-directeur -quebecois-dunifor-renaud-gagne-24-novembre-2021.

187   Patricia Rainville, "Appuyé de leaders syndicaux, le Bloc veut miser sur la forêt Qué-bécoise," *Le Droit*, August 26, 2021, https://www.ledroit.com/2021/08/26/appuye -de-leaders-syndicaux-le-bloc-veut-miser-sur-la-foret-quebecoise-c2d7a4c8c10cecod 64688816e80a2a34.

188   Unifor, "Unifor Requests Joint Meeting with Trudeau and Singh," September 22, 2021, https://www.unifor.org/news/all-news/unifor-requests-joint-meeting-trudeau-and -singh.

189   Prime Minister of Canada Justin Trudeau, "Delivering for Canadians," press release, March 22, 2022, https://www.pm.gc.ca/en/news/news-releases/2022/03/22/delivering -canadians-now.

190   Wilson, *New Kind of Union*, 20.

CHAPTER 7: HEAD-ON COLLISION

1   Robert Benzie, "Flanked by Union Leaders, Doug Ford Raises Ontario's Minimum Wage to $15 an Hour," *Toronto Star*, November 2, 2021, https://www.thestar.com/ politics/provincial/2021/11/02/flanked-by-union-leaders-doug-ford-raises-ontarios -minimum-wage-to-15-an-hour.html.

2   Chris Herhalt, "Unifor President Says 'F*** You' to Premier Ford in Televised Speech," *CTV News*, December 1, 2018, https://toronto.ctvnews.ca/unifor-president-says-f -you-to-premier-ford-in-televised-speech-1.4200849.

3   Martin Regg Cohn, "Doug Ford's Temporary Truce with Union Leader Shows the Enemy of My Enemy Is My Friend," *Toronto Star*, December 19, 2021, https://www.

thestar.com/politics/political-opinion/2021/12/19/doug-fords-temporary-truce-with
-union-leader-shows-the-enemy-of-my-enemy-is-my-friend.html.

4 Lana Payne, personal interview, March 31, 2023.

5 Fred Wilson, personal interview, December 15, 2022.

6 Buzz Hargrove, personal interview, November 17, 2021.

7 Ken Lewenza, personal interview, January 17, 2022.

8 Malcolm Allen, personal interview, November 16, 2021.

9 Robert Benzie, "Doug Ford Appoints Union Leader Jerry Dias to Head Auto Task
Force," *Toronto Star*, December 9, 2021, https://www.thestar.com/politics/provincial/
2021/12/09/doug-ford-appoints-union-leader-jerry-dias-to-head-auto-task-force.
html.

10 Unifor, "Update on Investigation into Breach of Constitution," March 25, 2022, https://
www.unifor.org/news/all-news/update-investigation-breach-constitution.

11 Unifor, "Confidential Workplace Investigation – Dias/MacDonald – Full Report,"
March 15, 2022, 13, in possession of the authors.

12 Ibid.

13 NEB member Dave Cassidy indicated an interest in being considered for the nomination at this meeting but did not take part in the vote. He subsequently became the first
candidate to challenge Doherty for the presidency.

14 Unifor, National Executive Board, minutes, April 11, 2022, 64–65, in possession of the
authors.

15 Unifor, "Update on Investigation."

16 Ibid.

17 Vanmala Subramaniam, "Retired Union Leader Jerry Dias under Investigation by
Unifor," *Globe and Mail*, March 14, 2022, https://www.theglobeandmail.com/business/
article-unifor-jerry-dias-retirement-union-announcement/.

18 Sara Mojtahedzadeh and Rosa Saba, "Unifor Whistleblower Reported Jerry Dias after
Being Offered $25K, Star Learns," *Toronto Star*, March 24, 2022, https://www.thestar.
com/business/2022/03/24/unifor-whistleblower-reported-jerry-dias-after-being
-passed-over-for-endorsement-star-learns.html.

19 Ibid.

20 Vanmala Subramaniam, "A Bag of Cash and a Bottle of Cologne: Inside the Undoing
of Unifor's Jerry Dias," *Globe and Mail*, March 25, 2022, https://www.theglobeandmail.
com/business/article-unifor-jerry-dias-national-president-undoing/.

21 Ibid.

22 Unifor, "Confidential Workplace Investigation," 14.

23 Tara Deschamps, "Toronto Police's Financial Crimes Unit to Investigate Former Union
Head Jerry Dias," *CBC News*, April 5, 2022, https://www.cbc.ca/news/canada/toronto/
unifor-jerry-dias-1.6408674.

24 Vanmala Subramaniam, "New Candidate Enters Race to Replace Jerry Dias as Unifor
President," *Globe and Mail*, April 12, 2022, https://www.theglobeandmail.com/business/
article-new-candidate-enters-race-to-replace-jerry-dias-as-unifor-president/.

25 "Unifor National Executive Board to Abstain from Endorsing a Presidential Candidate,"
Auto Recent, April 21, 2022, https://autorecent.com/2022/04/21/unifor-national
-executive-board-to-abstain-from-endorsing-a-presidential-candidate.

26 Subramaniam, "New Candidate."
27 Vote Dave Cassidy, "This Is Your Union," https://davecassidy.ca/#on-the-issues1.
28 Dave Cassidy, personal interview, January 20, 2023.
29 Scott Doherty, "Platform," https://www.scottdoherty.ca/platform#reporting via web. archive.org.
30 Forward Together, "About Lana," https://forwardtogether2022.ca/about/.
31 Unifor, "Confidential Workplace Investigation," 1, attached to Unifor, National Execu- tive Board, minutes, March 21, 2022, in possession of the authors.
32 Unifor, "Confidential Workplace Investigation," 24.
33 Unifor, National Executive Board, minutes, March 21, 2022, 73–74, in possession of the authors.
34 Ibid., 75.
35 Ibid., 89.
36 Ibid., 91.
37 Ibid., 94–95, 125–40.
38 Ibid., 135.
39 Ibid., 140.
40 Ibid., 140–41.
41 Ibid., 98.
42 Ibid., 116.
43 Ibid., 106.
44 Ibid., 109.
45 Ibid., 121.
46 Ibid., 112.
47 Ibid., 115.
48 Ibid., 122–23.
49 Ibid., 123.
50 Ibid., 6.
51 Unifor, "Confidential Workplace Investigation," 5.
52 Ibid., 6, emphasis in original.
53 Ibid., 14.
54 Ibid., 15.
55 Ibid., 17.
56 Ibid., 20.
57 Ibid., 16.
58 Ibid., 19.
59 Unifor, National Executive Board, minutes, March 22, 2022, 34, in possession of the authors.
60 Ibid., 36.
61 Ibid., 48.
62 Ibid., 54.
63 Ibid., 127.
64 Jerry Dias, "Statement to Unifor Members from Jerry Dias," *Cision Canada,* March 23, 2022, https://www.newswire.ca/news-releases/statement-to-unifor-members-from -jerry-dias-866565686.html.

65 Synopsis included in "Convention Motion May 2022," circulated as part of the NEB meeting on May 6, 2022, in possession of the authors.
66 Unifor, National Executive Board, minutes, April 11, 2022, 47, in possession of the authors.
67 Ibid., 48–49.
68 Ibid., 68.
69 Ibid., 49.
70 Ibid., 60.
71 Ibid., 80.
72 Ibid., 63–64, 74–76.
73 Ibid., 98.
74 Ibid., 105.
75 Ibid., 140.
76 Ibid., 141.
77 Rachel Lau, "Former FTQ-Construction Boss Found Guilty of Fraud," *Global News*, September 26, 2014, https://globalnews.ca/news/1585025/former-ftq-construction-boss-found-guilty-of-fraud.
78 Unifor, National Executive Board, minutes, April 11, 2022, 148, in possession of the authors.
79 Ibid., 163.
80 Ibid., 176.
81 Ibid., 177.
82 Ibid., 121.
83 Ibid., 179.
84 Ibid., 6–8.
85 Ibid., 7–8.
86 Ibid., 8.
87 Ibid., 17.
88 Ibid.
89 Ibid., 18.
90 Unifor Ontario Regional Council, "Ontario Regional Director Recommendations," March 9–10, 2022, Recommendation 2, Ontario Election 2022, in possession of the authors.
91 Graeme Frisque, "Doug Ford, Justin Trudeau Announce $1B in Subsidies for Stellantis to Build Electric Vehicles in Brampton and Windsor," *Toronto Star*, May 2, 2022, https://www.thestar.com/local-brampton/news/2022/05/02/doug-ford-justin-trudeau-announce-1b-in-subsidies-for-stellantis-to-build-electric-vehicles-in-brampton-and-windsor.html; Don Wall, "PCs 'Completely Aligned with LIUNA,' Says Mancinelli," *Daily Commercial News*, May 19, 2022, https://canada.constructconnect.com/dcn/news/government/2022/05/pcs-completely-aligned-with-liuna-says-mancinelli.
92 Solarina Ho, "Ontario's 'Right to Disconnect' Law: Who Qualifies and What Are the Loopholes?" *CTV News*, June 7, 2022, https://www.ctvnews.ca/business/ontario-s-right-to-disconnect-law-who-qualifies-and-what-are-the-loopholes-1.5936773; Mitchell Thompson, "Doug Ford's Plan to Help Gig Workers Makes It Easy to Misclassify Workers and Pay Them Less Than Minimum Wage," *PressProgress*, March 1, 2022,

https://pressprogress.ca/doug-fords-plan-to-help-gig-workers-makes-it-easy-to
-misclassify-workers-and-pay-them-less-than-minimum-wage/.

93 Dave Cassidy, personal interview, January 20, 2023.

94 Maureen Revait, "Ford Commits to Support the Windsor Assembly Plant," *Windsor News Today*, October 19, 2021, https://windsornewstoday.ca/news/2021/10/19/ford-commits-support-windsor-assembly-plant.

95 Dave Cassidy, personal interview, January 20, 2023.

96 Ibid.

97 Richard J. Brennan, "'Right-to-Work' U.S. States a Model for Ontario, Say Tories," *Toronto Star*, November 8, 2013, https://www.thestar.com/news/queenspark/2013/11/08/tories_say_righttowork_states_a_model_for_ontario.html.

98 Ontario, "Major Investments Secure Automotive Manufacturing Futures for Windsor and Brampton," press release, May 2, 2022, https://news.ontario.ca/en/release/1002141/major-investments-secure-automotive-manufacturing-futures-for-windsor-and
-brampton.

99 Quoted in ibid.

100 Quoted in ibid.

101 Unifor, "Doug Ford says ... " *Twitter*, April 20, 2022, 10:02 a.m., https://twitter.com/UniforTheUnion/status/1516794316538097666.

102 Unifor, National Executive Board, minutes, April 12, 2022, 125–28, in possession of the authors.

103 CBC Radio, "Who Are Union Members Supporting in This Election?" *Ontario Today*, May 11, 2022.

104 The ridings where Unifor supported the Liberals were Oakville, Oakville North–Burlington, Milton, Etobicoke–Lakeshore, and Mississauga–Streetsville.

105 Peter Kennedy, Gaétan Ménard, Fred Wilson, and Jim Stanford, "Reclaiming and Fulfilling the Unifor Dream," *Medium*, July 19, 2022, https://medium.com/@openletterunifordream/reclaiming-and-fulfilling-the-unifor-dream-534d16c6a2aa.

106 Unifor, National Executive Board, minutes, June 29, 2022, 89, in possession of the authors.

107 Sara Mojtahedzadeh and Rosa Saba, "Wads of Cash. 'Relentless' Pressure. Infighting at Unifor. Leaked Investigation Findings Reveal New Details of Jerry Dias Scandal," *Toronto Star*, July 20, 2022, https://www.thestar.com/news/investigations/2022/07/20/wads-of-cash-relentless-pressure-infighting-at-unifor-leaked-investigation-findings
-reveal-new-details-of-jerry-dias-scandal.html.

108 Scott Doherty for Unifor National President, Facebook page, July 20, 2022.

109 Vanmala Subramaniam, "Debate Erupts within Unifor over Executive Expenses as Union Looks to Replace Former President Jerry Dias," *Globe and Mail*, July 21, 2022, https://www.theglobeandmail.com/business/article-unifor-jerry-dias-expenses/.

110 Quoted in ibid.

111 Ibid.

112 Quoted in Mojtahedzadeh and Saba, "Wads of Cash."

113 Forward Together, "Campaign Platform: We Have So Much to Do," July 6, 2022, https://forwardtogether2022.ca/post/platform/.

114 Unifor, National Executive Board, minutes, June 29, 2022, 20.

115 Ibid., 36.
116 Ibid., 53.
117 Ibid., 57–58.
118 Rosa Saba, "Unifor National Convention Kicks Off with No Clear New Leader in the Wings," *Toronto Star*, August 9, 2022, https://www.thestar.com/business/2022/08/09/unifor-national-convention-kicks-off-with-no-clear-new-leader-in-the-wings.html.
119 Larry Savage, personal notes, Unifor national convention, August 8, 2022.
120 Ibid.
121 Ibid.
122 Carol Phillips, personal interview, November 22, 2022.
123 Dave Cassidy, personal interview, January 20, 2023.
124 Sylvain Martin, personal interview, February 15, 2023.
125 Dave Cassidy, personal interview, January 20, 2023.
126 Quoted in Sara Mojtahedzadeh and Rosa Saba, "'A Fighting Culture': Inside the Controversial Career of Former Unifor Head Jerry Dias," *Toronto Star*, March 18, 2022, https://www.thestar.com/business/2022/03/18/a-fighting-culture-inside-the-controversial-career-of-former-unifor-head-jerry-dias.html.
127 Quoted in Rosa Saba and Sara Mojtahedzadeh, "Jerry Dias under Investigation by Unifor for Alleged Constitutional Breach," *Toronto Star*, March 14, 2022, https://www.thestar.com/business/2022/03/14/jerry-dias-under-investigation-by-unifor-for-alleged-constitution-breach.html.
128 Robin V. Sears, "Union Leader Jerry Dias Does Not Deserve Public Humiliation," *Toronto Star*, August 3, 2022, https://www.thestar.com/opinion/contributors/2022/08/03/union-leader-jerry-dias-does-not-deserve-public-humiliation.html.
129 Carol Phillips, personal interview, November 22, 2022.
130 Ibid.
131 Rosa Saba, "No Charges against Former Unifor Head Jerry Dias Following Bribery Investigation," *CBC News*, May 25, 2023, https://www.cbc.ca/news/canada/windsor/unifor-jerry-dias-toronto-police-1.6854985.
132 Both quoted in Robert Fife, "Ex-Unifor President Jerry Dias Says He's Trying to 'Move On with My Life' after Bribery Allegations," *Globe and Mail*, June 26, 2023, https://www.theglobeandmail.com/politics/article-ex-unifor-president-jerry-dias-insists-he-never-took-a-dime/.
133 Fred Wilson, personal interview, December 15, 2022.

CHAPTER 8: THE ROAD AHEAD

1 Stephanie Ross, "Varieties of Social Unionism: Towards a Framework for Comparison," *Just Labour* 11 (2007): 16–34.
2 Lana Payne, personal interview, March 31, 2023.
3 Jim Stanford, personal interview, October 4, 2021.
4 Ibid.
5 Ibid.
6 Ritch Wyman, personal interview, February 28, 2022.

7   For example, Unifor threw its support behind NDP efforts in British Columbia and Alberta in their respective 2020 and 2019 provincial elections.

8   Carol Phillips, personal interview, October 5, 2021.

9   Malcolm Allen, personal interview, November 16, 2021.

10 Joel Harden, personal interview, November 9, 2021.

11 Hassan Yussuff, personal interview, October 18, 2021.

12 Andrew Jackson, personal interview, February 27, 2022.

13 Dave Cassidy, personal interview, January 20, 2023.

14 Hassan Yussuff, personal interview, October 18, 2021.

15 Hemi Mitic, personal interview, October 5, 2021.

16 Ibid.

17 Willie Lambert, personal interview, February 28, 2022.

18 Wayne Gates, personal interview, October 8, 2021.

19 Andrew Jackson, personal interview, February 27, 2022.

20 Andrew Jackson, *The Fire and the Ashes: Rekindling Democratic Socialism* (Toronto: Between the Line, 2021), 81.

21 Sam Gindin, personal interview, August 27, 2021.

22 Larry Savage, "Anybody but Conservative: Canadian Unions and Strategic Voting," in Stephanie Ross and Larry Savage, eds., *Rethinking the Politics of Labour in Canada*, 2nd ed., 88–110 (Halifax: Fernwood, 2021).

23 Larry Savage and Nick Ruhloff-Queiruga, "Organized Labour, Campaign Finance, and the Politics of Strategic Voting in Ontario," *Labour/Le Travail* 80 (Fall 2017): 247–71.

24 Lana Payne, personal interview, March 31, 2023.

25 Fred Wilson, personal interview, December 15, 2022.

26 Ibid.

27 Brent Farrington, personal interview, January 28, 2022.

28 Fred Wilson, personal interview, December 15, 2022.

29 Sam Gindin, personal interview, August 27, 2021.

30 Ibid.

31 Jim Stanford, personal interview, October 4, 2021.

32 Tod Rutherford, "The Canadian Automobile Industry: Work Reorganisation and Industrial Relations Change," *Employee Relations* 12, 2 (1990): 27–32; Canadian Auto Workers, "The CAW and Childcare," June 1995, https://riseuparchive.wpenginepowered .com/wp-content/uploads/2022/02/caw-1995-CAWChildcare-pamphlet-OCR.pdf.

33 Willie Lambert, personal interview, February 28, 2022.

34 Ibid.

35 Peggy Nash, personal interview, January 31, 2022.

36 Ritch Wyman, personal interview, February 28, 2022.

37 Elaine Bernard, "The New Democratic Party and Labor Political Action in Canada," *Labor Research Review* 1, 22 (1994): 107.

38 Stephanie Ross, "The Complexities of Worker Anti-unionism," in Stephanie Ross and Larry Savage, eds., *Labour under Attack: Anti-unionism in Canada*, 35–51 (Winnipeg: Fernwood, 2018).

39 David McGrane, *The New NDP: Moderation, Modernization, and Political Marketing* (Vancouver: UBC Press, 2019), 325.

40 Jim Stanford, personal interview, October 4, 2021.

41 Peggy Nash, personal interview, September 29, 2021.

42 Sam Gindin, personal interview, August 27, 2021.

43 Hargrove backed Svend Robinson in 1995, Peter Kormos and then Frances Lankin in 1996, and Joe Comartin in 2002.

44 For example, after the 2008 Alberta election, Alberta Federation of Labour president Gil McGowan issued a discussion paper that included the option of the provincial NDP and Liberals joining electoral forces in a "co-operative pact" designed to compete with the governing Conservatives more effectively. Graham Thomson, "Unity Pact Breathes Life into Politics," *Edmonton Journal*, May 6, 2008. In 2011, just months after the NDP formed the Official Opposition in the House of Commons, CAW president Ken Lewenza publicly called on the party to merge with the Liberals in order to create a united electoral alternative to Stephen Harper's Conservatives. Laura Payton, "NDP-Liberal Merger the Way to Win, CAW Says," *CBC News*, September 2, 2011, https://www.cbc.ca/news/politics/ ndp-liberal-merger-the-way-to-win-caw-says-1.1057208.

45 John Holloway, *Change the World without Taking Power: The Meaning of Revolution Today* (London: Pluto, 2002).

46 Paul Christopher Gray, "From the Streets to the State: A Critical Introduction," in Paul Christopher Gray, ed., *From the Streets to the State: Changing the World by Taking Power* (Albany NY: SUNY Press, 2018), 6.

47 Stephanie Ross and Larry Savage, *Building a Better World: An Introduction to the Labour Movement in Canada*, 4th ed. (Halifax/Winnipeg: Fernwood, 2023), 116–41.

48 Fred Wilson, personal interview, December 15, 2022.

49 Dennis Pilon and Larry Savage, "Working-Class Politics Matters: Identity, Class, Parties," in Greg Albo, Stephen Maher, and Alan Zuege, eds., *State Transformations: Classes, Strategy, Socialism* (Boston: Brill, 2021), 78–79.

50 Ibid., 88.

51 Matthew Polacko, Simon Kiss, and Peter Graefe, "The Changing Nature of Class Voting in Canada, 1965–2019," *Canadian Journal of Political Science* 55, 3 (2022): 663.

52 Allan Flanders, *Management and Unions* (London: Faber, 1970), 15. See also Stephanie Ross, "Business Unionism and Social Unionism in Theory and Practice," in Stephanie Ross and Larry Savage, eds., *Rethinking the Politics of Labour in Canada*, 2nd ed. (Halifax: Fernwood, 2021), 42.

53 Unifor, "Politics for Workers: Unifor's Political Project," paper presented to the Unifor Canadian Council, Vancouver, September 13–15, 2014, CAW/Unifor archives, Unifor National Office, Toronto.

54 Lana Payne, personal interview, March 31, 2023.

55 Ross, "Varieties of Social Unionism," 22.

56 Perry Anderson, "The Limits and Possibilities of Trade Union Action," in Tom Clarke and Laurie Clements, eds., *Trade Unions under Capitalism* (London: Fontana Collins, 1977), 334.

57 Sam Gindin, personal interview, August 27, 2021.

58 Bryan Evans, Carlo Fanelli, Leo Panitch, and Donald Swartz, "To Renew Working-Class Resistance, the Labour Movement Must Be Democratized," *The Bullet,* March 7, 2023, https://socialistproject.ca/2023/03/renew-working-class-resistance-labour -democratized/?fbclid=IwAR1af_l515RXAqwAZrSgePZT_pNO-bOoX5F2gyX8R5ois rILfqQCb6AraWQ.

59 Jane McAlevey, *No Shortcuts: Organizing for Power in the New Gilded Age* (New York: Oxford University Press, 2016).

SELECTED BIBLIOGRAPHY

Abella, Irving. *Nationalism, Communism and Canadian Labour: The CIO, the Communist Party and the Canadian Congress of Labour, 1935–1956.* Toronto: University of Toronto Press, 1973.

Aivalis, Christo. *The Constant Liberal: Pierre Trudeau, Organized Labour, and the Canadian Social Democratic Left.* Vancouver: UBC Press, 2018.

Allen, Bruce. "The CAW-CEP Merger: A Political Reflection." *Labour/Le Travail* 70 (Fall 2012): 225–28.

Anastakis, Dimitry. *Auto Pact: Creating a Borderless North American Auto Industry, 1960–1971.* Toronto: University of Toronto Press, 2005.

–. "Between Nationalism and Continentalism: State Auto Industry Policy and the Canadian UAW, 1960–1970." *Labour/Le Travail* 53 (Spring 2004): 89–126.

Anderson, Perry. "The Limits and Possibilities of Trade Union Action." In *Trade Unions under Capitalism*, ed. Tom Clarke and Laurie Clements, 333–50. London: Fontana Collins, 1977.

Aquanno, Scott, and Toba Bryant. "Workplace Restructuring and Institutional Change: GM Oshawa from 1994 to 2019." *Studies in Political Economy* 102, 1 (2021): 25–50.

Archer, Keith. *Political Choices and Electoral Consequences: A Study of Organized Labour and the New Democratic Party.* Montreal/Kingston: McGill-Queen's University Press, 1990.

Archer, Keith, and Alan Whitehorn. *Political Activists: The NDP in Convention.* Toronto: Oxford University Press, 1997.

Armstrong, Bromley L., with Sheldon Taylor. *Bromley, Tireless Champion for Just Causes.* Pickering, ON: Vitabu, 2000.

Avakumovic, Ivan. *The Communist Party of Canada: A History.* Toronto: McClelland and Stewart, 1975.

Babcock, Robert H. *Gompers in Canada: A Study in American Continentalism before the First World War.* Toronto: University of Toronto Press, 1974.

Barlow, Maude. *The Fight of My Life: Confessions of an Unrepentant Canadian.* Toronto: HarperCollins, 1988.

Barnard, John. *American Vanguard: The United Auto Workers during the Reuther Years, 1935–1970*. Detroit: Wayne State University Press, 2004.

Benedict, Dan. "The 1984 GM Agreement in Canada: Significance and Consequences." *Relations industrielles/Industrial Relations* 40, 1 (1985): 27–47.

Bernard, Elaine. "The New Democratic Party and Labor Political Action in Canada." *Labor Research Review* 1, 22 (1994): 99–109.

Blizzard, Christina. *Right Turn: How the Tories Took Ontario*. Toronto: Dundurn, 1995.

Bradford, Neil. "Ideas, Intellectuals and Social Democracy in Canada." In *Canadian Parties in Transition: Discourse, Organization, Representation*, ed. Alain Gagnon and Brian Tanguay, 83–110. Toronto: Nelson, 1989.

Brodie, Janine, and Jane Jenson. *Crisis, Challenge and Change: Party and Class in Canada Revisited*. Ottawa: Carleton University Press, 1988.

Burgess, Katrina. "Loyalty Dilemmas and Market Reform: Party-Union Alliances under Stress in Mexico, Spain and Venezuela." *World Politics* 52, 1 (1999): 105–34.

Callaghan, John. "Social Democracy and Globalisation: The Limits of Social Democracy in Historical Perspective." *British Journal of Politics and International Relations* 4, 3 (2002): 429–51.

Camfield, David. *Canadian Labour in Crisis: Reinventing the Workers' Movement*. Halifax: Fernwood, 2011.

Chamberlain, Neil. *The Labor Sector*. New York: McGraw-Hill, 1965.

Clarkson, Stephen. "Disaster and Recovery: Paul Martin as Political Lazarus." In *The Canadian General Election of 2004*, ed. Jon H. Pammett and Christopher Dornan, 236–64. Toronto: Dundurn, 2004.

Collombat, Thomas, and Magali Picard. "Third-Party Activism." In *Inside the Campaign: Managing Elections in Canada*, ed. Alex Marland and Thierry Giasson, 185–95. Vancouver: UBC Press, 2020.

Drache, Daniel, and Duncan Cameron, eds. *The Other MacDonald Report: The Consensus on Canada's Future that the Macdonald Commission Left Out*. Toronto: Lorimer, 1985.

Dreher, Axel. "The Influence of Globalization on Taxes and Social Policy: An Empirical Analysis for OECD Countries." *European Journal of Political Economy* 22, 1 (2006): 179–201.

Dunk, Thomas. "Notes on the Labour Movement and the Rise and Fall of the Pulp-and-Paper Industry in Anglophone Canada." In *Pulp Friction: Communities and the Forest Industry in a Globalized World*, ed. Michel S. Beaulieu and Ronald N. Harpelle, 70–84. Thunder Bay, ON: Centre for Northern Studies, Lakehead University, 2012.

Eaton, Jonathan, and Anil Verma. "Does 'Fighting Back' Make a Difference? The Case of the Canadian Auto Workers Union." *Journal of Labor Research* 27, 2 (2006): 187–212.

Ehring, George, and Wayne Roberts. *Giving Away a Miracle: Lost Dreams, Broken Promises and the Ontario NDP*. Oakville, ON: Mosaic, 1993.

Evans, Bryan. "From Protest Movement to Neoliberal Management: Canada's New Democratic Party in the Era of Permanent Austerity." In *Social Democracy after the Cold War*, ed. Bryan Evans and Ingo Schmidt, 45–98. Edmonton: Athabasca University Press, 2012.

–. "The New Democratic Party in the Era of Neoliberalism." In *Rethinking the Politics of Labour in Canada*, ed. Stephanie Ross and Larry Savage, 48–61. Halifax: Fernwood, 2012.

Fairweather, Chris. "'We Can't Just Wrap Ourselves in the Flag': Labour Nationalism, Global Solidarity, and the 2016 Fight to Save GM Oshawa." *Journal of Labor and Society* 25, 3 (2022): 367–94.

Flanders, Allan. *Management and Unions*. London: Faber, 1970.

Fowler, Tim. "Coordinated Strategic Voting in the 2008 Federal Election." *American Review of Canadian Studies* 42, 1 (2012): 20–33.

Gagnon, Georgette, and Dan Rath. *Not without Cause: David Peterson's Fall from Grace*. Toronto: HarperCollins, 1991.

Garrett, Geoffrey, and Deborah Mitchell. "Globalization, Government Spending and Taxation in the OECD." *European Journal of Political Research* 39, 2 (2001): 145–77.

Gidluck, Lynn. *Visionaries, Crusaders, and Firebrands: The Idealistic Canadians Who Built the NDP*. Toronto: Lorimer, 2012.

Gindin, Sam. "Breaking Away: The Formation of the Canadian Auto Workers." *Studies in Political Economy* 29, 1 (1989): 63–89.

–. *The Canadian Auto Workers: The Birth and Transformation of a Union*. Toronto: Lorimer, 1995.

Gindin, Sam, and Jim Stanford. "Canadian Labour and the Political Economy of Transformation." In *Changing Canada: Political Economy as Transformation*, ed. Wallace Clement and Leah Vosko, 422–42. Montreal/Kingston: McGill-Queen's University Press, 2003.

Gray, Paul Christopher. "From the Streets to the State: A Critical Introduction," In *From the Streets to the State: Changing the World by Taking Power*, ed. Paul Christopher Gray, 3–23. Albany, NY: SUNY Press, 2018.

Hargrove, Buzz. *Laying It on the Line: Driving a Hard Bargain in Challenging Times*. Toronto: HarperCollins, 2009.

Hargrove, Buzz, with Wayne Skene. *Labour of Love: The Fight to Create a More Humane Canada*. Toronto: McFarlane, Walter and Ross, 1998.

Heath, Jamey. *Dead Centre: Hope, Possibility, and Unity for Canadian Progressives*. New York: John Wiley and Sons, 2007.

Heron, Craig. *The Canadian Labour Movement: A Short History*, 3rd ed. Toronto: Lorimer, 2012.

–. "Labourism and the Canadian Working Class." *Labour/Le Travail* 13 (Spring 1984): 45–76.

High, Steven. "'I'll Wrap the F*** Canadian Flag around Me': A Nationalist Response to Plant Shutdowns, 1969–1984." *Journal of the Canadian Historical Association* 12, 1 (2001): 199–225.

Holloway, John. *Change the World without Taking Power: The Meaning of Revolution Today*. London: Pluto, 2002.

Horowitz, Gad. *Canadian Labour in Politics*. Toronto: University of Toronto Press, 1968.

Hoxie, Robert. "Trade Unionism in the United States." *Journal of Political Economy* 22, 3 (1914): 201–17.

Hrynyshyn, Derek, and Stephanie Ross. "Canadian Autoworkers, the Climate Crisis, and the Contradictions of Social Unionism." *Labor Studies Journal* 36, 1 (2011): 5–36.

Hyman, Richard. *Industrial Relations: A Marxist Introduction.* London: Macmillan, 1975.

Ibbitson, John. *Promised Land: Inside the Mike Harris Revolution.* Toronto: Prentice Hall, 1997.

Jacek, Henry, and Brian Tanguay. "Can Strategic Voting Beat Mike Harris?" *Inroads: A Journal of Opinion* 10 (2001): 55–65.

Jackson, Andrew. *The Fire and the Ashes: Rekindling Democratic Socialism.* Toronto: Between the Lines, 2021.

Jackson, Andrew, and Sylvain Schetange. "Solidarity Forever? An Analysis of Changes in Union Density." *Just Labour* 4 (2004): 53–82.

Jansen, Harold, and Lisa Young. "Solidarity Forever? The NDP, Organized Labour, and the Changing Face of Party Finance in Canada." *Canadian Journal of Political Science* 42, 3 (2009): 657–78.

Jenson, Jane, and Rianne Mahon, eds. *The Challenge of Restructuring: North American Labor Movements Respond.* Philadelphia: Temple University Press, 1993.

Kealey, Gregory S. *Toronto Workers Respond to Industrial Capitalism, 1867–1892.* Toronto: University of Toronto Press, 1980.

Keeran, Roger. *The Communist Party and the Auto Workers' Union.* Bloomington: Indiana University Press, 1980.

Korpi, Walter. "Power Resources Approach vs. Action and Conflict: On Causal and Intentional Explanations in the Study of Power." *Sociological Theory* 3, 2 (1985): 31–45.

Kumar, Pradeep, and John Holmes. "The Impact of NAFTA on the Auto Industry in Canada." In *The North American Auto Industry Under NAFTA,* ed. Sidney Weinstraub and Christopher Sands, 92–183. Washington, DC: Centre for Strategic and International Studies, 1998.

Laxer, James. 1996. *In Search of a New Left: Canadian Politics after the Neoconservative Assault.* Toronto: Viking.

Laxer, Robert. *Canada's Unions.* Toronto: Lorimer, 1976.

Laycock, David, and Linda Erickson, eds. *Reviving Social Democracy: The Near Death and Surprising Rise of the Federal NDP.* Vancouver: UBC Press, 2015.

Leier, Mark. *Where the Fraser River Flows: The Industrial Workers of the World in British Columbia.* Vancouver: New Star, 1990.

Lewchuk, Wayne, and Donald Wells. "Transforming Worker Representation: The Magna Model in Canada and Mexico." *Labour/Le Travail* 60 (Fall 2007): 107–36.

Lichtenstein, Nelson. *Walter Reuther: The Most Dangerous Man in Detroit.* New York: Basic Books, 1995.

Lipton, Charles. *The Trade Union Movement of Canada, 1827–1959.* 3rd ed. Toronto: NC Press, 1973.

MacLellan, Duncan. "Neoliberalism and Ontario Teachers' Unions: A 'Not-So' Common Sense Revolution." *Socialist Studies* 5, 1 (2009): 51–74.

March, James G., and Johan P. Olsen. "The New Institutionalism: Organizational Factors in Political Life." *American Political Science Review* 78, 3 (1984): 734–49.

Martinello, Felice. "Mr. Harris, Mr. Rae and Union Activity in Ontario." *Canadian Public Policy* 26, 1 (2000): 17–33.

Mazar, Alissa. "Paid Education Leave Program and Development: The Canadian Auto Workers Case Study." *McGill Sociological Review* 5 (2015): 19–42.

McAlevey, Jane. *No Shortcuts: Organizing for Power in the New Gilded Age.* New York: Oxford University Press, 2016.

McBride, Stephen. "The Continuing Crisis of Social Democracy: Ontario's Social Contract in Perspective." *Studies in Political Economy* 50, 1 (1996): 65–93.

McGrane, David. *The New NDP: Moderation, Modernization, and Political Marketing.* Vancouver: UBC Press, 2019.

McLean, James S. *Inside the NDP War Room: Competing for Credibility in a Federal Election.* Montreal/Kingston: McGill-Queen's University Press, 2012.

McLeod, Ian. *Under Siege: The Federal NDP in the Nineties.* Toronto: Lorimer, 1994.

Miller, Richard Ulric. "Organized Labour and Politics in Canada." In *Canadian Labour in Transition,* ed. Richard Ulric Miller and Fraser Isbester, 204–39. Toronto: Prentice-Hall, 1971.

Minkin, Lewis. *The Contentious Alliance: Trade Unions and the Labour Party.* Edinburgh: Edinburgh University Press, 1991.

Monahan, Patrick. *Storming the Pink Palace: The NDP in Power: A Cautionary Tale.* Toronto: Lester and Orpen Dennys, 1995.

Moody, Kim. *An Injury to All: The Decline of American Unionism.* New York: Verso, 1988.

Mordue, Greig, and Brendan Sweeney. "The Commoditisation of Automotive Assembly: Canada as a Cautionary Tale." *International Journal of Automotive Technology and Management* 17, 2 (2017): 169–89.

Morton, Desmond. *The New Democrats, 1961–1986: The Politics of Change.* 3rd ed. Toronto: Copp Clark Pitman, 1986.

–. *Social Democracy in Canada.* 2nd ed. Toronto: Samuel Stevens Hakkert, 1977.

Moschonas, Gerassimos. *In the Name of Social Democracy.* London: Verso, 2002.

Murnighan, Bill, and Jim Stanford. "We Will Fight This Crisis: Auto Workers Resist Industrial Meltdown." In *From Crisis to Austerity: Neoliberalism, Organized Labour, and the Canadian State,* ed. Tim Fowler, 129–65. Ottawa: Red Quill Books, 2013.

Naylor, James. *The Fate of Labour Socialism: The Co-operative Commonwealth Federation and the Dream of a Working-Class Future.* Toronto: University of Toronto Press, 2016.

Palmer, Bryan. *Canada's 1960s: The Ironies of Identity in a Rebellious Era.* Toronto: University of Toronto Press, 2008.

–. 1992. *Working Class Experience: Rethinking the History of Canadian Labour, 1800–1991.* Toronto: McClelland and Stewart.

Panitch, Leo. "Corporatism in Canada?" *Studies in Political Economy* 1, 1 (1979): 43–92.

–. "Globalisation and the State." In *The Socialist Register 1994: Between Globalism and Nationalism,* ed. Ralph Miliband and Leo Panitch, 60–93. London: Merlin, 1994.

Panitch, Leo, and Donald Swartz. *From Consent to Coercion: The Assault on Trade Union Freedoms*. Toronto: Garamond, 2003.

Patrias, Carmela, and Larry Savage. *Union Power: Solidarity and Struggle in Niagara*. Edmonton: Athabasca University Press, 2012.

Perlman, Selig. *A Theory of the Labor Movement*. New York: Macmillan, 1928.

Piazza, James. "De-linking Labor: Labor Unions and Social Democratic Parties under Globalization." *Party Politics* 7, 4 (2001): 413–35.

Pilon, Dennis, Stephanie Ross, and Larry Savage. "Solidarity Revisited: Organized Labour and the New Democratic Party." *Canadian Political Science Review* 5, 1 (2011): 20–37.

Pilon, Dennis, and Larry Savage. "Working-Class Politics Matters: Identity, Class, Parties." In *State Transformations: Classes, Strategy, Socialism*, ed. Greg Albo, Stephen Maher, and Alan Zuege, 76–97. Boston: Brill, 2012.

Polacko, Matthew, Simon Kiss, and Peter Graefe. "The Changing Nature of Class Voting in Canada, 1965–2019." *Canadian Journal of Political Science* 55, 3 (2022): 1–24.

Poulantzas, Nicos. "The Problem of the Capitalist State." *New Left Review* 1, 58 (1969): 67–78.

Quinn, Thomas. "Block Voting in the Labour Party: A Political Exchange Model." *Party Politics* 8, 2 (2002): 207–26.

Rae, Bob. *From Protest to Power: Personal Reflections on a Life in Politics*. Toronto: Viking, 1996.

Rapaport, David. *No Justice, No Peace: The 1996 OPSEU Strike against the Harris Government in Ontario*. Montreal/Kingston: McGill-Queen's University Press, 1999.

Reed, Louis. *The Labor Philosophy of Samuel Gompers*. Port Washington, NY: Kennikat, 1966.

Reshef, Yonatan, and Sandra Rastin. *Unions in the Time of Revolution: Government Restructuring in Alberta and Ontario*. Toronto: University of Toronto Press, 2003.

Rinehart, James. "The Canadian Auto Workers: An Inspirational Story." *Monthly Review* 50, 6 (1998): 58–63.

Roberge, Yvon. *Histoire des TCA Québec*. Montreal: Éditions Fides, 2008.

Robin, Martin. *Radical Politics and Canadian Labour, 1880–1930*. Kingston: Industrial Relations Centre, Queen's University, 1968.

Ross, Stephanie. "Business Unionism and Social Unionism in Theory and Practice." In *Rethinking the Politics of Labour in Canada*, 2nd ed, ed. Stephanie Ross and Larry Savage, 29–46. Halifax: Fernwood, 2021.

–. "The Challenge of Union Political Action in the Era of Neoliberalism: The Case of Ontario." In *Divided Province: Ontario Politics in the Age of Neoliberalism*, ed. Greg Albo and Bryan Evans, 522–48. Montreal/Kingston: McGill-Queen's University Press, 2018.

–. "The Complexities of Worker Anti-unionism." In *Labour under Attack: Anti-unionism in Canada*, ed. Stephanie Ross and Larry Savage, 35–51. Winnipeg: Fernwood, 2018.

–. "Social Unionism in Hard Times: Union-Community Coalition Politics in the CAW Windsor's *Manufacturing Matters* Campaign." *Labour/Le Travail* 68 (Fall 2011): 79–115.

–. "Varieties of Social Unionism: Towards a Framework for Comparison." *Just Labour* 11 (2007): 16–34.

Ross, Stephanie, and Jason Russell. "'Caterpillar Hates Unions More Than It Loves Profits': The Electro-Motive Closure and the Dilemmas of Union Strategy." *Labour/ Le Travail* 81 (Spring 2018): 53–85.

Ross, Stephanie, and Larry Savage. *Building a Better World: An Introduction to the Labour Movement in Canada,* 4th ed. Halifax/Winnipeg: Fernwood, 2023.

Rouillard, Jacques. *Le Syndicalisme québécois: deux siècles d'histoire.* Montreal: Boréal, 2004.

Rutherford, Tod. "The Canadian Automobile Industry: Work Reorganisation and Industrial Relations Change." *Employee Relations* 12, 2 (1990): 27–32.

Ryan, Sid. *A Grander Vision: My Life in the Labour Movement.* Toronto: Dundurn, 2019.

Sangster, Joan. *Dreams of Equality: Women on the Canadian Left, 1920–1950.* Toronto: University of Toronto Press, 1989.

Savage, Larry. "Anybody but Conservative: Canadian Unions and Strategic Voting." In *Rethinking the Politics of Labour in Canada,* 2nd ed., ed. Stephanie Ross and Larry Savage, 88–110. Halifax: Fernwood, 2021.

–. "Contemporary Party-Union Relations in Canada." *Labor Studies Journal* 35, 1 (2010): 8–26.

–. "From Centralization to Sovereignty-Association: The Canadian Labour Congress and the Constitutional Question." *Review of Constitutional Studies* 13, 2 (2007): 67–95.

–. "Organized Labour and Constitutional Reform under Mulroney." *Labour/Le Travail* 60 (Fall 2007): 137–70.

–. "Organized Labour and the Politics of Strategic Voting." In *Rethinking the Politics of Labour in Canada,* ed. Stephanie Ross and Larry Savage, 75–87. Halifax: Fernwood, 2012.

–. "The Politics of Labour and Labour Relations in Ontario." In *The Politics of Ontario,* ed. Cheryl N. Collier and Jonathan Malloy, 293–311. Toronto: University of Toronto Press, 2016.

–. "Quebec Labour and the Referendums." *Canadian Journal of Political Science* 41, 4 (2008): 861–87.

–. "The Shifting Landscape of Party-Union Relationships in Ontario." In *The Politics of Ontario,* 2nd ed., ed. Cheryl N. Collier and Jonathan Malloy. Toronto: University of Toronto Press, June 2024.

–. *Socialist Cowboy: The Politics of Peter Kormos.* Halifax: Roseway, 2014.

Savage, Larry, and Chantal Mancini. "Strategic Electoral Dilemmas and the Politics of Teachers' Unions in Ontario." *Canadian Political Science Review* 16, 1 (2022): 1–21.

Savage, Larry, and Nick Ruhloff-Queiruga. "Organized Labour, Campaign Finance, and the Politics of Strategic Voting in Ontario." *Labour/Le Travail* 80 (Fall 2017): 247–71.

Savage, Larry, and Charles Smith. "Public Sector Unions and Electoral Politics in Canada." In *Public Sector Unions in the Age of Austerity,* ed. Stephanie Ross and Larry Savage, 45–56. Halifax: Fernwood, 2013.

Smith, Doug. *Stickin' to the Union: Local 2224 versus John Buhler.* Halifax: Fernwood, 2004.

Smith, Miriam. "The Canadian Labour Congress: From Continentalism to Economic Nationalism." *Studies in Political Economy* 38, 1 (1992): 35–60.

Stanford, Jim, and Svend Robinson. "The New Politics Initiative: Open, Sustainable, Democratic." In *What's Left? The New Democratic Party in Renewal,* ed. Z. David Berlin and Howard Aster, 80–93. Oakville, ON: Mosaic, 2001.

Steed, Judy. *Ed Broadbent: The Pursuit of Power.* Toronto: Penguin, 1988.

Storey, Robert, and Wayne Lewchuk. "From Dust to DUST to Dust: Asbestos and the Struggle for Worker Health and Safety at Bendix Automotive." *Labour/Le Travail* 45 (Spring 2000): 103–40.

Sugiman, Pamela. *Labour's Dilemma: The Gender Politics of Auto Workers in Canada, 1937–1979.* Toronto: University of Toronto Press, 1994.

Swartz, Donald, and Rosemary Warskett. "Canadian Labour and the Crisis of Solidarity." In *Rethinking the Politics of Labour in Canada,* ed. Stephanie Ross and Larry Savage, 18–32. Halifax: Fernwood, 2012.

Tanguay, Brian. "Parties, Organized Interests, and Electoral Democracy: The 1999 Ontario Provincial Election." In *Political Parties, Representation, and Electoral Democracy in Canada,* ed. William Cross, 145–60. Toronto: Oxford University Press, 2001.

–. "Radicals, Technocrats and Traditionalists: Interest Aggregation in Two Provincial Social Democratic Parties in Canada." In *How Political Parties Respond: Interest Aggregation Revisited,* ed. Kay Lawson and Thomas Poguntke, 146–75. New York: Routledge, 2004.

Topp, Brian. *How We Almost Gave the Tories the Boot: The Inside Story behind the Coalition.* Toronto: Lorimer, 2010.

van Kersbergen, Kees. "The Politics and Political Economy of Social Democracy." *Acta Politica* 38, 3 (2003): 255–73.

Walchuk, Brad. "Changing Union-Party Relations in Canada: The Rise of the Working Families Coalition." *Labor Studies Journal* 35, 1 (2010): 27–50.

Walkom, Thomas. *Rae Days: The Rise and Follies of the NDP.* Toronto: Key Porter Books, 1994.

Watson, Chris. "The NDP Is in Big Trouble. So?" In *What's Left? The New Democratic Party in Renewal,* ed. Z. David Berlin and Howard Aster, 114–26. Oakville ON: Mosaic, 2001.

Wells, Donald M. "Origins of Canada's Wagner Model of Industrial Relations: The United Auto Workers in Canada and the Suppression of 'Rank and File' Unionism, 1936–1953." *Canadian Journal of Sociology* 20, 2 (1995): 193–225.

–. "When Push Comes to Shove: Competitiveness, Job Insecurity and Labour-Management Cooperation in Canada." *Economic and Industrial Democracy* 18, 2 (1997): 176–200.

Whitaker, Reg. "Introduction: The 20th Anniversary of the Waffle." *Studies in Political Economy* 32, 1 (1990): 167–71.

White, Bob. *Hard Bargains: My Life on the Line.* Toronto: McLelland and Stewart, 1987.

Whitehorn, Alan. "Jack Layton and the NDP: Gains but no Breakthrough." In *The Canadian General Election of 2004,* ed. Jon H. Pammett and Christopher Dornan, 106–38. Toronto: Dundurn, 2004.

–. "The NDP and the Enigma of Strategic Voting." In *The Canadian General Election of 2006*, ed. Jon H. Pammett and Christopher Dornan, 93–121. Toronto: Dundurn, 2006.

–. "The NDP Election Campaign: Dashed Hopes." In *The Canadian General Election of 1988*, ed. Alan Frizzel, Jon H. Pammett, and Anthony Westell, 43–54. Ottawa: Carleton University Press, 1989.

Wilson, Fred. *A New Kind of Union: Unifor and the Birth of the Modern Canadian Union*. Toronto: Lorimer, 2019.

Wiseman, Nelson. *Social Democracy in Manitoba: A History of the CCF/NDP.* Winnipeg: University of Manitoba Press, 1983.

Yates, Charlotte. *From Plant to Politics: The Autoworkers Union in Postwar Canada.* Philadelphia: Temple University Press, 1993.

–. "Unity and Diversity: Challenges to an Expanding Canadian Autoworkers' Union." *Canadian Review of Sociology and Anthropology* 35, 1 (1998): 93–118.

Yates, Charlotte, and Wayne Lewchuk. "What Shapes Automotive Investment Decisions in a Contemporary Global Economy." *Canadian Public Policy* 43, 1 (2017): S16–29.

Young, Walter D. *The Anatomy of a Party: The National CCF 1932–61*. Toronto: University of Toronto Press, 1969.

Zakuta, Leo. *A Protest Movement Becalmed: A Study of Change in the CCF.* Toronto: University of Toronto Press, 1964.

INDEX

activism: overview, 4–5, 13, 29, 89, 91, 118–19, 139, 249–57; agency and union structure, 7–8, 18–21, 256–57; anti-globalization protests, 17, 114–15, 116; anti-racism, 4, 13, 20, 25–26, 64; barricades and blockades, 171, 202, 246; boycotts, 171, 202; coalition building, 13, 91–92; Days of Action protests, 89, 93–99, 109–10, 116, 118, 167; demonstrations, 197, 202, 246; early history, 8–11, 29, 41–43; vs electoralism, 29, 89–95; GM Oshawa Matters campaign (2016), 197–98, 206; human rights issues, 4, 13–14, 25–26, 64; internal organizing for the future, 256–57; plant occupations, 54, 94, 143, 171, 246; political independence, 29, 42–43, 186–88; post-9/11 political climate, 17, 116–17, 119, 120; shifting trends, 4–5, 99, 116–20, 139, 143–44, 161, 246, 249–50; strikes overview, 29; value-action gap, 252–53. *See also* strikes; syndicalist direct action

Administration caucus: CAW system, 18–19, 153–60, 179–80, 234–35; UAW Canadian region system, 18–19, 31–32, 55, 59–60; UAW US system, 18–19, 26, 29–32, 55, 156. *See also* caucus system

agency and union structure, 7–8, 18–21, 256–57. *See also* Canadian Auto Workers (CAW), structure; Unifor, structure

Ahn, Jenny, 132, 140, 159, 170

aircraft industry, 42, 46

airlines, 109

Alberta: Notley's NDP government, 189, 194; strategic voting, 243, 308*n*7

Allder, Shinade, 223–24

Allen, Bruce, 142, 180

Allen, Malcolm: on CAW's structure, 154, 160; on Dias, 215; elections (2008, 2011, 2015, 2021), 162–64, 167, 169, 192, 211; on strategic voting, 132–33, 137, 163, 180, 215; on transactional politics, 151, 239; on union education program, 63

Amalgamated Transit Union (ATU), 199–200

American Federation of Labor (AFL), 9, 10, 25

Anastakis, Dimitry, 35, 37–38, 233

Anderson, Perry, 253

Angus, Charlie, 194

annual improvement factor (AIF), 56

anti-Conservative voting. *See* strategic voting

anti-globalization protests, 17, 114–15, 116

elections (1995, 1999, 2003, 2007), 83–86, 99–108, 123–24, 147; elections (2014, 2018, 2022), 3, 182–85, 201–2, 214, 225–29, 235; Hudak as leader, 182–84, 186–87; strategic voting against, 240–45. *See also* Ford, Doug, PC Ontario government; Harris, Mike, PC Ontario government; Ontario, provincial elections

proportional representation electoral system, 172

protests. *See* activism

public sector: Drummond commission on public services, 181; Ford's anti-labour policies, 201, 214, 227; Harris's anti-labour policies, 97, 99, 104; Hudak on job cuts, 184; Rae's Social Contract Act, 77–82, 85–86, 88, 91–92, 96, 107, 273*n*82; strategic voting, 99, 104, 123, 146; teachers' unions, 16, 95–99, 146, 181–82, 201; Unifor's membership, 178. *See also* Canadian Union of Public Employees (CUPE); Ontario Public Service Employees Union (OPSEU); Public Service Alliance of Canada

Public Service Alliance of Canada, 115, 135, 193

Pupatello, Sandra, 144, 182

Quebec: overview, 22, 66, 86–88; aircraft industry, 42, 46; auto industry, 45–47, 114; BQ-CAW relations, 22, 66, 86–88, 125–26, 129, 133–34, 162, 168; BQ-Unifor relations, 187, 204, 211; CAQ government, 211; CAW Quebec Council, 45–47, 59; CEP labour movement, 186–87; elections (1988, 1993, 2004, 2006, 2008), 69–70, 82–83, 125–26, 133–36, 162, 164, 168–69; elections (2011, 2015, 2019, 2021), 168–69, 187, 204–5, 211; free trade issues, 67, 69–70, 270*n*6; Liberal sponsorship scandal, 125–26, 135; nationalism, 45–47; NDP relations, 22, 32, 45, 66,

69–70, 82–83, 87, 168, 204; PQ (Parti Québécois), 45, 46, 83, 121, 187; QFL, 45, 83, 86, 191, 296*n*69; referendums (1992, 1995), 83, 86–88; strategic voting, 135–36, 141, 191, 204, 296*n*69; Unifor, 177–78, 186–87, 204, 211, 224. *See also* BQ (Bloc Québécois)

Quebec Federation of Labour (QFL), 45, 83, 86, 191, 296*n*69

racism, 13, 20, 25–26, 64

Rae, Bob: career and legacy, 71, 102, 104, 107, 127, 248; as Liberal, 209; NDP leadership races, 95–99, 248; on unions, 80–81

–Ontario NDP government: overview, 21–22, 71–86, 88, 102, 107, 248; anti- and pro-union policies, 16, 72–75, 85–86, 102, 107; budget deficits, 74, 77–79; CEP support for, 180; coalitions against, 91–92; economic recession, 73–74, 76, 77, 88, 90; elections (1990, 1995), 71–72, 83–86; fiscal austerity, 78–82; Hargrove's relationship, 74–77, 85–86; labour leaders in government, 72; Labour Relations Act, 73, 78, 90, 92, 97; NDP-union relations, 16, 72–78, 80–81, 88, 91–92, 102; Pink Paper unions' support for, 80, 92–99, 110, 180; political independence, 76–78, 91; Social Contract Act (1993), 16, 21–22, 65–66, 77–82, 85–86, 88, 91, 97

Railton, Lionel, 208

Rak, Russ, 198

Ramsey, Tracey, 192, 211

Rastin, Sandra, 80, 92, 103, 105

Reaume, Art, 28, 264*n*22

Rebick, Judy, 115

Reform Party, 82

research project: overview, 14–17, 236–37; chapter summaries, 21–23; critical political economy approach, 15–16; methodology, 21, 236; "shifting gears," 4–5, 17, 19, 116–20, 143–44, 236–37; theoretical approaches, 14–17

United Steelworkers of America (USWA), 7, 32–33, 40, 70, 72, 96, 115, 149–50, 296n69
Unity (Administration) caucus (Unifor), 19, 179–80, 234–35. *See also* caucus system
USWA. *See* United Steelworkers of America (USWA)

Volpe, Flavio, 233

Waffle movement, 37–39
Walkom, Thomas, 76, 77
Wark, Shane, 221, 224, 228
Watkins, Mel, 37
Watson, Mike, 164
Wells, Donald, 148
White, Bob: overview, 44–45, 54–55, 68, 245, 248; anti-free trade, 66–71; on auto plant occupations, 54; CAW president, 4, 57; CAW's breakaway, 56, 68, 157; CLC president, 68, 74–75, 85, 91; coalition building, 91–92; Framework of Fairness issues, 150; on NDP-CAW relations, 62–63; NDP officer, 63, 68, 74, 248, 271n31; Quebec Council, 46–47; Quebec referendum (1995), 86–87; Rae's government, 79, 85; Reuther's influence, 26, 31; on social unionism, 62–63, 246; UAW Canadian region director, 44–45, 54–56; UAW-NDP alliance, 44–45; union education programs (PEL), 44
Whitehorn, Alan, 130
Whyman, Ritch, 138–39, 142, 239, 246
Wilson, Fred, 176–77, 179–80, 212, 215, 230, 234, 243, 249
Wilson, Gord, 71, 85, 96, 149
Windsor (ON): CAW's transactional politics, 144–45; Days of Action protests, 94; early history of unions, 5, 24–25, 27–28, 30, 37, 38, 54; elections (1999, 2007), 106, 144–45; Framework of Fairness, 151–52; free trade impacts

(1990s), 73; government support, 141; layoffs (2006), 137, 141, 143; Stellantis plant, 226–28; strategic voting, 144–45, 185, 205, 229
Witmer, Elizabeth, 181
women in unions, 6, 13, 20, 177, 178. *See also* Nash, Peggy; Payne, Lana, Unifor president; Phillips, Carol
working-class politics: overview, 4–6, 8–14, 250–51; anti-power politics, 248–49; Canadianization of, 5–6; caucus system, 19–20; CCF, 9–10, 26–30, 32, 41, 260nn29–30; coalition building, 13, 91–92; Communists, 9–10, 27–30, 32, 263n14; democratic capacities, 255–57; direct action by working class, 54; early history, 8–11; internal organizing for the future, 256–57; merger of Liberal-NDP as proposal, 196, 248, 309n44; NDP overview, 10–11, 32–33, 63–64; sectionalism, 5, 236–37, 241, 246–47, 251, 256; shifting trends, 4–6, 19, 116–20, 143–44, 236–37; social justice issues, 4, 13–14, 20, 25–26, 64; strategies, 7–8, 9, 236–37; transactional politics, 7, 15, 140–45, 151–52, 236–40; union education programs, 44, 63; unions' roles, 236–37. *See also* NDP (New Democratic Party); social unionism
Working Families Coalition, 123–24, 146–47, 184
World Trade Organization, 114–15
Wynne, Kathleen, Liberal Ontario government, 182–85, 201–2, 204

Yates, Charlotte: CAW-Liberal ties, 27–28, 47; CAW-NDP ties, 33, 38, 43, 47–49; CAW's breakaway (1985), 26, 55, 59–61; CLC and strategic voting, 51; on Framework of Fairness, 151; internal union dynamics, 18, 59; on strikes, 42

Printed and bound in Canada by Friesens
Set in Perpetua and Minion and by Apex CoVantage, LLC
Copy editor: Robert Lewis
Proofreader: Caitlin Gordon-Walker
Indexer: Judy Dunlop
Cover designer: Alexa Love
Cover images: iStock